Praise for the series:

It was only a matter of time before a clever publisher realized that there is an audience for whom *Exile on Main Street* or *Electric Ladyland* are as significant and worthy of study as *The Catcher in the Rye* or *Middlemarch*. . . . The series, which now comprises 29 titles with more in the works, is freewheeling and eclectic, ranging from minute rock-geek analysis to idiosyncratic personal celebration—*The New York Times Book Review*

Ideal for the rock geek who thinks liner notes just aren't enough—*Rolling Stone*

One of the coolest publishing imprints on the planet—*Bookslut*

These are for the insane collectors out there who appreciate fantastic design, well-executed thinking, and things that make your house look cool. Each volume in this series takes a seminal album and breaks it down in startling minutiae. We love these. We are huge nerds—*Vice*

A brilliant series...each one a work of real love—*NME* (UK)

Passionate, obsessive, and smart—*Nylon*

Religious tracts for the rock 'n' roll faithful—*Boldtype*

Each volume has a distinct, almost militantly personal take on a beloved long-player. . . . The books that have resulted are like the albums themselves—filled with moments of shimmering beauty, forgivable flaws, and stubborn eccentricity—*Tracks Magazine*

[A] consistently excellent series—*Uncut* (UK)

The nobility—and fun—of the project has never been questioned . . . a winning mix of tastes and writing styles—*Philadelphia Weekly*

Reading about rock isn't quite the same as listening to it, but this series comes pretty damn close—*Neon NYC*

The sort of great idea you can't believe hasn't been done before—*Boston Phoenix*

We . . . aren't naive enough to think that we're your only source for reading about music (but if we had our way . . . watch out). For those of you who really like to know everything there is to know about an album, you'd do well to check out Continuum's "33 1/3" series of books.—Pitchfork

For reviews of individual titles in the series, please visit our website at www.continuumbooks.com and the series blog, 33third.blogspot.com

Titles available in this series:

Dusty in Memphis by Warren Zanes
Forever Changes by Andrew Hultkrans
Harvest by Sam Inglis
The Kinks Are the Village Green Preservation Society by Andy Miller
Meat Is Murder by Joe Pernice
The Piper at the Gates of Dawn by John Cavanagh
Abba Gold by Elisabeth Vincentelli
Electric Ladyland by John Perry
Unknown Pleasures by Chris Ott
Sign 'O' the Times by Michaelangelo Matos
The Velvet Underground and Nico by Joe Harvard
Let It Be by Steve Matteo
Live at the Apollo by Douglas Wolk
Aqualung by Allan Moore
OK Computer by Dai Griffiths
Let It Be by Colin Meloy
Led Zeppelin IV by Erik Davis
Exile on Main Street by Bill Janovitz
Pet Sounds by Jim Fusilli
Ramones by Nicholas Rombes
Armed Forces by Franklin Bruno
Murmur by J. Niimi
Grace by Daphne A. Brooks
Endtroducing... by Eliot Wilder
Kick Out the Jams by Don McLeese
Low by Hugo Wilcken
Born in the U.S.A. by Geoffrey Himes
Music from Big Pink by John Niven
In the Aeroplane over the Sea by Kim Cooper
Paul's Boutique by Dan LeRoy
Doolittle by Ben Sisario
There's a Riot Goin' On by Miles Marshall Lewis
Stone Roses by Alex Green
In Utero by Gillian G. Garr
Highway 61 Revisited by Mark Polizzotti
Loveless by Mike McGonigal
The Who Sell Out by John Dougan
Bee Thousand by Marc Woodworth
Daydream Nation by Matthew Stearns
Court and Spark by Sean Nelson
69 Love Songs by LD Beghtol
Use Your Illusion I & II by Eric Weisbard
Songs in the Key of Life by Zeth Lundy
The Notorious Byrd Brothers by Ric Menck
Trout Mask Replica by Kevin Courrier
Double Nickels on the Dime by Michael T. Fournier
People's Instinctive Travels and the Paths of Rhythm by Shawn Taylor
Aja by Don Breithaupt
Rid of Me by Kate Schatz
Achtung Baby by Stephen Catanzarite
If You're Feeling Sinister by Scott Plagenhoef
Swordfishtrombones by David Smay

and many more to come . . .

Greatest Hits Volume 2

edited by David Barker

continuum

NEW YORK • LONDON

2007

The Continuum International Publishing Group Inc
80 Maiden Lane, New York, NY 10038

The Continuum International Publishing Group Ltd
The Tower Building, 11 York Road, London SE1 7NX

www.continuumbooks.com

Library of Congress Cataloging-in-Publication Data for each individual title in the 33 1/3 series is available from the Library of Congress.

ISBN 978-0-8264-2876-9

Contents

Introduction vii
by David Barker

21 Armed Forces 1
by Franklin Bruno

22 Murmur 19
by J. Niimi

23 Grace 35
by Daphne A. Brooks

24 Endtroducing . . . 60
by Eliot Wilder

25 Kick Out the Jams 72
by Don McLeese

26 Low 89
by Hugo Wilcken

27 Born in the U.S.A. 109
by Geoffrey Himes

28 Music from Big Pink 134
by John Niven

29 In the Aeroplane Over the Sea 148
by Kim Cooper

30 Paul's Boutique 159
by Dan LeRoy

31 Doolittle 175
by Ben Sisario

32 There's a Riot Goin' On 191
by Miles Marshall Lewis

33 The Stone Roses 205
by Alex Green

34 In Utero 217
by Gillian G. Gaar

35 Highway 61 Revisited 236
by Mark Polizzotti

36 Loveless 254
by Mike McGonigal

37 The Who Sell Out 268
by John Dougan

38 Bee Thousand 283
by Marc Woodworth

39 Daydream Nation 305
by Matthew Stearns

40 Court and Spark 323
by Sean Nelson

Introduction

Welcome to the second collection of excerpts from Continuum's acclaimed, successful, and sometimes peculiar 33 1/3 series. For those who don't know, it's a collection of short books, each one dedicated to a particular album from the last forty or so years. Some of the books are straight journalism, some are intellectual critiques, some are miniature memoirs, and some are straight fiction. But all, we hope, are inspired by the album in question, and shed some light on what makes it special.

In this book, you'll find extracts from volumes 21 through 40 in the series—books that were originally published between April 2005 (Elvis Costello's *Armed Forces*) and December 2006 (Joni Mitchell's *Court and Spark*). Looking back on this period of the series, it definitely starts to veer toward what's commonly known as "indie rock." That was never part of the plan, but there's a fair amount of that in here: books on albums by Jeff Buckley, Neutral Milk Hotel (at the time of writing, the best-selling book in the series so far), the Pixies, Stone Roses, Nirvana, My Bloody Valentine, Guided By Voices, and Sonic Youth. As the series moves forward, you'll see more books on hip-hop, metal, the unclassifiable (Tom Waits, Throbbing Gristle), and, yes, on Celine Dion.

It struck me fairly early on, putting this series together, that many of the albums that writers most wanted to cover were records they'd first heard—and fallen in love with—during their adolescent years. What is it about pop music that lends itself so readily to teenage kicks? Is it the subject matter of the lyrics? (Sometimes, yes.) Is it the sense of rebellion? (A little, maybe.) It's certainly distinct from other popular art forms of the last few decades. Not that many people obsess over the films they first saw when they were teenagers, and neither do they keep talking about the novels they read at that age, or the TV shows that were on at the time. But the right music, if it finds you in those early teenage years, never lets go.

My own epiphany came early on in 1984, just after I'd turned fourteen, and it was entirely my sister's fault. I remember going to the record store in town—she bought an album that had a depressing, washed out photo of a guy's chest and stomach on the cover, and I bought the new album by Elton John. (The one that had "Passengers" and "Sad Songs (Say So Much)" on it. Check it out if you get the chance, it's a good record!) I distinctly remember being pleased with my purchase as it meant, in some way, that I was now more current than my parentsho had a whole bunch of Elton John albums at home, but *probably didn't even know this one was out yet*. Anyhow, that evening my sister handed me a tape and said, "See if you like this." As I lay in bed a little later in the darkness and pressed the play button on my crummy Walkman, I had no idea what was about to hit me.

"It's time the tale were told of how you took a child, and you made him old." I really had no idea what this man was singing about, or why his voice sounded like no other singer I'd ever heard, but after those first ten seconds I was completely floored. By the end of the song, I could barely breathe. It seemed to be a tale of somebody's innocence being forcibly taken away, and it felt to me as though I'd left my childhood behind in those six minutes or so. And as sad as that sounds, it was a wonderful feeling—childhood is great (or at least mine was) but I was ready to move on. As I pressed rewind and waited for the tape to rush back to the start, all I wanted was to hear that song over and over and over again. I must have listened to it at least fifteen times that night before falling asleep.

So perhaps it's that. If the right music finds you at the right moment, it can build a bridge to get you from where you were to where you want to be. And I think a lot of the books in the 33 1/3 series seize on that in some way, and try to get the heart of what made certain albums so transformative, so powerful, to so many people. I hope that some of the extracts in this book strike a chord with you, and that you'll want to explore further books in the series as a result.

David Barker

New York, August 2007

Armed Forces
by Franklin Bruno

Franklin Bruno's criticism has appeared in *The Believer, Slate, Salon, Best Music Writing 2003* (Da Capo), and *Listen Again: A Momentary History of Pop Music* (Duke University Press). After several records as a member of Nothing Painted Blue and as a solo artist, his most recent musical project is *Civics*, the debut CD by the Human Hearts (Tight Ship); he is also a recording and occasional touring member of the Mountain Goats. He has taught philosophy at UCLA, Pomona College, and Northwestern University; currently he is Visiting Assistant Professor at Bard College.

Unlike Sam Cooke and, later, Aretha Franklin and Al Green, **Ray Charles** did not cross over to secular stardom from a significant gospel career. But in combining a spiritual melody ("My Jesus Is All the World to Me") with a worldly R&B lyric—and a vocal style that split the difference—his 1954 recording of "I Got a Woman" became the template for modern soul. His 1962 album *Modern Sounds in Country and Western Music* was no less innovative. Dressing a genre often viewed as crude in lush string arrangements and vocal choruses would have been bold for a white performer of the time; for a black singer to wring a #1 pop hit ("I Can't Stop Loving You") from this synthesis was revolutionary.

Elvis Costello's own trawl through the country repertoire, 1981's *Almost Blue*, was widely viewed as an outsider's attempt to annex foreign territory; how much it owes to Charles' more successful one has gone unnoticed. Produced by Billy Sherrill, who got his start in the Muscle Shoals soul scene before heading to Nashville, *Almost Blue* again sets a rough vocal presence against the sort of smoothed-out backing that Charles introduced to the genre (and which Sherrill brought back home). This, at least, was the idea; EC later expressed disappointment that the countrypolitan polish was not more liberally applied. The album ends by confounding the distinction between black and white vernacular music with "Honey Hush," previously recorded both as jump blues (Joe Turner) and rockabilly (Johnny Burnette).

No stranger to career reversals, Charles forgave—"excused" is the better word—EC for his behavior in Columbus not long after the episode (*see Columbus,* p. 6). His on-the-record comment: "Anyone could get drunk at least once. Drunken talk isn't meant to be printed in the paper and people should judge Mr. Costello by his songs rather than his stupid bar talk." This leaves what the appropriate judgment ought to be entirely open.

Even more than on "Green Shirt," the arrangement and production of "**Chemistry Class**" seem imposed on the song from without. The verses alternate strictly between two instrumental textures, linked by an eight-note pulse carried first by piano, then by toms. The third verse switches the order of these units, setting up a dramatic approach into the final chorus. The choruses combine these opposing registers, and thicken the sound with an acoustic strum (and some precise piano/electric guitar interplay); ABBA's influence is, if anything, more pervasive than on "Oliver's Army." Dub/psychedelic touches from early in the album return: tremoloed guitar clouds the mix, and an atonal, arrhythmic howl of uncertain provenance dominates the fade.

The repetition of "if it wasn't for some *acciden—accidents*, some would never, ever learn," turns 4/4 time into 5/4 for exactly one measure—not that you have to count the beats to register this as a tear in the fabric. The Attractions could have learned to play the song this way, but they didn't. Bechirian created the effect by a tape splice of two copies of the recorded performance. "It was just an idea I had—I didn't know what anyone else would think of it. So I took a rough mix home, did the splice on a Revox, and brought it in. Nick and the band thought it was great, so we ran another copy of the master and spliced it into the final mix." Such touches are not exactly an EC trademark, though there have been others: on *Blood & Chocolate*, Lowe assembled "Battered Old Bird" from three performances in different tempos. In this case, the effect is self-referential—it *sounds* like an accident. Along with the darkness and wetness of the mix, it also ties the album's penultimate song to its opening track, with "Two Little Hitlers" as a dried-out coda. This is less evident in the US track order, where "Chemistry Class" sits next to "Moods for Moderns" in middle-of-Side-Two purgatory.

Beneath the disruption and ornamentation lies a simple form: three verses, three choruses. The verses are in EC's "knocked-together" mode, running over a five-chord progression with little effort to regulate meter or rhyme scheme. (The second verse is eight bars longer and cycles through the chords twice, but its harmonic relation to the chorus is identical to the others'.) The verse melody is conversational, contrasting with the richer chorus. The harmony opens up at the title, but this line and the next ("you don't know what you've started") are based of what has come before; what differs is EC's smoother phrasing, and the elaborate melisma on "mine." This sets the stage for the song's central melodic—and verbal—event: "Are you ready for the final solution?" The notes are held longer; "lu-tion" leaps up nearly an octave from "so," landing on the sophisticated sounding major seventh of the underlying (and out-of-key) C chord. The phrase subsides with a drawn-out "oh"—very much a pop-rock "oh," not a R&B/soul "ooh"—as a standard IIm–V–I transition leads back to the verse.

Even if we've already assimilated "white niggers," "Quisling Clinic," and "you'll never make a lampshade out of me," this hook is as disturbing as it is meant to be—genocide set to a wide-open pop tune, with a family resemblance to "Strawberry Fields Forever." Worse, it appears to be a near-pun; by association with the title, "solution" carries the sense of "combination of liquids" as well as the blander "answer." We can hear what EC is asking us all too well, but it is not obvious why. Throughout *AF*, EC tests popular music's lab equipment and his own growing mastery of it; here, this amounts to seeing just how bitter a pill he can sugarcoat.

In the *Rolling Stone*/*Ranters* interview, EC dismissed parts of *AF* as "glib," and commented further on its "charged language" in the Rhino notes: "Personal and global matters are spoken of with the same vocabulary; perhaps this was a mistake." Or, as Pamela Thurschwell has written, "One of Costello's most dubious and interesting moves is to take the imagery bequeathed by the Holocaust as the metaphorical fodder of modern existence." But with this song, set late in the album, it's no longer clear which way this metaphor is supposed to run. The surrounding verses, vivid but diffuse, are no help, touching on (among other things) scientific imagery, bad jokes about vocational school, and an oblique sense of sexual threat. Are the matters spoken of here personal, or global—or is asking this our first mistake?

The early live version—so early that the third verse is missing—on the Rhino bonus disc seems to have been included to back up EC's claim, in the liner notes, that the song reflected his disaffection with American audiences, particularly collegiate ones. The crowd is noisy, ignoring the dressing down they paid to hear. For all they care, he could be singing anything from "Cha-Dooky-Doo" to "Deutschland Über Alles"; no wonder he sounds like he wants to ruin their lives.

This extra information is interesting in retrospect, but it wasn't available to most listeners; even now, the *AF* version is more effective if its origins are left opaque. If there's more than a stunt here, it's what the stunt demonstrates: that the language, if not the fact, of atrocity has become so commonplace that it can be pulled from its proper context and incorporated into the triviality of a pop record, a mass market artifact disseminated indiscriminately to the many—very many, if all goes as planned—who will hear it. We ought decently to recoil from the chorus, and to some degree we do, thinking, "He's gone *too far.*" But most of us—EC's audience—let him get away with it, though we've just heard what we would normally agree to be the unique, unassimilable, unrepresentable tragedy of twentieth century history made, as Barthes would say, "childish, sophisticated, obscure." To the extent that we hear this question and keep listening, our implicit answer is "Yes."

This sort of stunt doesn't work in bars.

According to his friend Lord Beaverbrook, **Winston Churchill** "sang the popular music-hall melodies in a raucous voice, and without any regard for tune."

The success of **Eric Clapton** was built on his extension of blues guitar styles, and the innovations of Jimi Hendrix—who Clapton first encountered on the British tours managed by Stiff Records co-founder Dave Robinson—into a mastery of the extended, expressive solo. Clapton has also borrowed from the black music of the British Commonwealth: His 1974 cover of Bob Marley's "I Shot the Sheriff" reached many listeners unfamiliar with the original, and with reggae more generally.

Despite these debts, Clapton directed an anti-immigrant

diatribe to his audience at Birmingham Odeon, on August 5, 1976: "Do we have any foreigners in the audience tonight? If so, please put up your hands. I think we should vote for Enoch Powell." He also warned that Britain was in danger of becoming "a colony." The concert was not far from the site of Powell's 1968 "rivers of blood" speech; one wishes Bonnie Bramlett had been in the vicinity. His conciliatory letter to the English music paper *Sounds* ran, in part, with spelling and punctuation preserved:

> Dear everybody
> I openly apologize to all the foreigners in Brum . . . its just that (as usual) I'd had a few before I went on, and one foreigner had pinched my missus' bum and I proceeded to lose my bottle [. . .] and I think I think that enoch is the only politician mad enough to run this country. . . . yours eccentricly, e.c.

This episode was the seed for Rock Against Racism, which grew from the positive response to another open letter, published in *Sounds*, *Melody Maker*, *New Musical Express*, and the *Socialist Worker* later in 1976, signed by photographer Red Saunders and six others:

> [. . .] Come on Eric . . . you've been taking too much of that *Daily Express* stuff and you know you can't handle it. Own up. Half your music is black. You're rock music's biggest colonist. You're a good musician but where would you be without the blues and R&B? You've got to fight the racist poison otherwise you degenerate into the sewer with the rats and all the money men who ripped off rock culture with their cheque books and plastic crap. We want to organize a rank and file movement against the racist poison in music. We urge support for Rock Against Racism. P.S. Who shot the Sheriff Eric? It sure as hell wasn't you.

Clapton did not get the message. In a December 1978 *Melody Maker* interview—a few pages away from the announcement of RAR's first national tour—Clapton called Powell "a prophet . . . the only one telling the truth for the good of the country," adding: "The racist business starts when white guys see immigrants getting jobs and they're not." The same issue contained a full-page "thank you" from his promotion company for his recent soldout European tour—with "Special Guest Star Muddy Waters."

"**Clean Money**" was the last *AF* outtake to surface, first on *Taking Liberties/10 Bloody Marys*, and a few months later as a b-side to "Clubland." What if it *had* opened *AF*, as originally planned? The seventh-chord voicings and vocal arrangement, derived from "Taxman," would have seemed a self-conscious invocation of *Revolver*—another beat group's "leap" toward sophistication and variety. By EC's account, the track's power-pop charge was absorbed from Cheap Trick's *In Color*, another tour-vehicle standby; but once the other songs had undergone their studio transformation, this guitar-led rave-up must have seemed trad by comparison. The words, obscure as they are—what is clean money, and is there any?—would have announced the connections made in "Busy Bodies" that much sooner. In retrospect, the song's most remarkable feature is how smoothly its lyrics fit, with only light revisions, over the opening track of *Get Happy!,* the Supremes-inspired "Love For Tender."

Those curious about what disrespect for James Brown sounds like are invited to seek out "Chicken Funk," a 1976 single by Bay Area country-rockers **Clover**, paying special note to the repeated grunting of the title by frontman Huey Louis, later Lewis. The rest of the band—adrift in England, where they were managed by Stiff's Rivera and Robinson—backed EC on *Aim*, without credit. Only multi-instrumentalist John McFee has maintained this professional connection, sitting in on the Palomino dates mentioned earlier, as well as *Almost Blue* and 2004's *The Delivery Man*.

Columbia Records, the US label for *AF*, was founded in 1886 as a regional distributor for Edison equipment; the company began manufacturing "noiseless" shellac discs in 1921, and inaugurated their nationwide radio network (CBS) six years later. In 1948, Columbia introduced the ten- and then twelve-inch long-playing (LP) record, which eventually made possible, for good or ill, the "concept album." EC was signed to the label after publicity generated by a performance in front of its London office in July 1977 and was nearly dropped from its roster after the negative publicity generated on the Armed Funk tour.

EC's career-altering encounter with Bonnie Bramlett took place on April 15, 1979, around 2 AM, in a city named for the first European to make a commercial splash in the States. "The Columbus episode," "the Columbus incident," or—as though it were a Civil War battle—simply "**Columbus**" are the conventional labels for the affair. Most readers know the crux of the story: In the heat of some sort of drunken argument, EC described James Brown as a "jive-ass nigger," and Ray Charles as "nothing but a blind, ignorant nigger." (The last two adjectives are sometimes reversed; disturbingly, the insult seems to play off Charles' mother's famous line: "You're blind, not stupid.") One finds this much in even the shortest capsule biography of EC, often accompanied by Charles' exculpation, already quoted.

A transcript of EC's New York press conference two weeks later exists (and can be found, with running commentary, in Alan Jones' *Uncut* article on the episode, one of several sources synthesized below), but there was no tape running in the Columbus Holiday Inn lounge. Variations on the story are part of the story; it is as myth and rumor that the episode had and continues to have its effect. On the other hand, there is such a thing as too much distortion: some online versions name EC's interlocutor as Bonnie *Raitt*.

Known to be present were: EC, Bruce Thomas, Bramlett, Stephen Stills and his manager Jim Lindemith, band members including percussionist Joe Lala and organist Mike Finnigan (and his mother and brother, visiting the tour from nearby Troy), and a Japanese bartender named Eddie. Unidentified members of both bands' road crews were likely on hand; the other two Attractions and manager Jake Rivera, it seems, were not.

Thomas later recalled arriving at the hotel after the gig, for BBC Radio One: "I can remember seeing this other bus, and the general feeling was 'another group.' It was as if sailors came into harbour and saw another boat there. And then, whoa, 'It's Steven Stills!'" EC is more matter of fact in the *RS/Ranters* interview: "Bruce Thomas and I were in the bar after the show. . . . And we were *very drunk*. Well, we weren't drunk to begin with—we were reasonably drunk. And we started into what you'd probably call joshing. Gentle gibes between the two camps of the Stills band and us."

Costello's ungentle judgment of Americans raised the stakes: "We hate you. We only come here for the money. . . . We're the original white boys, you're the colonials." The May 5, 1979 *RS* "Random Notes" item, reported from information offered by Bramlett, gives this as a general pronouncement to the "barroom crowd"; in other reconstructions, it is a response to a fan's questions. Either way, this is fairly self-damning as insults go, splitting the difference between the view of British imperialism conveyed by "Oliver's Army" and the current album and tour's express end of "conquering America."

Most accounts now jump to EC, provoked or not, calling Joe Lala a "greaser spic." (Lala, a Florida-born Italian-American, was a leading session player until he developed tendonitis in the mid-80s; like Bramlett, he later became a character actor.) Some also have him calling Americans "just a bunch of flea-bitten greasers and niggers." By now, EC had left behind irony for straight abuse. In response, Stills either punched or pushed EC and left. Someone, maybe Thomas, called after him, "Fuck off, steel-nose," referring to Stills' coke habit and subsequent reconstructive surgery.

Much of the ensuing argument with those still in the bar was quasimusical. Thomas later paraphrased the tenor of his and EC's comments: "Jimi Hendrix had to come to England, The Beatles had to sell you Tamla Motown." Bramlett told *RS*: "I mean, here's this guy who looks like Buddy Holly, plays Chuck Berry licks and uses Elvis' name, saying American music was shit and this was 'a fucked country.'" (Certainly, "Pump It Up" derives from Berry's "Too Much Monkey Business" via Dylan's "Subterranean Homesick Blues," though it's questionable whether EC was guitarist enough to play Berry's actual *licks*.) Alan Jones may be extrapolating from Bramlett's account in having EC "badmouthing" his namesake and his look-alike without direct quotation.

At some point, Bramlett was the remaining representative of Stills' camp willing to engage EC. *RS* reported that she "opened the conversation by praising Elvis." Some biographies repeat this point, but it has slipped out of the received version. It makes little difference; EC wasn't offering or accepting any olive branches. Jones next has her accusing EC of "stealing and plundering from America's rich heritage of black music"—though not, one guesses, in just those words—"citing James Brown and Ray Charles specifically." The dismissal of Brown was the response; Bramlett next asked, "All right, you son of a bitch, what do you think of Ray Charles?"

One can only speculate as to whether Bramlett and EC knew exactly which parts of the just-mentioned "rich heritage" the other had borrowed. But it must have been obvious to both that the final question was a line in the sand—even this twerp won't knock The Genius; oh, won't I?—which EC immediately crossed. I hope that the ugliness of EC's remarks needs no further emphasis; Bramlett's questions appear to have been asked out of the presumption that her own position and attitudes were beyond reproach.

The *RS* version of what came next runs:

> "That's when I slapped him," Bramlett said. "I told him that anybody that mean and hateful had to have a little tiny dick. I told him, "Don't put the tongue on Ray Charles." Costello responded with a string of obscenities, causing Stills' band manager to fling him against the bar, setting off a brief rumble that ended with Costello retreating upstairs. . . . "This had to happen when I was trying to be a lady," lamented Bonnie, "Back when I was drinking, I woulda kicked his ass."

EC's exit line is usually given as "Fuck Ray Charles, fuck niggers, and fuck you!" Many retellings have Bramlett, before or after these words, not merely slapping him, but knocking him down or out. *People* described the free-for-all that followed as "a bench-clearing but punchless hockey brawl," with Lindeman battling EC's roadies and Eddie the bartender putting an end to the "fracas." Both Mike Finnigan (advised by his mother to keep out of the melee) and Bruce Thomas (a participant) have said that Bramlett dislocated EC's shoulder, though EC has since contended this was done by Stills' roadies; in the *RS/Ranters* interview, five.

The next morning, by EC's account, he only remembered what had happened once he noticed the pain in his shoulder. He wore his arm in a sling for the next several days, though there seem to be no reports of his not playing guitar at subsequent shows in Detroit, Dayton, Louisville, and Cleveland. By April 21, when the tour reached Harrisburg, Pennsylvania, *AF* had reached the Top Ten; Bramlett, meanwhile, had begun to call up, in Jones' words, "every newspaper, wire service and magazine on the East Coast." As write-ups began to appear, *AF* was rapidly dropped from radio playlists, and removed from some record stores. ("Quite rightly," EC told Marcus, "Until there was some explanation.") By Rochester, on the 25th, EC was opening sets with the then-unrecorded "I Stand Accused," even before the publication of widely read accounts in *RS* and the *Voice*. The press conference EC called to defuse the charge that he held the views his words had expressed took place at Columbia's New York offices on the 30th. This was a pitched battle of another sort, with EC facing fifty-odd writers, most of whom found the accused insufficiently apologetic and blithe to the subtleties of the situation. At one point, Robert Christgau explained to EC, "What you don't seem to understand is that by saying, 'I am not a racist,' you're not going to convince many people in this room, especially the black people, that you are not a racist. *That* is not what constitutes not being a racist." Earlier, asked how he came to use the most offensive language available, he replied, "Everyone's had occasions to go to absolute extremes . . . even to say things that you don't believe, you know. Ask Lenny Bruce," invoking the comedian's famous riff: "If President Kennedy got on television and said: 'I'm considering appointing two or three of the top niggers in the country to my cabinet'—it was nothing but 'nigger, nigger, nigger'—in six months 'nigger' wouldn't mean any more than 'good night, god bless you . . . '" Few were buying; even if this is an aim of *AF*'s "charged language," EC's "off-the-record" behavior was obviously not meant to defuse anything.

Despite the threats mentioned earlier, no shows were cancelled, and the *Voice* reported seeing "no pickets out front, no pickets of any sort" at the March 31 Palladium concert. At least one show of the next night's troika was protested, as EC recalled for Marcus:

> I'd been wandering around with this idea that the rest of world was reading my mind, just presuming that you don't always have to wave a huge banner saying, "I really like black people." Because you just end up looking like Tom Robinson or Joan Baez or something, a cause-monger. One branch of Rock Against Racism in Chicago were so surprised [by the Columbus story] that they wrote asking what the hell was going on. But in New York, they picketed our gig at the Bottom Line and handed out leaflets saying "Send them back to England" and so forth. And inside the pamphlet they were handing out as part of their own publicity, was a great big picture of us playing at Brockwell Park, at their rally, the year before. Still, the April Fools' Day shows came off smoothly enough. But Columbia turned down Rivera's request to hire out Shea Stadium after a radio call-in promotion attracted (by one report) 250,000 ticket requests. This was a bad omen: displeased by the storm

over Columbus, the label went to no great lengths to get *AF* back on the radio or in the stores.

Fred Scheurs' post-mortem in *RS*, archly titled "What'd I Say?" concluded that the Brits had stirred up enough ill will over the course of their travels—a near-riot after a truncated set in Berkeley, an insult to a sponsoring radio station in St. Louis, Rivera and tour manager Des Brown's bully-boy tactics with photographers just about everywhere—to make the current mess nearly unavoidable.

People, meanwhile, brought the story to an "Elvis who?" readership. Burt Reynolds graces the cover of the April 9 issue; a teaser for "The dark genius of John Cheever" runs just below another: "The songstress who bopped Elvis Costello." Though Richard K. Rein's piece duly notes that EC "is a member of an anti-racist group and has spoken out against neo-Nazi factions," it is largely a platform for Bramlett, "a longtime paladin of rhythm-and-blues." At one point, she seems to connect Vietnam, the civil rights movement, and the recent Havana Jam, which left her "feeling real proud of America after what we saw down there. A lot of my friends have died for this country and now we're trying to wade through the racism thing. Costello is destroying what we went through in the '60s. Blacks are the people I'm singing for." (With Stephen Stills? And the Allman Brothers? In 1979?)

Between the tour's final shows and his return to England, EC filmed a scene for the low-budget movie *Americathon*, lip-synching "Crawling to the U.S.A." in front of a back-lot mockup of Buckingham Palace. "There's one way out, there's only one way," runs the chorus; the song, recorded at a one-off Australian session, had been written in 1977, before his first US visit. Three months after World Elvis Costello Album Three was declared, he was crawling back, none too sure that he would ever return.

Columbia chose not to drop him; he would tour America next with *Trust*, in January 1981. But as late as the *RS/Ranters* interview, he was still "absolutely convinced" that his career had been defined and his music overshadowed by the episode and its aftermath: "The first thing that a lot of people heard about me was that incident. I think it outweighs my entire career." Marcus also asks if he has made any overtures of apology toward, for instance, James Brown. His answer: "What could I say? How could you explain such a thing? But there is nothing I'd like more."

Aim contains several well-documented soul references: the staccato chorus of "Alison" derives from the Spinners' "Ghetto Child," and The Ronettes' "Be My Baby" supplies the drum intro to "No Dancing." (Though, as EC told the Dutch magazine *OOR* in 1977, "You could just as easily say it's from 'Not A Second Time' from the Beatles.") But it takes someone like critic Douglas Wolk to trace "Blame It on Cain" to Roy Alfred and Del Serino's "That's It, I Quit, I'm Moving On," a minor 1961 hit for **Sam Cooke**. They can be superimposed on one another, harmonically and melodically, for the length of the verse, right up to "ah, but I never been accused" (in EC) and, "oh, honey that's not fair" (in Cooke). Lyrically, the songs are unrelated, though certain lines in "That's It . . . " would sound more at home on, say, *Blood & Chocolate* than on a Hugo & Luigi-produced Cooke side: "though your hair was all in place / somebody smeared the lipstick on your face / they smeared it every place."

"Motel Matches"—recorded for *Get Happy!* but first performed, with an earlier set of lyrics, on the Armed Funk tour—alludes to the sordid end of Cooke's career, by way of a 1959 George Jones hit: "Who Shot Sam?"

Barney Bubbles' original UK **cover** design is less significant for its iconography than for what it says about EC's professional position. The ability to commission a unique, costly package signified—as much to the label as to the audience—that, as of this record, he had become a commercial force to be reckoned with. (Despite the success of *Model*, this was as much bravado as fact; from the early Stiff days, Jake Rivera was notorious for spending the label's resources on profit-draining posters and promotional materials.) Photographic representation of the artist is entirely absent; ELVIS COSTELLO AND THE ATTRACTIONS and ARMED FORCES (in engraved-invitation script) are visible only in miniscule lines of type, crowded to the edges by the cover painting of elephants charging through the mist; a fair number of British consumers, it was assumed, would be on the lookout for this release, rather than being stopped in their tracks by EC's unlikely name and image while flipping through the bins. (Likewise, the sleeve has no informative, conveniently fileable spine.)

The front cover conveys an unmistakable sense of attack; otherwise, it is an oblique accompaniment to an album that contains few if any references to the natural world, much less to "human nature." This realistic (though cinematically framed) rendering contrasts with its stylized surroundings. Of the cover's fold-out flaps, the outer surfaces of three depict, quite literally, armed forces: American sailors dragging a cannon, Chinese soldiers shouldering rifles, and a wider "shot" of tanks on a sketched-in battlefield. These are interrupted by and/or framed against polka dots and kindred design elements; the fourth flap, divided into squares by an extra cut in the cardboard, bears primary-color representations of a sergeant's chevron.

The inner surface is decidedly abstract; the central square is the drip-image familiar from the Columbia release, with squiggles of black extending into the outer panels, which employ a range of devices—zebra-stripes, paw-prints, cartoon Mondrian. The whole package can be reassembled so that these surfaces appear as the record's outer shell; the effect is of art-historical modernism turned to the ends of commercial design.

The words at the top edges of the inner sleeve indicate which side is to be read first. OUR PLACE . . . centers on a photo of EC slumped over a diving board, as an unidentifiable body does the dead man's float in the pool below; around this, a number of identical rectangles are labeled with decorator colors (HYDRANGEA BLUE, FIREFLY RED), which seem to have no special relevance—though BLUE GRASS and BLACK BLACK are intriguing. EMOTIONAL FASCISM runs along the bottom edge; on the flip (. . . OR YOURS), the catalog number (RAD 14) occupies the same spot. The song titles, not given on the outer sleeve, surround another photo, this one of the band posing uncomfortably on the driveway of a suburban home, above the L-to-R legend STEVE ELVIS BRUCE PETE.

Besides the *Live at Hollywood High* EP included with early pressings, the package contains photographs of the individual musicians, on oversize six-inch square postcards. Bruce Thomas strikes a mock-Bond pose in front of a pink sports car, with a party girl attached to each leg; Pete Thomas, in vest and tie, stands blindfolded and headphoned in a nondescript hallway, punching a calculator (as in "Two Little Hitlers"?); Steve Nieve is snapped candidly at Disneyland, beside a sign reading SORRY—THIS ATTRACTION IS NOT IN OPERATION TODAY. The sole black-and-white shot is a formal studio portrait of EC, a cooler variation of the iconic front cover of *Aim*. Behind a Gretsch acoustic, the singer's stance is still knock-kneed, but he is clad in leather and Beatle boots, with a hint of the other Elvis' pompadour. Alongside the front cover's chevron, a slogan on the back of all four cards reads DON'T JOIN. Linked with the album title, this restates the order implicitly given in, most obviously, "Oliver's Army" and "Goon Squad." Here, it also suggests that EC's newly "attractive" image ought not to be trusted; there is a hint of Dylan's "Don't follow leaders, watch the parking meters."

The modest, more standardized packaging of the Columbia release reflects EC's lesser clout in the States—though even here a batch of copies were pressed on collectible gold-specked vinyl. The elephant panel is moved to the back cover, reduced to make room for a track listing and a legible rendering of the artist's name and album title, printed in a property-of-the-military stencil-font; these are repeated, along with a headshot of EC, on a sticker pasted to the shrinkwrapping. Bubbles' alternate front-panel spells or spills out the same information as though by accident, alongside a caricatured, jesterish profile, presumably meant as a stand-in for the singer.

Using this convenient element of the UK package as the US cover had other connotations. Bubbles—I am willing to speculate—would have been well aware of Abstract Expressionism's place as one of America's primary cultural exports after World War II. His mocking appropriation of the style is of a piece with the popified magnifications of Roy Lichtenstein's mid-60s "brushstroke" paintings, and with the British conceptual-art collective Art & Language's critical attempts to combine the drip technique with representational imagery, as in the 1979–1981 series *A Portrait of V. I. Lenin in the Style of Jackson Pollock*. In the GET MERCENARY print ad, EC holds a semiautomatic weapon to his own mouth, as though taking himself hostage; behind him, the "splatter" motif takes on yet another meaning.

In 1644–1645, long before "English Civil War" was a Clash song or "New Model Army" the name of a drab leftist Britpunk outfit, **Oliver Cromwell** dissolved the standing army of England, largely commanded by members of Parliament, via the Self-Denying Ordinance, and raised 22,000 men, recruited nationally, against King Charles I. This was the first armed force to base rank and promotion on merit rather than social standing, and the first composed largely of paid volunteers—egalitarian, but mercenary.

How closely does "Oliver's Army" resemble "**Dancing Queen**"? In most respects, not very; for one thing, it has none of the light funk syncopations of ABBA's 1976 multinational smash. The story repeated by EC and others is that his highest charting UK single might have been relegated to a b-side (or handed over to Lowe for his next solo album) if not for a crucial addition. "It didn't appear all at once," Bechirian says. "We already had a master take, and Steve had been going toward that part for a while by the time we did the overdubs." This is borne out by the finished record, which is resourceful but not as slick or precise as its model. Rhythmic chatter can be heard between two or more competing piano tracks, especially during the intro; where one drops out, it's a good bet that an underlying part conflicted harmonically.

ABBA's piano part—the record is so seamless that calling it Benny Andersson's seems strange—is the springboard for SN's, though they function differently. The earlier song uses the piano sparingly; at times, it simply emphasizes a rhythmic detail. SN plays the role of several instruments; his upward run at the end of the choruses resembles a string passage in "Queen." That the songs are in the same key (A major, before the final key change in "Oliver's") makes their most specific point of contact easier to describe: a descending three-note phrase, with each preceded by a grace note. There are slight differences of execution: SN plays fuller voicings, often attacking the notes three times for a grandiose light-classical effect.

In the intro to "Queen," (and in the vocal choruses, after "seventeen") this phrase, played in quarter notes, appears near the middle of a four-bar section, starting on the *fourth* beat of the third measure and extending over the first two beats of the next. It begins on the root of the home key, descending the major scale from there: A–G#–F#. In "Oliver's," the phrase is the climactic flourish of the piano-dominated intro; it begins on the *third* beat of the third measure of a four-bar section. Played twice as slowly, as half notes, it fills up all the space before the end of the section. Also, SN starts on the fourth of the scale and descends *toward* the root: D–C#–B. Quite naturally, given its rhythmic and harmonic placement, he invariably completes the series with a fourth chord, landing squarely on the tonic at the downbeat, before dropping out (in favor of organ) for the verse.

These technical differences reflect an aesthetic one. In "Dancing Queen," the phrase is one morsel of ear candy among others, disappearing without resolution. In "Oliver's

Army," the entire piano part is a neon arrow pointing back to EC's lyric and vocal.

Ray Charles' "**Danger Zone**" appeared in 1961, as the flip of "Hit the Road Jack." Both sides were written by Percy Mayfield, a 50s rhythm & blues star and Charles' favored staff writer at the time. It is a wonderful, underknown song, a straight 32-bar AABA with minor-blues touches brought forward in Charles' recording by Ellingtonian horns. Its overt sociopolitical import is unusual for commercial soul of the time (and for Charles at any time): "The world is in an uproar, the danger zone is everywhere." That uproar is, in part, over civil rights, but the bridge also indicates Cold War anomie: "that's why I'm so afraid / of the progress that's been made / toward eternity." Charles performed the song in Berlin in 1962, at a sports arena once used for Nazi rallies; his valet Duke Wade felt "like Hitler was there his damn self."

EC and band covered the song for a 1983 BBC session, later released on the *Punch the Clock* bonus disc. The choice is of a piece with his concerns at the time: recorded in the year of "Pills and Soap" and "Shipbuilding," the session also includes a medley of "Big Sister's Clothes," an oblique anti-Thatcher song from *Trust*, and a dub cover of The Beat's gloriously unambiguous "Stand Down Margaret." Four years after Columbus, this is the first time EC approaches a song associated with Charles, though one many listeners would not recognize. (See, by contrast, "Sticks and Stones.") EC would perform the song more convincingly on a 1989 acoustic tour, but this early performance doesn't quite come off. The radio-studio mix is bland, and the most moving lines in Charles' rendition are scarcely credible coming from EC: "I love the world like always, because the world is part of me."

After sorties to Japan and Australia, EC and the Attractions bivouacked at London's **Dominion Theater** for seven shows between December 18 and Christmas Eve, 1978. The stand was disappointing, displaying the band's exhaustion and their discomfort with a sit-down venue. But on the final night, the audience found an unexpected present on their seats: a teaser seven-inch of "Talking in the Dark" and "Wednesday Week," two outtakes from the forthcoming album. Copies were also given out in New York, during the March 31 one-night-three-clubs stunt; both tracks later appeared as b-sides for "Accidents Will Happen."

Built in 1929, the 2,000-seat Dominion had hosted early talkies, variety shows, and the London runs of *South Pacific* and *The Sound of Music.* (As of this writing, it houses *We Will Rock You*, a *Mamma Mia*-zation of the Queen catalog.) Jake Rivera's timing and choice of venue was pointed: on the eve of launching *AF*, EC was made to demonstrate his drawing power in a location associated with the forms of showbiz his persona and music had so far defied, with a name meaning, in the context of British imperialism, "self-governing territory."

Talk about your blonde on blonde: peel back the skin of "Dancing Queen," and one finds the sun-bleached bones of the Beach Boys' "**Don't Worry Baby**." As a double a-side with "I Get Around," this was a #1 hit (#7 UK) in June 1964; "Oliver's Army" is in some respects a reshuffling of its devices. EC's verse melody resembles Brian Wilson's chorus—the single-voiced "answer," more than the harmony group. Both songs use a classic 8-bar/4-bar, verse/pre-chorus form, diverging at the chorus. ("Don't Worry Baby" has no distinct bridge, only an instrumental verse.) The songs are in different keys, but both begin with the same I–IV–V progression, though Wilson's arrangement moves the bass, rather than the whole chord, under the final change.

After this, the relationship is subtler. "Don't Worry Baby" remains in its home key until the end of the pre-chorus, using a passing chord underneath, for example, "when she makes *love to me*" to modulate up from E to F# for the chorus, returning under the "ooh-ooh" passage. "Oliver's Army" changes key even earlier: the verse is in A, and an out-of-key passing chord (C#7, under "setting the world to right") moves the pre-chorus ("called careers information") into E—but a quick turnaround (at "occupation") brings the chorus back to the verse's key and chord progression, now played twice as fast. These are different modulations than those in "Baby," but the final verse's move up to B major—it's not elementary to say where in the unstable bridge progression this occurs—resembles Wilson's pre-chorus/chorus trick.

The use of a song by the 60s' great escapists as the grid for a *realpolitik* lyric is meant as a subversion; but it also brings something about the original to the surface. The vagueness of Wilson's chorus ("don't worry baby / everything will turn out alright") makes it easy to forget the framing narrative of the verses, in which a hot-rodding braggart is reluctantly forced into a face-saving drag-race: “but I can’t back down now / I pushed the other guys too far.” No reassuring “girl back home” figures in “Oliver’s Army,” but its soldier-of-fortune narrator plays out a parallel adventure story on the global stage.

Murmur

by J. Niimi

J. Niimi writes about music for the *Chicago Reader, SPIN, City Pages,* and *SF Weekly*, among other publications. In previous years he worked as a studio engineer, recorded eight albums as the drummer of Ashtray Boy, and hosted a weekly radio show on WHPK. He lives in Chicago with his wife and their two border terriers.

1.

The four members of R.E.M. loaded their guitars and drums into a decrepit van in mid-January of 1983 and left their home of Athens, Georgia, heading north on I-85. The 200-mile drive took them to Charlotte, North Carolina, where they would begin work on their as-yet-untitled full-length debut album. Vocalist Michael Stipe would later give it the title of *Murmur*, picking it from a list he read somewhere of the seven easiest words to say in the English language.

It was a drive they'd made many times already. Aside from numerous road trips there for club shows—their reputation as a great live act was already spreading throughout the Southern Atlantic states with an unchecked momentum—they'd also recorded a seven-inch single and an EP with North Carolina native Mitch Easter at his Drive-In Studio in Winston-Salem, so named because it was located in his parents' converted garage space. Easter had recorded the band's "Radio Free Europe" single there in April 1981, and the *Chronic Town* EP six months after that. The band had also met their manager Jefferson Holt after a July 1980 gig in nearby Carrboro where Holt was working the door—R.E.M. was filling in for Pylon, who couldn't make the show. At the time, Holt was managing a record store and was starting to book local shows for out-of-town bands, with a particular interest in the burgeoning Athens scene. It was through Holt that the band decided to work with Easter at Drive-In, after Holt had asked his friend Peter Holsapple for some suggestions about cheap recording studios. The R.E.M. guys were already big fans of Holsapple's band, the dB's, which helped clinch the decision.

Easter's home studio was primitive, but its relaxed atmosphere (guitarist Peter Buck tells stories of Easter's mom bringing the band coffee and donuts), coupled with Easter's complementary pop sensibilities, made it an ideal place for R.E.M. to begin addressing the problem every nascent band encounters: how to translate their road-hewn material to vinyl. This wasn't much of a concern for the band when they recorded their first single with Easter—the "Radio Free Europe"/"Sitting Still" seven-inch, released in a tiny initial pressing of about a thousand copies by their friend Johnny Hibbert on his new "label," Hib-Tone Records. It wasn't even so much of a concern after the band signed to I.R.S. Records and released *Chronic Town*—the label was fine with the idea of starting the band off with an EP release that would break listeners' ears in, while giving the band time to further hone their songs and develop their studio sound. But with the surprise buzz created by "Radio Free Europe" (voted #1 single in the *Village Voice*), as well as the rising cult popularity of the *Chronic Town* EP (especially in England), I.R.S. was now expecting R.E.M. to come up with an album that could capitalize on that underground buzz and parlay it into national recognition. At the same time, the band did not want to make a record that pandered to any of the prevailing radio chart trends: Euro-synth pop, hair metal, and light-rock balladry. More importantly, they simply couldn't even if they had to. *Murmur* was a giant gamble in a sense, but it was their only choice, and as far as the band were concerned, they had little to lose.

Peter Buck was born in California and moved to Roswell, Georgia in 1971 at the age of fourteen. He attended Emory University in the Atlanta suburb of Decatur from 1975 to 1977, eventually dropping out to take a job at Wuxtry Records in Athens the following year (where he continued to work off and on until about 1986), teaching himself guitar in his spare time by playing along with records.

It was while working at Wuxtry that Buck struck up a friendship with Michael Stipe. Stipe was born in Decatur, Georgia, but moved around in his childhood due to his father's army career, living briefly in Germany and attending high school in Southern Illinois, near East St. Louis. Stipe moved to Athens in the late 1970s to study art at the University of Georgia, and met Buck in early 1979. Stipe and his two sisters were regulars at Wuxtry, and he would come in to browse the racks and talk about bands with Buck, who often noodled around on his guitar while manning the counter. Eventually the conversation came around to starting a band themselves.

Buck was living in a deconsecrated church on Oconee Street in Athens, the former St. Mary's Episcopal Church, which was sublet by Dan Wall, Buck's employer at Wuxtry. The dilapidated church was subdivided into crude bedrooms, with a large space in the back perfectly suited for band practices (as well as some of the college town's notoriously raucous parties). Buck's roommate and sometime girlfriend Kathleen O'Brien introduced him to her friend Bill Berry, whom she had met in the UGA dorms. Berry was born in Minnesota and moved to Macon, Georgia with his family in 1972 as a young teen.

It was back in Macon that Berry first encountered Mike Mills, a fellow high school student. Mills is arguably the band's closest thing to a "native" Southerner: though he too was born in California, like Buck, Mills's parents moved to Georgia while he was still a baby. As a teenager Mills was a clean-cut straight-A student, while the teenage Berry was something of a long-haired stoner, and the pair did not get along well until the day they both happened to show up at the same band audition and reluctantly decided to bury the hatchet (as Berry had already set up his drum kit and thus couldn't bail out of the rehearsal). The two ended up becoming best friends, playing together in a few different bands (including one called the Frustrations, which included a local guitarist by the name of Ian Copeland). The duo eventually moved to Athens together in 1979 to enroll at UGA.

The four future members of R.E.M. were finally introduced to one another by Kathleen O'Brien in the fall of 1979. It was a less than auspicious beginning: Stipe was put off by Mills's falling-down drunkenness, but he did like Berry's now-famous monobrow, which Stipe credits for tipping the scale in his decision to join up with the two Maconites. A few months later,

O'Brien was planning a party at the church on Oconee Street in celebration of her birthday, to be held on April 5, 1980. She had gotten the popular local band the Side Effects to agree to play, but she now needed an "opening act." She asked the as-yet-unnamed (in fact, barely formed) R.E.M. to play as well. The band was thrilled at the prospect and said yes, though they had only a couple of half-hearted, beer-soaked rehearsals under their belt by this point.

Buck and Stipe had written a few tentative songs together before they met Berry and Mills. Together the four of them worked out a few more originals, as well as a slew of covers, rehearsing in the back of the church during the Winter of 1979–80. After O'Brien's invitation to play came in February, the band kicked up the pace, cobbling together a set's worth of songs in the weeks before the party, deciding at the last minute on the name Twisted Kites (after discarding such other possibilities as Negro Eyes and Cans of Piss—though some band members claim that they played the party without any name at all).

About three hundred people showed up at the church that night, surpassing even O'Brien's expectations: the birthday gathering was now an Event. After the Side Effects finished their set, Twisted Kites/R.E.M./untitled took the stage, playing about twenty songs, roughly half of them originals, to a wildly enthusiastic (and profoundly drunk) crowd. The band was so well received that night, in fact, that the crowd goaded them into playing their entire set a second time. Among the covers reportedly included in the set were "Honky Tonk Women," "God Save the Queen," "Secret Agent Man," the Troggs' "I Can't Control Myself," and the Monkees' "(I'm Not Your) Steppin' Stone." Among the band's originals that night (also documented on the early bootleg *Bodycount at Tyrone's*, recorded about six months after the party—a fairly representative cross-section of the band's early material[1]) was a nascent version of "Just a Touch," which appeared in final form on *Lifes Rich Pageant* in 1986.

Their earliest material was fast, brash, and goofy. Most of the lyrics were first person narratives from Stipe directed, interestingly enough, toward women subjects (or possibly *against* women subjects, as some R.E.M. historians believe). There's a liberal use of the rock pronoun *baby*, and plenty of *I don't wanna*s à la the first Ramones record. The band settled on the name R.E.M., picked from a dictionary—it didn't have any trite "punk" connotations, and Stipe really liked the periods. Plus, like *Murmur*, it was easy to pronounce.

The band was an almost instant hit on the Athens scene. But as they started to venture out of town, they realized that maybe they weren't just a local beer-party phenomenon. With encouragement from Jefferson Holt—who had moved to Athens to manage the band—they decided to try and record a demo to send out to clubs and record labels. The band's first "recording session" was held on June 6, 1980, a couple months after their gig at the church party, in the back of the Decatur branch of Wuxtry Records, where Buck had worked as a student at Emory. It was a stop-off on the afternoon of their first out of town gig at the Warehouse in neighboring Atlanta, essentially a rehearsal for the show, and they bashed through eight songs while Wuxtry owner Mark Methe videotaped them. (While the band never used the tape, which sounded like crap, the murky audio track of the session has shown up on various bootlegs over the years as *first demos*.)

Holt suggested they make a proper recording to showcase their newer songs, so they booked a day at engineer Joe Perry's Bombay Studio, a small eight-track setup in nearby Smyrna, in February of 1981. Within a matter of hours the band laid down eight songs, including skeletal versions of "Radio Free Europe," "Sitting Still," and "Shaking Through." Though the tapes have never been made public, the results were apparently less than stellar—Holt urged the band not to send them around and went looking for another studio and engineer. At the suggestion of Peter Holsapple, Holt called Mitch Easter.

Easter recorded the band's seven-inch on April 15, 1981, in his garage studio setup. The band wisely decided to focus on just a few songs, rather than banging out a whole mini-set as they did at Bombay, so they recorded "Radio Free Europe" and "Sitting Still," as well as a third song, "White Tornado"—a quasi-surf instrumental they had just written. The band slapped together a few hundred handmade cassettes of the three songs (plus a "dub mix" of "Radio Free Europe" that Easter had later spliced together, half-jokingly) and sent the tape out to clubs, labels, magazines, and just about anyplace else they could think of. Hib-Tone released the seven-inch of "Radio Free Europe" b/w "Sitting Still" in July 1981; of the initial pressing of 1,000 copies, 600 were sent out as promos, and a total of around 6,000 additional copies were later pressed by popular demand (amazingly, since the first pressing mistakenly omitted any contact info for the label). The band was annoyed with the muddy-sounding mastering job (Buck smashed one of his copies and nailed it to a wall in his house), but the single spurred a critical buzz for the band, garnering wide-spread plaudits and landing on a number of year-end Top 10 lists. R.E.M. started to get letters from labels, most of which made them laugh. They threw them in the fireplace and kept playing.

* * *

The band played a high-profile show in Atlanta that previous winter—their biggest yet—opening for the Police at the Fox Theater in December 1980. They landed the prestigious gig through Bill Berry's old friend from Macon, Ian Copeland (brother of Police drummer Stewart Copeland), to whom Berry had been sending the band's rehearsal and demo tapes. Ian was now running F.B.I., a successful booking agency that handled the Police, among other I.R.S. acts, and had been bugging his brother, Miles Copeland, the president of I.R.S., to sign R.E.M. Miles had heard the band's cruddy demo cassette and wasn't that impressed, but he eventually capitulated in the face of Ian's hyperbolic praise, dispatching I.R.S. VP Jay Boberg to New Orleans in March of 1982 to check out the band in person. The show that night was at a drug-infested dive called the Beat Exchange, where the toilets in the bathrooms were clogged with used syringes. The night was by all accounts a disaster—the Rastafarian sound man wandered off before their set started, and the band, uncharacteristically, suffered from horrible stage fright. But Boberg was sold, and upon returning to LA he advised Miles Copeland to sign R.E.M. The band adjourned to the label's New York office in May 1982 to sign a five-record deal. I.R.S. bought the master tapes the band had recorded with Easter and released *Chronic Town* in August 1982, with plans for a full-length album release the following spring.

* * *

Reflection Sound Studios in Charlotte looks pretty much like any recording studio that dates to the early 70s, when audio electronics began to enter the consumer market—a market that included both the people who consumed music and the people who wanted to make it themselves. Only five years earlier, recording studios were still building their own equipment with solder and sheet metal. Beyond companies with the wherewithal to employ engineers (real engineers, with professional training in electrical and mechanical engineering), having a viable recording setup not backed by radio revenues was the domain of amateur hobbyists, some of whom served in military capacities (like the army signal corps, where unlimited access to cutting-edge technology first whetted these hobbyists' appetites for audio experimentation).

With advancements in the electronic manufacturing industries (centered around the refinement of the transistor), these folks could now buy high-quality, reasonably priced mass-produced gear in place of their primitive homebrew inventions or costly, hard-to-come-by European products designed for broadcast applications and state-funded budgets. Now they were able to get down to what they wanted to do in the first place beyond all the soldering irons and the oscilloscopes, which was to make music. In turn some of these people built commercial recording studios to subsidize their dual interest in what was essentially folk technology and folk art. Though it's easy to take both for granted today, without independent studios there would be no independent music.

Not being affiliated with any particular record label or company, Reflection Sound Studios serviced a wide range of musical genres and clientele. It was outfitted with a modest array of professional grade recording equipment and musical gear, and could be rented by the hour or by the day by anyone, with or without the services of one of its house engineers. Reflection's layout was typical of many studios at the time, a plan that's still commonly used today in the construction of studios: A central control room contains all the recording equipment, adjacent to a larger studio room where the band plays, with a soundproofed double-pane glass window connecting the two and providing a sightline between the engineer and the band. The control room at Reflection is elevated slightly above the level of the live room, looking down into it, and is accessible by a small staircase in the hallway outside the live room.[2]

Inside the live studio room, connected by another door and window, is a smaller, closet-like "isolation booth," an enclosed, acoustically treated space where loud things like amps or a drum kit can be placed so as not to interfere with the other instruments. Like a lot of studios, Reflection also has a smaller second studio room, although R.E.M. did not utilize it on *Murmur*—in fact, there were other sessions in progress there during the recording of the album. The band even dropped in on one Studio B session during a lull in *Murmur* to contribute handclaps to another band's record. As far as the studio was concerned, R.E.M. was just one anonymous group out of many that were booked at Reflection over the course of January and February 1983—probably less notable by virtue of being a rock band.

Running an independent recording studio in any city is a treacherous business, but especially so in a small city off the mainstream record industry's map—Charlotte is a good seven-hour drive from Nashville and ten hours from New York City. Luckily, Reflection's setup was ideally suited to its bread-and-butter clientele—Southern gospel and soul groups. Reflection's main live room, Studio A, is an open thirty- by forty-five-foot wood paneled space designed in such a way that not only can it accommodate a modern gospel choir and band (plus its drummer in the isobooth), the room's acoustical properties are uniquely suited to the genre as well. The room is "live," or acoustically reflective, enough for voices to sound natural singing in it, but controlled enough to allow engineers to capture their sound with relative ease, without the technical problems that often arise when there are a lot of microphones capturing a lot of people producing a lot of sound in one enclosed space. As *Murmur* engineer Don Dixon put it in recording slang, "[Reflection's Studio A] was just the right combination of live and dead." The main room's sonic properties probably lent themselves to the duality of the studio's name: a space designed with a sensitivity for acoustical reflection, as well as the more spiritual kind—much like a church or a cathedral. In 2003, two Grammy Award-nominated gospel albums were made at Reflection.

While anyone would be hard-pressed to describe R.E.M. as a gospel act, it's interesting to think about how the studio's legacy might have resonated with the band during their stay at Reflection. They were still in the Bible Belt, but they were now in a different house of devotion, where soul musicians came to make Christian records (and vice versa)[3], a place that also happened to be sanctioned by musically like-minded hipsters like Dixon and Easter. It's reasonable to imagine that the band must have thought about their own devotion and austerity in such a place, both in terms of the band's sound and the personal life that each was starting to give up in the name of music.

Murmur was a new kind of sacrifice for a band that was becoming accustomed to sacrifice—after all, being in a band, as anyone who's ever been in one can attest, is not so much about freedom as it is about the giving up of one kind of burden for another. If the open road and the creative lifestyle do afford an escape of sorts, going into the studio is an equally profound time of confrontation, a kind of reckoning. The most intense recording sessions are fueled by an energy that's a lot like religion—a concentrated time when individual needs and egos are put aside in the attempt to galvanize a higher collective mind, especially when the stakes are high, as they were for R.E.M. by 1983. By comparison, the making of *Chronic Town* was a sleepover. Here the four of them lived together like monks in the squalor of a cheap hotel room for three weeks; rock stars don't steal ketchup packets from Burger King just to have something to eat with the stale tortillas they scavenge from the back of the van. But what they ate and how they slept only defined their existence—their lives during those weeks were defined at Reflection. There was penance and ecstasy and catharsis. It sucked, but how much more could it suck otherwise? Which is probably an even better description of what church is for.

It ought to be remembered that R.E.M. wrote most of their early songs in the pew of a dilapidated church, where skylight angled down on them through holes in the collapsed ceiling. Birds alighted from their amps when they came to practice. Peter Buck even used the phrase "spooky gospel" to describe the sound of *Chronic Town*'s "Gardening at Night." Buck lived in a church, but Stipe would have been comfortable there too—he was christened John Michael Stipe, after John Wesley—a choice informed by his Methodist grandfather who was a preacher in Georgia. A year after the *Murmur* sessions, during the recording of *Reckoning*, Stipe jokingly grabbed a gospel album out of a closet at Reflection and sang its liner notes over the backing track of "Seven Chinese Brothers" as a warm-up exercise. Beyond the parts where Stipe cracks up and his cadence falls off, it's startling how effortlessly Stipe could make lines like "the joy of knowing Jesus" fit the music, as if his vocal delivery had always been an arcane kind of preaching masked only by his usually obtuse lyrics.[4] In fact, there's an underlying sense of the grandson-of-a-preacher-man throughout *Murmur*'s imagery and language. In "Pilgrimage," Stipe sings, "speaking in tongues / it's worth a broken lip," bringing Pentecostal notions of authenticity to bear on his own cryptic lyrical style. "Talk About the Passion" has the quasi-Christian refrain "not everyone can carry the weight of the world." And the existential turmoil in "Perfect Circle" is resolved in its chorus of "heaven assumed"—a notion later revisited, in Classical terms, in the idea of "dreams of Elysian" from "West of the Fields."

But Reflection was also a good choice because it was geographically convenient for everyone involved. The band was already comfortable making the trek from Athens. They set up shop at the nearby Coliseum Motel on Independence Boulevard, sleeping two to a cot. They didn't enjoy the comfort of sympathetic fans and their beds this time around, but they also didn't suffer from the distraction, or the fatigue of vertical sleep in a smelly van. Mitch Easter and Don Dixon lived about an hour's drive away in the Winston-Salem area, and made the daily commute. On most days they worked from noon to midnight, going their separate ways at the end of the day (except for one detour to a local moviehouse to see the movie *Strange Invaders*, in which their song "1,000,000" makes a brief appearance).

Charlotte was cheap then as it still is today. If the band had opted to make the album in New York or LA, most of their tiny budget probably would have been blown in the first week—nowadays, R.E.M. probably spends *Murmur*'s budget on a typical album's catering bills. And this was one tight budget indeed. Easter and Dixon reportedly split a $3,000 advance between the two of them in order to make the record, with the total budget for the record topping out at a paltry $15,000. As Dixon told me:

> We were on a very strict budget—both Mitch and I took substantial pay cuts to do the record—but we believed in the band, and believed that the studio was a good value. It was handy to all of our home bases, it was out of the mainstream music cities—so the label couldn't pop in whenever they wanted—and it allowed for a certain *je ne sais quoi* that appealed to the band.

And beyond money and geography, Reflection was the obvious choice for more artistic reasons. Although the band wanted to continue working with Easter as producer, they both knew it was time to move up from the garage to a more versatile and more hi-fi environment. Although Easter was well versed in studio practice and was sympathetic to R.E.M.'s ideas, he wasn't totally comfortable bringing the band into a new studio as the primary engineer. Easter knew and trusted Dixon, who already had experience at Reflection as an engineer and as a recording artist.

Reflection had a number of technical advantages over Mitch's home studio, where *Chronic Town* and the "Radio Free Europe" single were recorded. Unlike a lot of independent studios, Reflection had an inside connection with the sales reps at MCI, the manufacturers of top-end studio equipment—a relationship that not only ensured privileged access to state-of-the-art products, but also the specialized servicing necessary for the constant maintenance of complex and sometimes temperamental pro audio gear. In terms of nuts-and-bolts, Reflection's Studio A boasted a 36-input MCI 600 mixing console ("The snazzy one with the plasma display," as Easter recounts)—an industry workhorse that, beyond its clean circuitry and well-designed architecture, also allowed for increased tracking flexibility as compared with Drive-In's smaller Quantum 24-input console. The extra tracks gave the engineers and the band more elbow room in terms of instrumental tracking, sound treatment, and mixing. Reflection also featured a two-inch 24-track MCI tape deck, which offered sharper fidelity over Easter's one-inch 16-track, as well as more room for various engineering techniques, such as retaining multiple takes of Stipe's vocals in order to edit the best parts of each down to one superlative final track.

Still, it would be somewhat simplistic and disingenuous to say that R.E.M. was "limited" by the parameters of Easter's home recording setup on their earlier recordings. The transcendent, organic production on the Easter-produced *Chronic Town* EP not only makes you doubt that the band's vision could ever have been realized had they gone the more conventional route in 1982 (big label/big studio/big producer . . . and they had numerous offers along these lines), but also that the EP would ever have garnered a fraction of the oddball mystique that ultimately gave the band the agency and leverage to make *Murmur* and make it on their own terms. This was before indie rock (and even "college rock"), so the irony may be lost now that back then the easiest and most direct way to make a record was to *get* a major label contract, not to be so quixotic and dumb as to try and make one yourself. Yet this is exactly what Easter and the band had succeeded in doing, against most odds.

Chronic Town succeeded as a fully realized expression of R.E.M.'s aesthetic because Easter was one of the craftiest engineers in the 80s in terms of being able to thrive within technical (and budgetary) limitations—not to mention the fact that Easter was working with an exceptional band with exceptional song material. Still, Easter's studio space was only barely conducive to recording ("a twenty-four-by-twenty-four-foot exgarage with extremely hard walls and a low ceiling," as he describes), and judging from R.E.M.'s earlier abortive attempts at recording (and in well-appointed places like New York's RCA Studios), Easter's resourcefulness and attentive ears were the main things that made up for what were otherwise extremely modest circumstances. Reflection's equipment, on the other hand, allowed Easter and the band to exercise a similar creative freedom in the studio but with fewer logistical worries. The increased fidelity was only a plus—not to mention the fact that Easter was freed up by Dixon's presence behind the console, now able to focus more of his energies on things like arranging and production, as well as being able to jump in front of a mic when he felt like it to lay down an overdub or two on guitar or the vibes.

In terms of its other tech knickknacks, Reflection's modest arsenal showed discreet taste, even by 2005 standards. The studio boasted an excellent collection of high-quality vintage microphones (like the vacuum-tube Neumann U47, whose globe-like foam windscreen reminded Stipe of Angela Davis), as well as choice signal processing gear like compressors (a couple of UREI 1176s, which are an engineer's '65 Mustang), exotic new digital delays (like the Lexicon Model 200, at the time the Lamborghini Countach of digital reverbs), and a few cherry perks, such as the studio's tube EMT plate reverb.[5] As Easter said, "Reflection was essentially comparable to any studio anywhere, gear-wise." As such, Dixon and Easter didn't find it necessary to bring any of their own gear, except for a few signature musical instruments. Easter brought along his white Fender Electric XII twelve-string guitar (a gift from his father when he turned thirteen; Peter Buck did not own an electric Rickenbacker twelve-string at this point, contrary to fan myth), as well as his trusty Danelectro electric sitar (which Buck had used in the *Chronic Town* session, most prominently on "Gardening at Night"). Easter's Electric XII can also be heard on many of Let's Active's early recordings.

Peter Buck's workhorse amp—his Fender Twin—was broken at the time, so Easter loaned him his checkerboard-grill Ampeg Gemini II for the session, which was used on most tracks, alongside the studio's little solid state (i.e., transistor rather than tube-driven) Kasino amp. Guitar-wise, Buck had brought his maple-glo Rickenbacker 360, which he had also used on the *Chronic Town* session. Mike Mills had been using a Dan Armstrong bass up to the time of *Chronic Town*, but Easter lent him his Rickenbacker 4001 bass on an early garage session, and by the time of the *Murmur* sessions Mills had bought his own. Mills played through the studio's trusty Ampeg B-15, which was set up in the hallway outside the live room. Dixon recalls Bill Berry using the studio's Sonor drum kit, set up in Studio A's isolation booth, which everyone called the "Tiki Hut" for its cedar-shingled conical ceiling. Easter remembers wanting to set Bill up in the main room, but Berry, in his ratty Steel Pulse T-shirt, liked the weird little space and was excited to play drums in there—it was how he envisioned a studio session was supposed to be.

Easter, Dixon, and the band availed themselves of the studio's two pianos (a modern Yamaha and an old upright "tack" piano—so called because of the thumbtacks inserted on its hammers to compensate for the dark sound of its enclosed harp), its Hammond B-3 organ, its Wurlitzer, and the somewhat unusual presence of a vintage Musser vibraphone. These instruments played a big part in *Murmur*'s sound, and in resolving the band's aesthetic concerns. Dixon explains:

> I wanted to create a Stax-like sound in the balance of the overall mix. Vocals as part of a drum-driven groove. A big reason for this was the desire on the part of the band for the guitars to be very clean. Guitars were kind of "out" at the time, and fuzz guitars were scary to the band and the label. The best model I could think of to keep a heavy groove was the sound of old Stax records. With [these organic-sounding instruments] as part of the studio's standing arsenal, we had the tools we needed to accomplish that.

As is common studio practice, the band recorded the basic tracks for most songs playing together live—drums, bass, and guitars, and probably a "guide vocal" from Stipe—with the instruments acoustically isolated from one another. Buck's guitar amp was set up in the main room, Berry's drum kit was in the isolation booth, Mills's bass amp was in the outside hallway, and Stipe was in the space under the stairwell behind the control room (he didn't want anyone to see him sing). The band monitored themselves over headphones. Often in recording sessions, a band might start by recording the basic tracks for all the songs on the album, then go back and overdub the rest of the instruments and the vocals. However, for the *Murmur* sessions, the band proceeded one song at a time, recording all of its tracks—the live tracks as well as the overdubs—before moving on to the next song. For the most part, the band would record the basic tracks together, then one person at a time would work with Dixon and Easter on overdubs, while the rest of the band played pool in the other room or went to get something to eat. Generally the band was able to nail most songs within a few takes, having played most of the album's material exhaustively over the preceding months on the road.

The majority of *Murmur*'s live tracks were recorded using standard "close miking" technique, where a microphone is placed directly in front of an instrument in order to capture a clean and up-front sound. But in terms of overdubs, Easter and Dixon sometimes took advantage of Studio A's natural acoustics by employing "room miking," or placing a microphone at a distance from an instrument. This technique can be used to create a sense of space in a recording, or to create unusual effects. Reflection had a number of sound processing devices that could electronically recreate the sound of a room—or a gymnasium or a dungeon, for that matter—but Dixon and Easter's use of room miking was in line with the band's insistence on clean, natural sounds and acoustic, organic-sounding instruments. Devices such as digital reverbs and delay units offer the engineer many options as far as "juicing up" the sound of a recorded track, but often they can sound artificial and obtrusive. On *Murmur* Easter and Dixon strike a harmonious balance between electronic effects and natural ones.

Going into the *Murmur* sessions, the band already had a finished version of "Pilgrimage" in the can, recorded a few weeks earlier by Easter and Dixon as a "test" song over the course of a day or two at Reflection. Though the band was adamant about working with Easter and Dixon, I.R.S. had wanted proof that the two were right for the job. Reportedly, the label wasn't that excited at how "Pilgrimage" turned out, but the band stonewalled them anyway, booking time at Reflection in January 1983 to begin work on the album with Easter and Dixon. The crew worked on the album on and off for about a month over the course of January and February. Since the studio's log book from this period is missing, accounts of the actual amount of time spent in the studio vary: Buck has said it was as low as "about fourteen days," while other estimates have it at around sixteen or seventeen days total, and one accounting puts it as high as twenty-four days.

By all accounts, the album sessions went smoothly—the band played great; Dixon, Easter, and the band got along well (beyond a few heated disagreements about arrangement and production details), and despite a generous amount of beer-quaffing the band was all about business. They disagreed about certain minor decisions, but the band's democratic philosophy prevailed: one of their "rules" was that each member had full veto power about any decision, no matter how minor. Easter describes the atmosphere of the *Murmur* sessions, both within the band, and between the band and Dixon/Easter:

> Jeez, it was pretty civilized. Michael may have sort of been a little removed as the most high-falutin' Artiste in the sense that he had a sort of big-picture view of the sound and was not remotely interested in some "awesome" sound if he thought it was overbearing. Probably all the rest of the band (and I) might've been a little more teenage/rock 'n' roll in our sensibilities. They'd get a little grumpy, like during the "Perfect Circle" first-listen, but no big deal.
>
> Overall, they were as respectful of each other as any band I can think of, which was remarkable since they really were sort of different "types." They seemed to always grasp the importance of their identity as a unit, and protecting that was important, and that's probably part of why they could seem stodgy at times. They didn't want the outside world to mess them up! Within the band, those guys would mildly insult each other, etc. but it was never mean-spirited. . . . In general, they all seemed seriously dedicated to the effort.

Dixon was similarly impressed with the band's sense of identity, as well as the tempered confidence they displayed about their strengths and limitations as a band:

> Again, this was an era when you had to be able to play to record. These guys could all play. Would they collectively have made a great Steely Dan cover band? No. Were they creative and musical? Yes. Did they have one of the most unique (and therefore controversial) sounds around? Yes. Were they misunderstood by many fellow musicians, the kinds of guys who would go to the music store and play Joe Satriani licks to show off? Yes.

NOTES

1. It's almost comical to listen to the *Murmur* songs on the band's early bootlegs. The songs were all there, but the playing is so spastic it's almost hard to believe these guys had aspirations beyond punk. Live, they tried to perform record-collector kitsch as "new wave," and in the confines of the Oconee Street church it made sense, but on these early boots they sound lost—simply *geeks* as opposed to *record* geeks, let alone rock stars or even rockers. But the band was developing confidence in their songwriting sensibilities much faster than confidence in their performative abilities. After *Murmur*, they could now hear their songs in a way that finally let them perform these songs to satisfaction—you can hear the difference on post-1983 bootlegs—and this eventually fed back into their songwriting, enriching it, and they began to have a clearer idea of how to play the songs they wrote, and vice versa.
2. Reflection Sound is still in business: you can view pictures of its facilities at www.reflectionsound.com.
3. The album *Carolina Soul Survey: The Reflection Sound Story* (Grapevine, 2002) chronicles the history of Southern soul acts that recorded at Reflection in the 1970s.
4. This version of the song was eventually released as "Voice of Harold" on *Dead Letter Office* (I.R.S., 1987).
5. Mic geeks might be interested to know that Easter and Dixon hated Shure SM57s, and instead used its red-headed cousin, the SM7, for instrumental tracking—a dumb analogy would be to say that it's a bit like preferring RC over Coke. For ambient room miking, the crew often forsook the sportier AKG C 414 in favor of the more proletarian Electro-Voice 635A, according to Easter—"a cheap omni dynamic, and one of our favorites."

Grace

by Daphne A. Brooks

Daphne A. Brooks is Associate Professor in the Department of English and the Center for African-American Studies at Princeton University, where she teaches courses on African-American literature and culture, performance studies, critical gender studies, and popular music culture. She is the author of *Bodies in Dissent: Spectacular Performances of Race and Freedom, 1850–1910* (Duke University Press, 2006).

Chapter Three
New Electric Mysticism

> As soon as the EP came out . . . I was dying to be with a band. I was dying for the relationship, for the chemistry—you know people, the warm bodies. Male or female. Bass, drums, dulcimer, tuba . . . any way that the band would work out . . . I was hoping . . . marching bass drum or whatever.[1]

In the wake of the Sin-é buzz, Jeff Buckley turned his attention to Columbia Records and contemplated signing with a major label. The home of Miles Davis, Bob Dylan, Thelonious Monk, Mahalia Jackson, Ella Fitzgerald, and Buckley's close friend Chris Dowd's former band, ska-punk veterans Fishbone, Columbia possessed the kind of musical legacy that impressed upon the spirit of Jeff as he continued to define his own goals and intentions as an artist. Feeling the spirit of "the blood that [ran] in the veins" of that label's legacy, Buckley signed a recording contract with Sony Music/Columbia Records in the fall of 1992. Soon after, he began to imagine the kind of album that he wanted to make.[2]

As a stop-post on the road toward developing a vision of his first major recording project, Buckley and Columbia agreed to roll tape on Jeff live at Sin-é, as a way to document this critical early period in his career. In the summer of 1993 the performances that would comprise Columbia's *Live at the Sin-é* EP were recorded, capturing Jeff in his loose, adventurous, solo electric troubadour mode. To Buckley, however, the EP was, at its simplest, "just a love note . . . to Sine." He admitted that "at first, [he] didn't even want to record all that material." In fact, he would firmly maintain throughout his career that the Sin-é period "was really just a way station . . . just something" he was doing in order to get to some place else in his musical process. So with a "love note" on the wind and at the urging of Columbia A&R executive Steve Berkowitz, Jeff turned his attention toward producing his first full-length album.[3]

Who could provide the roadmap in the studio for an artist as mischievous and uncategorizable as Jeff Buckley? Even Berkowitz admits that getting Jeff to commit to a sound on record was shaping up to be a challenge since he "didn't want to choose because he didn't want to negate any part of himself." Enter a most unlikely character to sit at the helm of recording Jeff Buckley's album. Recording engineer Andy Wallace seemed, at first glance, an odd match to work with East Village eclecticism. At 46, the critically acclaimed Wallace had grown in stature as a recording wizard who had worked mostly with hard rock and metal icons such as Ozzy Osbourne. Wallace had also produced the Run-D.M.C. classic rap revision of Aerosmith's "Walk this Way," and he was perhaps best known in the 90s for having served as the sound mixer on Nirvana's era-defining *Nevermind* in 1991. Nonetheless, it was to Wallace that Berkowitz turned in the fall of 1993, believing him to be a good match for Jeff since the project "needed someone who" could "take small and particular things and create large soundscapes" that matched the epic quality of Jeff's musical interests. "Andy," Berkowitz recalls, provided "flow, openness, easiness, creativity." He would become, in fact, the perfect figure to help Jeff "edit his ideas into the way this music sounds now." At the urging of Berkowitz, Jeff contacted Wallace and the two agreed to a recording partnership resulting in *Grace*.[4]

Stir-Frying the Band

> Infiltrate alien territory and BE A SINGER FRONTING A BAND. . . . Like you use to, Jeff. Fuck the legacy, you are you.[5]

> The next album will have a band. I wanted to do live shows to get my ideas together. But I can only get so far by myself. For recording, I need ideas from other people.[6]

> It was "like stir fry: fresh ingredients . . . really hot . . . and really quick."—Matt Johnson, drummer[7]

In the exhilarating period between arriving in New York City and convincing Shane Doyle to let him play weekly gigs at Sin-é, Jeff Buckley experimented with playing the front man in a downtown outfit that seemed a natural outgrowth of his forays into East Village experimentalism. Former Captain Beefheart guitarist Gary Lucas, Jeff's collaborative partner from the St. Ann's benefit performance, had invited him to sing lead in his band Gods and Monsters, an electric "twenty-first century folk" ensemble (as David Browne refers to it) whose mystic leanings drummed up the ghosts of cosmic prog-rock icons like Genesis and Yes, crossing them with raga influences and Jimmy Page flourishes. It was a musical match that seemed to make perfect sense for Jeff.

Yet surprisingly, it was also a short-lived New York City band experience for the California transplant. By the spring of 1992, Buckley made a decision to break with Lucas, dramatically finishing off what would turn out to be one of the band's final gigs by singing solo after his band mates had retired from the stage.

> But now I must find my own voice and work hard in a special direction without distraction, without the guitar player calling in the media cavalry before there's anything for them to really shout about.[8]

That "special direction" had led Jeff perhaps more rapidly than even he expected to the point of choosing and defining his own vision as a recording artist in the summer of 1993 as he prepared to go into the studio that fall. Having settled on Andy Wallace as a producer for the project, Jeff turned back to the issue of performing with a band and emphasized to Wallace and others his firm conviction that working with a group of musicians was a critical and necessary component in his aim to reach his larger goals as an artist. "The object of going solo," he once explained, "was to attract the perfect band. All my favorite music has been band music. I love listening to Bob Dylan, Robert Johnson and Thelonious Monk alone, but, the fact is, there are so many other areas you can go with other instruments going at the same time."[9]

In the summer of 1993 and just two months before the slated September commencement of his recording sessions, Jeff Buckley began to assemble the group that would ultimately travel through recording *Grace* and touring in support of that record for the next two and a half years. Soon after meeting bassist Mick Grondahl at a Columbia University café gig, Jeff connected with drummer Matt Johnson, a friend of Rebecca Moore's. As Johnson recalls it, the three "played together for only a couple hours" and "that night he said I want you to make my record . . . and that was that pretty quick . . ."[10]

Each in their early to mid-twenties and possessing a downtown, handsome, disheveled *je ne sais quoi*, Jeff, Mick, and Matt came together rapidly to create a core performing unit. Remarkably, they went from meeting each other and forming as a group to recording within less than a month and, according to Berkowitz, they had played together less than ten times before heading into the studio to begin production.[11]

> We didn't have to explain anything. It was sort of already understood. . . . We really connected emotionally and musically and as friends. And I never really felt like oh I'm a side man or professionally I'm not part of the process artistically or professionally. It was just like—"yeah, we're a band." And it just felt great.—Mick Grondahl, bassist[12]

The trio had only six weeks to rehearse before making the trek to Woodstock, New York to record and thus spent much of that time in the East Village jamming and beginning to gel as a unit. As a group they were traveling at lightening speed toward evolution as a three-piece creative organism fluidly, fearlessly, and brilliantly coming into its own in a compressed amount of time.

Into the Woods: Burning & Building at Bearsville

> I'm trying to learn from the great teachers . . . and trying to pay tribute to them. But now I have to burn away all these others and get down to what I really am inside.[13]

> The setting is great because it's outside Manhattan. . . . Because I'm an easily distracted person, and I can't sleep. . . . It's like being on a pirate ship. There's nothing to do but make this ship sail.[14]

The "clean slate" that was Jeff's new band, as Andy Wallace refers to it, traveled north of the city, into the woods and up to Bearsville Studios near Woodstock, New York for what was originally to have been a five-week period of recording. The environment seemed ideal for encouraging "interdependence, living together, eating together" and steering the curiosity-seeking Buckley away from the distractions of city life. Instead, he channeled all of his buoyant energy and endless fascination to revise and to experiment into the recording sessions that Wallace worked to harness. "He was," Wallace observes, "always on to something new . . . which was brilliant, it was great. But it was an important aspect of getting the record accomplished to keep him focused. . . . Things were always changing . . . "[15]

The studio setup actually was geared toward capitalizing and building on the ever-changing and evolving energy, intimacy, and momentum of Jeff's performance style. The aim was to "break down the idea of division between the recording room and the control room: just play music." "They didn't come in to record," Berkowitz adds, "but to play music." They were working toward that ideal, ineffable place where there is "no division between the moment of creation and getting everything down on tape."[16]

Toward this goal, "the room was set up in a way where there would not have to be stoppage. You wouldn't have to stop and to get out other guitars and get out other amps and re-mic everything."[17] Wallace and the group set up two different full band recording situations—for louder and softer ensemble playing with two different sets of drums all miked up and set to go at any time. Wallace was always ready with tape rolling. An additional third performance area with microphones was set up with a riser, similar to a small stage in a café. From time to time, Jeff would sit down and play songs. There was no set plan or schedule for these recordings, but these sessions clearly provided a fluid bridge between Buckley's solo work and the structure for his new experimentation with the band.

Five cover songs from this setup—"Lost Highway," "Alligator Wine," "Mama You Been on My Mind," "Parchman Farm," and "The Other Woman"—capture the dynamic musical environment in which Jeff immersed himself while making *Grace*. Taken together, these cover songs expose the foundations of Buckley's prodigious musical knowledge. His interpretation of "Lost Highway" (a song made popular by Hank Williams) imports the self-scrutiny of country-folk into an open, sonic existential journey. "Alligator Wine" finds the singer playfully dabbling with the southern gothic blues-folk melodies of the eccentric Screaming Jay Hawkins. His sweetly homespun cover of Bob Dylan's "Mama You've Been on My Mind" reveals Jeff's indebtedness to the eloquent poetry of that artist. And a stretched-out cover of Mose Allison's "Parchman Farm Blues" appears to most closely resemble Mississippi bluesman Bukka White's interpretation of that song, in which White reflects on racial and class discrimination and the cold brutality of the Parchman Farm State Penitentiary.

> They were just jamming more. . . . He was also at the same time, I think, trying to grab hold of things that worked arrangement wise.—Andy Wallace[18]

> I very much like listening to arrangements of things, anything from Duke Ellington to Edith Piaf, the small orchestra with the singer. I like Um Kalsoon.[19]

One of the most unheralded miracles to all who were present in Studio A Bearsville during the fall 1993 recording sessions was the emergence of Jeff Buckley as a gifted composer with sophisticated ideas for an artist of his age. Like "a Gil Evans or a Brian Eno" Jeff began, during these sessions, to use "sound, studio, overdubs, space, and dimension to make an entire soundscape." He "imagined and worked out the entire musical composition—instrumentally, lyrically, the space that it took up."[20]

Even so, the first few weeks of recording were slow going as the band continued to take shape and as Jeff refined his musical focus. He was determined, for one, to make an album that was not limited to "one-sound," and thus he gradually moved through the process of jamming and experimenting with Grondahl and Johnson to formulate his vision.[21] Although the recording sessions at Bearsville lasted six weeks, Berkowitz recalls a significant turning point—what he refers to as "the moment"—when the "greatness" of which Jeff was clearly in possession came into full view and asserted itself in the studio. The band had recorded a bluesy track entitled "Forget Her" and had subsequently begun to show signs of developing intense texture, depth, and experimentation as a band. New sounds began to erupt out of Jeff as the group began to flourish and push past the foundation of his solo style and material. Berkowitz appealed for two more weeks in the studio, and the seeds of some of *Grace*'s most complex and sophisticated compositions were planted.[22]

Released on August 23, 1994, as another summer of grunge was pulling to a close, *Grace* would quietly assert an elegant shift in the popular music landscape. Stringing together influences as diverse and far-flung as Nusrat Fateh Ali Khan and Leonard Cohen, Led Zeppelin and Nina Simone, Benjamin Britten and the Cocteau Twins, *Grace* scored rock revolution in an entirely different key.

Screaming Down from Heaven: New Electric Mysticism

> He possesses "a voice that manages to be both angelic and metal edged, pretty yet eager to travel strange, atonal regions where the buses don't run."—Dana Darzin, *Rolling Stone*[23]

> Psychedelia is a resurgence of Romanticism's pastoralism and pantheism. Above all, psychedelia is the quest for a lost state of grace.—Simon Reynolds and Joy Press, *The Sex Revolts*[24]

In 1994 it took a whole lot of guts to open a major-label, full-length debut rock album with a five-minute, forty-two-second "song about a dream," a slow-burning howl of a track lamenting the departure of a mistress with hair like "black ribbons of coal." But into this twisted fairytale universe Jeff Buckley hurls us on "Mojo Pin," a jagged, crescendo-bending, elliptical tornado of a song that has you wading through the hummingbird serenade of Buckley's lullaby falsetto all the way into "memories of fire" and the wonderland world of ugly addiction. In this scorched-earth kingdom of an abandoned lover's malaise, "Mojo Pin's" singer beckons his listeners to travel with him to the center of a wild, disorienting lyrical and sonic field of play. This was no *Nevermind*, no *Ten*, no *Live Through This*—seminal records of the era that each respectively announced their arrival with bursts of guitar-driven voltage and aggressive, nerve-rattling vocals. Rather, the dreamscape of "Mojo Pin" unfolds gradually, slowly introducing minute and exquisite musical detail so as to spin a mystic and mysterious web from its first few atmospheric seconds.

Weird, intriguing, and unwieldy, think of this lead-off *Grace* track as Jeff Buckley's great "icebox laughter" masterpiece. It was Steve Martin (the ramblin' man, himself) who pointed out that "icebox laughter" is bestowed upon the very best, most offbeat films. At 3 a.m. as you stand with the fridge door ajar staring blankly into the glare of the icebox, that film you saw six hours ago bears down on you with its subtle yet shrewd wit and humor, and voilà, you are left in convulsions on the kitchen floor, overcome with a case of borderline hysterical laughter.

Like the best "icebox laughter" films, "Mojo Pin" has a way of mystifying upon initial spins. With the rhythmic wobble of an open-tuned guitar and harmonics that create a light, bright, airy sound, the song introduces us to Jeff Buckley in all his lyrically and musically oblique glory. Maybe it was that spacey, quirked-out vibrator bar, the swell of Buckley's lead vocals, the folkie strumming, but "Mojo Pin" was always the most daunting and disturbing Jeff Buckley tune to me. Lurching and lunging, busy and dissonant, it initially felt to me almost like impenetrable cosmic granola crunch.

But for all its oddball, rhythmic shifts and Zeppelinesque power chords, "Mojo Pin's" vocal details finally seduced me, held me, astonished me at the refrigerator door: the Qawwali octave slides that give the song its eastern flourishes, the Plant-like howling at the height of the song's final crescendo. This was some kind of mystical whirlpool of "violent romanticism," a song that—despite your best intentions, you might find yourself rocking your neck to in its final, headbanging minute and a half. A song that you might never be able to hum on your own, but one whose off-the-wall, quirky sonic noises and schizophrenic vocals might very well knock around in your head for days on end, at the foot of the icebox or in your dreams.

Originally entitled "And You Will," "Mojo Pin" had first seen the light of day with Gods and Monsters, although Jeff's lyrics for the song had been kicking around at least as early as 1989 in his Los Angeles notebook scribblings.[25] While working with Lucas, Buckley had arranged to match his lyrics to the guitarist's music, and a solo version of the song eventually surfaced on the *Live at the Sin-e´* disc. The collaboration gained new life on *Grace*. At Bearsville, Buckley invited Lucas up to contribute what he refers to in the *Grace* credits as his "magical guitarness," and the work between the two on "Mojo Pin" as well as the title track appears to have lent the album some of its most distinctly dense and detailed musical textures.

If Jeff had been sensitive to utilizing space and environment imaginatively and resourcefully in his live solo sets, "Mojo

Pin" is evidence of his ongoing interest in developing textural instrumentation and detail as a musician. Within moments of its opening, the track mixes frequencies and plays with bell-tone harmonics while marking tonal shifts, changing rhythms, and finally kicking into a very warm sound that makes use of the entire stereo field of sound. "Mojo Pin's" eastern guitar flourish drones unfold into shimmering cosmic ambience while Jeff's honey-rich tenor rises to the surface, shifting into falsetto and swelling into the pitch with the vibrator bar on the guitar. In an early act of extraordinary vocal finesse, he vocally matches, in these early minutes, the highest harmonics on the track. Here and elsewhere, Buckley makes mad use of changing time signatures and vocals unafraid to "travel strange, atonal regions."

Stretched out in bed and wracked with febrile visions, the singer of "Mojo Pin" is awake yet dreaming, emotionally naked yet also mysteriously opaque. Sinuously bending and twisting as the "rhythms fall slow," Grace's explosive opening track—an oblique tale of desire, desertion, hunger, and dependence—bursts, after nearly four fitful minutes, into fully majestic vocal ecstasy. Filled with contrasts, this is a song that, on the one hand, lyrically tells a tale of a weak and passive body that craves to "keep . . . whole," one that will "never be safe from harm," and yet musically, "Mojo Pin" is sonically bold, ambitious, disruptive, and filled with brazen risks.

It is a song that recalls the kind of "psychedelic malaise" of Nick Cave's Birthday Party days in full bloom. Yet it also announces the arrival of a new "electric mysticism," one that would break free of that genre's escapist conceits by "reinventing psychedelia . . . as a reflection of inner conflict rather than transformed reality." If old-school psychedelia celebrates a "cult of passivity, indolence and sleep," Jeff's music turns those tropes around, upside down, and inside out. Unlike psychedelia, which embraced "a cult of immobility," Buckley remains mobile, fluid, unpredictable, spontaneous, and enlivened on "Mojo Pin." The vocal shifts alone on the track, leaping from Nusrat-inspired octave slides to Plantish throat singing toward the close of the track, bear witness to the depth of Buckley's originality and fearlessness as a singer.[26]

It's no wonder then that Jimmy Page and Robert Plant were so smitten with the music of Jeff Buckley. It is no secret to anyone that "Mojo Pin" is perhaps the greatest testimony on *Grace* to Jeff's love affair with Led Zeppelin. Like that group, he and Lucas and band follow suit here by "disturb[ing] the boundary between voice and guitar" and by using "voice as 'another instrument . . . geared along the lead guitar's screaming highs." Like Led Zeppelin, "Mojo Pin's" musical ensemble "worked to strike a balance of power between their respective instruments."[27]

At the same time, "Mojo Pin" is in every way a departure from the Plant-Page paradigm of Jeff's boyhood days. If Led Zeppelin all but wrote the book on heavy metal masculinity and "the racialized nature of rock's favored mode of phallocentric display, with the electric guitar as a privileged signifier of white male power and potency," Buckley's "Mojo" persona calls attention to the feverish vulnerability of a wounded man-child, wrapped in a blanket, swooning and yearning for affection. His opening vocals owe perhaps more to Judy Garland in all her earnestly pubescent, "Somewhere Over the Rainbow" elegance than to the full-throttled, "manly" excess Plant squall that he slides into toward the song's end. Taking its share of left-field twists vocally as well as musically, "Mojo Pin" is a track that rages "with the vocal triumphalism of someone for whom failure seems to hold no special terror."[28]

At the heart of "Mojo Pin" is the very mystery of the title. Buckley reportedly gave many answers, including his assertion that "the song title was 'a euphemism for a dropper full of smack that you shoot in your arm.'" David Browne speculates that the song "could have easily been about a drug addiction or, most likely, the addictive, feverish pull of love." But what seems most likely is that "Mojo Pin" is about the inevitable relationship between the two. The track leaps through anxiety, existential fragmentation, burning desire, abandonment, betrayal, psychic torture, and the detritus of love, its sadomasochistic brutality, delivering "welts . . . of scorn" and "whips of opinion." It vividly evokes the pulsating promise of a drug hit, where "white horses flow" and offer the singer his sole relief, a poor substitute for the "precious, precious silver and gold" high of intimacy itself.[29]

In its vertiginous spin, "Mojo Pin" masterfully oscillates between volume swells on vocals to mimic the sound on the guitar and guitars late in the track mimicking the vocals. As a listener, you can't help but remain locked in the cyclical power of the track. With its exquisite arrangements filled with tiny guitar parts and disorienting rhythmic structures, the song conjures, as scholar Reggie Jackson argues, the sonic feel of narcotic transmogrification. That is, it aesthetically mimics the cyclical experience of a narcotic-altered state. One need only think of the ebb and flow of volume swells to imagine the rush of a smack high or how the swirling guitar loop kicking in at the close of the track mirroring the repetitive cycle of a drug habit in order to trace the way that "Mojo Pin" manifests the condition of addiction.

Parody? Dark comedy? Jeff Buckley had often sardonically mocked the rock-star clichés of drug dependency and self-annihilation (most likely as a way to distance himself from his father's tragic demise). And though rumors would linger about Buckley's own drug use (which David Browne points out was, at best, slight and occasional), "Mojo Pin" bears witness to an artist using his sheer musical power and artfulness to triumph over paralysis, lethargy, and waste. More still, in order to absorb the true immensity of the song, one should to listen to "Mojo Pin" in conversation with the rest of the album. *Grace* is the answer to tortured stasis. It is an album that embarks on a great quest to realize one's purpose and meaning in life. By the time Buckley hits his screeching "wrong notes" on "Mojo Pin" he has used this daring opening song to announce his own rebirth as an artist. "Born again from the rhythm, screaming down from heaven, ageless, ageless," he opens the door to his difficult "sound painting," pulls us into his arms and onto a new musical plateau.

Like a Prayer: "Grace" in Flight

> This is a song "about not feeling so bad about your own mortality when you have true love."[30]

> I try to make my music *joyful*—it makes *me* joyful—to feel the music soar through the body. It changes your posture, you raise your chin, throw your shoulders back, walk with a swagger. When I sing, my face changes shape. If feels like my *skull* changes shape . . . the bones *bend*. "Grace" and "Eternal Life" . . . are about the joy that music gives—the, probably *illusory*, feeling of being able to do anything. Sex is like that. You become utterly consumed by the moment.[31]

> Relentless . . . endless joy peaking into tears, resting into calmness, a simmering beauty. If you let yourself listen with the whole of yourself, you will have the pure feeling of flight while firmly rooted to the ground . . . Be still and listen to the evidence of your holiness.[32]

Whirling, galloping, spinning like the hands of a clock gone haywire, like a ballroom dance couple on crank, "Grace" moves brilliantly and relentlessly away from the bad mojo and runs straight into the shimmering light, into the "calmness" and "simmering beauty" of love's naked secrets about life. From a dizzyingly askew song chronicling a quagmire of addictions to a soaring anthem about love's ability to clarify one's purpose in life, *Grace* the album moves swiftly from exhortation and lament to its rapturously ascending title track, an electric prayer exulting in the transcendent powers of human intimacy. While "Mojo Pin" unleashes a difficult, mid-tempo lament filled with musical breaks, ruptures, and oscillations between grand cacophony and hushed vocals, the title track builds swiftly toward an emotional pinnacle. Lucas's agile guitar riffs evoke "the clicking of time," while Buckley's smooth, dulcet vocals ascend toward the transcendent peak of the chorus. A big anthem of a song that dissonantly chronicles the euphoria of trusting love and fearing not the certainty of death, "Grace" unveils the full power of Jeff's vocals, as they seem here to almost fly, traversing space and time.

> *Life* and *death*: they are one, at core entwined.
> Who understands himself from his own strain
> presses himself into a drop of wine
> and throws himself into the purest flame.
>
> —Rainer Maria Rilke[33]

Like "Mojo Pin," "Grace" had evolved out of Buckley's Gods and Monsters period, and Lucas lent his guitar work to the track. In both cases, Jeff had matched early notebook musings and poetry to Lucas's music. Originally entitled "Rise Up to Be," the song that would become "Grace" has dark philosophical leanings, but was ultimately evocative of the transcendent Qawwali spirit that Jeff had come to adore and respect through his Khan fandom. It celebrates, as Buckley would claim of Nusrat's own music, "the evidence of your holiness," by documenting the intense simultaneous communion and melancholic departure of two lovers forced to separate. According to David Browne, "Grace" was "inspired by the time he and Moore said their goodbyes at the airport on a rainy day."[34]

"Grace" emerges essentially as a prayer affirming and manifesting the endless and elliptical beauty of humanity itself. Both musically and lyrically, the song performs the task of putting the soul in flight and embracing the Rilkean awareness of life and death as forever sensually entwined. Indeed, the similarities between Buckley and Rilke are somewhat profound, particularly with "Grace," which calls upon themes found in John J. L. Mood's popular anthology, *Rilke On Love and Other Difficulties*, a collection that Buckley owned. Like the poet who would contemplate the connections between life and death, Jeff Buckley would on "Grace" urge his lover to "drink a bit of wine" and "wait in the fire." In the glory of human connection, this mortal existence finds its eternal fullness in the elemental wonders of earth, wind, and fire.[35]

In many ways a song about learning to fly, "Grace" is also about grandly harnessing the power to travel, to cross boundaries, to create an inclusive musical space that replenishes the soul. It is also a song that creates an altogether new place outside of musical convention. To be sure, rock is nothing if not a genre "born to run," populated by rebels who are always set alight, always indulging in fugitive velocity and the "rhapsodic exaltation of motion." But on "Grace," Jeff Buckley rebuilds the idea of rock flight. The traction of his vocals alone ignites a different kind of departure on the track. Think of "Grace" as the answer to "Mojo Pin's" state of paralysis, the affirmation that you will, indeed, "rise up to be."[36]

> It's still kind of like a regal visitation just to have someone arrange for strings . . . Just to hear a chord progression with strings makes it really different . . . [37]

> The arrangements of, say, the strings on *Grace*, that was mainly down to Karl [Berger, who wrote string arrangements for "Grace"], and then I'd sometimes come in with "Maybe you should bend that note here," or I'd go [suggesting a rhythm] "Klah, klah, klah, klah, klah, klah."[38]

Filled with bursts of spinning guitar sunshine and fleet guitar picking in the vein of Led Zeppelin's more folky, jangling strumming numbers, and yet simultaneously crossed with dissonant breaks, guitar hammer-ons and pull-offs, and rushes of reverb, "Grace" evokes the feeling of mystic flight through the rays of the sun and the light of the moon. "Clouds" hover ominously overhead in the first few lines of the song, waiting to "fly" the singer away. The song's shimmering purity and regal elegance are even further enhanced by the string arrangements of Frankfurt Philharmonic conductor and jazz vibraphonist Karl Berger, who lent his work to several tracks on the album. Together Berger and Jeff developed "a good chemistry" with one another in order to work out a richly realized series of arrangements, particularly on "Grace," "Last Goodbye," and "Eternal Life." As Wallace maintains, "It was not a matter of 'give me a tape and I'll write all of the string parts.' Jeff was very involved in going over melodies with him. And Karl certainly did a lot of compositional work on it. But Jeff also added to that compositional work quite a bit—actively and as a filter—saying 'I like this idea better than that idea.' But he also had a lot of ideas himself about where he wanted to go. And Karl was more than happy to incorporate that . . . "[39]

The strings on "Grace" add intensity, depth, and dimension, as well as a kind of delicate sense of fragility to the song at its most tender moments. At a late turning point in the song, as Buckley is reminded of "the pain" he might "leave behind," the strings dance lightly, pizzicato across the sound field, just for a second, as if to remind the listener of the very ephemeral nature (the "clicking" of time) of life itself once again. Here and elsewhere, Berger's work holds together the epic beauty of the song's very core.

Sweeping and panoramic in sound and image, the scope and size of "Grace" creates space for Buckley's vocals to rise powerfully, full of color and dimension—even as his lyrics call attention to a "fading voice" singing "of love." This is sly, Jeff Buckley irony at its strongest. Like a ruse, the proclamation of weakness here only calls greater attention to the sheer power, majesty, and aesthetic eclecticism of what the singer is actually doing in song. The ornamentation and layers of vocal detail on "Grace" are in themselves an extraordinary feat. Queue up the background sound on one's stereo, and one can hear Buckley's vocal dubs creating the sound of choral backup singers, hushing and humming, quietly yet forcefully pushing the melody along. A little over three minutes into the track, he pushes a steadily rising falsetto to its mammoth peak and then artfully twists the mellifluous contours of his voice by adding an overdriven mic or dirty vocal. Yoked in with these warm, high-rising, humming background voices, Buckley's voice comes alive here like Frampton to create a bit of gorgeous, weird, funky talk-box-sounding harmony, setting the track sonically onto yet another plane.

> Hearing *Grace* influenced musicians to push past their own limits. *Grace* made beauty cool again.[40]

"Grace" is most beautiful as a song because of its exquisitely rendered imperfections, most fully realized in Buckley's offbeat vocals. The singer moves from mellifluous virtuoso singing to guttural screech and howl. This is the sound of an artist using his sophisticated vocal control to evoke the sound of letting go completely, like a sanctified member of the choir. Listen to "Grace" and you are witnessing Jeff Buckley in full, regal holy-roller mode, reincarnated in the guise of millennial rock singer testifying before a congregation. What saves Buckley's performance here from slipping into an "I wanna know what love is" Lou Gramm—or even Clay Aiken "Bridge Over Troubled Water"—moment is that he seems more than capable of taking the true spirit and pure essence of singing soulfully—of singing from the soul—in order to create music that is his own signature sound, not derivative in the least.

The "flanged guitar" emerging late on "Grace" puts Buckley's vocals and the song itself on its final cosmic flight. Set against images of "fire," "falling rain," "bright lights," and a woman "weeping" on his arm, the track reaches its final ethereal crescendo, ending on a ravishingly over-the-top Qawwali vocal flourish, harmonized, layered, and recalling the sexy, surfeiting vocals of Prince in his sensuous "Take Me With You" / "Darling Nikki" mode. What might, upon first listen, sound like self-absorbed vocal excess and Buckley indulging in the extravagant wealth of his own vocal prowess emerges as a moment of lavish vocal expenditure translated into spiritual articulation. Like that sacredly profane Minneapolis artist, Jeff Buckley reveals on "Grace" his interest in mixing the sensual with the divine, the romantic with the gothic, the ordinary with the ethereal. Like a prayer, "Grace" ends by landing in worshipful, musical praise, in effect by creating a grace note of embellishment that pushes the recording early on to its spiritually ecstatic limits. "Grace" is the sound of a singer stepping into the light and into communion with the universe.

Dreaming in the Round

> The band launched into "Dream Brother," the fabled paean to its Buckley père, although according to its author [it concerns] his close friend, ex-Fishbone keyboards and trom-

bone player Chris Dowd. Claims Buckley, "I just wanted to sing about a man instead of a girl."—*Q* magazine[41]

Track number ten, "Dream Brother," rounds out the circle of *Grace* with a return to the mystic power chords and the floating, fantastical imagery of the album's first two songs. Beginning and ending in dreamlike repose, the album stretches all the way from the opening feverish haze of a love and drug addict to the exiting vision of twin brothers sleeping beneath the wings of a mysterious "dark angel." On the one hand, "Dream Brother" embodies all of the big, roving, epic images of classic pastoral psychedelia. This is Led Zeppelin's tricked-out Garden of Eden, a fractured Arthurian kingdom of green-eyed maidens with butterscotch hair and "tears scattered round the world."

With cathedral-chiming vocals, tabla, and vibes and "the droning fluidity" of Indian raga music, "Dream Brother" is as cosmic and oceanic as the best of Can and Pink Floyd, as ethereally rhapsodic as the floating wonder music of Buckley favorites the Cocteau Twins. Flowing and rippling with windswept rhythm guitar strumming and pushed back vocals in the mix with reverb, "Dream Brother" evokes the feeling of being carried out to sea, of in every way "falling asleep" with "the ocean washing over." Indeed, its very mix of "cosmic and oceanic imagery" might invite the most obsessive (and wrongheaded) fans to thematically compare the track to the elder Buckley's cult favorite *Starsailor* album.[42]

But like most Jeff and Tim comparisons, such a facile coupling would miss the point of the song entirely. Beyond the obvious differences that say, for instance, as Ann Powers argues, Jeff "relaxed into weirdness" in ways that his father . . . never could," "Dream Brother" is both a final renunciation of a father's misguided acts and an attempt to right the wrongs of the father by way of counsel to a friend.[43] Anyone jonesing for even the faintest allusion to the absent Tim Buckley could, however, find clues in the chorus's clear-eyed admonishment to not "be like the one who made me so old / Don't be like the one who left behind his name." Apparently written to close friend and fellow musician Chris Dowd, the song offers parting advice to a youthful parent whose family was "waiting," just as Buckley had waited for his own parent, "and nobody ever came." Then in spite of its initial flirtation with psychedelia's languid passivity and escapism, "Dream Brother's" core narrative ultimately affirms a vision grounded in the focused here and now rather than the far out and hallucinatory.

"Dream Brother" is, then, a full embrace of manhood, fatherhood, the ability to love, to protect, to be fully connected to one's lover and children. In this way, the song emerges as an act of grace in that it bestows divinely "regenerating, inspiriting, and strengthening influence" upon a friend; it imparts "mercy, clemency, pardon and forgiveness" on a loved one, and it looks to a faith in spiritual brotherhood as a form of salvation.

Aiming for the heavens, Jeff Buckley could—and often did—open live shows in support of *Grace* with versions of this song, the track at the end of the album, which is itself a beatific beginning. On any given night he might hover like a Qawwali in the lowest register of his high tenor voice in his live "Dream Brother" performance, finally pushing toward elevation and sounding more like holy heretic, hitting gloriously sick, fitful, recklessly punk opera high notes that could turn the beat of rock hall culture all the way around. Those soaring falsetto notes that may sound old hat now in the new millennium at a Coldplay show were anything but in 1995. Live and plugged in with band, the dream brother Buckley found an even higher plane on which to climb on his *Grace* tours ("The Unknown," "Mystery White Boy," and "Hard Luck"), re-exploring and reinventing the album tracks one by one, night by night for two and a half years and 307 shows.

Grace Notes Live: Surfing the Open-Tuned Universe

> It's just about being alive, my songs. And about . . . emitting sound. It's about the voice carrying much more information than the words do. The fact is, there are so many other areas you can go with other instruments going on at the same time. You can reach a trance-like state . . . [44]

> He was "a fantastic guitar player as well, which no one ever mentions. He used a lot of open tuning and jazz and blues. . . . He wasn't concerned about 4/4 rock/pop geared at the charts."—Bernard Butler[45]

> A lot of our shows just seem like huge, pleasurable, messy kissing sessions, where you're so filled with passion that every move you make on the body . . . sends it into pleasure. That's mostly what it's like; then the songs just happen by themselves. I guess it's all just about giving up to certain states of being. I imagine the reason the Qawwalis are so excellent is that they live their life in

> order to be in that state. They're not your typical young, white rock dude.[46]

Any God-fearing sensually open-minded individual on earth who was in the music hall the night that I was when Jeff Buckley sang what came to be known affectionately by fans as the infamous "chocolate-orgasm" version of "Mojo Pin" had to have hit a pleasure-driven trance state of incredulity while watching and listening to that ludicrously erotic performance. With seven minutes of simmering, sexual innuendo and metaphor unfolding into a concatenate six-minute version of the original album intro track, this "Mojo Pin" finally shed the Led Zeppelin echoes of "bewitching, spell-binding" femme fatalism and the classic cock-rock obsession with the tricks and traps of "feminine miasma."[47] With "Mojo Pin" live Jeff Buckley effectively worked to reverse the curse put upon woman, to conjure a little sexual mojo as sacred and profane as Prince at his "Dirty Mind" spiritually erotic pinnacle.

Merging the carnal with the spiritual, Jeff Buckley in performance "revolted against the proper model of masculinity that is upheld by" rock's royal patriarchy. In his live performances on the *Grace* tour in particular, Jeff created a "new rock archetype" by screwing with the "masculine selfaggrandizement" of blues and rock.[48] He took the occasion to play outside the lines of "4/4 rock/pop geared at the charts," and dared to flout gender and racial boundaries even more brazenly than he had done in the studio. As was the case on the album, in concert Buckley found ways to explore the self without exploiting women's abjection and myopic heterosexual desire. Summoning the electric elixir of his "voice, guitar, body" (a note he signed at the bottom of a 1993 set list, for instance), as well as the "mind," Jeff turned his shows into occasions to examine the self and connections to others through musical desire, romantic love, spiritual longing, and sexual reciprocity.[49] Nowhere is the latter more apparent than in the live performances of "Mojo Pin," where drug addiction and love's rejection transforms into gynocentric pleasure seeking.

> Music comes from a very primal, twisted place. When a person sings, their body, their mouth, their eyes, their words, their voice says all these unspeakable things that you really can't explain but that mean something anyway. People are completely transformed when they sing; people look like that when they sing or when they make love. But it's a weird thing—at the end of the night I feel strange, because I feel

> I've told everybody all my secrets.[50]

In his thirteen-minute-plus versions of "Mojo Pin" live, Buckley would use the occasion to "warm up and work his way into the song he had learned from studying Nusrat Fateh Ali Khan." A vocal melisma both jarring and magnetic, spectacularly bombastic and intimately seductive, Buckley's voice initiates a kind of ambience. Like ambient music, which is "spatial," it establishes a kind of "echo and reverb" to create "an imaginary psycho-acoustic space."[51]

Buckley's affinity for open tuning and for picking close to the bridge pick-up of his modified guitar had the effect of generating harmonics and tones rolled off so very brightly. What's more, his great skill and imagination as a guitarist allowed him to work with his band to create big, ethereal, and atmospheric sound spaces. This was ambient music that recalled Eno in its immensity yet was ultimately much more corporeal and spiritually pixilated. If Brian "Eno's music equates the state of grace with stasis, repose," Jeff Buckley's live shows pushed this ambience onto a volatile, constantly transmogrifying plane.[52]

While Eno often described an interest in avoiding bombast and experimented with sounds that evoked the abstract image of languid, lounging Gauginlike women, Jeff expressed an interest in balancing the hard with the soft, the bombast with the flow. In his reoutfitted ambience, Buckley was more interested in worshiping and absorbing the radiant power of the feminine, the "If I Was Your Girlfriend" / "Nothing Compares 2 U" / iconic Prince women who could strut and seduce, belt and holler, hum and harmonize. This female power emerges in Jeff Buckley's ambient world, a world that does indeed "disorient the listener and refuses rock's thrust-and-climax narrative structure in favour of a more 'feminine' economy of pleasure, i.e. plateau after plateau, an endlessly deferred climax."[53]

> Apparently orgasm is the only point where your mind becomes completely empty—you think of nothing for that second. That's why it's so compelling—it's a tiny taste of death. Your mind is void—you have nothing in your head save white light. Nothing save that white light and "YES!"—which is fantastic. Just knowing "Yes."[54]

A performance that took shape on the concert hall venue leg of the *Grace* tour, this "Mojo Pin" allowed Jeff to flex his Sin-é gig muscles and to unveil his finesse in collaborating within a live environment. As he had learned in the coffeehouse, "to his ears, no melody or rhythm was separate from the sounds going on in the background." Buckley would himself insist, "It's not like music begins or ends. All kinds of sounds are working into each other . . . if you're open to hearing the way music interacts with ambient sound, performance never feels like a rote experience."[55] In his revised performance of "Mojo Pin," he used ambient sound then to open up the song's latent eroticism and to make sexuality palpable at the outset of his concert.

> Qawwali is among the forms of music in which religion and sex seem most closely intertwined . . . [56]

With trancelike vocals that would meld with and melt into the crowd, bringing his audience to full attention, Buckley used his voice in his extended "Mojo Pin" performance to reorder desire and pleasure by singing: "Love turn me on, let me turn you all over. With my thumb on your tongue, rest your heal on my shoulder. Your love melts like chocolate on the tongue of God."

Legs wrapped around a lover's neck, a mouth tasting a divine sweetness like no other. Instead of an "obsession with dominance, power, and sexual aggression," so characteristic of conventional rock erotic expression, Buckley offers a lyrical articulation of cunnilingus and opens his concert set by revising rock's male narratives of heterosexual conquest.[57] Instead of "cock rock," he redefines the terms of giving and receiving literal and figurative pleasure against an atmospheric wall of extended harmonics and shimmering, amplified tones. Open-mouthed and elevating his voice in a slowburning rise, he morphs in this performance into *both* sex partners as they hit the pinnacle of wordless ecstasy in song.

> It's pretty special sometimes, the way a song affects a room, the way you're in complete rhythm with the song. When you're emotionally overcome, and there's no filter between what you say and what you mean, your language becomes guttural, simple, emotional, and full of pictures and clarity.[58]

The key to this "Mojo" performance then is twofold: it both revels in the ambient and it puts to work the immense uses of voice. Guitar wonks were always quick to point out that Buckley's musicianship was often overshadowed by the majesty of his vocals. But live in performance as well as on *Grace*, it's more than apparent that the two—voice and guitar—were always heavily entwined, reciprocal, responding. Jeff Buckley was known for performing with two main guitars, an early 1990s Mexican Telecaster and a Les Paul Gibson with dual humbucking pick-ups. In either case, he was able to strike an ethereal effect and (most likely with the Telecaster) create a bright, jangly sound. With open tuning he had the ability to work with more pitches on his guitar, to sound more drone, and to create a rich, full, textured sound. Through open tuning, he could use the same pitch in different gages with a clean setting and lots of reverb to at times conjure an almost organist, churchy aesthetic.[59]

In Jeff Buckley's ambient guitar universe, he created a sanctuary full of heat, fire, and intensity in song. You could feel engulfed by the wash of a big, sweeping sound, one that was held together by the magnetism of voice. If, as some pop music scholars have noted, rock music's lead singer operates traditionally as mentor/shaman to young men in search of defining and expressing their masculinity, then Jeff Buckley brilliantly mixed up these archaic dynamics in rock space and rewrote the utility of rock frontmanship. Still a conduit of hopes and desires, he also challenged mainstream audiences to respond in new ways to the music. He demanded something different from listeners and he created a kind of transgressive space that went beyond stylish posturing to forge intense connections with his audience. The live shows became the occasion to watch the birth of a new rock archetype for men and women alike. He was doing something with more than words.

> I've always felt that the quality of the voice is where the real content [of a song] lies . . . Words only suggest an experience, but the voice is that experience.[60]

> Words are really beautiful, but they're limited. Words are very male, very structured. But the voice is the netherworld, the darkness, where there's nothing to hang on to. The voice comes from a part of you that just knows and expresses and is. I need to inhabit every bit of a lyric, or else I can't bring the song to you—or else it's just words.[61]

Live in concert, Jeff Buckley showed that he was unafraid to experiment with repetition in words, moans and yelps that reinforced the concept of wordless mantra. Extraordinary live versions of "Grace," for instance, evolved into full-throttle exorcisms with Buckley bouncing off the walls vocally, howling and screeching like a preacher man caught in an orchestral tempest. On certain nights he might push the grace note far outside of the bounds of the song, leaping vocally into a heated repetition, a controlled spectacle of artfully losing control with the voice, a kind of beautiful cross between Linda Blair, Al Green, and Freddie Mercury in the round.

On tour, Jeff was moving swiftly and brilliantly toward incorporating the spirit of Qawwali, its celebration of the utterance to create something of a living mash-up, part ambient utterance and "jouissance rock," part Sufi divine music, part Liz Fraser / Bjork / Kate Bush Euro-gynocentric worldless profundity and aversion to the WORD, part R&B singing, part gospel call and response. He was crafting performances that called attention to the elasticity of voice and its power to reconfigure space in connection to other human beings. With a voice that was, as Johnny Ray Huston once called it, "expansively sexy," Jeff Buckley used powerful vocalizing in concert to challenge the preeminence of the electric guitar "as an instrument of mastery that amplifies the masculinity of the band's performers."[62]

> His voice was very, very commanding and at the same time hypnotic and it would flood the stage and not only cast a spell on the audience but a lot of times on the band as well. . . . That was something that Jeff induced—for you to leave yourself and just let the music flow through you.—Michael Tighe, guitarist [63]

Holy departure. In the live performances of *Grace*'s wraparound tracks, a new electric mysticism was born.

NOTES

1. Jeff Buckley as quoted in "The Making of Grace," *Grace* Legacy Edition DVD (Columbia Records 2004).
2. Mary Guibert as quoted in *Everybody Here Wants You*, dir. Serena Cross (BBC, 2002).
3. Jeff Buckley as quoted in "Interview with Jeff Buckley," *Live at the Sin-é* Legacy EditionDVD (Columbia Records 2003).
4. Author's phone interview with Steve Berkowitz, June 28, 2004.

5. Unpublished notebooks, September 16, 1989, courtesy of Mary Guibert and the Jeff Buckley estate.
6. Jeff Buckley as quoted in Steve Tignor, "A Live Thing," *Puncture* (1st Quarter 1994).
7. Matt Johnson as quoted in *Jeff Buckley: Amazing Grace*, dir. Nyala Adams (2004).
8. Jeff Buckley, "Letter to Elaine Buckley," Jeff Buckley exhibit, Rock and Roll Hall of Fame, Cleveland, OH, 2003.
9. Jeff Buckley as quoted in Sony *Grace* press release.
10. Matt Johnson as quoted in *Mystery White Boy: The Jeff Buckley Story* (BBC 2), September 25, 2004.
11. Author's interview with Berkowitz.
12. Mick Grondahl as quoted in "The Making of Grace," *Grace* Legacy Edition DVD (Columbia Records), 2004.
13. Jeff Buckley as quoted in *Live at the Sin-é* Press Release, Columbia Records.
14. Jeff Buckley as quoted in "The Making of Grace," *Grace* Legacy Edition DVD (Columbia Records), 2004.
15. Wallace as quoted in ibid.
16. Author's interview with Steve Berkowitz, June 28, 2004.
17. Steve Berkowitz, as quoted in "The Making of *Grace*," *Grace* Legacy edition DVD (Columbia, 2004).
18. Wallace as quoted in "The Making of Grace," *Grace* Legacy Edition DVD (Columbia), 2004.
19. Josh Farrar, "Interview," *DoubleTake* (February 29, 1996).
20. Jeff Buckley as quoted in author's interview with Steve Berkowitz, June 28, 2004.
21. Browne, *Dream Brother*, 202.
22. Author's interview with Steve Berkowitz, June 28, 2004.
23. Dana Darzin, "Jeff Buckley, New York City, Jan. 12, 1994," *Rolling Stone*, February 24, 1994.
24. Simon Reynolds and Joy Press, *The Sex Revolts: Gender, Rebellion and Rock 'n' Roll* (Cambridge, MA: Harvard UP, 1995), 158.
25. Browne, *Dream Brother*, 140–141. Jeff Buckley, "Mojo Pin," unpublished notebook entry, November 22, 1989, courtesy of Mary Guibert and the Jeff Buckley estate.
26. Reynolds and Press, 92, 160–166. *New York Times*, "Love Songs that Reflect Maturity."
27. Steve Waksman, *Instruments of Desire: The Electric Guitar and the Shaping of Musical Experience* (Cambridge, MA: Harvard UP, 1999), 252.
28. "Feral: Jeff Buckley: A Cool and Clever Cat," Q, March 1995.

29. David Nagler, "Music and the Search for Eternal Life: Jeff Buckley Says Grace."
30. Jeff Buckley, "Grace," *Live at the Sin-é* Legacy Edition (Columbia Records, 2003).
31. Jeff Buckley as quoted in Caitlin Moran, "Orgasm Addict," *Melody Maker*, May 27, 1995, 12–13.
32. Jeff Buckley, unpublished notebook entry, courtesy of Mary Guibert and the Jeff Buckley estate.
33. Rainer Maria Rilke, "Life and death: they are one," John J. L. Mood, ed. *Rilke on Love and Other Difficulties: Translations and Considerations* (New York: Norton, 2004), 83.
34. Browne, *Dream Brother*, 140.
35. John J. L. Mood, "Introduction," ed. *Rilke On Love*, 49. Jeff Buckley home library archive, courtesy of Jeffbuckley.com.
36. Reynolds and Press, 61.
37. Jeff Buckley as quoted in "The Making of Grace," *Grace* Legacy Edition DVD (Columbia), 2004.
38. Jeff Buckley as quoted in Josh Farrar, "Interview with Jeff Buckley," *DoubleTake* (February 29, 1996).
39. Wallace as quoted in "The Making of Grace," *Grace* Legacy Edition DVD (Columbia), 2004.
40. Bill Flanagan, "A Decade of Grace," Liner Notes, *Grace* Legacy Edition (Columbia), 2004.
41. "Feral: Jeff Buckley: A Cool and Clever Cat," *Q* Magazine, March 1995.
42. Reynolds and Press, 183, 157, 185–187.
43. Ann Powers, "Strut Like a Rooster, Fly Like an Eagle, Sing Like a Man," *Revolver* (May/June 2001).
44. Jeff Buckley as quoted in Aidin Vaziri, "Jeff Buckley," *Raygun* (fall 1994).
45. Bernard Butler as quoted in Jim Irvin, "'It's Never Over': Jeff Buckley, 1966–1997," *MOJO*, August 1997, 38.
46. Jeff Buckley as quoted in Josh Farrar, "Jeff Buckley Interview," *DoubleTake* (February 29, 1996).
47. Reynolds and Press, 24–25.
48. Ibid, 16–23.
49. Jeff Buckley, 1993 Set List Notes, Jeff Buckley exhibit, Rock and Roll Hall of Fame, Cleveland, OH, 2003.
50. Jeff Buckley as quoted in *Live at the Sin-é* Sony Press Release.
51. Browne, 256. Reynolds and Press, 176.
52. Reynolds and Press, 201.
53. Ibid, 177.
54. Jeff Buckley as quoted in Caitlin Moran, "Orgasm Addict,"

Melody Maker, May 27, 1995, 12–13.

55. Ehrlich, "Jeff Buckley: Knowing Not Knowing," *Inside the Music: Conversations with Contemporary Musicians about Spirituality, Creativity, and Consciousness* (Boston, MA: Shambhala Publications, 1997), 154–155.
56. Ibid, "Nusrat Fateh Ali Khan: A Tradition of Ecstasy," *Inside the Music*, 117.
57. Sheila Whiteley, "Little Red Rooster v. The Honky Tonk Woman: Mick Jagger, Sexuality, Style and Image," ed. Sheila Whiteley, *Sexing the Groove: Popular Music and Gender* (London and New York: Routledge, 1997), 73.
58. Jeff Buckley as quoted in Ehrlich, "Jeff Buckley: Knowing Not Knowing," *Inside the Music*, 155.
59. My thanks to Reggie Jackson for his helpful input with regard to Jeff Buckley's guitar aesthetics here and throughout this project.
60. Jeff Buckley as quoted in Paul Young, "Talking Music: Confessing to Strangers," *Buzz* (Fall 1994).
61. Jeff Buckley as quoted in Ray Rogers, "Jeff Buckley: Heir Apparent," *Interview* (February 1994).
62. Reynolds and Press, 201, 378–380. Waksman, 223.
63. Michael Tighe, transcript of on-line chat with Michael Tighe, courtesy of Jeffbuckley.com.

Endtroducing . . .

by Eliot Wilder

Eliot Wilder is a writer and editor, having spent more than ten years at the *Los Angeles Times* and five years as editor and senior writer for *Amplifier*, an alternative music magazine. He is also a musician and songwriter and is currently promoting his latest album, *The Sentimental Education*. He lives in Boston.

An interview with Josh Davis, aka DJ Shadow

Do you remember the first rap record you bought?
It was *Street Beats, Volume Two*, which came out in '83. It was a Sugar Hill Records compilation that was designed as a gateway into the world of Sugar Hill. It was $7.99 for two records and I split the cost with a friend of mine. And we would share custody of it. My friend, he came from a wealthy household and thought he was into rap and then got it and decided he wasn't. So it was perfect for me because I knew he wasn't going to keep it.

Who was on that album?
It had West Street Mob, who sampled Apache, Grandmaster Flash and the Wheels of Steel, and the Funky 4 + 1. I really like the song "Break-Dance Electric Boogie" by the West Street Mob because it had a lot of scratching in it. Shortly after that came Run-D.M.C.'s [eponymous 1984] first album. It was seen as being punk and cutting edge because it was so raw. And the cover was real cool, too.

And I also remember, around this time, that's when I decided to first tune in to the college radio station in Davis, called KDVS. Davis is a university town, and KDVS very much catered to, obviously, college tastes. The very first time I tuned in, I heard "World War III" by the Furious Five. But then the next record they played was by Camper Van Beethoven, which didn't make sense to me. So I asked my dad, who I always felt was a little more hip when it came to music, if he knew of any station in the Bay Area that might play just rap. He told me about KSOL, which was a long-time independent black radio station. I took his advice and that night I tuned in and I heard—and somewhere, I've still got a tape of this as well—"AJ Scratch" by Kurtis Blow being mixed with "One for the Treble" by Davy DMX. And, you know, I was sold. So now I had a lot of access to the music. I was hearing it in cars. I was hearing it on KSOL. I was hearing it on KDVS. My brother was into it, so he would get tapes from people at his school. This was all between '83–'84.

It wasn't until I started shopping at a Tower [Records] in San Jose—again, thanks to my dad—that the world of the 12-inch opened up to me, really. But, you know, as I've now learned, so many important, pivotal records from the first 7 years of rap never made it—were never distributed to California.

Why?

Well, many of them were never distributed outside of Harlem or the Bronx or Brooklyn let alone halfway across the country—or all the way across the country. It's sort of the nature of what was going on. It was so neighborhood-driven back then. But, by the same token, a lot of important early Miami-based records never left Miami. A lot of important early LA records never left LA. I quickly started to understand how it all worked with distribution and all that stuff.

In the mid-80s, I started watching an independent TV station up in San Jose that would show videos for hip-hop records by Run-D.M.C., the World Famous Supreme Team and Grandmaster Flash. I was able to see people scratching on video. Somehow hearing scratching and seeing what it looked like—it made sense to my experiences touching vinyl and making it do things. The whole technological thing came back 360 because it seemed like such an out-there concept. And it was very much a stamp of hip-hop. It was something only hip-hop embraced and only hip-hop seemed to do. And this is way before the idea of genre meshing.

So now it's late '84, and that's when I got my first turntable.

What was it?
What I asked for was a Sears combination turntable, radio tuner and dual cassette deck, so that I could dub all of Stan Green's tapes, so I could dub my own records and so I could still listen to the radio and dub mixes off the radio. By now I knew all the DJs names on KSOL. And I had also, by this point, figured out when the main guy who plays rap on KDVS, when his show was. His name was Oras Washington. He was a black guy from Richmond, California, who went to school at UC Davis. His real interest was groups like the Time, but I think he decided that one way he could make his mark was to play hip-hop and rap and make a show out of it.

By now I was able to take in a lot of stuff. I stopped buying comic books. I stopped buying video games. I stopped spending my money on all the other things that kids at that time spent money on and started saving my money for records. And that pretty much became my spending pattern until I was off to college. I'd save almost all the money I had, sell my comic books, sell whatever, [laughs] to be able to buy records. Stan and I worked out a thing where we'd go to a store, and he'd buy two singles, and I'd buy two singles, so that between us we had four new 12-inches to record off each other. With the Sears turntable, the first thing I did was try to see how it worked for scratching. And, of course, I didn't understand that you needed to have a mixer, and that belt-drive turntables don't quite work the same as direct-drive turntables do, and that has to do with the motor in the turntable. If you pull back on the turntable with a belt, the belt slips, and it doesn't speed back up again very fast, so you have to push it along. What I did figure out is that, if I held the little selector knob in between "tape" and "phono," I was able to dub a tape and scratch over the top of it. It was like a glitch in the way that the turntable operated. I had wanted my own stereo for so damn long that, when I got this thing, I absorbed it. It became part of my bloodstream. I touched every knob and fiddled with the thing endlessly and sat there at the radio.

Just out of curiosity, could you tell me what you think is the difference between turntablism and scratching?
Turntablism is the description of scratching that's supposed to make people who don't listen to hip-hop sit up and go "Hmm, maybe it is real music." Scratching, to me, is just what it is. Turn-

tablism has this virtuosic aspect to it, and to me, that's when things start to turn jazzy. And I'm not a huge fan of when things turn jazzy. Because when I think of jazzy, I think of Wynton Marsalis. He came to speak at my African-American Studies class at UC Davis when I was a freshman. I remember him just standing up there, and just dissing rap for 20 minutes straight, and just loving the response he was getting from the lily-white audience. As if they were so thrilled that finally a black guy was speaking out against rap. I remember just sitting there thinking, Oh this sucks. I was venting about it afterward in class. Ever since then I've had this thing against people who over-intellectualize everything and make it an in-crowd-only thing. So, any time anything starts getting jazzy—and you are going to have to say it [whispers] "jazzy"—I run in the other direction because "jazzy" to me isn't where it's at.

Do you recall some of your early mix tapes?
I started out by imitating my heroes. "Step Off" by Grandmaster Flash had a scratch solo in it. A lot of records were starting to have scratch solos. And I would imitate the scratching that they were doing. But the big X factor and the big question mark, in my mind, was, "OK, even if I can achieve the same patterns, what sounds are they using? What are these records that they're scratching?" I was trying to figure out what was going on on "One for the Treble" and "Step Off." Both of those records scratched the same sound, which I learned, a few years later, was the stab at the beginning of the break on "Ashley's Roach Clip" by the Soul Searchers.

I didn't understand that there was a whole culture that was very underground, and very few people knew about this stuff back then. It was an underground culture in New York City and Philly, pretty much exclusively, where there was the whole break-beat thing and all these DJs. The records that they were playing—those were the sounds I was hearing. And I didn't know what the sounds were. I started realizing that I can do what they're doing—I just couldn't make it sound the same because I didn't have these records. I didn't have these break-beats. I didn't have these stabs, you know, these horn stabs that punctuate the one on the break-beat. And that's what everybody would scratch on. Or certain phrases, or certain sounds. All these classic scratch sounds. I didn't know what the hell all those things were. And that became my next obsession: unlocking this secret knowledge. But it was like the knowledge was nowhere to be found. I mean, you couldn't get on the Internet and find out what this was. You couldn't read a book and find out what this shit was. I couldn't talk to anybody in California, save for probably a few New York transplants living in LA that I didn't know, that could explain this to me, any of this shit. But then I read David Toop's *Rap Attack*. That book helped connect a lot of dots for me. I started to understand a little bit more about the evolution of the music and the culture.

Were you ever able to get your hands on the music itself?
In certain cases, yeah. One time I had to special order from a distributor list at Barney's, an independent record store in Davis. I asked the guy that was working there, who seemed to be sympathetic when I would buy rap records, I said, "Look, there's a bunch of records that I want. Is there a way that you guys can order them in?" And so he showed me the distributor list, and I pretty much checked off anything that sounded like it might be rap. And it took like six weeks, and then finally some of them came in. I remember, in that shipment were two records that were important to me. This is about mid-'85, I'd say. One was "What I Like" by 2 Live Crew, and the other one was "Techno Scratch" by Knights of the Turntables. Play "What I Like" yourself and you'll hear why I went nuts. Because there's so many different scratches and cuts in it!

When did you get into buying older records?
In '87. I went into the only used record store in Davis and bought records like "Dance to the Drummer's Beat" by Herman Kelly, which is a classic break-beat, and James Brown's *Payback* double album. All these records were $3. They were cheap because there was no real market for that stuff outside of the Bronx and Manhattan and Brooklyn, where hip-hop DJs were being gouged by local record dealers for these classic break-beats. But back in California, nobody was that into it.

I started making tapes of some James Brown records and things like that, around '87, to complement my normal hip-hop diet. And the only person that seemed to really devote himself to the same passion was my friend Stan. He got into listening to soul and Parliament and stuff like that. But, to me, rap sounded like the soundtrack to my life, in a weird sort of way, even though I didn't live in New York and couldn't really identify with a lot of what was being talked about. It was so dynamic and so powerful back then that I just didn't see the need to listen to much else.

In the summer of '88, I made a tape of my dad's copy of *Hot Buttered Soul* by Isaac Hayes and the song "Hyperbolicsyllabicsesquedalymistic." At around five minutes into it, there's a riff from Public Enemy's "Black Steel in the Hour of Chaos." But, you know, the Public Enemy album hadn't come out yet. And then, when it did, and I heard that, that's the first time I went, "Oh, shit, I could have, theoretically, hypothetically, hooked this beat up." Because I felt like, damn, Public Enemy's the most progressive rap group out, and I'm like almost caught up to them. In my own funny way, that's how I thought about it. I mean, obviously, I've never made a record as good as that record. But, in my own mind, I was thinking, that from a production point of view or a DJ point of view, that I at least was on the right track.

When did you first put your stuff out there?
I would listen to Oras Washington and his KDVS hip-hop show. He'd always ask for people to call in with requests. One day, I did, and I asked for some pretty obscure and hardcore New York record, and he was like, "Damn, who's asking for this out there?" [laughs] I introduced myself over the phone.

At that time, I was 14. I looked up to Oras because he was older than me, and he was trying to mix, and he was playing a wide variety of good stuff. And at some point, I asked him if I could come and sit in and watch him do the show. And he said, "By all means." So I did. And, you know, he was about 23, and I was this real skinny white kid. I think he was tripping out about my dedication to the music. And also, at a certain point, I was brave enough to play him one of my little mixes I had done on my Sears system. I tried to do my own version of the instrumental side of 2 Live Crew's "What I Like." Oras said, "OK, I'll play it. Do a 20-minute mix, and I'll play it." And I recently found that tape. [laughs]

I gave him the tape, and then I went home and turned on the radio and started taping. All of a sudden, Oras goes, "And now we've got a special treat. We've got, Davis's own Josh, and he's got a mix." Just to really help my nerves, the tape didn't start right away. I was worried he was going to yank it, you know what I mean, like I blew my shot? I knew I had cued it up just right, and I couldn't figure out what happened. Maybe he rewound it or something. Oras got on the mic. He's like, "Oh, it should be coming on here in a second." My heart was sinking. And then finally it did come on. Me, I was going over the waves. Then I felt like, if I was at home taping it, maybe somebody else was.

It was also the first time I got to be around a DJ who deejayed for a living. He was in school, but he would do weddings and parties and spin at clubs. He let me come over to his house and use his Technics 1200, which were $500 turntables back then and well outside my reach financially. It was like being born to be a racecar driver and, for the first time, being in a Ferrari. As soon as I got on the Technics, it was like I was channeling these guys. I couldn't do what some of them could do, but I could do what others could do. And I started to develop my own little style. But again, it was still about imitation at that point.

In 1988, a huge rap show was coming to Oakland Coliseum with Def Jam artists like Run-D.M.C. and Public Enemy. Oras asked if I wanted to go. I thought that there was no way my parents would let me go. But my parents, in retrospect, were really encouraging and they understood that I was passionate about this music. So they let me go.

Unfortunately, we didn't get into the show. We were also supposed to get hooked up backstage, and we didn't. But afterward we went to the Holiday Inn, where all the groups were staying, and I got to meet everybody from Chuck D and Flavor Flav to Eric Sermon and Terminator X. I got their autographs. Flavor was walking around with a Muppet Babies boom box, listening to Public Enemy's "It Takes a Nation of Millions," which hadn't come out yet. People were coming up to me saying, "Hey, man, check out my tape." Like, "You must be somebody." I felt like an equal, in a certain sense. I felt like people were looking at me like, "Oh, you could be in the biz," or, "You're a DJ? OK, cool. Check out my new record." Nobody had ever treated me like that before.

All of a sudden there was a huge melee. I remember Oras running around the lobby going, "Josh, where are you, man? Don't do this to me!" I was following him going, "I'm right here! Stop! I'm right here!" And he just kept running around in circles because he couldn't see me. Then bottles were flying and all kinds of shit was jumping off. The cops showed up, and the last thing I saw was these two dudes pull up in a Cadillac and pop the trunk. And that's when I went, "It's time to go!"

Yeah! [laughs] Wow.

I don't know what happened or what that was all about. We were driving home, and Oras was like, "Ah, man, I'm so sorry." But I was completely OK. It was my hip-hop moment.

That was my first experience with the industry, with meeting managers and label reps and promo men; it was my preview to the back end. It was like somebody raised the curtain up and said, "All right, you can only hang out here for about four hours, and then you've got to go sit on the other side where the rest of the people sit." I was hooked, in a whole other sense. Chuck D's looking at me like, "Damn, how old are you?" I said to him, " 'Rebel Without a Pause,' when you looped this and that. . . . " He's looking at me like, "Goddamn, how do you know this shit?" Back then, I think I had the attitude like, if you're into rap, shouldn't you know this?

That's cool that Oras opened up that world to you. Was there anyone else early on?

In '89, I met a guy named Chris Rivers. Like Oras, he was a black guy from the Bay Area who ended up at UC Davis. He was aware that I could scratch, and there were only a few people in Davis that could scratch. I think that, in retrospect, I must have come off as some sort of idiot savant about hip-hop because I was so fanatical and so wide-eyed—I must have exhibited a lot of enthusiasm. Chris introduced me to a rapper named Swee D. He had a little home studio with a four-track and a keyboard. And this dude laid down vocals. And then I did a scratch. And what we ended up with would have to be the first released project that I was in any way involved in. It was cassette only. Swee D also said, "Let me see if you can dance, too." That was the first experience I had with being in a room with people and them saying, "Do it like this. OK, you're going to lay out here, come in here."

When did you get your first serious recording equipment?

In late '88, I was hanging out with a friend of my brother, who had a primitive four-track tape recorder, and he told me about a new Yamaha that was coming out, an MT-100. It was the affordable option as far as four-track tape recorders go. I became fixated on that because I started thinking about the mixes I'd be able to do. So I started saving up money. I had a $10 allowance every week, and somewhere in there, around late '89, I worked at a pizza parlor. Eventually, I was able to take it home. From that point on I started messing around with looping beats. I didn't have a sampler. Basically, I had two cheap, belt-drive JVC turntables. And when I got the four-track, what I would do is take an old record with a break and, if you can imagine,

I would be cuing it, in my headphone, and then I'd punch in to record on the four-track on, say, track one. And say the beat just goes "boom t-gat t-boom boom-boom gat," and say that's all I wanted or that's all that existed on the record. So then I'd punch out in time. "Boom t-gat t-boom boom-boom." Right? Stop the tape, rewind the tape, pull the record back, cue it to the top, and play the tape, so it'd go "boom t-ba t-boom boom-boom ba," punch in, "boom t-ba t-boom boom-boom ba," and I'd play the record again. Then maybe, on the next track, I'd find a vocal scratch. Then, on another track, I'd layer something else. So, with this technique, I was able to make crude beats, which weren't always accurate because it depended on if I was exactly accurate in my punch and my cuing.

The earliest tape I have that was made with the MT-100 is from April 1990. I remember doing something with Gil Scott-Heron's "The Revolution Will Not Be Televised," which is something that a couple other people had already used. But that was back in an era where it wasn't considered a sin to use what other people had used. Although, I know that when I heard things that hadn't been used before, that's when I really started getting interested. At first, you try to make beats that sound like the beats that you like on records. In the same way, when you first start scratching, you're imitating the scratches that you've heard. I was trying to make beats that sounded like stuff that was out on Def Jam or Profile or Tommy Boy.

Another guy Oras introduced me to was a rapper named Paris. He was the first person to put me in a real studio. He was from San Francisco and he had his own little label, called Scarface. He put out a couple records that I liked. One was "This Beat Is Def" by a group called ATC. It was better than your average Bay Area stuff, which, to me, just didn't have the right kinetic energy. It didn't bump, the way stuff from the East Coast or LA did. Paris and I got along pretty well. He put out an EP called *By Night*, which was incredible. It had a full-color jacket and looked professional. Then I didn't see him for a while. Next thing I knew, I saw his video on MTV. He'd gotten on Tommy Boy and he'd put out an album called *The Devil Made Me Do It*. It was very much in the spirit of Public Enemy—some would say maybe a little too much.

By the time I connected with him again, he was not getting along with Tommy Boy, and, in fact, he eventually ended up getting off the label. He was starting work on his next album and he remembered that I was out there making beats and could scratch. He also had a falling out with his DJ and needed some scratching. Turns out, I had just gotten a $1,800 Cadillac Sedan de Ville and was able to drive the 2½ hours to East Palo Alto, where his studio was. I'd bring a bunch of records with me, and he'd be in there working on tracks. I did scratches and made a lot of beats for him. If you look at the liner notes on *Endtroducing...*, I thank Paris for "teaching me 'the game.' " What I meant by that was he taught me that you have to kind of watch your back, when it comes to making beats for people, and how you choose to get paid. Because, in retrospect, I got shanked. But I have absolutely no hard feelings about it.

He jerked you around?

Well, the way it worked was that basically he'd call me up and be like, "I need some beats." Paris would bullshit me and talk about how funny my hair was. He'd be like, "Yeah, you're not doing shit. Hook that beat up." I'd play him a few things that I was working on, some samples I thought were cool. And he'd say, "That one sucks. That one sucks. This one's cool." Then he'd say, "Yeah, run that onto cassette for me." A lot of times, he'd end up just sampling off the cassette I gave him. [laughs] And basically, he would pay me a finder's fee for samples. But, like I said, back then, I wasn't complaining because he was dealing with me mostly straight. I think deep down he respected what I was about.

Overall, Oras, Paris and Chris Rivers were probably the three people, between '86 and '91, that were the main positive forces in my musical evolution. Chris introduced me to a lot of people that helped further my understanding of sampling and deejaying and records and what it's about to be down with a crew. I thank him pretty profusely on the *Endtroducing...* liner notes. He never said a discouraging word and always had time for me. There were so many people, early on in my career, that helped me above and beyond the call. I can only assume that it must have been my enthusiasm that attracted them to me. Because, in some ways, it doesn't make any sense, how accommodating and how helpful people were. All these guys were older to me. They seemed worldlier. They all had cars and they zoomed around to parties, and I felt like, "Wow, these cats are really doing it." I felt like I was faking it.

When did you start at UC Davis?

In the summer of 1990. Oras had graduated in '89, so there

was about a year-and-a-half period where there was no hip-hop on the radio at Davis, at least none of any substance. One day I happened to be at Tower Records in Sacramento, buying 12-inches. I saw a playlist from KDVS by a guy named DJ Zen. I was looking at his list, and I was like, "Damn, this guy knows what he's doing." It's an informed list. It wasn't some stupid shit. I went, "OK, wow, somebody's back at KDVS like doing stuff again. I'd better check it out." I noted what time his show was on and I started tuning in. And at some point, just like with Oras, I called him up, and I started talking to him. I went to the station and checked out his show. It was good. He wasn't trying to mix like Oras had. He was just playing stuff. And he definitely had a political slant, as well, which, back then in hip-hop that was very normal. For people with an ax to grind or that needed a soapbox to stand on, hip-hop was a convenient conveyor of the message at the time. To some degree, it took a little bit of the fun out of it, but some of the music was still compelling, and some of the politics was compelling, so it was all good. Jeff and I started hanging around, and eventually I asked him if I could play some of my things. And he was intrigued to learn that I was a DJ and could scratch, and he started playing my stuff on the air, little tracks here and there that I had been working on on the four-track.

I worked on tracks my whole freshman year. I thought that maybe I could mix like some of the guys I heard on KMEL. I thought that I could scratch like a lot of the people that I heard on record and that although my beats were not as tight as people who were using samplers, at least I was using interesting stuff. I sat down at a computer because my neurons were really firing back then, as they do when you first start college, and I wrote all this propaganda about how I was going to take over the hip-hop business. Not in an arrogant way or a pushy way. I tried to put it in political terms—that I was trying to start a musical revolution, and who's going to join me, kind of thing. It was a little manifesto, very much along the lines of something that would have made DJ Zen happy.

Around this time I went to KMEL, which was very influential in the urban market in San Francisco. Somehow, I got a meeting with the program director. I strolled right into his office and said, "You need to hire me. Your mixes are getting weak. You know, I'm what you need." The guy was looking at this 18-year-old kid, just like, "This guy's hilarious. I'm going to give him a shot." I started doing real complicated four-track mixes that go on for 45 minutes. Immediately, I would call a label like Tommy Boy, Profile, Wild Pitch, Rap-a-Lot, and they'd say, "You do mixes on KMEL? Let's get you all our product immediately." Because they knew that KMEL was a big, important force. It was a great calling card. Suddenly, everybody was my friend [laughs], all these radio promo guys at all the labels. So now, not only was I getting records from these people, but also I was getting posters, stickers and any type of promo item that any of them came up with. In return, I put their music on the air because that's what it's all about.

I sent one of my demos to *Source* magazine, which then was very much underground. They had a column called "Unsigned Hype," and it was where people would send their demos and hopefully get a little write-up and then try and parlay that into a deal. I submitted a tape to "Unsigned Hype." It's interesting because, I think it would have been '98 or '99, *Source* did a 10-year issue that featured profiles of everybody that had been in "Unsigned Hype" that went on to do anything. And I was in that. I was glad they didn't forget about me! [laughs] But people like Notorious B.I.G. started out there. It was cool to see all that company.

Kick Out the Jams

by Don McLeese

Don McLeese has written about rock for the alternative weekly *Chicago Reader*, as the award-winning pop music critic for the *Chicago Sun-Times* and *Austin American-Statesman* and as a frequent contributor to *Rolling Stone, Request*, and other national music magazines. He is now an associate professor of journalism at the University of Iowa, and a senior editor at *No Depression*. He continues to contribute to national music, literary and general-interest publications.

You Must Choose, Brothers and Sisters . . .

Even with the benefit of more than thirty-five years' hindsight, it's hard to render the MC5's next six months as more than a whiplash blur. So much happened so quickly that the band's thrill ride from local legend to national notoriety to rock laughingstock feels like an acid flashback.

By the end of July 1968, the band was little-known beyond the Detroit/Ann Arbor axis. By the end of August it had launched its legend as the only band gutsy enough—or goofy enough—to risk the wrath of Chicago at the Democratic National Convention.

Toward the end of September, the band signed with Elektra Records.

At the end of October, it recorded its debut album, live at the Grande.

Toward the end of December, the 5 took its show on the road, making a disastrous pre-release swing through the East Coast, alienating both the most powerful club promoters and the most radical street anarchists in the process.

At the beginning of January, *Rolling Stone* ran a rapturous, delirious (and barely comprehensible) cover story on the 5—a month before *Kick Out the Jams* was even released.

By the end of February, *Kick Out the Jams* had hit-bound momentum, heading toward the Top 30 with sales approaching 100,000 copies.

By the end of March, Elektra Records dropped the band, just weeks after releasing the album. Too much controversy. Too much trouble. Though the label had made a sizable investment in promotion and had benefited from an avalanche of publicity, the MC5 could take their revolution elsewhere.

Rarely has a bigger buildup incited a stronger backlash. Almost overnight, the MC5 went from "next big thing" to heavily-hyped pariah. The band was too aggressive, too chaotic, too confrontational, too extreme. Too full of themselves. Their revolution was nothing but a joke, or so went the prevailing wisdom within the rock world. Maybe all this high-energy, fist-pumping, foot-stomping, rabble-rousing bullshit worked in Detroit, but that was Detroit. Rock was smarter than this. More sophisticated. Rock was aspiring toward art. The MC5 weren't artists. The MC5 were crazy.

* * *

John Sinclair had begun greasing the wheels for the band's roller-coaster rise (and fall), a month before the 5's breakthrough at the Democratic convention. In the underground version of smoke signals, his breathless accounts of the 5's revolutionary exploits from his columns in various Detroit-area rags had made their way into New York's *East Village Other*. When he traveled east in July on the band's behalf, bringing copies of "Looking at You" as a calling card, he found kindred spirits and willing co-conspirators (as they would soon be credited on *Kick Out the Jams*) in Dennis Frawley and the irrepressible Bob "Righteous" Rudnick. The two shared a column in the EVO and a weekly radio show called "Kokaine Karma."

In addition to providing the MC5 with both print and play, they introduced Sinclair to Danny Fields, the crucial connection in taking this regional phenomenon to the next level. Working for Elektra Records, scenester Fields had a job that hadn't existed within the music industry a couple years earlier and wouldn't a couple years later. His title was director of publicity, spreading the word among the emerging rock press, but his unofficial role was "house hippie," mediating between the underground and the record industry that was trying to capitalize on it.

There was no doubt that rock and roll was in the midst of a sea change—from am to fm, from singles to albums, from British Invasion to San Francisco psychedelia, from teen mags to rock mags and underground papers—and that the music industry would need to change as well. Elektra was committed to changing. The well-respected boutique label had established its identity with a stable of folk artists including Judy Collins, Phil Ochs, Tim Buckley and Fred Neil. The New York-based company had recently made its move into rock by venturing into the West Coast underground to sign Los Angeles acts such as Love and the Doors. Each combined counterculture credibility with commercial potential; both had already cracked the Top 40 with hit singles.

It was Fields's job to keep Elektra ahead of the curve, as rock continued to change faster than one would ever suspect from the clueless mainstream media. He had to know not only what was big now, but what could be big six months from now.

As he'd learned from Frawley and Rudnick, the MC5 were huge in Detroit and extending their reach across the Midwest, generating the sort of response typically reserved for the likes of the Who and the Stones, wiping the stage with touring headliners whose heavily hyped reputations couldn't withstand the band's high-energy assault. With minimal airplay and no national reputation, the band would pack the Grande, drawing three or four thousand screaming maniacs who were convinced that rock couldn't get any more kickass than this.

Yet Detroit was Detroit—in other words, nowhere. The Midwest typically followed trends rather than starting them. At the time, the nation's airwaves were dominated by the likes of Simon and Garfunkel—whose *Bookends* and soundtrack to *The Graduate* both topped the charts through the first half of '68. Such music couldn't even pass as rock by the high-energy standards of the Motor City. While the music industry was searching for cities whose scenes could be packaged as successfully as San Francisco's psychedelia, Detroit was considered a much tougher sell than Boston (where one label was hyping the "Boss-town" sound, and Elektra had recently signed Earth Opera).

The sighing of Simon and Garfunkel through "Old Friends" and the raging of the MC5 through "Kick Out the Jams" seemed to exist within separate musical universes. At a time when rock aspired to maturity, refining itself into art, a spirit of elitism was leading the music toward the literary, the sophisticated, the conceptually complex, the improvisational, the expansion of consciousness. With its blast-furnace urgency, the blue-collar populism of the MC5 was plainly and powerfully at odds with all of that. It was the rock of the drag strip, of the street gang, of the clenched fist, not the rock of the library, the conservatory, the concert hall.

If rock were ready to march to the beat of a different drummer, that drummer didn't appear to be Dennis "Machine Gun" Thompson. Yet whatever was happening in Detroit was strange enough and strong enough to merit a first-hand look. Even the force of Sinclair's personality and the enthusiasm he generated with his wild tales of rock and roll revolution couldn't prepare Fields for what he encountered that September on a scouting mission to the Motor City.

"It was a midwesternized version of anarchy," he remembers in *Please Kill Me*. "Tear down the walls, get the government out of our lives, smoke lots of dope, have lots of sex and make lots of noise" (p. 48).

There was nothing like this in New York: the commune of macho militants and the women doing their sewing, cooking and sexual bidding (feminism had yet to imprint itself on the radical consciousness), the rock concert as revolutionary rally, the band at the vanguard of an aural assault on the culture at large. Fields had never experienced rock like this; no one outside the MC5's force field had.

After visiting with the band at the Ann Arbor commune and witnessing the 5 all but levitate the Grande, Fields called New York to tell label owner Jac Holzman he had to sign them. And not just them. He had also seen the Stooges over the weekend at Wayne Kramer's insistence, and Fields wanted both bands. Holzman said to offer twenty grand for the big band and five grand for the "little brother" band.

Everyone was ecstatic. Fields had signed the most exciting bands he would ever discover. The MC5 were ready to rampage across the country. Sinclair would have a national platform where he could wage his revolution. The Stooges were finally taken seriously by someone; the "little brothers" had a record deal of their own. What Elektra was buying into was more than one very exciting band. They were signing the Grande, the audience, and blue-collar Detroit and the whole notion of high-energy rock.

With their debut album, the MC5 would confront some crucial challenges: How could the band extend its radical domain from the Rust Belt across the nation at large? How could this music transfer its galvanizing energy from live performance to vinyl? Was it possible for the whole world to channel the power that the 5 and their fans had generated at the Grande?

For such a radical band, Elektra decided on a radical approach. At a time when even great live acts such as the Who and the Stones were employing studio technology to enhance their recordings, adding dimensions that couldn't necessarily be duplicated onstage, the label decided to capture the 5 in all their sweaty, messy glory—live at the Grande, where the crowd was almost as amped as the band. For this music, the audience was like rocket fuel. Introducing a band with a live album was a risky proposition, but if you were willing to sign the 5, there was no sense in playing it safe.

Just a week and a half earlier, the band had opened a weekend bill for Kensington Market and Pacific Gas & Electric at the Grande. Now the band would storm the stage as conquering heroes, in a headlining, two-night Halloween extravaganza at the Grande, with the Psychedelic Stooges opening. To ensure a pair of packed houses in the middle of the week, the Thursday of Halloween and the warm-up night before, both shows would be free, with the tapes rolling.

"Kids knew if they went to see the MC5, something extraordinary would happen," explained Sinclair to *DISCoveries* magazine. "I figured if we could record live, in our stronghold, to a packed crowd going wild, then we'd be able to capture it" (Dec. 1995, p. 26).

Even so, there was too much at stake to work without a net. The band received assurances that if they weren't pleased with the recording, if they somehow suffered an off night (or two), the tapes would not be released. And Elektra decided to hedge its bets by additionally taping the band in an empty ballroom on the Thursday afternoon between shows. A few tape splices are obvious, between the "Motherfuckers!" and the roaring riff that opens "Kick Out the Jams" and the "high society" rant and the beginning of "Motor City Is Burning," though if the label were interested in homogenizing the 5 to contemporary standards, it would have fixed the spot where Thompson drops the beat in "Rocket Reducer No. 62 (Rama Lama Fa Fa Fa)." Whatever was used from the afternoon session, it's plain that the label and the band were intent on presenting the music—and the crowd—in all their crazed energy and chaotic glory rather than cleaning up the mess.

For those who'd already experienced the incendiary excitement of the band in the flesh, listening to that debut recording is like the difference between a wall-sized Jackson Pollock splatter canvas and a reproduction reduced to a page. Or like viewing something on a small-screen TV that you'd seen on an IMAX. It can give you an idea of what the original experience was like, but the scope, scale and impact couldn't come close to measuring up. If you were there, you couldn't deny the power of the experience, or resist it.

Some of those who were introduced to the 5's music by the album tended to respond like gapers at a car crash or onlookers at a street brawl. Hard to turn away, hard to comprehend. The first side of the album (and this is definitely an artifact of an era when vinyl albums had sides) is a rush of adrenalin, a roar of testosterone, and a revolutionary testimonial to the dick that stays hard all night long. Whatever John Sinclair envisioned for his guerrilla assault, the band plainly believed mainly in the power of the penis, the revolution as group grope.

From the start, the crowd is pumped, carrying a higher charge before the band even takes the stage than most concerts generate with the encore. First comes the invocation by "spiritual advisor" Brother J. C. Crawford (aka John, aka Jesse), the emcee as street preacher, merging James Brown's "Star Time" intro with a gospel call-and-response and a militant's call to arms:

> Brothers and sisters, I wanna see a sea of hands out there . . . I want everybody to kick up some noise, I wanna hear some revolution. . . . Brothers and sisters, the time has come for each and every one of you to decide whether you are going to be the problem or you are going to be the solution! You must choose, brothers, you must choose. It takes five seconds, five seconds of decision, five seconds to realize your purpose here on the planet. It takes five seconds to realize that its time to move, it's time to get down with it. Brothers, it's time to testify. And I want to know—are you ready to testify? *Are you ready!!* I give you a testimonial. THE MC5!!

The crowd erupts as four of the five come bucking out of the chute, the guitars charging and drums pounding behind Wayne

Kramer's breathy falsetto on "Ramblin' Rose." It's a song about sex. With two notable exceptions on the album's second side, every cut on "Kick Out the Jams" is a song about sex—sex as stamina, sex as conquest, sex as manhood, sex as rock and roll. "Love is like a ramblin' rose," Wayne squeals. "The more you feel it, the more it grows." The second time he sings the line, he rubs the crotch of his skintight satin pants. The band and the crowd are ready to explode; the set is barely two minutes old.

The explosion comes with the fuse hit by the belated emergence of the fifth of the MC5, the bushily afro'd Rob Tyner. Stomping to center stage, he introduces the band's signature anthem with a series of pregnant pauses, "And right now . . . right now . . . right now . . . it's time to . . . KICK OUT THE JAMS, MOTHERFUCKERS!!!" Again, the song is about sex—sex as getting down, sex as getting stoned, sex as going crazy, sex as partying all night long if you're man enough to do it. Mostly, it's about the sexual power of being in a rock and roll band. It should have been a bigger hit than "We're an American Band" by Grand Funk Railroad, one of the many bands inconceivable without the 5. (By appropriating the all-American iconography while eliminating the politics from the equation, Grand Funk would prove far more commercially successful at spreading the high-energy ethos to the lowest common denominator.)

While the rhythm section has yet to finish with "Kick Out the Jams," the guitars are already surging into "Come Together," a song that has little in common with John Lennon's Chuck Berry rewrite that would later open *Abbey Road*. The longest sustained orgasm this side of Donna Summer, the song is about sex as cosmic rhythm and energy, "the dance from which all dances come," as Tyner moans, the drums pound and the guitars spurt.

After a pause to allow Tyner to catch his breath (and indulge in a brief Donald Duck impression), the multiorgasmic 5 launch into the album's centerpiece and the anthem that would remain the highlight of their live sets, "Rocket Reducer No. 62 (Rama Lama Fa Fa Fa)." This is the supercharged 5 in all their garage-band glory, with pedal to the metal and flight plan to the stars. Between the way the verses lurch and the choruses soar, the band generates so much kinetic energy that it fulfills the most grandiose claims ever made for the music.

The revolutionary message? "Rama lama fa fa fa": "I said wham, bam, thank you ma'am, I'm a born hell-raiser and I don't give a damn. I'm a man for you, baby. Yes I am for you, baby."

Not exactly a dialectic manifesto, but Che Guevara never rocked like this.

Four songs, fourteen and a half minutes of high-energy epiphany and raw sexual release. Then comes the second side, which remains the second side even in the CD era, another set of four cuts as diffuse as the first four are focused. In the vinyl era that spawned the album, you'd listen to both sides of a release at least once but then come to favor one side over the other. I'd guess that most of the more than 100,000 who bought *Kick Out the Jams* played side one 25–50 times for every time they turned the album over.

When Kramer helped compile Rhino's *The Big Bang! Best of the MC5* in 2000, the anthology included side one in its entirety and omitted side two in its entirety. Yet listening to the second half of the album can still offer flashes of revelation, where every note on side one left an indelible imprint decades ago.

"Borderline," one of the band's first originals and the B side to its second single, launches the B side of the album with the closest thing the early 5 were likely to come to a tender love song—sex as confusion. It even invokes the term "make love," a different sort of physical sensation from the "rama lama" thrust of side one.

From there, the set makes a sharp left turn into radical rabble rousing, when, from out of nowhere, Crawford returns to exhort, "Brothers and sisters, I wanna tell you something. I hear a lot of talk from a lot of honkeys, sitting on a lot of money, saying they're the high society. But, if you ask me, this is the high society, this is the high society!"

However high the crowd was by this time, the twelve-bar plod of "Motor City Is Burning" immediately brings them down. Despite the most politically incendiary message on the album, an expression of celebration of the riots, invocation of firebombs and "si-REENS," disdain for the "pigs" and solidarity with the Black Panthers, there's barely evidence of any audience reaction as the band tames itself to the strictures of standard blues. "I may be a white boy, but I can be bad, too," boasts Tyner at the fade, before prophesizing that Detroit is the harbinger of urban destruction to come: "They'll all burn! They'll all burn!"

So much for politics. The band is back on familiar territory though forging new musical ground with "I Want You Right Now." What Detroit called "Heavy Music" (in a regional anthem by Bob Seger) the world would soon know as "heavy metal." Over six minutes of proto-metal sludge, the MC5 provide the bridge here between the Troggs and Black Sabbath. In the early punk uprisings of the mid-to-late 70s, punk and metal had little in common but mutual disdain. Yet the MC5 provided a template for each, and a prophetic example of how they would come to revel in a shared sonic sensation, driven by the visceral noise of the electric guitar.

In its climactic finale, credited to MC5 and Sun Ra, "Starship" takes rock where it had never gone before and has rarely ventured since (though the psycho-progressive likes of Pink Floyd and Hawkwind would take tamer trips through the cosmos). There's barely an interval from the heavy, heavy sexual slurp of "I Want You Right Now" into the transformation of the guitars into Flash Gordon rayguns, as Tyner starts the count-down to blast off for "Starship." Through his out-of-body mantra of "leaving the solar system," the music proceeds through screams and crashes into an eerie euphoria, taking the 5's front man to the outer limits of his beloved science fiction. It's a long way from the burning ghettos of the Motor City.

It's impossible to know how this music might have fared independent of Sinclair's revolutionary hype, partly because the hype escalated considerably between the recording of the album and its release. Wayne Kramer later insisted that the band was dissatisfied with its performance, intimidated by the pressure of the rolling tape and felt that Elektra's decision to release this version of the live set represented the label's first breach of faith.

By the time the label unleashed *Kick Out the Jams*, the musical dynamic had become overshadowed by the political posturing. Just as the beatnik Artists' Workshop had mushroomed into hippie Trans-Love Energies, the mood toward a more militant radicalism saw Trans-Love morph into the White Panther Party in the wake of the live recording. The very day after the Halloween taping, Sinclair issued a proclamation as "Minister of Defense" of this Caucasian auxiliary to the notorious Black Panthers, whose rejection of non-violence and move toward armed "self-defense" had become white America's worst nightmare.

"We're as crazy as they are, and as pure," boasted Sinclair. "We're **bad**. This is our program." The ten points that followed ranged from the surreal ("We demand the end of money!") to the prophetic ("Free access to the information media—free the technology from the greed creeps!"). The point that generated most of the response, from laughter to outrage, was an expansion of the guerrilla war as point 2: "Total assault on the culture by any means necessary, including rock and roll, dope and fucking in the streets."

By the time of the album's release just three months later, the identification of the MC5 with the White Panther Party was absolute. The gatefold liner showed three of the bare-chested 5 with White Panther buttons pinned right on their skin, with Sonic Smith slinging a strap of bullets across his chest as a fashion accessory. The liner notes by Sinclair, identified as "Minister of Information, White Panthers" rather than the band's manager, raised the rhetorical ante:

> The MC5 is totally committed to the revolution, as the revolution is totally committed to driving people out of their separate shells and into each other's arms. . . . The MC5 will make you feel it, or leave the room. The MC5 will drive you crazy out of your head and into your body. . . . They are a working model of the new paleocybernetic culture in action. There is no separation. They live together to work together, they eat together, fuck together, get high together, walk down the street and through the world together. There is no separation. . . . Separation is doom. We are free men, and we demand a free music, a free high energy source that will drive us wild into the streets of America yelling and screaming and tearing down everything that would keep people slaves.
>
> The MC5 is that force.

No Middle Ground

Inevitably, *Kick Out the Jams* proved as polarizing as it was pulverizing. The music forced listeners to take sides in a way that rock rarely had before. This wasn't merely a matter of intramural factionalism, like a preference for the Stones over the Beatles, or for the S&M strains of New York's Velvet Underground over the peace-and-love psychedelia of the San Francisco bands. Rock was big enough to encompass those divisions; fans could find room in their record collections for both the Beach Boys and Bob Dylan.

The MC5 represented a different sort of breach, at a time when confrontation and polarization were at their politico-cultural peak. "You're either part of the problem or part of the solution," radical militants insisted, castigating more temperate souls as wishy-washy liberals, unwilling to commit to the necessity of bringing the war home. As J. C. Crawford harangued a crowd of potential commandos in his intro to *Kick Out the Jams*, "You must choose, brothers and sisters . . . "

With the MC5, there could be no middle ground. Either this incendiary explosiveness was the ultimate rock experience—maybe the ultimate life-transforming experience—or it was artless, mindless noise. Either it was a flight into the visionary future or a Neanderthal return to brute force, pure physicality. As Detroit critic and early band champion Dave Marsh wrote in *Creem* (later anthologized in his *Fortunate Son*), either "the MC5 had to be defined as the very best rock and roll band in the whole world or else no good at all."

Punk would eventually require a similar choice—you couldn't apply the same standards to the Sex Pistols as you did to the Beatles or the Stones—but punk hadn't arrived to provide a frame of reference for the MC5. For the 5 to triumph, the world would need to change, rock would need to change, the music industry would need to change, the audience would need to change. Maybe the molecular structure of the universe would need to change.

Some of that would happen, when the likes of the Ramones and the Clash shattered the complacency of rock almost a full decade later, but by then it was too late for the 5. The band was remembered, when remembered at all, as something between a curiosity and a footnote.

* * *

As it turned out, it made a huge difference whether you were introduced to the music of the MC5 from the stage or from the page. For those of us who had gotten our initiation to the band first-hand—as Marsh had, as I had, as Norman Mailer had, as thousands of rabid Motor City fans had—this music was an irresistible force. You could no more deny the power of the MC5 than you could analyze the aesthetics of a nuclear explosion. You just needed to experience it, and your sense of rock's possibilities, of life's possibilities, would never be the same.

Hearing too much about this music before actually hearing it not only raised expectations, it generated resistance—the cultural equivalent of the equal and opposite reaction. Paced by the propaganda of John Sinclair, the hype surrounding the band was every bit as over-the-top as the music. A buildup as big as the one the 5 received almost guarantees a big backlash. The more that people read about not only the revolutionary impact of the music but the revolutionary rhetoric surrounding it, the greater the skepticism the MC5 had to overcome when they took their show on the road.

"Before their record even came out, they had been the most publicized group in the history of American rock," proclaimed Danny Fields, in a bit of hyperbole worthy of John Sinclair, "but it's real, they're the best. The prejudice against them comes from the literate literary crowd; the best reviews of their music are in the high school underground papers, 'cause those are the kids who know what it's supposed to be and what rock is about" (*The Age of Rock* 2, p. 168).

The divide was geographic as well as generational, for the red-hot, blast-furnace intensity of this band from the industrial Midwest didn't play nearly as well to the cooler sophisticates on the coasts. Among the East Coast rock-crit intelligentsia, those who had traveled (often at Fields's behest) to see the 5 on their home turf were duly impressed, with the influential Jon Landau of Boston and Richard Goldstein of New York among the early converts. Yet the farther the band surged from its home base, the more disdain it received from rock and roll's smart set.

"In Detroit, we ruled," wrote Wayne Kramer in the notes to Rhino's anthology, *The Big Bang! The Best of the MC5*. "Our fans were the blue-collar shop rats and factory kids, and they connected with the energy and the release in the MC5's live shows. But our band was generally despised outside of the industrial Midwest."

A big part of the problem was that the music wasn't allowed to stand on its own. The MC5 weren't just a band; they were a movement, the musical vanguard of the militant White Panther Party. In order to embrace this music, you apparently had to commit to the destruction of Western civilization as we knew it. Against a backdrop of bullets in the air and fornication in the streets, even the primal power of "rama lama fa fa fa" hardly stood a chance.

Too many people ended up taking the White Panther Party seriously—as if there really were a party and a platform to be reckoned with—and dismissed the MC5 as a joke. Yet the White Panther Party was really the joke (as the Black Panthers were quick to recognize, distancing themselves from their Caucasian comrades), while the music of the MC5 was the real deal, the most exciting rock that many of us would ever experience. It was the music that was revolutionary, not the stoned, slapstick rhetoric accompanying it.

Other bands would have killed for the amount of pre-release publicity the band generated, but that publicity all but killed the MC5. The month before *Kick Out the Jams* was issued, *Rolling Stone* elevated the band to "next big thing" status with an exhaustive five-page January 4 cover story, including an annotated set-list sidebar by John Sinclair (a close friend of the late John Coltrane, the story suggested). Introducing the nation to the likes of Wayne "Cramer" and "Bob" Tyner, writer Eric Ehrman proclaimed the band a "total destroy experience."

"The MC-5 are attempting to politicize and liberate the minds of our culture," he wrote. "This radical musical action stems from the one-dimensional automobile factory environment of their Detroit home (their name stands for Motor City Five) and it is spreading rapidly with the popularity of the band."

Of the subculture surrounding the band, he continued,

> The commune is quite a successful endeavor and it welcomes anyone who wants to participate and do their thing. Chicks live with the 5 and also provide the domestic energies to make clothing for concert wear, keep the place tidy and make some of the most destroy barbecue ribs and chicken that you can chomp on. Anyone from the area can walk in, sit down at the 30-foot long harvest table and scarf down some really destroy food, absolutely free.

Though the piece—*really destroy!*—has somehow been omitted from the magazine's subsequent anthologies of literary highlights, it made a big splash. It got lots of people talking about a band that few of them had heard. It ensured that the release of the band's debut would be heralded as an event. "If you hear of some notoriously freaky band coming to your town with a trail of policemen, narcs, freaks and guerillas, it'll be the MC-5," the feature concluded. "Don't just sit and watch—KICK OUT THE JAMS!"

The word was out. And for better and worse, the MC5 helped spread that word. During the weeks between the interview with the *Rolling Stone* reporter and the publication of the cover story, the band began rampaging its way toward the East Coast on a pre-release promotional tour, aiming to ignite their musical revolution that would set the nation on fire. Since the MC5 had been positioning themselves at rock's radical vanguard, they were a magnet for radicals and anarchists who were determined to "liberate" rock from the reactionary music industry.

Foremost among them were a notorious group of confrontational street activists known as the Up Against the Wall Motherfuckers. More commonly called the Motherfuckers, they traveled from their native New York to hitch their wagon to the promotional engine of the band whose "Kick Out the Jams, Motherfuckers!" plainly signified kindred spirits. The Motherfuckers were there in full force when the MC5's first eastern swing commenced on December 15 at the Boston Tea Party.

Commandeering the stage during the 5's set, the Motherfuckers harangued the crowd that it was being ripped off (as recounted in *Mansion on the Hill*, p. 170), and that the music, in the argot of the day, should be "free." The crowd should tear down these walls of oppression. The diatribe incensed Boston promoter Don Law, who heard himself branded a rip-off artist and an enemy of the people from his own stage. The MC5 had made their first big enemy among the industry's power elite, and were effectively "banned in Boston."

Next stop was New York's Fillmore East, where promoter Bill Graham was even more of a hardliner when it came to hearing his investment become a target for the rhetoric of half-baked revolution. A fracas with the Motherfuckers at Graham's hall turned violent the night of the 5's New York debut, with the promoter himself suffering a broken nose during the brawl. (He claimed that Rob Tyner had hit him with a chain, though the band's resident quasi-intellectual was an unlikely perpetrator.)

Having alienated two of rock's top promoters, the band found itself caught in the crossfire from the radical flank. In typical record company fashion, Fields had ordered limos to squire his new signees around Manhattan. In the wake of the Fillmore brawl, as the Motherfuckers saw the band flee the scene in their stretch limo, the breech between White Panther rhetoric and rock-star privilege couldn't have been greater. While positioning themselves as such a radical threat to the music industry and the culture at large, the MC5 could never be radical enough for the militants who saw the music as a means to a political end.

"The streets are full of ranting anarchists and Maoists, and up pulls a shiny black limo to carry 'the people's band' away," Fields recounted to Ben Edmonds in *Mojo* (September 2002). "Everything went wild at that point. There was a riot. The band were seen as traitors to community values because I hired these limos. But I always did, because it made sense for large numbers of people. I was so naïve I didn't see it as a flagrantly provocative political gesture. I should have hired armored tanks."

On the eve of the debut album's release, not only was the band blacklisted on both coasts—since Graham was such a major player in California as well as New York—but its street cred had taken a major hit as well. The stench of hype pervaded the exhaustive, over-the-top *Rolling Stone* cover package, as if the MC5 and the powers behind them were trying to put something over on a rock and roll community too savvy to fall for this promotional campaign of revolutionary drivel. It became increasingly easy to turn the band into caricature, especially for those who had yet to experience the cataclysmic impact of the music and now never would experience it fresh, without strong preconceptions.

Yet with all the promotional momentum behind it, the February release of *Kick Out the Jams* attracted the curious along with the converts in sufficient numbers that it paid quick commercial dividends. By the first week in March the album had already cracked Billboard's Top 200 albums, debuting at number 173. Two weeks later, the album had surged into the Hot 100, at number 97 with a bullet. "Kick Out the Jams" had already established itself as a smash single in the band's native Detroit, rising to number two on the weekly WKNR survey.

(The rest of the radio station's top five suggests an alternate universe, with "Dizzy" by Tommy Roe topping the chart, and "Twenty-Five Miles" by Detroit soulster Edwin Starr, the chirpy "Build Me Up Buttercup" by the Foundations and the bubblegummy "Indian Giver" by the 1910 Fruitgum Company trailing in the wake of the furious 5.)

It was in the midst of this ascent that Sinclair and band decided it was truly time to bring the war home. The album's inflammatory liner notes and "Motherfucker" exhortation had met resistance from Hudson's, a downtown department store that occupied the same position of prominence in Detroit as Macy's in New York or Marshall Field's in Chicago. During a period before the proliferation of both national chains and hip, indie retailers (where record stores doubled as head shops), department stores exerted the same sort of influence on music retailing as the conservative Wal-Mart does today.

With Hudson's refusing to stock the album, the hometown heroes launched a counter-attack. The band took out a full-page ad in the underground Ann Arbor *Argus* exhorting, "KICK OUT

THE JAMS, MOTHERFUCKER! and kick in the door if the store won't sell you the album on Elektra. FUCK HUDSON'S" (vol. 1., no. 2). The ad carried Elektra's logo and Sinclair sent the bill to the label for payment. Since the band had also relied on Hudson's for musical and performance gear, it stopped payment on its account, stiffing the store for more than $1,600, sending a letter of defiance and a copy of the ad to the retailer.

Hudson's responded to what looked like an Elektra-sponsored ad by pulling all of the label's stock from its racks. The label was aghast, realizing the outrageous lengths to which the band would go, determined not to let such radical excess interfere with the ascent of a hit album. Fearing more reprisals such as Hudson's, the label decided to offer retailers a censored version of the album, with "motherfuckers!" replaced by "brothers and sisters!" on "Kick Out the Jams" and Sinclair's liner notes removed. Even before the "clean" copies were ready, the label recalled the "dirty" copies. Instead of having a choice between the two versions, stores had no copies.

As retailers, radicals, promoters, even their own label turned against them, the band suffered another body slam with the review of the album in the April 5 *Rolling Stone*, which hit the stands mid-March. Just weeks after anointing the band as rock's next big thing, the vanguard of an impending revolution, *Rolling Stone* now dismissed the debut album as sounding like "a bunch of 16 year olds on a meth power trip . . . more like Blue Cheer than Trane [John Coltrane] and [Pharoah] Sanders . . . and a ridiculous, overbearing, pretentious album."

It was the first review ever published by Lester Bangs, whose own influence and notoriety would soon eclipse the 5's (at least in rock-crit circles) and who would soon do a critical about-face on the band and Detroit high-energy rock in general. Moving to Detroit to join Marsh and others at *Creem*, he became one of the staunchest defenders of the band he had reviled.

Of his experience seeing the 5 in concert after moving to Detroit, he wrote to friends, "They weren't just fantastic, they wuz cataclysmic, and it's only now I completely and finally understand why so many people lose their cool and objectivity over this band," as reprinted in *Let It Blurt*, the Bangs bio by Jim DeRogatis. "THERE IS NO BETTER BAND ANYWHERE!" (pp. 67–68).

Yet it was Bangs's original assessment that spoke the loudest, establishing the party line on the MC5 as a band beneath contempt, one that discerning listeners could never take seriously. It was as much a review of the hype surrounding the band—including *Rolling Stone*'s buildup—as it was a response to the music.

Though the album was heading onto *Billboard*'s Top 30 with sales approaching 90,000, Elektra decided there was more risk than reward in continuing to work with this band. It had become plain that there were irreconcilable differences between a band intent on waging a cultural revolution and a label attempting to market that revolution for commercial profit.

Two weeks after the review, the next issue of *Rolling Stone* carried the news that Elektra had cut the MC5 loose. It quoted Elektra's owner Jac Holzman, "I want to make clear that the 'revolution' will be won by poetics and not by politics." The label that would stand behind a "poet" such as the Doors' Jim Morrison, who had apparently exposed his poetic penis to a Miami concert crowd, wanted nothing more to do with the MC5. When Danny Fields argued about the hypocrisy, he was booted from the label as well.

Meanwhile, the rumors of the band's antics onstage and off became increasingly outlandish (and perhaps even true). During my freshman year at the University of Wisconsin in Madison, I heard that Tyner had shocked a Seattle audience by defecating on the stage. That their concerts were turning into orgies in which the band eagerly participated. That the burning of an American flag was becoming as much of a performing signature as the Who's Pete Townshend smashing his guitar.

The more notorious the band became, the more peripheral the music seemed.

Low

by Hugo Wilcken

Hugo Wilcken is a Paris-based, Australian-born writer and translator. His first novel, *The Execution*, was published by HarperCollins in 2002. ("A remarkably accomplished debut heralding the arrival of a noteworthy talent"—*Publishers Weekly.*) It was well reviewed, and has since been translated into Dutch and German. A second novel, *Colony*, was published in August 2007.

what can I do about my dreams?

In mid May, David Bowie and Iggy Pop retired to the picturesque Château d'Hérouville, forty kilometres northwest of Paris, to rest up for a few days after the tour. The Château had been converted into studios by the well-known French film composer Michel Magne in 1969. While winding down there with Iggy, Bowie met up with the Château's manager and chief sound engineer Laurent Thibault, former bassist with the ultimate prog rock group Magma. The two talked late into the night. Much to Thibault's surprise, Bowie seemed well acquainted with Magma's peculiar oeuvre, which mostly consists of a series of concept albums about a planet called Kobaia—with many of the songs sung in native Kobaian. By the end of the night, Bowie had agreed to put down two hundred thousand francs to book the studios for the months of July and September (they were already taken for August). He'd already recorded *Pin-Ups* there, in 1973, and would eventually record most of *Low* at the Château as well.

From there, Bowie moved to a large house at Clos-des-

Mésanges, near Vevey, Switzerland. The move had been engineered by his wife, Angie, partly to get him away from Los Angeles, but largely for tax reasons. Bowie was supposedly settling down to family life with his five-year-old son and wife. But by this stage, their marriage (outrageously open even by seventies rock marriage standards) had more or less broken down in a morass of recriminations and jealousies. Angie had in particular taken against Bowie's assistant Corinne Schwab, whom Bowie used to shield himself against the people he didn't want to see. "Coco kept the irritating people out of his life," his friend and producer Tony Visconti said in 1986, "and Angie had become one of them." Often, Bowie would simply disappear altogether without telling Angie, sometimes to Berlin, and with only Coco in the know. It enraged Angie. The couple's living arrangements became increasingly complicated; while Angie was away in London, Bowie would stay at the house, but when she was home, he'd book into a nearby hotel.

The idea had been to relax after the tour, but Bowie was clearly the sort who thrived on nervous energy, not relaxation. At Clos-des-Mésanges he amassed a library of 5,000 books and threw himself into reading them. Bowie had always been the intellectually curious autodidact, having left school at sixteen. But now it became something of an obsession. During the tour, Bowie had travelled around Europe in a kind of cultural rage, going to concerts, visiting galleries, learning everything he could about art, classical music and literature. It was a reaction against America, but there was also an element of replacing one mania for another (albeit far healthier) one.

A life of leisure in the Swiss Alps for the workaholic Bowie was another mirage, and when Iggy Pop showed up they began to rehearse what would result in Iggy's first solo venture, *The Idiot*, produced and cowritten by Bowie. He had admired Iggy's proto-punk band the Stooges from early on; had got them signed to his then manager's company, Mainman; had mixed the classic Stooges album *Raw Power*, had continually boosted Iggy Pop in the press. The two had become close in Los Angeles, when a washed-up Iggy Pop had checked himself into a mental asylum. "I think he respected me for putting myself in a loony bin," Iggy said in 1977. "He was the only guy who came to visit me. Nobody else came . . . nobody. Not even my so-called friends in LA . . . but David came." (At this time, back in England, Bowie's schizophrenic half-brother, Terry, had already been interned in a mental institution for some years.)

Various studio sessions during 1975 had produced little of worth (there'd been the dirgelike "Moving On," never released, plus a couple of tracks that ended up on *Lust for Life*, changed beyond recognition). But Bowie had invited Iggy on the *Station to Station* tour, and early on in the soundchecks they'd come up with "Sister Midnight," based around a Carlos Alomar riff. Bowie had written the first verse and Iggy the rest, recounting an oedipal dream he'd once had. There was slippage between what was Bowie's and what was Iggy's, and Bowie had played "Sister Midnight" a few times live on tour, but it eventually became the first cut on *The Idiot*, as well as the first real fruit of their fertile (and later not so fertile) partnership.

Bowie remained in Clos-des-Mésanges for most of June, working, painting and reading. He paid visits to Charlie Chaplin's wife, Oona, who lived nearby. ("This intelligent, very sensitive fellow who came from the same part of London as Charlie, walked in and wanted to talk. I really am very fond of him.") He was often seen out and about in local bars and restaurants, dressed simply and generally keeping his head down. But by the end of the month he'd had enough, and decamped with Iggy Pop back to the Château d'Hérouville.

The sixteenth century Château was a former coach staging post and stables, built in the ruins of a castle, and was said to be the setting for secret trysts between Frédéric Chopin and his lover George Sand. Its vast wings contained some thirty bedrooms, rehearsal rooms, kitchens, a dining hall and a gaming room. Outside there was a swimming pool, tennis courts, a beautiful complex of fountains and waterfalls and even a mini-castle, complete with its own moat. The grounds were enormous and one had the impression of being completely isolated and deep in the countryside, despite the fact that Paris was less than an hour away.

It was the first ever residential studio suite—a concept that was much copied afterwards. Two studios were located in outhouses, probably former stables, while a third was in the right wing. In 1976, it cost 5,500 francs (£550, $1,000) per day to hire a studio at the Château, not including tape, which was expensive back then (700 francs for a 50mm roll). Session musicians would get around 1,000 francs for a day's work. The studios were very state-of-the art for the era; the one Bowie used for *The Idiot* and *Low* had an MCI-500 console and the first Westlake monitors to be installed in Europe. Originally opened in 1969, the Château studios had taken a few years before building up an international reputation, which eventually came when Elton John recorded *Honky Château* there in 1972. Since then, the Château's ever-expanding clientèle counted the likes of Pink Floyd, the Grateful Dead, T-Rex, Rod Stewart, Bill Wyman, Cat Stevens and the Bee Gees plus dozens of French artists.

Bowie and Iggy Pop settled in at the Château; their idea was to record when the mood took them, but to basically take it easy. On the face of it, they made for unlikely friends. Although there were certain things in common—both rock performers, both in something of a personal and artistic impasse, both struggling with drugs and mental health problems—it was basically a case of opposites attracting. Bowie was the sexually ambiguous English dandy; Iggy Pop the hyper-masculine American rocker. Career-wise, Bowie was riding a tidal wave, his fame largely transcending the rock world. By contrast, Iggy Pop was at an all-time low, flat broke, without a band and without a recording contract, until Bowie used his weight to get him one at RCA. Bowie was the consummate professional: even during the nightmare of his cocaine addiction, he still toured his albums, touted himself regularly in the media, starred in a movie and, of course, made records that many consider his finest. Iggy Pop, on the other hand, was erratic, disorganised, had no self-discipline, wouldn't turn up to studio sessions, hadn't put out a record in years—and was essentially heading for a massive fall without the helping hand of someone of Bowie's calibre.

It would seem that Iggy Pop needed Bowie a hell of a lot more than Bowie needed him. But Iggy had a certain underground cachet that Bowie probably envied. "I was not executive material like him," Iggy Pop said in 1996. "I couldn't do the things he seemed to do so well and so easily. Yet I knew I had something he didn't have and could never have." The Iggy persona was about danger and violence, urban edge, outlaw posturing, rawness, unrestrained liberty to the point of nihilism . . . in short, a blunt instrument of American masculinity, and the polar opposite of what Bowie was about at the time. "David always had a weakness for tough guys," was how his friend Marc Bolan bitchily put it. Likewise, Iggy Pop had been intrigued by the "British music-hall, pure vaudeville" quality he'd seen in Bowie the first time they'd met. In other words, it was a perfect match of alter egos.

There was a touch of Tom Ripley in the way Bowie adopted those he admired, as if they were another role to be played. Bowie had already sought out and befriended another American hard man, Lou Reed, in rather similar circumstances. Lou Reed's former band the Velvet Underground was of course a legendary nexus of the sixties New York scene, but by the early seventies Reed was down on his luck and in desperate need of a leg up. Enter David Bowie, who talked Reed up in the media and produced *Transformer* (1972)—which did indeed transform Reed's career through the classic hit "Walk on the Wild Side." The album is largely about New York's gay and transvestite scene, and the glammed-up Bowie certainly helped bring out Lou Reed's inner drag queen. In a sense, he did the same for Iggy Pop, suffusing Iggy's balls-out rock routine with a more ironic, cabaret sensibility, giving him a veneer of sleazy European sophistication.

For Bowie, *The Idiot* wasn't just about resurrecting Iggy Pop's stalled career. It was also a dry run for *Low*, with which it would be recorded almost back-to-back, in the same studios. In fact, the recordings overlapped. Sound engineer Laurent Thibault: "Low was recorded after *The Idiot*, but *Low* came out first. David didn't want people to think he'd been inspired by Iggy's album, when in fact it was all the same thing. There were even tracks that we recorded for Iggy that ended up on *Low*, such as 'What in the World,' which was originally called 'Isolation.' " (You can hear Iggy's backing vocals on "What in the World.") Bowie produced *The Idiot*, played many of the instruments and cowrote all the songs—the lyrics largely written by Iggy and the music by Bowie. "Poor Jim [Iggy's real name], in a way, became a guinea pig for what I wanted to do with sound," Bowie explained later. "I didn't have the material at the time, and I didn't feel like writing it all. I felt much more like laying back and getting behind someone else's work, so that album was opportune, creatively." Iggy Pop agrees: "[Bowie] has a work pattern that recurs again and again. If he has an idea about an area of work that he wants to enter, as a first step, he'll use side-projects or work for other people to gain experience and gain a little taste of water before he goes in and does his . . . and I think he used working with me that way also."

As with *Low*, the recording was all done at night, from around midnight on. Bowie covered keyboards, saxophone and most of the guitar parts; the other musicians were Michel Marie on drums and Laurent Thibault on bass. Phil Palmer, nephew of Kinks frontman Ray Davies, played guitar on "Nightclubbing," "Dum Dum Boys" and "China Girl." Carlos Alomar wasn't present, but the rest of Bowie's rhythm section (Dennis

Davis and George Murray) turned up a few weeks in. According to Robert Fripp, Bowie had asked him and Eno to attend as well, but "it so happened that David and Iggy had a dispute and the project was postponed." Keyboardist Edgar Froese of Tangerine Dream was also at the Château, but apparently had to leave before recording had got properly under way. And Ricky Gardiner, guitarist with prog rock group Beggar's Opera, had also originally been asked to lend a hand on *The Idiot*, but "then I had this last-minute phone call saying that it was no longer necessary for me to go, and that Mr Bowie sent his apologies," he later recalled. A few weeks later, he got another call summoning him to the Château, "asking could I go off . . . and perform miracles on the new album?" That new album was of course *Low*.

In the studio, Iggy would sit writing lyrics on the studio floor, surrounded by books and piles of paper. But musically, it was Bowie who was in control. He'd arrived with bits of instrumentals recorded on minicassettes, which he'd play to the musicians. The way he directed them was autistic to say the least: "I'd continually ask him if what we were playing was OK," recalled Laurent Thibault in 2002. "He wouldn't reply. He'd just stare at me without saying a word. That was when I realised he was never going to reply. For example, Bowie would be playing a Baldwin piano hooked up to a Marshall amp. Michel gets up from his drumkit to see what Bowie's up to. Bowie still won't say a word. And I'm recording it all. David would listen back to the tape, and once he was happy with the results, we'd move on to the next thing. After a while, we stopped bothering to ask him anything." They recorded quickly, without it ever being explicit whether they were working on Iggy's album or Bowie's.

According to Thibault, *Low*'s signature crashing drum sound was conceived in these sessions as well. The Château was the first in Europe to have an Eventide Harmonizer, which is an electronic pitch-shifting device—you could raise or lower the pitch of any instrument directly without having to slow the tape down, as had been previously necessary. Bowie apparently decided to hook the Harmonizer up to the drums, with astonishing results. This account doesn't really square with Visconti's, though (as we'll see a little later on). And listening to *The Idiot*, although it does seem that some songs have a treated drum sound (particularly "Funtime"), it's not nearly as evolved or as startling as what Visconti developed for *Low*.

At the time, Iggy Pop excitedly talked up *The Idiot* as a cross between Kraftwerk and James Brown. That's an exaggeration, and would actually be a better description of the first side of *Low*. *The Idiot* is still mostly a rock album—replete with heavy metal–style licks—and doesn't really play off a pop sensibility in the way *Low* does. But Bowie's genre-thieving, magpie sensibility makes itself felt. A funk feel creeps in on most tracks; synthesisers fill out the sound (sometimes mimicking strings, sometimes as sound effects); an early use of a drum machine features on "Nightclubbing"; and the dissonant, wandering lead guitar lines (mostly played by Bowie) are pretty similar to what Ricky Gardiner achieved on the first side of *Low*. The experimentalism is most apparent on the final track, "Mass Production," with its looped industrial noise. "We made a tape loop using David's ARP," recalled Laurent Thibault, "but it sounded too erratic and David didn't like it. So I had the idea of recording it on a quarter-inch tape, and once he was satisfied, I set up a loop so huge we had to set up mic stands right round the console. As the loop went round, you could see the little white joining tape, making it look like a toy train. David sat on his swivelling chair for three quarters of an hour, just watching the tape circle go round and round the four corners of the room, until finally he uttered the word 'record.'" (Of course, this was in the days before sequencers—nowadays you could do all that on a computer in a few minutes.)

The Idiot also finds Iggy Pop straining towards other idioms, experimenting with his voice: "To work with [Bowie] as a producer . . . he was a pain in the ass—megalomaniacal, loco! But he had good ideas. The best example I can give you was when I was working on the lyrics to 'Funtime' and he said, 'Yeah, the words are good. But don't sing it like a rock guy. Sing it like Mae West.' Which made it informed of other genres, like cinema. Also, it was a little bit gay. The vocals there became more menacing as a result of that suggestion."

Iggy's catatonic, lugubrious croon—like a drugged-up Frank Sinatra—is one of the signatures of the album. As on *Station to Station*, the crooning comes over as a form of alienated male hysteria. The emotionally skewed quality of the album is apparent right from the first track, the superb "Sister Midnight." A funk bass and riff play against dirty, dissonant guitars, while Iggy Pop's basso profundo contrasts weirdly with Bowie's falsetto yelps. The lyrics set the tormented, psychiatric tone of the album, as Iggy recounts a dream in which "Mother was in my bed, and I made love to her / Father he gunned for me, hunted me with his six-gun."

There's a relentlessly disturbing feel to the album that would be too much to take if it weren't for the camp touches and stabs of dark humour scattered across most of the tracks. The autistic worldview of *Low* is one in which relationships are an impossibility; on *The Idiot*, relationships are not only possible, they're a mutually destructive addiction. Songs kick off with a vision of happy codependence, only to sink into rupture and depression or violence. "China Girl" (reprised by Bowie six years later as a cheesy pop song, but excellent here) uses the analogy of East and West, as Iggy corrupts his oriental lover with "television, eyes of blue" and "men who want to rule the world." (The song also alludes to Bowie's messianic delusions: "I stumble into town, just like a sacred cow, visions of swastikas in my head, plans for everyone.") Even the jokey, cabaret-style "Tiny Girls" (a risqué title given Iggy Pop's sexual proclivities of the time) ends with the sour message of a world where even the "girls who have got no tricks" ultimately "sing of greed, like a young banshee." Relationships are power struggles in which lies and deception are the weapons, and the strong crush the weak.

There's misogyny, but also plenty of self-hate in there too—in fact it's pretty much the sort of album you'd expect two junkies running away from deteriorating relationships might make. But the songs are mostly leavened with irony and humorous touches. The exception is the eight and half minutes of the final track—nothing on the rest of the album matches the sheer nihilism of "Mass Production." (Eno described listening to the album as akin to sticking your head in concrete, which is not true at all, except perhaps for this one track.) Crunching, industrial synth sounds fight distorted guitars over the genocidal imagery of "smokestacks belching, breasts turn brown." Iggy Pop croons against the backdrop of suicide ("although I try to die, you put me back on the line"), begging the lover who thanklessly saved him to "give me the number of a girl almost like you," since "I'm almost like him." The estrangement from the self is now complete, and the song collapses in a morass of detuned synthesisers and grinding noise.

Bowie's stylistic *imprimatur* is all over the album. Even the title's literary allusion is more Bowie than Pop. The cover is a black-and-white shot of Iggy Pop in a karate-style pose inspired by the painting *Roquairol* by the German Expressionist painter Erich Heckel—a Bowie-esque reference. Not only did Bowie write most of the music, he also suggested song subjects and titles, and generally kick-started Iggy's imagination. For "Dum Dum Boys," "I only had a few notes on the piano, I couldn't quite finish the tune," Iggy Pop recounted later. "Bowie said, 'Don't you think you could do something with that? Why don't you tell the story of the Stooges?' He gave me the concept of the song and he also gave me the title. Then he added that guitar arpeggio that metal groups love today. He played it, and then he asked Phil Palmer to play the tune again because he didn't find his playing technically proficient enough." The danger of the album being perceived as Bowie's was something Iggy Pop was well aware of, and shaped his work on their following collaboration, *Lust for Life*: "The band and Bowie would leave the studio and go to sleep, but not me. I was working to be one step ahead of them for the next day. . . . See, Bowie's a hell of a fast guy. Very quick thinker, quick action, very active person, very sharp. I realised I had to be quicker than him, otherwise whose album was it going to be?"

And yet, the influence was definitely not just a one-way street. The harsher, messier guitar sound is something that infused *Low* and was further developed on *"Heroes"*. Bowie was also particularly impressed with Iggy's way with words: "'[China Girl]' has an extraordinary lyric, and it was really sort of thrown out as he was writing it," Bowie recalled in 1993. "It was literally just thrown out on the recording session, almost verbatim. He changed maybe three or four lines. But it was an extraordinary talent that he had for spontaneous free thought."

Iggy Pop's lyrics pointed Bowie towards a new way to write, which shows up on *Low* ("the walls close in and I need some noise" ["Dum Dum Boys"] sounds a bit like a lost line from "Sound and Vision"). On previous albums, you got the feeling that Bowie's efforts to escape cliché had him resorting to ever more baroque constructions and *recherché* imagery. And sometimes, he went too far ("where the dogs decay defecating ecstasy, you're just an ally for the leecher, locator of the virgin king"). But with Iggy Pop, there's no sixth-form cleverness. He pulls off the trick of avoiding cliché while keeping it simple, direct and personal. Death stalks the seventies work of both Bowie and Iggy Pop, but Bowie has nothing quite so blunt as "though I try to die, you put me back on the line." Instead, he locates the death impulse in the mystique of rock 'n' roll suicides, of lovers jumping in the river holding hands, and so on. Such romantic imagery is eschewed on *Low*.

The Idiot is a blistering album that brought out the best in both of them. It was no great commercial success at the time, but then again no commercial concessions had been made in its creation either. Nonetheless, in its way, *The Idiot* turned out to be just as influential as *Low*. It's hard to imagine the curdled croon of Joy Division's Ian Curtis if Iggy Pop hadn't got there first. And "Mass Production" is almost a template for Joy Division (and quite probably the last song Ian Curtis ever heard as well—*The Idiot* was still spinning on the turntable when his wife discovered his lifeless body). If Iggy Pop was the godfather of punk, then *The Idiot* was the sound of Iggy keeping a step ahead (with Bowie's help of course), shepherding a new generation towards the post-punk scene of the late seventies and early eighties.

Bowie was still suffering from mental problems—from paranoia and black magic delusions. On several occasions he'd turned up at the hospital at nearby Pontoise, convinced he was being poisoned. Another time, Iggy Pop playfully pushed him into the Château swimming pool. Visibly shaken, Bowie decided to abandon the recording sessions on the spot—months before at a party in Los Angeles, the actor Peter Sellers had warned him of the occult danger of "dark stains" at the bottom of swimming pools. The sessions were held up for several days, until Iggy persuaded him to return. Sound engineer Laurent Thibault also got on the wrong end of Bowie's paranoia. Thibault basically coproduced the album and comixed it as well, with Tony Visconti, but Bowie left him (and all session musicians) off the credits. Bowie had got it into his head that Thibault had smuggled a journalist into the Château, although in fact he'd known all about it and probably arranged it. "David wasn't there for the interview, but he told me a journalist was coming and told me what I had to say to him," recalled Thibault. "Then after, when David returned to the Château, he threw the copy of *Rock 'n' Folk* [a sort of French *Rolling Stone*] at my face as he got out of the car. He said he didn't know there was a traitor among us.... The journalist had asked the names of the musicians. David had been happy to share the information, but had changed his mind since, he didn't want anyone to know. He then told me that this French article might appear internationally, that what I'd said would be taken at face value, and that, consequently, he couldn't put my name on the record sleeve. Of course, my jaw dropped to the ground, and on the way back to Paris, he said that it'd teach me a lesson."

In August, with the Château already booked for another band, *The Idiot* sessions moved on to the Munich Musicland studios, owned by Giorgio Moroder. Bowie met up with Moroder and his producer partner Peter Bellote, the architects of the synthetic eurodisco sound that was sweeping Germany at the time. There were never any plans to work together at that time (they would do years later), but viewed from a certain angle, Moroder and Bowie weren't so very far apart in what they were doing. Moroder was using the New York disco sound and marrying it with synthesisers and a thumping robotic beat to create a particularly European-flavoured dance music. And the following year, Moroder and Bellote would produce Donna Summer's hugely influential synth disco anthem "I Feel Love," which impressed Eno greatly at the time.

According to Bowie, he and Eno started meeting up at around this point. Bowie: "At our regular sound swap-meets in 1976, Eno and I exchanged sounds that we loved. Eno offered, among others, his then current fave, Giorgio Moroder and Donna Summer's military R&B and I played him Neu! and the rest of the Düsseldorf sound. They sort of became part of our soundtrack for the year." This sounds a little unlikely—Eno would have already heard Neu! by the summer of 1976, since he'd already met and worked with Neu! guitarist Michael Rother (Rother's other group, Harmonia, had been championed by Eno as early as 1974).

In any case, Neu! was certainly a part of Bowie's musical landscape at the time: "I bought my first vinyl *Neu! 2* in Berlin around 1975 while I was on a brief visit," he later recalled. "I bought it because I knew that they were a spin-off of Kraftwerk and had to be worth hearing. Indeed, they were to prove to be Kraftwerk's wayward, anarchistic brothers. I was completely seduced by the setting of the aggressive guitar-drone against the almost-but-not-quite robotic/machine drumming of Dinger. Although fairly tenuous, you can hear a little of their influence on the track "Station to Station." Indeed, in the summer of '76 I called Michael Rother and asked whether he would be interested in working with myself and Brian Eno on my new album entitled *Low*. Although enthusiastic, Michael had to decline and to this day I wonder how that trilogy would have been affected by his input."

Again, Bowie is muddling a few things up here. He wasn't in Europe at any time in 1975, so presumably it was more like the spring of 1976 that he first got hold of a Neu! album. (That perplexes me, since I too detect a Neu! influence on "Station to Station.") And Michael Rother recalls being contacted by Bowie in 1977 for the *"Heroes"* sessions, not for *Low*. According to a 2001 interview with Bowie in *Uncut* magazine, it was one "Michael Dinger" who had been Bowie's first choice for guitarist on Low. Bowie no doubt means Klaus Dinger, the other half of the Neu! duo. Bowie had supposedly called him up from the Château, but Dinger had politely refused.

Rother and Dinger had originally played in Kraftwerk, but left in 1971 to pursue their more organic sound, recording three influential albums (*Neu*, *Neu! 2* and *Neu! 75*). The Neu! sound was about textures, and about stripping things back to simple structures until you arrived at a spacey, meditative groove, often referred to as *motorik*. (Eno: "There were three great beats in the 70s: Fela Kuti's Afrobeat, James Brown's Funk and Klaus Dinger's Neu! beat.") *Motorik* was basically a steady 4/4 rhythm that would often fade in slowly, but what made it different was that there were no tempo changes, no syncopation and minimal variations. The guitars and other instrumentation accompanied the beat, rather than the other way around. It was very human, a pulse that simply went on and on, inducing a trancelike state of mind and the gentle welling of emotion. "It's a feeling, like a picture, like driving down a long road or lane," Klaus Dinger explained in 1998. "It is essentially about life, how you have to keep moving, get on and stay in motion."

Bowie mentions Neu! quite a bit at this time, but I don't hear anything on *Low* that sounds too much like them (although "A New Career in a New Town" is something of a tribute to Neu! offshoot La Düsseldorf). Nonetheless, there is a convergence in the approach of bands like Neu! and what Bowie was to do on *Low*. The feeling that a lot of German artists had then of being forced to start again with a blank page after the betrayals of a previous generation, of having to pare it all down to nothing in order to see what will emerge, all that resonates on *Low*. The rock star moves and masks partially give way to a junky trying to kick the habit while living above an auto repair shop in an immigrant quarter of Berlin. "Nothing to say, nothing to do . . . I will sit right down, waiting for the gift of sound and vision."

Another element that the Bowie of *Low* shares with German bands like Neu! and Can is the willingness to treat music as soundscapes, rather than structured songs with their melodic "narratives." That very much informs tracks like "Weeping Wall" or "Subterraneans." These have an emotional quietude about them as well, quite different from the histrionic register that Bowie more often retreated to on earlier albums to express emotion. Many of the German bands also shared a strategy of radical repetition overlaid with experimentation. There was Neu!'s *motorik* rhythm, Kraftwerk's robotic beats, but also Can's endless grooves on songs like "Halleluwa," that sound like a long jam but were in fact carefully reconstructed in the studio with tape loops. Bowie and Eno were converging on similar studio-driven ideas of repetition-plus-experimentation.

From Munich, the *Idiot* sessions moved on to Berlin, and the Hansa-by-the-wall studios. The nucleus of the *Low* team assembled there for some final work on *The Idiot*—rhythm section Carlos Alomar, Dennis Davis and George Murray, as well as producer Tony Visconti, whom Bowie had called in to mix the *Idiot* tapes. He'd wanted Visconti to produce, but he hadn't been available, so Bowie had done the job himself aided by Laurent Thibault. Visconti found the tape quality to be fairly poor—a "salvage job"—and did the best he could with what he was given. (In retrospect, *The Idiot*'s slightly muddy sound adds to rather than detracts from the album.)

This was the first time Bowie had worked at Hansa-by-the-wall, where he and Visconti would later mix *Low* and then record its follow-up *"Heroes"*. The studio was only twenty or thirty metres from the Wall: "From the control room we could see the Wall and we could also see over the Wall and over the barbed wire to the Red Guards in their gun turrets," recalled Visconti of his time working at Hansa. "They had enormous binoculars and they would look into the control room and watch us work, because they were as star-struck as anyone. We asked the engineer one day whether he felt a bit uncomfortable with the guards staring at him all day. They could easily have shot us from the East, it was that close. With a good telescopic sight, they could have put us out. He said you get used to it after a while and then he turned, took an overhead light and pointed it at the guards, sticking his tongue out and jumping up and down generally hassling them. David and I just dived right under the recording desk. 'Don't do that,' we said because we were scared to death!"

It was the charged, John Le Carré aspect of Berlin as it was then. "The thing about all those Bowie/Eno/Iggy/Hansa albums was the mythology that went with their creation," mused New Order drummer Stephen Morris in 2001. "Why was a studio overlooking the Berlin Wall so important?" The Wall provided almost too much symbolism for one city to bear. All cities construct myths around themselves—but in the Berlin of the sixties and seventies, the myth was in danger of smothering the city under it. This was Berlin as the decadent outpost of the West—dangerously cut off and etiolated, frozen in the aftermath of disaster, a city that continued to pay for its sins, where paranoia was not a sign of madness but the correct response to the situation. The symbolism of the Wall was as much psychological as it was political. Not only was it a microcosm of the Cold War, it was also a mirror you could gaze into and see a looking-glass world, utterly like yours but utterly different as well. It divided mentalities, and expanded schizophrenia to the size of a city. And the Wall was just one of many layers of the myth of Berlin.

waiting for the gift

With *The Idiot* mixed, Bowie retreated to his home in Switzerland, where Eno shortly joined him. Together they started writing and throwing around ideas for the new album, then provisionally called *New Music: Night and Day* (a title that caught the concept of the two different sides, but which sounded rather pompously like the work of a minimalist composer). A few weeks before the sessions got under way, Bowie had put in a call to Visconti: "He phoned me up, it was actually a conference call, he had Brian on one line, himself on another," Visconti later told Australian broadcaster Allan Calleja. "I was in London, and David and Brian were in Switzerland I think, where David used to live. David said: 'We have this conceptual album here, we want to make it really different, we're writing these strange songs, these very short songs.' It was conceived right from the beginning that one side was going to be pop songs and the other side was going to be ambient music in the style of Brian and Tangerine Dream and Kraftwerk." Actually, it seemed that the original idea had been not so much pop songs for the first side but raw rock songs, with minimal studio intervention. That would have emphasised two completely different approaches, probably at the expense of any sonic unity at all. But perhaps Bowie had got the raw rock idea out of his system with *The Idiot*, and working with Eno was always going to be more about pop.

The idea was radical experimentation. Visconti again: "The three of us agreed to record with no promise that *Low* would ever be released. David had asked me if I didn't mind wasting a month of my life on this experiment if it didn't go well. Hey, we were in a French château for the month of September and the weather was great!" Bowie asked Visconti what he thought he could contribute to the sessions; Visconti mentioned the pitch-shifting Eventide Harmonizer he'd just got. Bowie asked what it did, and Visconti famously replied that "it fucks with the fabric of time!" Bowie was delighted, and "Eno went berserk. He said: 'We've got to have it!' "

Brooklyn-born, Tony Visconti had started out playing in various bands in New York and elsewhere across the country, carving out a reputation on the circuit as a proficient bass player and guitarist. He'd put out a couple of singles as part of a duo with his wife Siegrid, but when the last single flopped he took up a job as a house producer with a New York label. Shortly after, he relocated to London, where he met a not-yet-successful David Bowie at the early stages of his career. Together they recorded *Space Oddity* (excluding the title track) and *The Man Who Sold the World*, although Visconti missed out on the albums that propelled Bowie into bona fide rock stardom (*Ziggy Stardust*, *Aladdin Sane*). But he'd hooked up with Bowie again to mix *Diamond Dogs* and produce *Young Americans*, Bowie's first smash hit in the States.

Visconti had come of age as a producer in late sixties London, a crossover period where producers were becoming a lot less like lab technicians and more like an invisible member of the band, the one with a handle on the technology that would drive experimentation. George Martin's mid-sixties work with the Beatles was clearly one kind of template for Visconti. Instead of the live takes of the early Beatles albums, Martin would take different instrumental, vocal and percussion tracks and build them up, layer upon layer, over a number of sessions. In other words, the process started having a more direct influence on the content. Visconti has singled out "Strawberry Fields" as the moment where "George showed us once and for all that the recording studio itself was a musical instrument." The Beatles had recorded two versions of the song, one more psychedelic, and one more understated, with classically inspired instrumentation. Lennon liked the beginning of the first and the end of the second; the trouble was they were recorded at slightly different speeds, and the keys differed by a semitone. Martin speeded up one version, slowed down the other, then spliced the two together. "This track was the dividing line of those who recorded more or less live and those who wanted to take recorded music to the extremes of creativity," Visconti later commented to *Billboard*. Here, you can already see the intersection of Visconti's and Eno's vision of the studio, even if they're converging from different standpoints.

The fact that Visconti hadn't come up through the ranks at a studio but had started off as a musician also gave him a different, more hybrid take on the duties of a producer. He could play several instruments, and was excellent at arrangements. It was another area where he had at first looked to George Martin: "I would read Beethoven and Mozart and learn the voicings from how they voiced the string section, and I'd apply that. And then I'd listen to George Martin, and I'd say, 'That's what he did. He listened to Bach. . . . ' He's taking something classical and old and tried and true and putting it in a pop context, so I just worked it out. And I just imitated him for a few years until I developed some tricks of my own." All this cross-disciplinary expertise meant that Visconti tended to play a greater role in the studio than most producers. On Bowie albums, Visconti is not only sound engineer and mixer, but often scores the arrangements (the cello part on "Art Decade," for instance), and sometimes sings and plays various instruments as well.

The *Low* sessions kicked off at the Château on September 1st, without Eno for the first few days. The assembled band was the R&B rhythm section Bowie had had since *Young Americans*, namely Carlos Alomar, George Murray and Dennis Davis. On lead guitar was Ricky Gardiner, a suggestion of Visconti's, after Bowie's other choices had fallen through (Visconti and Gardiner had been working on demos for what would become Visconti's only solo album, *Inventory*). The main keyboardist was Roy Young, formerly of the Rebel Rousers; he'd also played with the Beatles in the early sixties. Young had first met Bowie in 1972 when they'd played on the same bill; Bowie had wanted him for *Station to Station*, but had given him too short notice. Then, in the summer of '76, Young had been playing in London when Bowie had called him from Berlin, asking him to come over. Apparently Bowie had originally wanted to do *Low* at Hansa, but then changed his mind, probably because he'd already paid upfront for studio time in France. In any case, a few days later he called Young again to switch the venue to the Château.

Bowie's and Visconti's working methods crystallised on the *Low* sessions. They would start late. (Eno: "It was all overnight, so I was in a kind of daze a lot of the time, days drifting into one another.") As with *The Idiot*, Bowie came into the studio with various bits and pieces on tape—*The Man Who Fell to Earth* material; leftovers from the *Idiot* sessions; stuff he'd recorded at his home in Switzerland—but no complete songs written, and no lyrics. In other words, the studio was very much part of the writing process. To begin with, the rhythm section would be told to jam with a loose chord progression. There might be minimal direction from Bowie or Visconti, and some experimenting with different styles, but basically they'd simply keep kicking the progression around until something emerged that developed into an arrangement. Carlos Alomar: "I'd get together with the drummer and the bass player and we'd work on a song, maybe reggae, maybe slow or fast or up-tempo, and we'd let David hear it three or four different ways, and whichever way he wanted to do it, we just did it. . . . Basically he says: 'How about something like this?' 'OK fine.' I just start grooving and start playing until I came up with something, and that ability has been like the saving grace." The rhythm section provided the seed bed for most of the first side, and Bowie was generous with writing credits if he thought one of the musicians had come up with a defining element of the song. Alomar already had credits for his riffs on "Fame" and "Sister Midnight." On *Low*, Bowie cut credits for "Breaking Glass" three ways with bass player George Murray and drummer Dennis Davis.

This initial backing-track phase was very quick and in the case of *Low* took only five days, after which Dennis Davis and George Murray played no further part in the proceedings (in fact, by the time Eno turned up at the Château, they'd already left). Once Bowie was happy with the backing tracks, work with the overdubs could begin—essentially recording guitar and other solos. Alomar would normally have come up with an initial solo to hold the rhythm section together, but then record a new one later. Ricky Gardiner and Roy Young would be recording their parts too. On *Low*, these were generally further electronically treated by Visconti, Eno or Bowie (there's not a lot of "natural" sound on *Low*), so this is where the sessions would enter a more experimental, nebulous phase. Some of it was about treating instruments as the musicians were playing, with Visconti using the Harmonizer, various tone filters, reverbs and a panoply of other studio tricks.

Eno would mostly be using a portable synth he'd brought along with him. Visconti: "He has an old synthesiser that fits into a briefcase made by a defunct company called EMS. It didn't have a piano keyboard like modern synths. It did have a lot of little knobs, a peg board and little pegs, like an old telephone switch board to connect the various parameters to one another. But its *pièce de résistance* was a little 'joystick' that you find on arcade games. He would pan that joystick around in circles and make swirling sounds." (This synth lives on, and Bowie even used it on a recent album, *Heathen*: "Some years ago, a friend very kindly bought me the original EMS AKS briefcase synth that Eno used on so many of those classic records of the seventies. In fact, it was the one he used on *Low* and *"Heroes"*. It was up for auction, and I got it for my fiftieth birthday. . . . Taking it through customs has always been a stomach-turning affair as it looks like a briefcase bomb in the x-ray. Eno got pulled out of the line on several occasions. I wouldn't even dream of taking it through these days.")

This was also the phase where Eno would often be left alone in the studio to lay down a "sonic bed." Eno: "I was trying to give some kind of sonic character to the track so that the thing had a distinct textural feel that gave it a mood to begin with. . . . It's hard to describe that because it was never the same twice, and it's not susceptible to description very easily in ordinary musical terms. It would just be doing the thing that you can do with tape so that you can treat the music as malleable. You have something down there but then you can start squeezing it around and changing the colour of this and putting this thing much further in front of something else and so on."

Where the rhythm section was about finding the groove that worked—in other words, locating the pattern—Eno was more concerned with breaking those patterns that the mind instinctively slotted into, when left to its own devices. One of the methods that he and Bowie used on *Low* was the "Oblique Strategies" he'd created with artist Peter Schmidt the year before. It was a deck of cards, and each card was inscribed with a command or an observation. When you got into a creative impasse, you were to turn up one of the cards and act upon it. The commands went from the sweetly banal ("Do the washing up") to the more technical ("Feedback recordings into an acoustic situation"; "The tape is now the music"). Some cards contradict each other ("Remove specifics and convert to ambiguities"; "Remove ambiguities and convert to specifics"). Some use Wildean substitution ("Don't be afraid of things because they're easy to do"). And several veer towards the Freudian ("Your mistake was a hidden intention"; "Emphasise the flaws").

The stress is on capitalising on error as a way of drawing in randomness, tricking yourself into an interesting situation, and crucially leaving room for the thing that can't be explained—an element that every work of art needs.

Did the Oblique Strategy cards actually work? They were probably more important symbolically than practically. A cerebral theoretician like Eno had more need of a mental circuit-breaker than someone like Bowie, who was a natural improviser, *collagiste*, artistic gadfly. Anyone involved in the creative arts knows that chance events in the process play an important role, but to my mind there's something slightly self-defeating about the idea of "planned accidents." Oblique Strategies certainly created tensions, as Carlos Alomar explained to Bowie biographer David Buckley: "Brian Eno had come in with all these cards that he had made and they were supposed to eliminate a block. Now, you've got to understand something. I'm a musician. I've studied music theory, I've studied counterpoint and I'm used to working with musicians who can read music. Here comes Brian Eno and he goes to a blackboard. He says: 'Here's the beat, and when I point to a chord, you play the chord.' So we get a random picking of chords. I finally had to say, 'This is bullshit, this sucks, this sounds stupid.' I totally, totally resisted it. David and Brian were two intellectual guys and they had a very different camaraderie, a heavier conversation, a Europeanness. It was too heavy for me. He and Brian would get off on talking about music in terms of history and I'd think, 'Well that's stupid—history isn't going to give you a hook for the song!' I'm interested in what's commercial, what's funky and what's going to make people dance!" It may well have been the creative tension between that kind of traditionalist approach and Eno's experimentalism that was more productive than the "planned accidents" themselves. As Eno himself has said: "The interesting place is not chaos, and it's not total coherence. It's somewhere on the cusp of those two."

The final stage of the recording would be the actual generation of a song. Bowie would experiment in front of the microphone, trying out different voices with different emotive qualities, eventually finding the one that would fit the song. There would be suggestions from Visconti and Eno, but this phase was more uniquely Bowie's show than any other's. Once he'd found the voice, the rest would slip into place—a melody line would materialise; the lyrics would find their shape. Some songs ("Sound and Vision," "Always Crashing in the Same Car") had extra verses, but when Bowie listened back he decided he didn't like them and they got wiped. In a way, he was doing everything backwards: nailing the context first, and finding the content afterwards. And ultimately, the lyric was as much texture as voice intonation or instrumental background—to the point that the words in "Warszawa" are literally in an imaginary language, the semantic content bleached right out of the lyric.

Born in the U.S.A.

by Geoffrey Himes

Geoffrey Himes has written about music on a weekly basis in the *Washington Post* since 1977. During that time he has also written about pop music for *Rolling Stone, Paste, The New York Times, Jazz Times,* the *Nashville Scene*, the *Oxford American,* and other outlets. He won ASCAP/ Deems Taylor Awards for Music Feature Writing in 2002 and 2005. His stage musical, *A Baltimore Christmas Carol,* was produced in 2005, and his songs have been recorded by Edge City, Billy Kemp, and the Kinsey Report.

Chapter One
Nowhere to Run

Bruce Springsteen is best known for his most public acts. It's in the concert hall—more than on the stereo or the screen—that he engages his audience as few other performers ever have. It's on the stage that he makes his deepest impression, not only singing his hits, but also telling stories, digging out forgotten songs, shouting like a preacher, clowning like a vaudevillian, whispering like a confessor and leaping about in flagrant disregard for his own safety. From the seats, his fans respond with almost equal fervor until each show, larger than life and longer than a baseball game, reaches its climax of happy, communal exhaustion.

And yet, the most important moments of his career have taken place in utter solitude. His most crucial decisions, the ones that have most shaped his art and career, have taken place not on stage but at home. They've taken place in the privacy of those rooms where he has sat with an acoustic guitar and a notebook and tried to write the next line of words and the next measure of music for the next song.

His most enduring work has been that of a writer not an entertainer, an inventor not an interpreter. If his artistic persona has been an unlikely combination of Elvis Presley the performer and Bob Dylan the songwriter, the Dylan half defined the space where the Presley half would operate, not the other way around. A writer's work takes place far from an audience, and anyone seeking to understand Springsteen's work has to investigate those solitary moments. The most important of all those moments took place in the waning weeks of 1981 as he sat alone in his house in Colt's Neck, New Jersey, and wrote "Born in the U.S.A."

He had been trying to write a song about a returning Vietnam veteran. Those veterans—suffering from bad memories, a lack of work, lingering wounds and a lukewarm welcome—seemed to crystallize the betrayal of the American dream that was much on Springsteen's mind that winter. But he was having trouble with the song. It was easy to describe the character's problems but much harder to figure out the man's response. Somehow the old solution, jumping in a car and roaring down the highway, seemed inadequate. If that wasn't the answer, what was?

After all, the freedom of the road was not just Springsteen's favorite songwriting theme; it was his way of life. Just three months earlier, he had finished a 347-day, 145-show, 59-city tour, traveling with his six bandmates and more than twenty backstage hands, playing almost every other night in a basketball arena full of 20,000 people. It had been eleven months of constant crowds, constant companionship. Now he was rattling around in an empty house in rural Jersey, trying to make sense of it all.

On June 5, for example, he had played London's Wembley Arena with his longtime backing group, the E Street Band. Springsteen opened the show, as he did at most stops on the tour, with "Born to Run," the song that had made him famous. He took the stage in his just-another-guy-down-at-the-gas-station outfit of motorcycle boots, blue jeans and a plaid, snap-button shirt with the sleeves rolled up to the elbows. He was as short and wiry as ever, and his sideburns spread down from his curly dark hair to his lower jaw. He counted off, "Uh, one, two . . . ," Max Weinberg hit a drum roll, and the rest of the band jumped on the drummer's back with the unison four-bar melody that was one of the most recognizable pop hooks of the 70s.

Even on stage, the two guitars, tenor sax, glockenspiel

synth, bass, drums and piano created a wall of sound worthy of Springsteen's hero, Phil Spector. The lyrics were equally exaggerated, contrasting the daytime's cagelike existence of sweaty jobs and diminishing dreams with the nighttime's liberation of driving down a New Jersey highway toward the beach and the amusement park as you and your girl straddled a chrome-wheeled motorcycle. When the options were presented like that, the choice was obvious: "We gotta get out while we're young, 'cause tramps like us, baby, we were born to run," and the song accelerated like a chopper with a boot stomped on the pedal.

This romantic vision of a life divided between daytime traps and nighttime escapes set the mood for the whole evening. If the days offer scant opportunities for demonstrating your worth, what choice do you have but to "Prove It All Night"? Why? "Because the Night" belongs to us. If work, school and home provide no platforms for such proof, where can you go? "Out in the Streets," down "Thunder Road," wherever your "Hungry Heart" leads.

Springsteen didn't invent this fantasy; he inherited it. From Chuck Berry singing of driving with "No Particular Place to Go" in 1964 to Bob Seger singing of driving out to "Fire Lake" in 1980, the lure of the escape hatch had always been a central myth in rock 'n' roll. You didn't have to give in to your parents' rules, your teachers' definitions, your preacher's don'ts, your classmates' rejections or your boss's orders. You could grab the car keys and light out for a new territory where the camaraderie was real, the music was righteous and the sex was good. It was an update of the American frontier myth for a new generation.

From Elvis Presley singing "Good Rocking Tonight" in 1954 to the Clash singing "White Riot" in 1977, rock 'n' roll claimed immediate, total gratification as a birthright—and if it were thwarted, the response was rebellion, not stoicism. Rock 'n' roll may have grown out of blues, gospel and country music, but it refused to accept their working-class fatalism or their Christian faith in delayed gratification. The first generation of rock 'n' rollers may have played the same instruments in much the same way as older blues and country bands, but this refusal distinguished rock 'n' roll from its predecessors and defined it as a genre. Born in the shadow of an atomic bomb that made delayed gratification seem an absurd joke, rock 'n' roll promised its listeners that they could have it all right now.

The rock 'n' roll promise was an amplification of the American dream. The latter offered this contract: if you go to school, work hard and obey the law, you'll get a decent paycheck, a safe neighborhood and a nice house with a spouse and kids. The contract was backed by the frontier myth: if you can't realize the American dream here, you can find it out in the open spaces of the unbuilt West.

The rock 'n' roll promise raised the stakes: if you stay true to your friends and ideals, if you live every moment to its fullest, you can find work that not only pays well but also keeps you thinking; you can mix true love and hot sex; you can be a nonconformist individual and still belong to a community of family and friends. And it offered a similar contract guarantee: if you can't find it here, hit the road and look for it there. Few artists had ever articulated this promise as passionately and seductively as Springsteen had in the mid-70s.

"My whole life," Springsteen told *Rolling Stone* in 1978, "I was always around a lot of people whose lives consisted of just this compromising—they knew no other way. That's where rock 'n' roll is important, because it said that there could be another way. That's why I write the kind of songs I do."

"There's no halfway in most of the songs," he added in the same interview, "because I don't approach what I do in that way. There's just no room to compromise. I think, for most musicians, it has to be like life or death or it's not worth it. That's why every night we play a real long time and we play real hard. I want to be able to go home and say I went all the way tonight—and then I went a little further."

Life without compromise is an intoxicating fantasy, but a fantasy just the same. If you examine the results rather than the prospectus, you'll find that no one gets everything they want; reality isn't constructed that way.

But the fantasy is necessary. If you're a young person facing a world full of adults telling you to curb your desires, a pop song that tells you that you have every right to those desires—even if it misleads you about what it will take to achieve them—is invaluable, because it keeps you hoping, keeps you fighting. Rock 'n' roll insisted you could have more than a slice; you could have the whole pie. You can't, but if you believe you can, you're likely to eat a lot more pie than you would otherwise. This rock 'n' roll fantasy may not be entirely true, but it's an indispensable lie.

That vision was certainly invaluable for Springsteen himself. Born in Freehold, New Jersey, on September 23, 1949, he had grown up in a home where money was scarce; books were scarcer; work was drudgery, sex went unmentioned, and friends were few. Doug Springsteen was an Irish-American who worked as a bus driver, factory worker and prison guard; Adele Springsteen was an Italian-American who worked as a legal secretary; they sent their kids to Catholic schools and rarely socialized outside the family.

On January 6, 1957, though, when Bruce was seven, he saw Elvis Presley on the "Ed Sullivan" TV show and, like St. Paul on the road to Damascus, was "blinded by the light." In Presley's swaggering confidence and carefree joy, the third grader heard the promise of a fuller life, a life where you got to eat the whole pie. He became addicted to the radio, searching for variations on that promise from girl groups like the Ronettes, surf groups like the Beach Boys, soul singers like Gary U.S. Bonds and greaser bands like Mitch Ryder & the Detroit Wheels. In 1963, he bought a pawnshop guitar for $18 and devoted himself to it as if it were his door out of a small room.

He joined his first real band, the Castiles, in 1965, when he was fifteen. At the end of 1968, he dropped out of Ocean County Community College and joined the hard rock quartet Earth. In 1969, he formed a similar band called Child. By the time they changed their name to Steel Mill and drove out to California, the band included Springsteen, drummer Vini Lopez, keyboardist Danny Federici and bassist Steve Van Zandt. In 1971, there was a short-lived group called Dr. Zoom & the Sonic Boom, followed by the Bruce Springsteen Band.

In March of 1972, Springsteen signed a management contract with a pair of New York songwriters, Mike Appel and Jim Cretecos; in May he auditioned for the legendary John Hammond Sr.; in June he signed with Columbia Records and immediately went into the studio with his current band (Lopez, Federici, bassist Gary Tallent, keyboardist David Sancious and saxophonist Clarence Clemons). The first album, *Greetings from Asbury Park, N.J.*, was released in January 1973. The second album, *The Wild, the Innocent and the E Street Shuffle*, soon followed in September. The third album, *Born to Run* (featuring Springsteen, Federici, Tallent, Clemons, keyboardist Roy Bittan, drummer Max Weinberg and Van Zandt on guitar), finally emerged in 1975.

Fueling these early bands and early albums were Springsteen's own versions of the vision offered by Presley, the Ronettes and the rest in songs such as "Rosalita," "Growin'

Up" and "Spirit in the Night." The ultimate version was "Born to Run," which did for countless youngsters what Presley's "Jailhouse Rock" had once done for a seven-year-old Bruce Springsteen. When he declared that rock 'n' roll had saved his life, it wasn't an idle claim. If your dreams were being squelched in the here and now, rock 'n' roll told him, you could seek out the there and tomorrow.

But where was this there? When was this tomorrow? If you were born to run, where did you run to? When did you get there? Rock 'n' roll, like most fantasies, was always a little hazy on these details, and Springsteen's early writing was no different. It was almost as if the over-the-top arrangement of "Born to Run" and its dreamlike lyrics, all the overheated imagery of "mansions of glory" and "madness in my soul," were necessary to keep reality at arm's length.

After all, if you roar out of Freehold, New Jersey, on your motorcycle and cruise down Highway 9, where are you going to end up? In another small, blue-collar New Jersey town. What makes you think life is going to be any different in this town than in the one you just came from?

These were the questions Bruce Springsteen wrestled with each afternoon as he awoke in another New Jersey town, Colt's Neck. It was December 1981, and he was trying to write the songs for his next album. A fantasy that's easy to embrace when you're fifteen (as Springsteen was in early 1965 when he joined the Castiles) or twenty-four (as Springsteen was in mid-1974 when he wrote "Born to Run") is harder to swallow when you're thirty-two (as he was at the end of 1981). It was hard to let go of a fantasy that had meant so much to his life, but it was impossible to write another version of it. He had seen too much.

Springsteen would seem to be living proof that the fantasy could come true. He had just scored a #1 album (*The River*) and a #5 single ("Hungry Heart"). He was financially set; he enjoyed strong friendships with his guitarist (Steve Van Zandt) and his manager (Jon Landau); and he had found immensely satisfying work, a way to express himself to millions of listeners.

But the rock 'n' roll promise was not that a few people could get the whole pie if they were extremely talented or extremely lucky; the promise was that everyone should have a full life. It was supposed to be a birthright, not a lottery prize. As Springsteen crossed the boundary of thirty, he watched as many of his old friends became hemmed in by dead-end jobs, troubled marriages, drug problems or worse. He couldn't accept the argument that it was their own fault.

"One of the things that was always on my mind," Springsteen told *Rolling Stone* in 1984, "was to maintain connections with the people I'd grown up with, and the sense of the community where I came from. That's why I stayed in New Jersey. The danger of fame is in forgetting, or being distracted. You see it happen to so many people. . . . I believe that the life of a rock 'n' roll band will last as long as you look down into the audience and can see yourself, and your audience can look up at you and see themselves—as long as those reflections are human, realistic ones."

There was something wrong with a society that made a full life so difficult to achieve. Something was wrong with a rock 'n' roll fantasy that suggested that merely wanting the dream was all that was required. Nothing brought these issues into focus more sharply than Vietnam, the first rock 'n' roll war. The Vietnam veterans were the most dramatic example of everyone who had been let down by the American dream and the rock 'n' roll promise. All the disappointments that happened to anyone else happened to them—only more so.

Springsteen himself had escaped the draft, thanks to a 1968 motorcycle accident and a heartfelt impersonation of a crazy person at the induction center. His objection to the war at that point wasn't so much political as it was musical; it threatened the only thing in the world he cared about: a career in rock 'n' roll. But many of the guys he had grown up with hadn't been so determined or so lucky.

He described his day at the draft induction center to *Rolling Stone* in 1984: "I remember being on that bus, me and a couple of guys in my band, and the rest of the bus was probably 60, 70 percent black guys from Asbury Park. And I remember thinking, 'What makes my life, or my friends' lives, more expendable than that of somebody who's going to school?' It didn't seem right."

"I had no real political standpoint whatsoever when I was 18," Springsteen says in Dave Marsh's biography, *Bruce Springsteen—Two Hearts*, "and neither did any of my friends. The whole draft thing, it was a pure street thing. You didn't want to go. You didn't want to go because you'd seen other people go and not come back. The first drummer in my first band, the Castiles, enlisted and he came back in his uniform and he was, 'Oh, here I go; I'm going to Vietnam.' Kind of laughing and joking about it and that was it. He went and he was killed. There were a lot of guys from my neighborhood, guys in bands."

Bart Hanes, the Castiles' drummer, went to Vietnam and did not come back. Those who did return weren't having an easy time. There were the health problems and nightmares, and now, in 1981, as the Reagan recession settled over the land, it was hard to find a job good enough to pay the mortgage. As he watched his old friends struggle, Springsteen must have peppered himself with questions: Why did they have to go and not me? Why do these guys who seemed so full of life ten, fifteen years ago now seem so sad, so weary? What can rock 'n' roll possibly say to them now? Can a car, a girl and a guitar make any difference? What can my own songs say to them? Or for them?

The Viet vets had it tougher than most, but as Springsteen's baby-boomer buddies—male and female, vets or not—drifted into their thirties, they faced similar challenges: reclaiming the thrill of Saturday night, finding a reason to get up in the morning, finding a reason to believe. Where was the full life rock 'n' roll had promised them? Did the promise expire when you reached thirty? No, Springsteen wasn't ready to accept that.

One of the songs he was working on was called "Vietnam." It was sung from the first-person perspective of a Vietnam veteran returning to his hometown to receive something less than a hero's welcome. The first two lines describe his airplane touching down on the runway and, when no one meets him at the terminal, the lonely taxi ride back home. In the second verse, the hiring man down at the factory shakes his head sadly and tells the out-of-work protagonist, "Son, understand, if it was up to me . . . "

There's a photo of one of Springsteen's 1980s writing rooms in the CD booklet for the album, *Tunnel of Love*. He sits, with a guitar in his lap, in a plain wooden chair by a plain wooden desk. On the desk is a small fan, a hinged lamp, a double-slot cassette deck, a direct-input box for the guitar cord, a small microphone, a set of headphones and half a dozen pens propped up inside a roll of duct tape. His writing room at Colt's Neck must have been very similar.

One can imagine Springsteen sitting in his chair with his acoustic guitar on his right thigh, playing through the song one more time. It sounded a lot like Randy Newman's "Have You Seen My Baby"; it had Newman's imitation of Fats Domino's New Orleans music and it turned Newman's line, "I'll talk to strangers if I want to, 'cause I'm a stranger, too," into Springsteen's line, "All I seen was strangers . . . and nobody was stranger than me."

Something's not right, Springsteen must have decided. The bouncy, happy-go-lucky music didn't fit the anguished lyrics at all. Even the lyrics by themselves were problematic. The chorus tells the protagonist, "You died in Vietnam." Maybe Springsteen intended the song as a modern ghost story; maybe the chorus is a metaphor for the way many veterans were treated as barely acknowledged, living corpses. In either case, the whole thing sounded too defeated. To tell the protagonist that there's no hope would merely add to his burden instead of relieving it.

OK, Springsteen might have told himself, I've got this character who went to Vietnam to shoot people and get shot at in return. Now he's back in New Jersey without a job or prospects. What happens next?

To answer that question, Springsteen tried to learn everything he could about the Vietnam veterans. He talked at length to every vet he met. He read *Born on the Fourth of July*, Ron Kovic's vivid memoir of serving in Vietnam and then coming home in a wheelchair to protest the war (in 1989 it would become a movie starring Tom Cruise and directed by Oliver Stone). He read Henry Steele Commager and Allan Nevins's *A Pocket History of the United States* to understand the historical context for the war.

The more Springsteen investigated the situation, the more he wanted to do something about it. He had his manager, Jon Landau, contact Bobby Muller, a wheelchair-bound paraplegic like Kovic. Muller, an alumnus of Vietnam Veterans Against the War, had founded in 1978 the Vietnam Veterans of America, a group agitating for the rights of those former soldiers who were now being neglected by the nation they fought for. By 1981, despite a notebook full of newspaper clips, the organization was struggling, unable to open an office or to put out a regular newsletter.

Springsteen was intrigued and he invited Muller to a July 1981 show at the Byrne Arena in New Jersey. After the show, the two men sat down for a fifteen-minute chat that ended up lasting forty-five. Muller was a lifelong rock 'n' roll fan; Springsteen was fascinated by the war and its aftermath, so they had a lot to ask each other. Within days Springsteen called Muller with an offer: he would devote his opening show in Los Angeles on August 20 to raise funds for the Vietnam Veterans of America.

That night he took the stage at the Los Angeles Sports Center without a guitar and tried to frame the evening's issue for his fans. "It's like when you feel like you're walking down a dark street at night," he said from the stage, "and out of the corner of your eye you see somebody getting hurt or somebody getting hit in the dark alley, but you keep walking on because you think it has nothing to do with you and you just want to get home. Well, Vietnam turned this whole country into that dark street. And unless we're able to walk down those dark alleys and look into the eyes of the men and the women that are down there and the things that happened, we're never going to be able to get home."

A few minutes later, Muller wheeled out onstage in his chair and gave a short speech that ended, "It's a little bit ironic that for the years that we've been trying, when the businesses haven't come behind us and the political leaders have failed to rally behind us, that when you remember the divisions within our own generation about the war it ultimately turns out to be the very symbol of our generation, rock 'n' roll, that brings us together."

With that the E Street Band took the stage and played Creedence Clearwater Revival's "Who'll Stop the Rain," a 1970 song the veterans had adopted as their anthem. Songwriter John Fogerty had used rain as a metaphor for all the confusion, pain and darkness that falls into everyone's life (though some have leakier roofs than others). Like the rain itself, these miseries come from beyond our sight and arrive beyond our control. As Springsteen sang it that night, the song seemed to ask why that suffering—especially the extraordinary affliction of war veterans—has to keep falling like rain generation after generation. "I wanna know," he cried, "who will stop the rain? I wanna know."

He did want to know. For he was not just a celebrity fundraiser; he was also a writer. It's a celebrity's job to raise money for worthy causes, but it's a writer's job to put into words what is difficult to express. So Springsteen kept trying to write a song that clarified the dilemma of the Vietnam veteran.

Between 1981 and 1983, Springsteen worked on six different songs about Vietnam veterans. He took the first two lines of "Vietnam" and used them to start "Shut Out the Light," the bleak, droning tale of Johnson Leneir, a Maryland veteran who comes home to his wife and parents. Johnson wakes up from a battlefield nightmare at four am with uncontrollable shakes and begs his wife, "Throw your arms around me in the cold dark night." This song became the B-side of the "Born in the U.S.A." single and was part of the 1998 *Tracks* box set.

Another song, "A Good Man Is Hard to Find (Pittsburgh),"

describes the widow of a Vietnam soldier. She's sitting by her Christmas tree, listening to Christmas songs on the radio and looking at a photo of "him in his dress greens and her in her wedding white." The gently rolling country-pop music reinforces the lyrics' evocation of domesticity, but that only makes the key lines bite harder. How, the woman wonders, is she going to explain to her sleeping daughter "about the meanness in this world"? That meanness led to this harsh assessment of the war: "she thinks how it was all so wasted and how expendable their dreams all were." This song didn't emerge until 1998 on *Tracks*.

"Highway Patrolman" is sung from the perspective of someone like Springsteen who didn't go to Vietnam, but saw many of those close to him go and come back changed. The narrator is Joe Roberts, a Michigan state trooper who had a farm deferment from the draft. But his brother Frankie, never one for manual labor, got drafted, went over to fight and came back drinking more than ever. Meanwhile, Joe married Frankie's girlfriend Maria, and when the farm failed in 1968 took a job as a cop. More than once Joe finds himself caught between his duty to his badge and his soft spot for his brother. The insoluble dilemma of that choice is echoed in the fatalistic sadness of the Woody Guthrie-like folk music. The song became a centerpiece of the *Nebraska* album.

"Brothers Under the Bridges," has only an oblique connection to Vietnam; it's the tale of fourteen-year-old boys who idolized the older teenagers who raced their hot-rods and cuddled up with their girls and beers beneath the train trestles. Only in the last verse, as the adult narrator remembers those days, does he allude to the fate of those hot-rodders: "now I hear a cry in the distance and the sound of marching feet come and gone." The song's galloping, anthemic music was eventually put to new lyrics and became "No Surrender."

In 1995, however, Springsteen recycled the title, slowed the music way down, altered the melody, and turned it into a narrative with explicit references to Vietnam. It's sung from the perspective of a veteran who came home in 1972 and wound up homeless, sleeping in a mesquite canyon beneath a California highway overpass with a small camp of fellow vets in the same predicament. Both versions of "Brothers Under the Bridge" were finally released on *Tracks*.

He also wrote some new verses and a new chorus for "Vietnam," keeping the same, Randy Newman-flavored music. Perhaps, he must have thought, if I figure out how this guy ended up in Vietnam, I'll have a better grasp on what happens to him when he returns. "I was born in the shadow of the Glendale Refinery," he wrote; "the air was so dirty, you could hardly breathe." The protagonist was from New Jersey, just like the author, but why didn't this character escape the army?

"I had just turned eighteen," Springsteen wrote in the second verse; "I got in a roadhouse jam. They gave me the choice: the barracks or the jailhouse; with my country I did stand." He recycled the airport imagery from the first draft but changed the location from Newark to Saigon: "The runway rushed up at me; I felt the wheels of the plane. The heat hit me in the face, then I stood in Vietnam."

These details improved the song, but the music was still inappropriate and the lyrics were still too wordy. Springsteen's first three albums had overflowed with words, as if he were under the mistaken impression that the more words you cram into a line—especially the more fancy words you use—the better lyricist you are. Many gullible listeners and critics agreed—these are the same sort of folks who believe a guitarist can be judged by how many notes he crams into a sixteen-bar solo, as if Black Sabbath's Tommy Iommi were a better guitarist than Steve Cropper or Robbie Robertson.

Springsteen knew better. He had learned that lyric writing, like playing the guitar, has little to do with technical dexterity and everything to do with producing an emotional reaction in the listener. The strongest reactions are often created by lyric phrases that pick out a few sharp details and imply the rest. He had learned that Dylan was the rare writer who could be verbose and still make every word count—an anomaly to be admired but not imitated. Since 1977, Springsteen had been whittling away at his verbiage, trying to tighten up his lines and achieve the taut distillation achieved by writers such as Hank Williams, John Prine and Chuck Berry. At the end of 1981, Springsteen was getting close to that level.

So he was looking for a succinct phrase that would sum up his character's problems and hopes, that would explain why this kid from the shadow of the refinery would end up in a courtroom and on a plane to Saigon, why this kid had any reason to believe that things might get better soon.

It was during this time period that Springsteen received a screenplay from Paul Schrader, who had written the scripts for *Taxi Driver* and *Raging Bull*, and who had directed *Blue Collar* and *American Gigolo*. This latest screenplay was about a guy who works in a Cleveland factory by day and plays guitar in a bar band by night. His sister sings in the band but she is also a single mom who is constantly arguing with her sick mother and long-suffering brother about whether she's raising her son properly.

"The script sat on my writing table," Springsteen recalls in *Songs*, "until one day I was singing a new song I was writing called 'Vietnam.' I looked over and sang the top of Paul's cover page, 'I was born in the U.S.A.' . . . I later gave Paul a song called 'Light of Day,' and the film was released under that title."

Schrader had wanted to know if Springsteen was willing to follow in the footsteps of his hero Elvis Presley and try movies. Springsteen was one of those Elvis fans who believed that Hollywood had led Presley astray, and he wasn't going to let that happen to him. But he was intrigued by Schrader's title: *Born in the U.S.A.* After all, Springsteen had a history with titles that began with the word "Born."

There was something about that word, whether it was in his own "Born to Run," Kovic's *Born on the Fourth of July*, Creedence Clearwater Revival's 1969 "Born on the Bayou," Steppenwolf's 1968 "Born to Be Wild," T. Rex's 1973 "Born to Boogie," Rare Earth's 1971 "Born to Wander," Sandy Posey's 1966 "Born a Woman" or Johnny Cash's 1958 "Born to Lose." And there were movies such as Jimmy Stewart's 1936 *Born to Dance*, Robert Wise's 1947 *Born to Kill*, Nicholas Ray's 1950 *Born to Be Bad* and the 1966 kids' movie *Born Free*.

The power of these titles is their ability to suggest that people have traits and destinies that they never chose, that they were born with. Those qualities may be suppressed, these songs, books and movies imply, but they can never be erased; and sooner or later they will reassert themselves. It's not that you chose to be wild, to run, to dance, to wander, to kill, to be an American or to be a woman; that's just the way you were born. Society may try to squelch that destiny—you may try to avoid it yourself—but eventually that innate trait will shape your life.

Just as no one chooses to be born, no one chooses to be born in the U.S.A. But if you are, the rest of your life is profoundly shaped by that circumstance. You are born into a distinctive landscape, a certain standard of living, a particular way of talking and getting around. You inherit a mythology of stars and stripes, cowboys and Indians, guitars and saxophones, stone walls and white picket fences, horses and cars, crowded sidewalks and open roads. You absorb an expectation that the

American dream is your birthright. You are ushered into a reality where that dream often goes unfulfilled.

And, if you were a male born between 1940 and 1954, you faced the prospect of being drafted into the Vietnam War, not because of anything you did, but simply because you were born in the U.S.A. If you did serve in that war and returned home to neglect and worse, you refused to accept it; you insisted on your right to a healthy, meaningful future for the same reason—because you were born in the U.S.A. So it was natural that Springsteen would marry Schrader's title to his ongoing quest to write a Vietnam song.

"Born in the U.S.A."—the phrase was so pithy and evocative that all he had to do was repeat it four times and he had his chorus. In its ability to sound like both a sentence of doom and a hopeful declaration of optimism, it was infinitely better than "you died in Vietnam." But the song's music was still wrong; the verses were still too wordy, and the story didn't quite cohere.

He got rid of the Newman-ish music (which wound up with the "don't talk to strangers" line in "Love Is a Dangerous Game," an early version of "Pink Cadillac"). Springsteen came up with a new hard, driving guitar figure reminiscent of John Fogerty's riff for Creedence Clearwater Revival's "Run through the Jungle." Springsteen borrowed the chorus melody from the old black spiritual, "Wade in the Water," also the source for Fogerty's similarly titled "Born on the Bayou." Alone in his house in Colt's Neck, Springsteen was still playing everything on unaccompanied acoustic guitar, but it was already obvious that this was a rock 'n' roll number.

He both expanded the scope and distilled the language of the song's pre-Vietnam section. The song's protagonist, who might have been one of the writer's teenage buddies, was born in a small New Jersey burgh, "a dead man's town," in the years after World War II. He was born into a working-class family that had neither the money nor the knowledge to steer him toward college and away from the draft. Everything started right there, in the maternity ward, when he was born in the U.S.A.; the first kick he received was when he dropped out of the womb onto the table with a thud. It was the first handicap of many.

Turned off by strange books and snobby classmates, the protagonist gets bored at school and gets into trouble. Before long, he feels like "a dog that's been beat too much." With no other way to make a name for himself, he starts stealing cars and breaking into houses. He inevitably gets caught and finds help. But the conclusion is not as bleak and t is in "Nebraska," "Factory," "Point Blank" or stead the conclusion is resilient and defiant: not going to run away, but he's also going to get in remind you that he's cool.

l, of course, is no assurance that the American me true for you. But believing in your right to that initely preferable to deciding that the dream is a jecting both naïve romanticism and cynical despair, has to confront both the very real obstacles to that the legitimacy of that dream. To contain both those in the same piece, the songwriter has no choice but o the modernist solution—irony, the juxtaposition of ld be and what is. He has no choice but to write like

rrowing lines from Williams and Holland–Dozier–Hol- ringsteen completed his transformation as a lyricist literary diction of Bob Dylan (which dominated Spring- first three albums) to the populist vernacular of Jerry Curtis Mayfield and Merle Haggard (which dominated gsteen's subsequent work). His lines became shorter and even; his language became plainer; he relied less on l dazzle and more on implication. His narrators and char- s now spoke as real people conversed, how they might ak if they could turn their innermost feelings into words.

There's nothing inherently wrong with literary diction—Dylan Smokey Robinson use it brilliantly—but it's very difficult to ld effectively, and the vernacular approach fits Springsteen's ts better. His talent, it turned out, was not wordplay but rather escription and dialogue. His ability to sum up a man's life in e short, plain-speech lines of "Born in the U.S.A." is a much more impressive writing achievement than the out-of-control verbiage of "Blinded by the Light."

Now that he at last had the words for his best Vietnam veteran song, he had to record a demo version. Springsteen asked Mike Batlan, his guitar tech from the last tour, to set up a basic tape deck at the Colt's Neck house so the singer could tape all the new songs he was writing. Batlan brought in a thou- sand-dollar, four-track Teac Tascam Series 144 tape recorder and hooked up his boss's old Gibson guitar echo unit to give the tape some reverb. He showed Springsteen how to run the simple equipment and then left him alone. On the tape of "Vietnam," for example, you can hear Springsteen let go of the

himself tangled up "in a little hometown jam." The judge offers him the age-old choice for a poor kid in trouble: the barracks or the jailhouse. So our protagonist ends up with a rifle in his hand and orders for Southeast Asia.

He serves his rotation of duty in the jungle and comes home, hoping to get his life back on track. He drives over to the oil refinery where his dad and his dad's pals all had good union jobs. But the personnel man at the refinery explains that they're not hiring on account of the economy. The man shakes his head slowly and says helplessly, "Son, if it was up to me . . . "

The protagonist gets back in the car and drives over the Veterans Administration office. Surely the government would help him out after all he had done for his country. But the VA official explains that there's no funding for the kind of job refer- rals and counseling he's seeking. The VA guy shakes his head just as sadly as the refinery guy and asks the young veteran to be realistic: "Son, don't you understand?"

No, he doesn't understand. Why did he spend two years of his life in a country he had never heard of shooting at farmers he didn't know? Why is his nation turning its back on him now that he's back? He never wanted to go in the first place. And why did his older brother have to die over there? Look, he has a Polaroid snapshot of his brother in his wallet. See how young and hopeful he was? See his Vietnamese girlfriend? He had promised to take her away from the prostitution and sewing fac- tories of Saigon and bring her back to a brick house in Jersey. Why did he have to die?

What, the protagonist continues, am I supposed to do now? I can't find a job; I can't keep a girlfriend; I can't sleep through the night without the nightmares waking me up, and most days I can't get out of bed before noon. What am I going to do next?

At this point in writing the song, Springsteen must have leaned back in his chair and pondered how to answer that question. Seven years earlier, the answer would have been simple: find a friend, jump on a motorcycle and shout to the world: "We'll run till we drop; baby, we'll never go back." But in the present story, that answer seemed foolishly romantic. Where could the protagonist drive his motorcycle where the nightmares and memories wouldn't follow? Where could he go that the employment prospects for an untrained high school dropout and moody Vietnam vet would be any better? And how will things at the refinery and the VA office ever change if people keep running away from them?

It was at this point that Springsteen wrote the most important lines of his career. "I'm ten years burning down the road," he scribbled. "Nowhere to run, ain't got nowhere to go. / Born in the U.S.A. / I was born in the U.S.A." In those few words, a career-long investment in the romantic fantasy of escape came crashing down around him. Thirty years of rock 'n' roll mythology and 400 years of faith in the American frontier came crashing down as well. No road is long enough and no frontier is distant enough to escape some problems, he must have realized. Some problems can be found in every corner of America, and some problems you carry within you wherever you go. You can't always outrun your disappointments; at some point you have to make a stand and fight back.

The words, "Nowhere to run," came from the title of Martha & the Vandellas' 1965 top-ten hit. In that song, written by the Eddie Holland–Lamont Dozier–Brian Holland team, the singer has nowhere to run from heartbreak after a boyfriend has abandoned her. She can't look in the mirror because his face is there; she can't sleep at night because he's in her dreams. This was the flip side of the rock 'n' roll promise: because the stakes were higher, the losses could be, too. And because the singer was still a teenager in high school, the option of flight was impossible.

Springsteen took this phrase from teenage heartbreak, which rarely lasts more than a few weeks, and applied it to adult despair, which can last for years. But Springsteen transformed the phrase from a confession of hopelessness into something more ambiguous. If this character is going to stop running, is he going to surrender or is he going to turn and fight? If you're "born down in a dead man's town," is being born in the U.S.A. a blessing or a curse?

Springsteen answered these questions by borrowing another song title, from Hank Williams's 1948 hit, "I'm a Long Gone Daddy." Williams's song was a swaggering kiss-off to a woman who thought she had the singer under her thumb; before she knows it, Williams sang, he'll be "long gone" out the door. Springsteen drops the leaving but retains the swagger, using "gone" in the beat-poet sense of being "cool" or "far out." "I'm a long gone daddy in the U.S.A.," his protagonist sings, as if confident that all the hypocritical judges, hard-assed sergeants and head-shaking personnel officers in the world can't break his spirit.

"I was born in the U.S.A.," he repeats twice, as if echoing

Woody Guthrie's
one can chase him
as to anyone. Why
"dog that's been bea
he shouts, summoni
Elvis Presley, "I'm a co

Being born in the U
and it's that rich ambiva
Springsteen's greatest so
of America, as George W
neither is it an indictment of
have argued. In a mature rom
a partner because he or she
you ignore those flaws; you fi
with your eyes wide open. The s
tism. And "Born in the U.S.A." m
patriotic song ever recorded.

"I grew up in this small town," Sp
in Greensboro, North Carolina, on
I was sixteen, man, I hated that tow
minded and small-minded. I used to g
coln Transit to New York City, and it use
I got out at Port Authority. It was like, 'Oh,
owns me up here.' I'd go down into the
was a lot easier to breathe.

"When I finally got out of [Freehold], I sa
coming back.' But as I got older, I used to c
road, and I'd drive back down through town, an
of my old friends, see what their lives were like
would always carry a part of that town with me n
I went or what I did. When I was a kid, I guess,
belonging to something, because if you admit that
something that means you've got some responsibil

"Like if you stand and you say, 'Well, I'm an Am
means you've got some responsibility to America, t
that you live in. In this country we've got plenty of thi
proud of and plenty of things to be ashamed of. Unless
at both, unless you look at the bad stuff as well as th
stuff, there's no way it ever gets better."

In the final chorus of "Born in the U.S.A.," Springsteen s
the problem of realism vs. optimism. The song still describe
the obstacles to the American Dream: the handicap of be
born poor, the choice of war or prison, the lack of jobs, the la

guitar halfway through and flip the page in his notebook before he plays the second half of the song.

"I sat in a chair," Springsteen explained in *Songs*, "singing and playing into a couple of microphones. With the two tracks left, after I sang and played the song, I could add a harmony or hit the tambourine. Sometimes I added a guitar. On four tracks that was all you could do. I mixed it through a guitar Echoplex unit onto a beat box, like the one you take to the beach."

"I was trying to get them to sound right," Springsteen amplified. "That's what would deepen the images. I thought of John Lee Hooker and Robert Johnson—records that sounded so good with the lights out. I wanted to let the listener hear the characters think, to get inside their heads, so you could hear and feel their thoughts, their choices."

On January 3, 1982, Springsteen and Batlan mixed the best songs from the new work the singer had been recording on the four-track down to a two-track cassette on a portable boom box. The latter tape presented fifteen songs in this order: "Bye Bye Johnny," "Starkweather (Nebraska)," "Atlantic City," "Mansion on the Hill," "Born in the U.S.A.," "Johnny 99," "Downbound Train," "Losin' Kind," "State Trooper," "Used Cars," "Wanda (Open All Night)," "Child Bride," "Pink Cadillac," "Highway Patrolman" and "Reason to Believe."

Nine of these songs would be released on *Nebraska* exactly as they were mixed that day. "Born in the U.S.A.," "Downbound Train" and "Child Bride" would be substantially rewritten (the last as "Working on a Highway") and would appear on the *Born in the U.S.A.* album. "Pink Cadillac" and "Bye Bye Johnny" would be re-recorded and seriously considered for the *Born in the U.S.A.* album, only to be bumped at the last moment to the B-sides of the "Dancing in the Dark" and "I'm on Fire" singles. "The Losin' Kind" has never been released.

Springsteen sent the tape to Jon Landau later that month with a note explaining that these were the most finished of the more than twenty songs he had written in the three-and-a-half months after *The River* tour ended. "The only thing I looked for in the songs," Springsteen wrote in the accompanying note, "was that it someway break a little new ground for me. They all don't do this; some I just got a blast out of, but I think a good amount do or at least try. They may not hit you right away or may seem a little foreign."

They seemed more than a little foreign, with their country-folk feel and bleak mood, but they hit Landau right away.

The manager was impressed by the songs' emotional power and immediately focused on his favorite tunes: "Atlantic City," "Nebraska," "Mansion on the Hill" and "Johnny 99."

Landau later admitted that he dismissed "Born in the U.S.A." as one of the tape's lesser songs, even though the lyrics were already exactly the same as they would be on the famous single. Because the new lyrics were so pared down, they relied on implication, and those implications were getting lost in the pell-mell rush of the riff and bluesy slide-guitar lead. The music drove the song forward so briskly and relentlessly that it sounded as if the protagonist were being pushed off a cliff. It was too pessimistic to work as a rocker, and it was too rocking to work as pessimism.

This was the danger of replacing rock 'n' roll fantasy with rock 'n' roll realism: Reality can be very depressing. It's one thing to predict great things for your twenty-year-old self and your twenty-year-old friends, to believe that you can live your lives as "gypsy angels . . . built like light . . . too loose to fake," dancing "all night to a soul fairy band" and getting kissed "just right like only a lonely angel can." It's quite another thing to look at what really happened to your pals by the time they reached thirty-two, to examine the jobs and marriages they actually have, to consider the wounds they carry from foreign wars and domestic disputes.

Springsteen had certainly been thinking about all this in the years since *Born to Run*. The title track of the next album, 1978's *Darkness on the Edge of Town*, is sung by a man who has lost his money and his wife and spends his time racing cars without joy. "Everybody's got a secret," that narrator admits, "something they just can't face." The title track of the next album, 1980's *The River*, is sung by a guy who had to marry his pregnant girlfriend at nineteen, drop out of school and take a construction job. The job dried up; the marriage withered, and he wonders, "Is a dream a lie if it don't come true, or is it something worse?"

That question, a paraphrase of the Langston Hughes poem "Dream Deferred," must have been hard for Springsteen, rock's leading purveyor of dreams, to write. He spent much of 1981 through 1984 trying to answer it. He wanted to know what it felt like to be thoroughly alienated from the American dream and the rock 'n' roll promise. As he scribbled lyrics in his lined notebook at his writing table in Colt's Neck, he tried to put himself in the shoes of Vietnam veterans, their widows and their brothers. How do you find a "Reason to Believe" in songs like these?

"For the *Born to Run* record," Springsteen told Marsh, "I established a certain optimism. After that I felt I had to test those things to see what they were worth. . . . I decided to move into the darkness and look around and write about what I knew and what I saw and what I was feeling. I was trying to find something to hold onto that doesn't disappear out from under you. Eventually it led up to *Nebraska*, which was a record about the basic things that keep people functioning in society, in a community or in their families or in their jobs. The idea is that they all break down. I was interested in finding out what happens then—what do my characters do, what do I do?"

If the romantic fantasies of Springsteen's early songs were flawed by their refusal to think beyond the first night of escape down the road, many of his new songs were flawed by their inability to offer their characters any hope at all. The songwriter needed to find a way to accommodate real lives and genuine hope in the same song. He found the solution in the irony of "Born in the U.S.A.," where the narrator is buffeted by denial on every side but who still believes he can find the life he deserves if he just stands his ground. Why? Because he's "a cool rocking daddy in the U.S.A."

The words were right, but there was still something wrong with the music. After all, if Landau couldn't grasp the song's irony in its present form, it was unlikely that a seventeen-year-old kid in suburban Connecticut was going to get it while doing his homework as the record played on the stereo. No, the music needed to be revamped. Instead of a nonstop tumble of words, the vocal needed pauses, so the words could sink in. It needed to build the tension in the verses with a melody that never lands on the root and then release that tension in the chorus. It needed the stomping beat and the call-to-arms hook of a rock 'n' roll anthem such as Bob Dylan's "Like a Rolling Stone," the Rolling Stones' "Jumpin' Jack Flash," the Who's "Won't Get Fooled Again" or Elvis Costello's "What's So Funny 'Bout Peace, Love and Understanding."

So Springsteen sat back down in the writing room of his Colt's Neck home, lifted the acoustic guitar back onto his right thigh and fooled around with various chords and rhythms, pulling out examples from his encyclopedic knowledge of rock 'n' roll history, till he found what he needed. Starting with a hollow

B chord, he moved to a full B chord and then to a combined B/E chord. It almost sounded like a one-chord vamp and that gave the song its tension, but the slight alterations in the chord gave the song a forward movement, and the few times the melody actually touched down on the B, it released all that tension in glorious fashion. The song was finally finished; all he had to do was take it to the band.

By now, it was May 1982, and the studio sessions for turning the January demos into full-band tracks had bogged down. The E Street Band had gathered at the Power Station studio in Manhattan to translate those cassette tapes into arrangements that could be released as an album. They worked on Landau's favorite songs from the tape—"Nebraska," "Atlantic City," "Johnny 99" and "Mansion on the Hill"—but even after multiple takes, they couldn't match the intensity of the demos.

Everyone was getting frustrated, so Springsteen shifted gears by pulling out the song that his coproducers (Landau, Chuck Plotkin and Steve Van Zandt) had forgotten about: "Born in the U.S.A." Springsteen flipped through his notebook till he found the song, and he quickly taught the band the new, minimalist chords and marchlike rhythm. After a couple of run-throughs, Springsteen stepped up to the mic and they started to record.

"We just kind of did it off the cuff," Springsteen told Marsh. "I went in and said, 'Roy, get this riff.' And he just pulled out that sound, played that riff on the synthesizer. We played it two times and our second take is the record. That's why the guys are really on the edge. You can hear Max—to me, he was right up there with the best of them on that song. There was no arrangement. I said, 'When I stop, keep the drums going.' That thing in the end with all the drums, that just kind of happened."

Danny Federici hits an anchoring piano chord, and Roy Bittan immediately answers with the two-bar synth figure that will dominate the song. The sound is vaguely Asian, resembles the brass fanfare of an army band, and yet has that sizzle of a mid-80s synthesizer. Coproducer Chuck Plotkin and engineer Toby Scott give Max Weinberg's snare drum so much reverb that it sounds like an artillery shell exploding every time he hits it. In the beginning that's all there is: Federici's chord on the one-beat, Bittan's six-note motif beginning on the two-beat, and Weinberg hitting the two and four beats as hard as he can. It's hypnotic in its repetition, but in its refusal to resolve it creates an expectation for something else.

On the fifth repetition, Springsteen's voice comes in, singing at the top of his range, "high and lonesome," as the bluegrass guys say, but with a ragged rawness as if he were at the end of his rope like his character. "Born down in a dead man's town," he hollers, "the first kick I took was when I hit the ground." He gives us three rhymes in two lines and echoes down with dead and kick with took; the language may seem simple, but he has far greater control of it than he ever did on his word-drunk early songs. The first word he sings is born, reminding us that some factors in our lives are beyond our control, are set in place as soon as we pop out of the womb.

In that light, the chorus' four repetitions of the title line are ironic indeed, turning the familiar boast into a bittersweet lament. Yet there's a grandeur to the chorus music that implies that there's still some boastfulness left in the claim. At this point, it's still just piano, synth, snare drum and vocal, but the rest of the band comes crashing in on the first line of the second verse—Springsteen's guitar, Weinberg's full drum kit, Van Zandt's guitar and Tallent's bass.

The second and third verses provide the song's plot about getting into trouble with the law, getting shipped off to Vietnam and returning home to refusals at the refinery and the VA office. After the third verse comes the song's bizarre bridge, a flashback to Nam. The first two lines, "Had a brother at Khe Sahn / fighting off the Viet Cong," follow the first two lines of the verse melody, but the melody for the third line, "they're still there and he's all gone," descends as if into an abyss, and there's no vocal at all on the fourth line, as if the singer is too overcome by loss to even talk about it. It's a totally unconventional structure, but it captures the reaction to a needless death as few other songs ever have.

That line about the Viet Cong taking over Vietnam while his brother lies in his grave bluntly declares that America lost the war and that its soldiers died in vain. That statement, coupled with the first verse's allusion to the war's underlying racism (the narrator is sent "off to a foreign land to go and kill the yellow man") were shocking statements to make in the realm of popular culture in 1984. As I write this in 2005, as America is in the midst of another misbegotten war, they seem just as bold and just as rare.

The flashback bridge continues with another couplet tied to the verse melody: "He had a woman he loved in Saigon / I got a picture of him in her arms now." But once again the narrator is too overcome by memories of his brother to continue, and the third and fourth lines of music go by without vocals.

After the bridge, most of the band drops out of the arrangement and we're back where we started—synth, snare drum and vocal, with bass instead of piano this time. Against this stripped-down backdrop, the narrator pulls us back to the present, as he ponders his fate in the bright glare of the orange flames sprouting from the tips of New Jersey's oil refineries and in the shadow of the New Jersey state prison, where he almost ended up before and where he might end up again. What should he do? Hit the road as if he were born to run? Give up on the American Dream and return to his criminal ways as if he were Johnny 99?

He will do neither. Both are forms of escape, and he decides, in the echo of Weinberg's thundering snare, that he has nowhere to run. He's going to follow the example of Vietnam veterans such as John Kerry, Ron Kovic and Bobby Muller; he's going to stay right where he is and try to make it work. "I was born in the U.S.A.," Springsteen sings again and again over the spare backing, as if unsure whether that's a good thing or bad. But then the rest of the band rejoins the arrangement with a triumphant charge, and the implication is clear: for all its failures and cruelties, the United States is still home, still a place worth loving, still a dream worth pursuing rather than abandoning.

"I'm a cool rocking daddy in the U.S.A.," Springsteen cries exultantly in the final line, and the band is indeed rocking at this point. In fact, it keeps playing for a minute and twenty-four seconds after the lyrics end. The guitars reinforce the synth riff, but Weinberg, Federici and Tallent all start playing freely against the groove and Springsteen starts wailing wordlessly. This juxtaposition of repetition and improvisation perfectly echoes the song's contrast of fate and freedom.

After forty-five seconds, the groove falls apart; Federici and Van Zandt drop out; Weinberg solos madly against Bittan's exposed synth riff. It's as if the narrator's confidence has faltered before the problems he faces. But Springsteen shouts out, "One, two, three, four"; the band pulls the song back together; the narrator's poise is restored; and they go out cool and rocking. And it's over.

It was the finest four-and-a-half minutes that Bruce Springsteen has ever spent in a recording studio. And it was all made possible by the decisions he made in his writing room at his Colt's Neck home.

If he had been Elvis Presley, with Sam Phillips as his producer and Colonel Tom Parker as his manager, as soon as they finished the song, they would have taken the acetate down to the local radio station and played it on the air that night. It would have been in the stores two weeks later, and it would have been a giant hit within a month. But Springsteen wasn't Elvis Presley; he wasn't working with Phillips or Parker, and it would be two full years before the greatest recording of his career would be heard by the wider world.

Music from Big Pink

by John Niven

John Niven toured and recorded as guitarist in the Wishing Stones—their sole LP *Wildwood* (Heavenly Records 1992) owes more a passing debt to the music of The Band—before becoming an A&R man and working with acts like Travis, Mogwai, and Sígur Ros. Over the years he has written about music, film, and sport for various publications. In 2003 he sold his first screenplay and cowrote and directed the award winning short film *Tethered* (British Film Council/ Frozen Tundra Films).

Three

"We spent our whole lives at sea . . ."

Bob Dylan's arrival in town had made Woodstock about as cool as any place in the known universe. But in a low-key way—this was way before the festival and all the stupid shit that happened later when the hippies came.

I'd been up to his house once, toward the end of last fall, and it was because of that night that I eventually got to know the guys in The Hawks. Tommy, Alex and me had been drinking in Deanie's one Saturday night when this girl Chrissie, who we kinda knew but didn't like (she was beautiful—button nose, straw-blonde hair, Disney freckles, perky little titties—but a real star-fucker), came in and asked us if we could get any smack. I had a little in the house that I wasn't going to sell, but I asked her who it was for anyway.

"This film guy," she said, then added in a stupid, stagey whisper, "he's staying up at Byrdcliff. At Bob Dylan's place."

Twenty minutes later we peeled off Camelot Road and up Dylan's driveway. A sign on the gate said:

IF YOU HAVE NOT TELEPHONED, YOU ARE TRESPASSING.

"Shit, maybe we should have called."

"Oh, it's OK," she said casually. "Bob's not here. Didn't I say? He's down in the city with Sara for the weekend." I looked at her and thought, you fucking *cunt*. But I didn't say anything. Fuck it. Get to see the place anyhow.

We parked in front. Dylan's house was this huge chateau ("Turn of the century," said Chrissie, like a tour guide) built along the side of Mead's Mountain. A rambling, classy old place of cedarwood, stone and mahogany shingle. I followed her off toward a little outbuilding that looked kinda like a garage and I could hear music—Motown—coming from inside.

Chrissie pushed the door open. The garage had been turned into a poolroom where a huge, twitchy guy, maybe in his mid-thirties, and a younger couple were shooting some eight ball. The big guy shuffled over and held out a massive paw. "*Hi. I'm Howard*," he shouted over the music. The couple—a stunning, exotic, dark haired chick and a tall, cool looking guy in shades and a sharp houndstooth check jacket, both about my age—nodded hellos but didn't really pay us much attention. "Come on," said Howard as he led me off, "let's go in the house."

You bond with people fast when you take dope. Fast and shallow. We'd snorted some of the smack—there wasn't much but it was really good; Chinese fuckin' crazy powder—and this Howard guy was talking and talking.

"What we're uh . . . excuse me, man . . . what we're trying to make here is something that'll really . . . really freak people out. It'll be like this trip that . . . where . . . where's ah, yeah . . . man, that is some nice junk you have there, some *nice* junk . . . where you from? Canada? The boys are all from Canada you know, I . . . oh, here we are . . . "

He was messing about with reels of film that had been shot on Dylan's tour of Europe earlier that year; the one where people were losing their minds because he had a backing band with him. They had a machine (a Moviola it was called) set up in one of the bedrooms. It was like a big, metal reel-to-reel tape deck, but for film. It had a little TV screen on it and you could run the film back, forward or whatever.

In the car Chrissie had said Howard had been here a couple of months, working with Bob (again with the fuckin' "Bob") and trying to edit all this footage into an hour-long television special. The original guy who was doing it had quit over in England having been driven nuts by Dylan, and I think old Howard was starting to go a little crazy too, stuck up here on the mountain. What with the smack on top of whatever he'd been doing earlier, he was pretty wasted by this point. He ranted and raved as he rooted through those cans—boxes and boxes of them—until he eventually found what he wanted and started feeding the film into the machine. "Here. Look at this."

He pulled me toward the tiny screen. Footage of a steam train crossing the English countryside gave way to a bunch of fans shuffling into a Dylan show, then a brief shot of a wasted-looking Dylan in a dressing room somewhere, then back to another train shot, then some cops, then another show. It went on like this for a while, no one clip lasting for more than a few seconds. Man, you couldn't even hear the songs properly.

"You see what I'm saying? Each section, every sequence, will fall together with a musical, an orchestral logic. In the same way individual notes form chords."

Shit, tell me these guys weren't doing drugs up here. The movie was a fuckin' mess.

"Err, yeah," I finally said. "It's pretty . . . radical."

"Hey, you're goddamn right it's radical. This is going to blow people's minds. Anyone can make a fucking documentary. That's why we had to sack Don. It's like I've been telling Bob, we have to . . . "

"I—sorry man—where's the john?"

"Oh, right across the hall there."

Lightheaded from the junk I waltzed off, grateful to be away from the yabbering and get a look around. The place was like a hotel in France or someplace. Antiques up the ass. A load of paintings—abstract, unfinished looking canvases—leaned here and there against the furniture, against the walls. To my left was this huge, dark living room. A little way inside an enormous book was opened up on a lectern. The kinda thing they'd have in a church. I tippy-toed over and stood there for a minute, wasted, just looking at it. A couple of pages were bookmarked and I turned to one: Revelations. As I was trying to figure out what this might mean for the next Dylan record a voice behind me said, "Can I help you?"

I turned. The guy from the poolroom—the guy in the houndstooth check jacket—was standing in the doorway watching me. The pointed, burning tip of a joint dangled from his lips and glowed in the shadows.

"Umm, no. I was just . . . " I gestured toward the lectern.

"Should you be in here?" he said evenly.

Fuck. "Sorry. I was only . . . I . . . like, who are you?"

He just smiled—an enigmatic, unfriendly smile—and walked off. The fucking prick was real calm. From down the hall a girl was calling something to him in a French accent.

I went back into the Moviola room where my new buddy had some more footage up.

"Hey," he said as I walked in, "I got some foil here. It's a waste snorting that stuff."

On the screen Dylan was in a hotel room somewhere playing a song I didn't recognize on one of those new Fender acoustics. "We got hours of this shit to cut," said Howard. "Who needs to see another documentary about a bunch of guys playing the fucking guitar, right?"

The camera panned across to the other bed. Facing Dylan, looking sick as a dog, yellow as a Manhattan cab, and picking out an intricate lead part on an old Martin was the guy who'd just basically told me to fuck off. "Who's he?"

"Robbie? He's Bob's guitar player. You met him back there in the pool room."

"Riiiight," I said.

That was how I met Robbie Robertson.

The guy was cold.

* * *

I'm telling you, man, he was *cold*. None of the other guys were like that. Garth was a bit distant, but not in a mean way. He was just older and weirder than everyone else. Later on I figured out that Robertson's thing was something he'd gotten from Dylan, or Grossman, or both: that it's cool just to be, like, *silent* most of the time. You'd say something, something obvious or pleasant—like a couple of times I tried to give him some production tips, just a little advice—and he'd look at you from behind those pebble glasses like you'd fuckin' grown horns, man. Or just look right through you like you weren't there. Like Dylan did. But, the guy's guitar playing? Holy shit. I mean, forget about it. He was only the same age as me, maybe just a year older, but he could make that Fender fuckin' *talk* to you, man.

The first time I really heard him play, like up close and personal, was one night when a few of us were sitting around the living room at the pink house, everyone stoned and drunk and wasted and passing joints, bottles and guitars around. Robbie didn't hang around getting fucked up and playing tunes as much as Rick and Richard and—later—Levon would. He had his old lady at home and he hung with Dylan and Grossman more than the others did, but he was there that night.

Richard was singing something, some Ray Charles tune (we all loved Ray Charles, and Richard could sing the shit out of that stuff), and there were a few of us sitting on the floor listening. Robbie was perched on a chair, nodding along, just listening with an acoustic guitar cradled in his lap, when, from nowhere, he leaned forward and just . . . *drilled* this fucking solo out. Shit, it was like a bird flying—his left hand swirling up the neck in a beautiful flurry, finishing on this real high note way up on the b string, his thumb and guitar-pick popping off the string together, making this unbelievable ringing, crying harmonic and bending the string so far I thought it was gonna bust. His right hand was raised up above the neck, fluttering in the air like a shot bird, while the left hand wrung the last bits of feeling from the sustained note.

One of the girls sitting cross-legged on the floor went, "Whoa!" I looked over at Bill Avis—my expression *saying what the fuck?* He just smiled. He'd seen it all before. But me . . . I mean, I was stoned and all, but, shit, my jaw was on the fucking floor. So, although we didn't really get along, I had to admire the guy. As a musician.

* * *

It was late now, up here in Bob Dylan's big old wooden mansion in the mountains. Howard and I smoked up the last of the junk—chasing the brown-black gobs around the sizzling foil with a yellow straw—and he put an old blues record on, Elmore James or something, while he did whatever he had to do with those rolls of film. I lay back on the couch, nodding out and in; the heroin making the music drip like molasses from the speakers, great slabs of bottleneck clanging and swooping over my head and swimming through my vision.

After a while Chrissie came and got me and I gave Howard my number and we left. She drove my car—the radio off, the top down and the blue night air all around us as the big Lincoln whipped by the Ashokan Reservoir. I was so high I felt like I could hear the pumps and valves humming beneath the surface, the uncountable pebbles and rocks clacking together as they sifted and moved beneath millions of gallons of clear mountain water.

Also down there, flaking and eroding on the reservoir floor, were the remains of the town of West Hurley where old Walter Travers grew up. He said it was the city's fault. In 1898 its boundaries expanded; Manhattan joining with the other boroughs to form New York City. One of the things New York City needed was a billion gallons of fresh water every day. So the men came up here. They had maps, geological charts, strange tools, instruments and vision. They commandeered ten thousand acres of Ulster County. They dammed the Esopus River. They cleared the Travers family and two thousand other people from their homes. Then they brought the water down: leveling West Hurley and ten other villages, covering 13 square miles and creating the Ashokan.

The water flowed downhill, through the Catskills aqueduct, through broad pipes sunk 300 feet beneath the bed of the Hudson, through Silver Lake and Staten Island, and into Manhattan, nearly a hundred miles away. The water flowed downhill, seeking its lowest level, seeking the city, while the artists and musicians flowed uphill into the mountains, seeking . . . well, maybe just seeking. There had been a real nice bakery in West Hurley too, said Walter.

I was smiling, stretched out there in the passenger seat, feeling like I'd made an important connection and enjoying being driven down through the dark hills toward town by this beautiful girl who I didn't really know or like.

Four
"I'm pushing age 73 . . ."

There were a lot of people like us in Woodstock: kids in their early twenties with no responsibilities, a little money from doing whatever, and a taste for what Johnny Becker used to call "high quality mood tailoring ingestibles." Most of us came from different parts of the country, drawn to the town (usually via New York) in the summers by the cheap rent/nice houses/Bob Dylan combo. Alex and Tommy were from Ohio, Chrissie and her friends were Californians, Johnny B came from Detroit, The Hawks—except Levon—were Canadians, Warren and Jeannie were New Englanders. It was a real mix. You know how they say that Manhattan is this island off the coast of America? We all felt that we were like this island off the shore of Manhattan.

Johnny B was a real junkie, the first guy I ever saw popping a needle between his toes. But he was cool and fucking funny, super-smart and real sarcastic. He'd been busted on a dope possession charge in San Francisco in '66 and had jumped bail to run east. He was renting this little place off the Glasco Turnpike that had no heating, so he became a regular fixture at our place during the winter. Man, seeing Johnny B go at it with little Tommy—that was some funny shit.

We were all sitting around getting stoned one night and Johnny convinced Tommy that the commies were putting bromide in the American water supply. Just tiny amounts, nothing you could really detect, just enough, over time, to make you impotent.

"I'm telling you T, by the year 1980 this generation of American males will have dicks like acorns. We'll be ejacualtin' nothing stronger than fresh air."

"What's ejaculatin'?"

"He means coming, Tommy," said Alex.

Tommy looked at Johnny. Then at us.

"Naw, man. The guvver . . . the guvvermint would tell us if that shit was going down."

"Are you crazy bro?" said Johnny. "They'd start the biggest panic in history. There's nothing they can do about it now anyways. It's a done deal. The commies are gonna come marchin' in here in about twenty years and they're gonna start fucking your sister, boy."

"Goddamn it Johnny, I told you before, don't be talking about ma sister like that!"

Me and Alex were crying, man.

"Yeah, there's gonna be this big Red commie sonofabitch with a schlong like a nuclear fucking missile schtupping your sister, Tommy."

"Fuck you, man!"

We had to pull Tommy back. Johnny B didn't know where to stop.

Now and again my mom would call. I don't know how she got the number. She called one night when Alex and me were stretched out wasted in front of the TV watching *The Smothers Brothers*. She started with the stuff about what everyone had been up to—Uncle Whatever had fallen down the stairs, Auntie Who Cares had to have her fuckin' womb removed (like you ever needed to hear about that kind of shit, man)—before asking about when was I going back to finish school.

I told her I wasn't sure the law was for me. That I still needed a little time out to clear my head. That I was thinking about—maybe—re-enrolling for another course next year, in the fall '68 semester.

"Maybe pre-med," I said.

Alex hooted—not at the *Smothers* show—and I threw a softball at him. "Y'know; like Dad," I said, not making it sound one way or another, but really knowing this would terminate the conversation pretty fuckin' quickly.

"Yes, well that would be wonderful Greg. But it's a lot of work you know, medicine."

"How is Dad?"

"He's fine." Yeah, right. "He sends his love."

"Listen, I gotta go, mom."

"OK. Take care of yourself."

"You too."

Alex tossed the softball back to me with the words "You, my friend, are a nasty son of a bitch" and started rolling another number.

Was I going back to school? Like fun I was.

Some weeks in the summer I was clearing four, five hundred bucks straight profit a fuckin' week. I was on first-name terms with people like Paul Butterfield and The Hawks. Even Dylan had nodded at me a couple of times. I had three or four different kinds of weed under the bed, a shoebox full of amphetamines and barbiturates in the closet. I had a little ceramic honeypot with a fat, happy bee on it on the top shelf of the dresser in the kitchen. I kept the junk there. "Time for a little honey," we'd say.

The news was on now, the same stuff you were seeing every fuckin' night: those big Huey's coming down in dusty clearings, body bags, maps, and troop statistics and stuff. My dad had been through this stuff. An army doctor, bouncing around islands in the Pacific in '44 and '45, coming in behind the Marines as they cleared out the Japs. His main job was popping enough morphine syrettes into kids to stop them screaming for their mothers while they bled out. One for pain, two for eternity, they used to say. Guys could still scream for a long while with four or five shells the size of a shot glass studded across their chests.

We weren't worried. I was Canadian—this shit with the slopes had nothing to do with me, man—and Alex was medical exempt on account of only having one kidney (or so he claimed). But Alex was worried for Tommy, probably because Tommy didn't have the good sense to be worried for himself. His number was getting low. He didn't even have college to fall back on. "What are you gonna do if they call you up, man?" I asked him one night. Tommy thought for a second.

"Man, old Tommy will be smokin' in Alaska so fucking fast you won't believe it."

"Uh, Tommy, Alaska is still, like, in the US," said Alex.

"Ain't it Canadia?"

"No, man."

"Ain't part of it in Canadia?"

"Shit, no Tommy."

"Damn. Where *is* in Canadia?"

"Vancouver? Quebec?"

"Yeah, that's what I meant. Vancooover," he strung the word out, enjoying the sound of it. "You watch. I'll haul ass up there, man. Sit tight in Vancooover. Don't you boys go worrying about old Tommy."

We were laughing our asses off, man.

According to Alex, Tommy's high-school SAT score was something like 211. Just 211. Shit, is that even possible?

* * *

I loved those goofy weekends up in the Catskills. On a Saturday afternoon Alex and me would sit out on the porch, grilling hamburgers, drinking beers, rolling joints: we were a regular counterculture Ozzie and Harriet out there with the barbeque, the Adirondack chairs, the smell of charcoal and pine.

Our place was just a few minutes from Tinker Street, so people would drop by, some of them picking up pills and powders and feel-good shit for the weekend, some just to say hi and hang out. Sometimes friends would come up from the city, although I didn't really encourage the likes of Fifth Floor Dave too much; I had a good thing going up here and I didn't need those guys moving in. (But they wound up coming anyway, by end of the decade there were probably more dealers than guitar players in Woodstock.) We'd all hang out in the yard getting stoned and throwing the football around until it got dark, then we'd stumble along the road to Deanie's and get ripped.

It was right after Halloween and we were out back having one of those Saturday afternoons—taking turns shooting up our jack-o'-lantern with Alex's .22 Woodsman—when a VW Beetle came clunking up the drive and Warren, this friend of Alex's from the city, got out with these two girls.

Two girls? Man, these two exotic looking creatures. The first one was a screech of red hair, a slash of orange lipstick. The second one was dressed head to foot in white Biba: billowing white shirt, thin, white cotton pants, head-scarf, white mules. She had coal-black bobbed hair, a bottle of Rolling Rock in one hand and a cigarette—in a thin black and gold holder—in the other. She looked about eighteen years old, looked like she'd stepped out of *Vogue*, or a Truman Capote book, or a fuckin' Dylan song. I thought, *You gotta be kidding me, Warren*.

She was skipping toward us, laughing at something the other girl was saying, when she tripped up and went fuckin' *flying* into the muddy lawn, the beer bottle catching on the cement path and exploding like a glass hand grenade. We ran to help her but she was flat out on her belly, howling with laughter. It took her a couple of minutes to get up. When she did, she was just destroyed. I mean, this chick had totally fuckin' obliterated herself in the space of two seconds—she'd cut her hand open and she was covered in blood, mud and beer. "Fuck, are you OK?" I said.

She wiped her palm on the seat of her pants, raking a huge bloodstain across them, before daintily offering her hand to me, "Hi, I'm Skye," she said. "Could I trouble you for a beer? A Rolling Rock if you have it?" Her accent was beautiful; pure Vermont, New England old money. I looked down at my hand, her blood all over my fingers. I was *gone*, man. Just real corn-ball love-at-first-sight gone.

Later, after we got her cleaned up, bandaged, and changed into one of my old T-shirts and Levi's, we all went out to Deanie's. It was rammed, bluegrass playing and waitresses going back and forth with steaks and chili. We were slamming tequilas and chasing them down with cold beers, all talking at once, the way you do when you're full of new people and speed and infatuation. Skye was nineteen, a sophomore at Columbia. We talked about Paul Butterfield's band and about the downers she'd gotten from her mom's bathroom cabinet. She knew her music and her drugs. She had a little beauty spot high up on her right cheek.

On the way to the john I ran into Rick at the bar. "Greggy! What's going on, man?"

"Ah, just pounding a few."

"Hey, come by our table. You gotta meet Levon."

I squinted across the room, through the smoke and music. A bunch of the guys were all around a big table in the corner: there was Avis, Richard, Howard, and a couple of guys I didn't know. One of them—lean, bearded—was telling a story, cracking the others up.

"Yeah, man, I'll come over."

"Who you with?"

"Uh, Alex and Warren and . . . " I gestured vaguely toward our table.

"Shit, man, who's the fox?"

Fuck. "Uh, Skye? I think she's . . . like she's Warren's girlfriend or something."

"Fuck. Bring her by."

"Yeah, sure."

Man, I didn't need cooze-hounds like Danko and Manuel fucking this up for me. But what can you do? They all wanted to meet the guys who played with Dylan so we went over and joined them. Levon, the drummer, the new guy, was a few years older than the rest, in his late twenties, and he was a real life, no-shit, Southerner. I'd never met one before. He started sentences with "Well, son," and finished them with "Yessir." You could have listened to him all night.

"Greg gets the best pot around here," said Richard, introducing me.

"Is that a fact?" said Levon. "Tell me son, have you ever come acrawss some weed called Chicago Green?"

I said I'd heard of it.

"Shit Greg, that there is some serious mary-jew-anna."

"Yeah?" I was a bit distracted. Over the other side of the table Rick was listening to Skye. Her face was animated, lit up, as she explained something to him.

"Hell yeah," said Levon. "Trust me on this one. I've smoked weed from New Orleans to Anchorage and that Chicago Green is the finest pot in the Yew Ess. If yew can ever lay your hands on some I'd sure appreciate it."

"Yeah, I'll call a guy I know."

"What you drinking there son?"

By midnight everyone was pretty totalled. The place had emptied out some and a few people, regulars, were ragging on the guys to sing something. A guitar and a mandolin appeared. While they tuned up I went and sat down next to Skye. "Having fun?"

"You bet. I didn't know you were so connected," she said, patting my leg kinda playfully.

"Oh, I'm full of surprises."

Levon said, "Well folks, this here is a song ma daddy showed me," and they went into it.

"Ain't no more cane, on the Brazos."

It was a song I'd heard before, an old chain-gang number recorded by Leadbelly, but it sounded like nothing I'd heard in my life. Levon was playing mandolin, Rick guitar, all three of them singing harmony on the opening chorus. It was the first time any of us had heard the three of them sing together, and their voices just fit perfectly. It was just the rawest sounding thing I'd ever heard from white men. There were people like Paul Butterfield doing this kind of stuff but, these guys, I guess with Levon being from the South and Richard having that Ray Charles thing, it was black-blues-white-country-soul all at once, man. Levon took the first verse, his eyes shut and his head down as he flailed at the little mandolin, the veins in his neck standing out as he growled out this song written decades before by some black guy who couldn't read or write.

"You should have been on the river in nineteen and ten.
They were driving the women, just like they drove the men."

He sang in the most perfect extension of his speaking voice. I thought this guy was the drummer, but here he was —playing mandolin, singing great. These guys, man, it made you wanna do something to yourself.

Richard took the next verse, his voice catching, quavering with hurt in his throat.

"Oh mister don't ya do me, like you done poor old Shine.
You drove that poor boy till he went stone blind."

I glanced to my left. It was like she was watching the second coming or something.

Rick took the last verse, singing it shamelessly right at Skye, and then they all brought it home together, letting the last almost-in-tune chord ring out true. As the applause started—instant and sincere—Richard scooped up his glass and drained off about a half pint of dark liquor, crunching the ice cubes, hanging his head in shyness. I sometimes wondered what it cost him singing those songs the way he did. Like, just singing for some friends and a few strangers in a bar he'd wring everything out of that lyric, chasing the melody through that high ghostly register he had.

They started closing up the place. No one was gonna follow that. Richard invited us back up to the pink house and suddenly we were out on the street in the rain and there was the usual hubbub of who was going with who and people were pulling on coats, climbing into cars. I looked around just in time to see Skye getting into Rick's Continental (The Confidential, he called it). The car was already full. Shit. Richard was getting in his car alone, but I wasn't getting in there. No way. No one was gonna ride with Richard, the way he drove.

Levon came out behind me with this girl Bonnie. He looked at the rain coming down. "Hell," he said. "Rainin' like a cow pissin' on a flat rock. You need a ride, son?"

I watched as Danko's car peeled off—Skye and Warren waving to me from the backseat—and nodded. Levon followed my gaze. "Shit, I guess we'd better get you back there quick. I wouldn't be leevin' young Rick alone with that one for too long!" I climbed into the passenger seat, Bonnie got in the back, and we took off behind Richard, his red taillights already disappearing into the distance. Somewhere ahead of him was Rick. "Don't worry; we'll catch 'em," said Levon, flooring it. We went hurtling out of town toward Saugerties, barrelling at seventy along those Ulster County backroads.

Levon was telling us about a motorcycle crash he'd had down in Arkansas recently (which wasn't exactly filling me with confidence) when we came to that sharp corner before Zena Road. It was a hard, downhill, left-hander. It dawned on me that Levon had only been in town a little while. "Hey," I said, "you might wanna . . . "

"Ah know, son," he flashed the lights to see if anything was coming round the corner headed in the other direction. When he got no answer he just floored it and we came screeching around the bend about as fast as you could without going off the road. Bonnie screamed.

I saw it all very fast: the cop car parked in the middle of the road, red and blue lights strobing in the night, Richard and the two cops right beside it, Richard's car nose-down in the ditch behind them. They turned, wide-eyed in our headlights, Richard shouting something and them leaping out of the way. Levon started to brake, but he realized he couldn't stop in time. So he just slalomed through everything: the cops and Richard and the cars. He almost made it too but then our front just caught the back of the cop car at about fifty miles an hour. I balled up and shouted "*Fuck!*," then there was breaking glass, crumpling metal, and Bonnie screaming as the car spun across the road.

We came to a stop ass-way round; facing back along to where

the cops and Richard were scrambling out of the ditch they'd jumped into. Man, we'd nearly killed all of them. There was broken glass all over the car. Levon got out shaky and headed over to Richard.

"Are you cut?" I asked Bonnie. She shook her head numbly.

"I don't think so."

I could see from here that Levon had demolished the police car, just smashed it to fuckin' pieces.

Bonnie was picking shards of glass from out of her hair and I was just getting around to thinking about how bad it would be if these cops searched me when Levon came back and perched down on the driver's seat. I could hear one of the cops shouting something to him.

"Are you guys all right?" he asked me.

"Yeah, are they OK?"

"They got a damn good scare. I . . . "

The cop grabbed hold of Levon's jacket and just tore him out of the fuckin' car, man. I had only known the guy a few hours but I'd already sensed that he wasn't the kind of guy you'd put your hands on.

Sure enough, Levon grabbed ahold of the deputy and ran him backwards, the two of them swinging and flailing at each other, pumped from the accident. Richard and the other cop ran over and the next thing you know the four of them are going at it like one of those crazy cartoon fights—fists and legs and heads and all of 'em rolling around in the wet gravel. "What the fuck, Greg?" said Bonnie.

I crammed the big bag of grass and the speed into the glove-box and got out, running across the road just in time to see one of the cops pull a mean looking blackjack out. As I shouted "Hey!" he brought it down hard on the back of Levon's head. He went straight down. This was fucking over, man. Richard put his hands up, saying, "OK, OK."

They cuffed them and took them off to the station and Bonnie and I finally got up to the pink house at about four a.m. Everyone had left or gone to bed. There was a T-shirt on the floor. My T-shirt. A little further along were my old Levi's. Further still, at the foot of the stairs, was a pair of white cotton panties. There was a tiny bloodstain on them. I stood at the foot of the stairs and listened. Sure enough—it wasn't a huge house—I could hear it all going on in a bedroom upstairs, Rick and Skye.

In the Aeroplane Over the Sea

by Kim Cooper

Kim Cooper is the editrix of *Scram*, an occasional journal of unpopular culture dedicated to celebrating unjustly neglected artists in the worlds of music, literature, film/TV, comics and bohemia. With fellow 33 1/3 scribe David Smay, she is co-editor of the anthologies *Bubblegum Music Is the Naked Truth* and *Lost in the Grooves: Scram's Capricious Guide to the Music You Missed.* A third-generation Angeleno, Kim offers offbeat bus tours of the city's crimes, literature and architectural gems through Esotouric, and blogs at the crime-a-day 1947project.

Listening Parties

Before they even left Denver, the band had sought out their peers' opinions on the record with a listening session at the studio for their local friends. Jeremy Barnes felt so detached from what they'd accomplished over the last weeks that he left the room during the playback. When he came back in, he found the locals speechless. It wasn't until several months later, when he heard a few of the songs on the radio in New Orleans, that the intensity of the recording really struck him, and he began to understand their reaction.

For Jamey Huggins, the completed album stirred mixed feelings. He'd already heard the songs dozens of times as Jeff Mangum worked out the lyrics and arrangements—adding words and moving them around, repeating or holding phrases, singing the horn parts long before the brass players had ever heard them. Once the songs were fairly static, he saw the band play them repeatedly as they tried the new material out in live settings, so when Jeff and company came back to Athens with tape copies for their friends, there was no way Jamey could listen objectively. "I was not prepared for half of the album to be stripped down to basically voice and guitar with very little or no effects or coloring to the sound from the studio. I kind of wanted it to bubble and bounce like the Apples or Olivia's recordings did. I wanted to hear Jeff's voice through heavy space echo, and Jeremy's drum sound defined and isolated. I was put off somehow. I basically wanted the songs to go into the board like a washing machine and rinse them out so I could see them clearer."

Later, as the power and loveliness of the album overrode his initial preconceptions, he recognized that it worked in ways he couldn't have anticipated. "What was I thinking?! I quickly came to appreciate that the beautifully blurry layers of madness that shot through the microphones and onto the tape were perfectly imperfect, raw and fierce, frantic and immediate. The whole thing just spins around the center: Jeff's voice."

Cover Art

There are no great records without great sleeves, and *Aeroplane*'s is a stunner. The front cover shows a group of old fashioned bathers—though with the odd cropping it's unclear if they are waving from the shoreline or drowning in the deeps. The central figure, a curvaceous lass in a gold-starred red costume, gazes out from a perfectly neutral visage, in place of her face an oversized, well used drum head. That same drum is found on the back cover, strung round the tallest of the stilt-striding musicians who march across a pastoral stage set unsuited to their blare. Externally, the name Neutral Milk Hotel appears only on the spine and on a sticker that Merge applied to the shrinkwrap.

The record cover was a collaboration between Jeff Mangum and Chris Bilheimer, R.E.M.'s staff designer. But the first bit of art came from the pen of Brian Dewan, a visual artist, inventor, filmmaker, carpenter and musician from New York. The iconic line drawing of the enormous Victrola soaring above a smoky city is his. Brian's first Elephant 6 collaboration came when Julian Koster asked him to provide drawings for posters to be inserted inside early singles by the Music Tapes. These singles had three-dimensional pop-up sleeves with mechanisms designed by Chris Bilheimer that Julian and his friends painstakingly cut out with x-acto knives—a fact Brian discovered when Julian asked if he could recommend a good die-cutter. Julian supplied Brian with words and drawings, and Brian adapted this material for the poster, which featured land- and waterscapes decorated with mysterious slogans like "March of the Father Fists" and "Every time you light a cigarette with a candle a sailor will not return from sea."

Not long after the Music Tapes commission, Brian got a call from Jeff Mangum, who identified himself as Julian's housemate. Would Brian be interested in doing some artwork for his new record? Intrigued by the tape he received, Brian agreed to draw two things for Jeff: a flying Victrola and a magic radio. That Victrola would become a shorthand symbol for Neutral Milk Hotel and *In the Aeroplane Over the Sea*, but first it was just one in a stack of potential graphic elements that Jeff brought to Chris Bilheimer when it came time to design the jacket.

Chris Bilheimer was a fine arts student at the University of Georgia when he stumbled onto his dream job with R.E.M. in 1993. Grateful for the opportunity to make a living making art (and to make art on the best equipment "Losing My Religion" could buy), he was a notoriously easy touch for indie artists needing record covers or poster design. Chris had told Jeff to call if he ever needed help; for *Aeroplane*, Jeff took him up on the offer.

Bryan Poole recalls that Jeff "was always into that old-timey, magic, semi-circus, turn-of-the-century, penny arcade kind of imagery," examples of which he'd find in thrift shops on his travels. Among the pieces that Jeff brought Chris was a vintage European postcard of bathers at a resort, and this was the image that Chris—working closely with Jeff—cropped and subtly altered to create *Aeroplane*'s front cover. The other source material included a book of historic circus posters, a clip art book of cloud formations, Will Hart's Elephant 6 logo and Brian Dewan's aerial cityscape.

Although Chris Bilheimer mainly works on computers, his aesthetic is more analog than digital. The disparate images selected for the album design ranged from Brian Dewan's crisp new drawings to the slightly grubby old postcard. How could all these pieces be given a visually cohesive look? Chris solved the problem by scanning the back of the postcard and using the foxed, spotted, off-white paper as the background against which all other images were screened. In this way, everything appeared to be about the same age and printed on similar paper, with the overall effect one of slow decay. Chris even left a splash of dirt on the postcard—just above the girl's waving hand—a touch that's easily overlooked on the CD cover, but obvious on the larger LP jacket. The CD contained a piece of art absent from the album, two reproductions of tiny human figures beneath dramatic clouds. These images appear on the back side of the single sheet of paper on which the CD cover was printed, with the mysterious numerals "205/6" a carryover from the back of the vintage postcard.

Instead of a standard lyric sheet, Chris arranged the song titles, lyrics (which Jeff provided) and other information like a broadsheet. Every song had a title except the one that starts "The only girl I've ever loved / Was born with roses in her eyes." He asked Jeff what to call the track. Jeff said he was thinking about calling it "Holland," or maybe "1945." Chris suggested he combine the two titles, which is how he named what would become his favorite song on the album.

Chris: "I wanted to have a little bit of a 'circus coming to town' feel without an obviously circusy-looking image. And so I laid out this whole thing and printed it out and crinkled it up and then scanned it back in and laid it on top of old paper. I work really hard to make things look like they weren't made on a computer. Even though I'm not using traditional graphic methods—it's the same reason bands like recording with tube amps and recording to tape instead of to hard drive—it has that tactile warmth to it. That's what I try to do with graphic design. Especially by designing something, printing it out, fucking it up and then scanning it back in." Most of the fonts used came from old typography books and were set by hand, although the headline is set in an especially handsome computer font derived from Vineta, an in-line shadowed Clarendon designed in 1973 by Ernst Volker.

Chris had agreed to help Jeff with the design prior to hearing the record. Once he did, he was "absolutely blown away by it. I thought 'holy crap, this is the best record in ten years!'" While this made him excited about the project, it also stirred up unexpected emotional responses. For example, during the design process, he and Jeff initially worked up a different back cover based around the lower portion of the vintage postcard, showing the woman bather's feet trailing off into the water. Chris was very attached to the image, but Jeff decided he didn't want to use it. Chris: "I remember almost wanting to start crying. And I was driving home, thinking, 'I really need to back off and not be so emotionally involved. It's not my record!' I learned a really good lesson about designing. And ultimately I think he made a good decision."

Although *In the Aeroplane Over the Sea* is not the most famous record Chris Bilheimer worked on, nor the best selling, it remains the design he's most proud of, and it occupies a prominent place in his portfolio, where music industry people regularly exclaim over it. Once he was bemused to find someone selling a "really crappy, kinda high schooly pencil sketch of the cover" on eBay, with a description claiming it was the original layout; he emailed eBay and got the auction pulled.

Even after the art was completed and the album released, Chris maintained a relationship with Neutral Milk Hotel, often seeing them play at house parties and formal gigs around Athens. Chris recalls, "There's three times in a row where I saw them live and I started crying. It was something you really couldn't put your finger on. The music was really beautiful, and the lyrics might have been obtuse and not something you could directly relate to, but there was something in Jeff's voice, just the sound of his voice, that encapsulated so many different feelings at the same time. It was just incredibly moving. I think the goal of most art is to transcend your medium or your surroundings—and that just happened at every show, for me, anyway."

The Neutral Milk Hotel Aeroplane Takes Off

Up on stage, the players tapped into a trancelike—but hardly calm—state where the unexpected was the norm. Performances turned frighteningly physical, bodies and instruments flying, blood bring drawn without anyone realizing they'd been hurt. Ben Crum says, "They are easily the best live band I ever saw. There was a powerful energy to their show that I really haven't seen anywhere else. It was definitely dangerous. There often seemed to be a very real chance that someone, probably Julian, would get hurt. Jeff was always doing things like picking him up and throwing him into the drums."

Julian soon discovered that their onstage behavior was frightening people in the audience. Fans wanted to talk with them after shows, but they'd hesitate, as if they were approaching dangerous, possibly demented people. This perception was a major impediment, since the band was hoping most nights to find an agreeable floor on which to crash. Sometimes it was only after Jeff, Jeremy, Julian and Scott settled in at a fan's house that they discovered their host was petrified of them. They found this disconcerting and troubling, and wondered how to handle the situation.

Still, it's hardly surprising that the sight of Julian playing piano with his nose, Scott with his fabulous cantilevered beard jumping around like an inflamed Viking, Jeremy flipping out behind the drum kit, Jeff falling into that drum kit when he wasn't howling words so intensely beautiful that they made jaded hipsters feel things they didn't necessarily want to feel, that all of this barely contained chaos would startle and worry people who came to it freshly.

There were nearly six months between the completion of the *Aeroplane* recordings and its February 1998 release. Merge planned a tour to begin on February 14 in Birmingham, starting out sharing stages with Superchunk and finishing with Of Montreal and the High Llamas. The band spent the time before the album's release gearing up for the tour. Their sets, which had averaged around 45 minutes, would need to be expanded to a maximum of 90 minutes for the road dates. Friends like John Fernandes and Will Westbrook were brought into the touring band and taught the horn parts, culminating in a marathon rehearsal session in a freezing practice space on the edge of town during the first week of February.

It was hard enough expecting a newly expanded band to play the songs from *Aeroplane* and those older Neutral Milk Hotel songs that had survived in the live show into 1998, but Jeff set additional hurdles for the players. Up until the week they left Athens, they were still trying to figure out how to incorporate an ambitious, horn heavy improvisational cover of Charlie Haden's "Song for Che" into the set. This would only infrequently be played, supplanting an original improvisational piece based on the colors of the rainbow that had sometimes found its way into the live performances in 1997.

Ben Crum, asked about the improvisational and collaborative aspects of the band, says, "Jeff guided it, but everyone had some freedom. Those guys didn't need much direction, though. Their instincts were good, and they knew how to complement the songs and stay out of the way of the songs and their direct route of communication to the listener." Jeremy Barnes concurs, "Jeff wrote the songs and we experimented as a band to come up with arrangements. Jeff was very open to our opinions and receptive to our ideas. We were much more collaborative than a lot of bands I can think of, where one leader does everything, and passes jobs along to others. I think Jeff had confidence in his musicians, so he could lead without necessarily telling us what to do. There were no weak links in the band, and everyone really admired each other's musical abilities."

Lance Bangs, who attended those final *Aeroplane* practice sessions, noticed how gentle and encouraging Jeff was with the other musicians, telling them that he loved them and that everything was going to be okay. "And he wasn't any kind of a taskmaster—never turning and glaring at anybody—it was never like that. Clearly, there was a love of his circle of friends that made it important for him to build this community and bring them along with him. And at any point that he'd wanted to, he could have gone out on his own and not had to split the money twelve different ways. It wasn't about that: it was about building this community of likeminded people and supporting their eccentricities. That was really inspiring, and kinda reestablished my faith in what the best part of music can be, building this protective enclave of misfits and lost kids. That really meant a lot to me, and added to my sense that it was really important to document this."

As Jeff and company took those new songs out more frequently, the Athens music community became aware that something really special had been born. On October 14, Jeff got up onstage at the 40 Watt, in a slot opening for the Tall Dwarfs' Chris Knox, and slew the room. Lance Bangs says, "There was a sense of all of us kinda realizing how special it was and making a point of not missing the shows, and not talking, not being as flippant as you might be if it was just some other band that happened to be playing where it wasn't as crucial to catch every note."

Neutral Milk Hotel would be on the road more than one day in four during 1998. February through April saw them canvass Florida, Alabama, Tennessee, Arkansas, Kansas, Missouri, Illinois, Indiana, Ohio, Pennsylvania, Washington D.C., North Carolina, New Jersey, New York, Massachusetts, Rhode Island, Connecticut, Virginia, South Carolina, Georgia, Louisiana, Texas, New Mexico, Arizona, Nevada, California, Washington, Oregon, Colorado and Minnesota. May was two nights in London, June three Florida dates, July a weeklong East Coast/Canadian tour sharing stages with Of Montreal, Elf Power, Papas Fritas and Marshmallow Coast (aka their Denver friend Andy Gonzalez). Then from August through October the band played Sweden, Norway, France, England, Brussels, Holland, Germany, Scotland and Ireland.

Although she played with Neutral Milk Hotel at nearly every show, Laura Carter's most significant role on the tour was that of mix-board translator, a position she'd first held for Olivia Tremor Control. For the first part of a Neutral Milk Hotel set, she'd sit with the soundman, physically handling the board and advising him of what to expect. "'Okay, next song, Julian's gonna throw that accordion on the ground and he's gonna pick up the banjo—the pickup's barely hangin' on, so if it starts to squeal, that's what it is!' It was more like talking them through what was about to happen, because so much was happening onstage that without someone helping, it was a wail or squeal and the soundman would look at twenty instruments onstage and not know what to dive for." Once the soundman was acclimated, Laura would jump onstage to play the songs on which she was featured, which were conveniently clustered near the end of the set. While ordinarily a club soundman might have been insulted to have a strange girl come up and tell him how to handle a band's mix, Laura's personable blend of humility and diplomacy managed to soothe hurt feelings before they erupted into attitude. She learned a lot and kept the sound from devolving into chaos on many a night.

But on some level, chaos was a friend to the band. Anyway, it was inevitable with so many disparate players, equipment that wasn't always in the finest repair, complex arrangements and complex personalities. Laura reflects, "It was always falling apart. Half the time, somebody would give Scotty a joint before the show and he'd get up there to nail that big trumpet part and blank out—or nothing would come out of the hole. There's always this struggle, but somehow I think when it came together, it was even more triumphant. Maybe the audience reacted even more to it, because it fails and gets a little bit stronger and by the third time you nail it and everyone's like, 'Yeah!' I think it made the audience pull harder for us, too, or engage more than if we had been perfect."

Neutral Milk Hotel traveled in two vans: a roomy rental van for the musicians, an old one for equipment. The expanded road band often included members of the Gerbils, Of Montreal and Elf Power, who also played their own sets. It became an ongoing comedy trying to keep a bunch of sleepy, distractible souls from wandering off during pit stops. In an attempt to shame the worst offenders into behaving themselves, the group came up with the nickname "Farkey," which described someone who might be hypnotized by the offerings in a convenience store, wander out the back door and be nowhere to be found when it was time to get back in the van. But with Neutral Milk Hotel quickly gaining a reputation as a band that never made it to gigs on time, it was pointless to single anyone out. They were a band of Farkeys. And when their numbers were swollen with guest horn sections, zanzithophonists and assorted others, well, as Bryan Poole sighs, eight years later but still sounding exasperated, "The more people you have, the greater the Farkeydom."

On February 7, the band headlined the final night of the Florida Popfest in Tallahassee in an Athens-packed line up that included the Music Tapes (featuring Static the television), Elf Power, Of Montreal and the Gerbils. Despite not taking the stage until 2 am and the new album not even being in stores yet, they played to a full room of ecstatic fans. It was a propitious beginning to the next phase in the band's existence.

In April, Lance Bangs joined the *Aeroplane* tour for the West Coast dates, traveling with Neutral Milk Hotel, Elf Power and the Gerbils from Los Angeles to San Francisco, Seattle and Portland, but not returning with them to San Francisco for the important April 18 Terrastock II gig, where they'd appear with several dozen like minded combos, including Elf Power, Olivia Tremor Control and the reunited Silver Apples.

The initial stop in San Francisco was over Easter weekend, with shows at Bottom of the Hill on Saturday and Sunday, and Monday off. Unlike other bands Lance had traveled with, the Elephant 6 crowd wasn't happy just doing radio station promos and hanging out in bars. They worshipped at the Saint John Coltrane African Orthodox Church in its old location on Divisadero, went thrift and record shopping, visited the Musée Mechanique and looked for the best burritos. They were, he thought, "like great, smart, exploratory tourists, seeing the best of the weird sides of the country." At one of those Bottom of the Hill shows, after a collision with Julian that took out the drums and a wall of monitors, Jeff tore his finger open, a terrible-looking wound for which he didn't seek medical attention. It didn't seem to inhibit his playing.

As public awareness of *Aeroplane* rose during the early part of 1998, Neutral Milk Hotel found themselves on the crest of a wave of popularity, facing ever larger and more passionate audiences. And the merch sales, always the touring band's lifeline between living fat or living skinny, increased as well. Laura Carter recalls, "But the money, that happened so fast. We'd always been where we were making $200 a night, and then just, like, suddenly, bam! bam! bam! bam! We were making more money off merch than off shows. We had Elephant 6

T-shirts, which we called 'the cash cow,' and we had the same NMH shirt that we're still selling, the maggots one. We would shut down the merch section during the show, and then just run back there after the last song."

This increased revenue triggered one of the most extreme instances of Farkeydom that would befall the band, the legendary Scott Spillane Pizza Hut Incident. The date was probably April 25, 1998, and Neutral Milk Hotel, Elf Power and the Gerbils were traveling between Minneapolis and Chicago to play a show at Lounge Ax. Laura Carter and Jeff were riding by themselves in the equipment van. Everyone stopped at a Pizza Hut for lunch, then got back on the highway. A couple hours into the trip, Jeff and Laura saw the other van make an abrupt U-turn. Laura says, "This is before the days of cell phones, and we're just like, 'What the fuck? We're gonna miss the show!' So we just keep driving with the equipment—if nothing else, we'll get it all set up for everybody."

Scott Spillane picks up the story. "That was scary! Two hours down the road when we realized we left the money in Pizza Hut. Funny thing was after driving back, we got there just as the shift changed. So we come in and everybody's different. 'Have you guys seen a black bag?' 'No.' Fuck! What do we do—they're ripping us off!! Freaking out. And I look back in the booth and I don't see anything. I'm thinking, how can we accuse these people of stealing?"

Laura: "He left somewhere between ten and twenty thousand dollars in cash, in a backpack, under the table."

Scott: "I dunno, it was quite a few thousand dollars. Probably three or four thousand bucks. But it was a black bag and it was actually sitting on the floor in the shadows, luckily. It was still there."

Laura: "So lucky. And they made the show. After that we instantly went to the bank and we'd get money orders and mail them back to ourselves."

The next night, they played the Blue Angel Café in Chattanooga, the last show of the tour before going home to Athens. That's where Bryan Poole witnessed the most devotional act of Neutral Milk Hotel fanship he ever saw, a girl who drove from Arkansas to give Jeff her grandmother's rosary, talked with Jeff for a little while and had to head home without even seeing the show.

The Farkeys were in force again come July 29, when Neutral Milk Hotel was booked to headline at Toronto's venerable Horseshoe Tavern. Bryan Poole reflects, "We'd always do these tours, Elf Power and Neutral Milk and Gerbils, I don't know how many people that is in total, twelve to fifteen people. Nobody can make a group decision, there's no consensus on what to do or where to go. It becomes a real problem. Neutral Milk Hotel was notorious for showing late to gigs, barely getting to gigs, more than a few times. We totally misgauged how long it was gonna take to get there, and then couldn't find our way out of Montreal. 'Ah, we're still like 250 km away, we're not making sound check. . . . It's 10 o'clock, we're still not there.' Elf Power's supposed to open the show. Ended up not getting to this club until midnight. Sold-out club. The owners were freaking out. We finally get there and they're like super excited, wild-eyed, waving us into the back alleyway, running to get the stuff on stage. There's people just packed, standing there, no equipment onstage—you can imagine, these people are there for a couple hours, staring at a stage with nothing on it. So Neutral Milk Hotel just went and played, and then Elf Power played afterwards. But the thing is, those were the best shows. They barnstormed the stage and the next day, the Toronto paper gave this outstanding review of how great it was. The live shows were always just really chaotic."

Paul's Boutique

by Dan LeRoy

Dan LeRoy is the Director of Literary Arts at Lincoln Park Performing Arts Charter School in Midland, PA. His writing has appeared in *The New York Times, Rolling Stone, Newsweek, Vibe,* the *Village Voice*, *National Review Online,* and *Alternative Press*. Mr. LeRoy is the co-author (with Michael Lipton) of *20 Years of Mountain Stage, a history of the National Public Radio show*, and his book *The Greatest Music Never Sold* will be published by Backbeat in autumn 2007. He is also a contributor to the forthcoming *But Prince Don't Moonwalk*.

Side Three
Play

In the spring of 1988, Tim Carr was in his office at Capitol Records when an attorney he knew called with a question. The Beastie Boys wanted off Def Jam. Did Carr want to meet with the band?

Given the success of *Licensed to Ill*, Carr could hardly have said no. But his reasons for agreeing to the meeting had to do with art, as well as commerce.

A Minnesota native who had moved to New York City in 1980 to work at the Kitchen Center for Performing Arts, Carr had first noticed the Beastie Boys when they were shedding their hardcore punk roots and turning to hip-hop with the underground hit "Cooky Puss." Carr could recall the Beasties, who had just added Adam Horovitz to their lineup from the Young and the Useless, performing at a Kitchen-sponsored concert with the equally unknown Sonic Youth.

At that time, Carr's life "was more Laurie Anderson and Glenn Branca and the experimental side of the downtown arts scene." Yet he was also managing pioneering rapper Fab 5 Freddy, and was on the forefront of the early-eighties mixture of hip-hop culture and high art.

Carr would make the move into the music business in 1986. "I started to bring bands to labels, because you could get Laurie Anderson a record deal when you could no longer get her a grant," he remembers. "I'd been selling acts to different A&R people, and they said, 'You should be in A&R.'"

He found a place at Capitol's New York office, which was "just an A&R outpost" for the label's West Coast headquarters. Carr would make an immediate impression with the first act he signed: the Los Angeles metal band Megadeth. Within six short months, Carr had become the head of Capitol's East Coast operation, at age 29.

When the Beasties visited his office, they first rifled through his record collection. Carr had just returned from Jamaica with a load of dancehall and ragga singles, and also had plenty of hip-hop vinyl on hand. That, he felt, made an impression on the group. "I don't think when they went into other A&R people's offices, that's what they saw." What Michael Diamond saw was a nervous executive thrust into an unenviable role. "He had to all of a sudden step into our world, and meet us on our own terms," Diamond says. "It must have been hard, especially in those days."

But Carr, like the Beasties, had a keen sense of the absurd, particularly as it applied to the music business. "I was sitting in this big chair," Carr explains, "when I really didn't deserve it." With some mutual understanding established, they got down to business. "They played me two pieces, 'Full Clout' and 'Dust Joint,'" Carr says. "And I said, 'We should do this.'"

Many of Carr's fellow staffers at Capitol disagreed. First, there was the small matter of the band still being signed to Def Jam. The Beasties had assured Carr their lawyer could extricate them from the contract, but no one was willing to take that assertion on faith. And even if the group could free itself from Def Jam's clutches, there were still serious questions about exactly what sort of prize Capitol would be winning.

"Everybody was really afraid. They said, 'The Beastie Boys are really Rick Rubin,'" Carr recalls. "Everyone felt he wrote their music and he created their persona." The band's bad-boy reputation also gave Capitol officials pause. A story that was still making the rounds concerned the group's banishment from Black Rock, the headquarters of CBS Records. The Beasties had been accused of stealing some company cameras at a 1985 press conference, and joined Ozzy Osbourne—who had bitten the head off a dove during a label meeting three years earlier—as the only artists unwelcome on CBS property.

Yet when Capitol decided to fly the trio to Los Angeles later that spring, the Beasties were on their best behavior, dusting off the social graces of their childhoods. Ad-Rock was the son of a painter and playwright Israel Horovitz; MCA's father and mother were an architect and a public school administrator, respectively; and Mike D was born to an interior designer and Harold Diamond, one of the country's best-known art dealers.

That background came in handy when the band met Capitol CEO Joe Smith. "It turns out that Joe Smith had bought a Brach[1] from Mike's father years before," Carr says. "Mike walked in and was like, 'You bought a Brach from my father,' and Joe Smith is like, 'What?!' And he realizes that this kid, who's this terror that he's been told about, is all of a sudden the son of the most important art dealer in New York."

After the Beasties broke bread with Carr, Capitol president David Berman, and Tom Whalley, the label's head of A&R, at a soul food restaurant in the Wilshire district, the braintrust left impressed. "They were, without a doubt, the smartest bunch of really arrogant kids I had ever met," Berman would later say. "I was like, 'They're too smart not to pull it off.'"

Yet what clinched the deal, in Carr's view, was the arrival of a competitor: MCA Records, chaired by the powerful Irving Azoff. "Columbia had pretty much spooked the competition," Carr says. But Azoff's bid, he thought, stirred Berman's competitive juices. "Irving and David Berman had a longstanding kind of competition. So David said, 'If Irving wants 'em, maybe I want 'em.'"

Having received less than $100,000 in royalties from the multiplatinum *Licensed to Ill*, the Beasties weren't going to come cheap. Their lawyer, Ken Anderson, was demanding a guaranteed $3 million, two-album deal, Carr says. "It was the equivalent of a $20 million deal today. It was just a huge deal." Especially for a group that Joe Smith was being advised was a one-hit wonder. "He said, 'Why are we doing this?' And David said, 'Tim believes in it. Tom believes in Tim. I believe in Tom and Tim. I wanna do it.'"

Azoff also jetted the band to Los Angeles, and was reportedly willing to meet the $3 million asking price. If Capitol matched, Carr thought, they would get the group—perhaps in part because of the rapport he had established with the Beasties. "My background as a record store clerk, and as a collector, and as a journalist and as a curator and as a manager and as a music fan," he says, "had made it so that I had the right computer bank to interface with the Beastie Boys."

That summer, the trio would officially choose Capitol,[2] triggering lawsuits at the federal and New York state levels from Def Jam and CBS, which believed it still had the Beasties under contract. When rumors of the band's label shopping had reached him weeks earlier, Rick Rubin had told the *New Musical Express* he wasn't sure if the group would record again. That brought an angry reply from Adam Yauch, who claimed Rubin was trying to "throw a monkey wrench" into the trio's plans to release a new single later in the summer and an album by Christmas 1988. The Beasties' response to Def Jam's lawsuit was equally swift: they countersued the label for breach of contract and breach of fiduciary duty, demanding their missing royalties.

This legal activity made Tim Carr's first meeting with Def Jam's Russell Simmons an awkward one. The setting didn't help: the encounter took place at the Tenth Street Baths, an East Village steam room frequented by a diverse clientele of music business-types and Russian mafiosi.

Simmons's right-hand man, Lyor Cohen, recognized Carr and pointed him out as "the guy who's stealing the Beasties from us." Simmons, Carr says, "didn't know who I was, and all of a sudden he's meeting me, naked, in this room. And he goes, 'You don't wanna get involved with me, man. You're gonna lose this battle. We've got them tied down in a very firm deal. This could be a lot more trouble than you want.'"[3]

That threat, Carr believed, would come back to haunt Simmons later, when it was repeated during depositions taken during Def Jam's lawsuit. But the band the two men were battling for was oblivious. The Beastie Boys had finally gotten paid, and were officially trading their Big Apple past for even brighter, wilder California dreams.

* * *

Under the terms of the deal with Capitol, Horovitz, Yauch and Diamond received an advance of about $750,000—minus their lawyer's fees—for *Paul's Boutique*. They wasted no time putting this long-awaited windfall to use, setting up headquarters on the ninth floor of the Mondrian, a luxury hotel on Sunset Boulevard.

A favorite stop for traveling rock stars, it was the perfect location for the Beasties to perfect their spendthrift philosophy.

"It was this whole thing that money doesn't matter," Tim Carr says. "And if it costs money, it's funner—especially if it's somebody else's money." Not that using their own money stopped the three from any pranks. "They would tip each other. Ad-Rock would order iced tea and charge it to Mike D's room, and give a $25 tip," Carr recalls. Of course, having some fun at their new labelmates' expense was better still. "We'd be sitting by the pool, and they'd yell to Bret [Michaels] from Poison, 'What room you staying in?' Then they'd sign tons of shit off on his room. I'd be going, 'God, is this really happening?'"

The band indulged in more than iced tea and tips, as Carr would learn during the trips he made to Los Angeles every six weeks or so. "It was the early days of cell phones, so the Beasties would walk around with these, like, walkie talkies and call each other, from one side of the bar to the other. And they all had unbelievable cars. These guys dove headfirst into the LA car culture. But everything they had was that way."

Capitol received an early warning of this attitude. One of the band's first official acts after signing to the label was to commandeer a conference room and arrange a phony "video casting call" to meet girls. "The record isn't even conceived of at this point," recalls Dike. "But what could be better than having 500 hot chicks show up in their bikinis?" The Beasties and their producers watched the aspirants dance to some of Matt Dike and the Dust Brothers' instrumentals, while seated at a table, "drunk, with huge joints, and stacks of money in front of us," Dike says.[4]

Such conspicuous consumption, combined with the Beasties' already larger-than-life image, quickly made them the toast of Los Angeles. "They were treated like gods," says photographer Ricky Powell, often referred to at the time as "The Fourth Beastie." "Wherever they went. Clubs, parties—you name it. They had a lot of female admirers, and a lot of male groupies, too."

Powell would be flown to California many times, one of several old friends—like Sean Carasov, Cey Adams and Max Perlich—who remained part of the band's inner circle. But the group was rapidly building an influential new group of acquaintances as well. "These kids were actors and musicians," Adams remembers, "the sons and daughters of Hollywood royalty." Among them were Balthazar Getty, the grandson of billionaire

J. Paul Getty; Mick Fleetwood's daughter Amy; and Karis Jagger, daughter of Mick.

"None of these kids had jobs, and they all had these huge houses and were driving these fancy cars," marvels Adams. "I was just amazed at the amount of wealth."

Two others who drifted into the Beasties' orbit were the children of folk singer Donovan: his son, musician Donovan Leitch Jr., and his actress daughter, Ione Skye. Leitch remembers 1988 as "a 24-hour party," beginning with leisurely breakfasts—"You never went with less than ten people," he says—where the band and its friends would map out the day. There were pool parties, frequent road trips to Lake Arrowhead and Joshua Tree National Park, and nights of clubbing at Matt Dike–affiliated spots like Enter the Dragon and Dirt Box.

Adam Yauch and John King, meanwhile, would frequently depart in the wee hours for some skiing. "Set the cruise control on the Mercedes to over 100 in the middle of the night, heading to Mammoth," recalls King. "Then, since the snow sucked there, we took off to Tahoe or Snowbird, which was awesome."

All this recreation, funded by Capitol, was helping the Beastie Boys recover the sanity lost during the last days of *Licensed to Ill*. But it was little wonder that the new album was taking shape at a less-than-frantic pace. Even the group's afternoon writing sessions at the Mondrian, work "which involved a good deal of red wine and marijuana," according to Mike Simpson, would soon become dominated by one of the Beasties' favorite sports. "We noticed that every day at a certain time, people would line up outside the Comedy Store, which is right across the street. So, someone—I don't know who—had the idea that it might be fun to throw eggs at these people. So it sort of became a daily ritual."

"One night . . . there was a line of people waiting to see Billy Crystal. And the Beasties went up on the roof, and lobbed from across the street. So these things hit like boulders," says Tim Carr. "And the Comedy Store called the Mondrian, and the Mondrian security and the police were there. And nobody was taking any blame for anything."

The egging would spread to drive-by excursions throughout downtown Los Angeles, and it even inspired a new song, "Egg Man." "There was a certain amount of research going into all these stunts," Carr admits with a smile. "But they knew no bounds."

The Mondrian staff would address the mounting disturbances in a "very politically correct letter" to the band. "It said that there were complaints of things falling out their window, and that if there was a problem with the window, they could have maintenance come up and address it," recalls Simpson. "It was just hysterically funny."

The man who would have to answer for the Beasties, Tim Carr, was beginning to disagree.

* * *

"It would be great, you know, if we could all just go to work every day and say, OK, we're gonna work in the studio from one o'clock until dah-dah-dah, and we're gonna finish the album in two months," Michael Diamond would tell a radio interviewer in 1989. "But it never works like that. . . . You might go for two weeks and get one day of work done. But that one day of work is very special, for very special people like ourselves."

It would be hard to better summarize the work habits of these very special people during the summer of 1988. The days ran together in Matt Dike's sweltering apartment as the seven collaborators tried out new ideas and foreign substances. Not surprisingly, that combination lengthened the sessions appreciably. An insider recalls that Adam Yauch, who often took the creative lead, "would drive everyone bananas" with his suggestions. "He'd take mushrooms and say, 'OK, let's run the whole mix through a guitar stompbox!' And you'd think, 'Will somebody fucking kill this guy?'" The band's drug use, by rock-star standards, was fairly benign. "Wine and weed" were the primary vices, according to Mario Caldato, who not-quite-jokingly calls the group's "friendly dealer, Hippie Steve," a major influence on *Paul's Boutique*. And to Ione Skye, the Beastie Boys' smoking and 'shrooming seemed worlds away from the heroin nightmares surrounding her boyfriend Anthony Kiedis's band, the Red Hot Chili Peppers. "It just seemed so much more fun, and less dark, around the Beasties," she says.

Another observer from the time adds, "People ask, do drugs ever help you create art? I'd have to say, listen to *Paul's Boutique*."

Which was exactly what Tim Carr wanted to do. Unfortunately, he couldn't. "Because they didn't finish anything!" he recalls. "Still at this point, 'Shake Your Rump' and 'Dust Joint' were the best tracks. And it was just like, fuck it, what is going on here?"

Part of the problem was that the Beasties, free to find a new direction, were no longer sure what to write about. This, contends Diamond, was not a situation unique to *Paul's Boutique*. "On every record we've had that. We sit down and we look at each other: 'OK, what the fuck are we gonna say now?'" The dilemma this time, however, was pronounced enough that Matt Dike remembers: "We had to write some of the lyrics for those guys when they first came out here, because they had such writer's block. I have some notebooks of things we suggested, just to get things moving."

While he waited, Carr amused himself by browsing the collector's fantasyland in Dike's apartment. The half-million records were the centerpiece, but there was also plentiful seventies memorabilia, nestled alongside valuable paintings by the likes of Dike's old boss, Jean-Michel Basquiat. "He just knew exactly what was the right stuff to have," Carr says admiringly of Dike. "The coolest Ohio Players album cover next to a Haring, for example."

That aesthetic, which dovetailed perfectly with the Beasties' own retro leanings, would heavily inform *Paul's Boutique*, as well as the band's future business venture, Grand Royal. And Carr appreciated that *something* was going on amidst all the tokes and tokens of a bygone age. It was just hard to say what. "This beat would go into this beat, but you never knew what was gonna come out of it. The Beasties had notebooks and notebooks, but each page began a new rhyme," Carr recalls. "The Dust Brothers were, like, splitting the atom. But it all existed as a thousand petri dishes."

Because the band was recording at Matt Dike's, with almost no real instruments, the potential savings were immense. But the Beasties were "still spending $30,000 to $40,000 a month," Carr says, with no manager to help rein in the multiple excesses—like the rental cars Horovitz kept crashing "doing those 'Streets of San Francisco'–type jumps, where you go over a hill and airborne," remembers Donovan Leitch with a chuckle.

Carr was, he admits, having the time of his life. His Midwestern common sense, however, was tingling. "It really felt like a freight train running out of control, downhill, heading toward the wall. And there was nothing I could do to stop it."

Yet the Dust Brothers, Dike and Caldato, who were pushing their equipment well past its boundaries, couldn't go fast enough. When *Paul's Boutique* was released, it became fashionable to compare the album to *Sgt. Pepper's* because of its evident ambition and air of psychedelia. What few critics realized was another, more pertinent, parallel. Just as George Martin and the Beatles had taken four-track recording as far as it could go on their 1967 magnum opus, the team behind *Paul's Boutique* was testing the absolute limits of still-embryonic technologies like computer recording and automation.

Looping and layering samples that synchronize perfectly has since become a simple task for anyone with a computer. In 1989, the process was laborious. "Basically, we would find a groove, and we would loop it, and then we would print that to tape, and we would just go for five minutes on one track of the tape," Simpson recalls. "And then we would find another loop, and we would spend hours getting that second loop to sync up with the first loop, and then once we had it in sync, we would print that for five minutes on another track. And we would just load up the tape like that.

"And once we had filled up the tape with loops, we would go in, and Mario had this early, early, mixing board that had this very primitive form of automation. It was pretty complex, but if you knew which tracks you wanted playing at any given time, you typed the track numbers into this little Commodore computer hooked up to the mixing board. And each time you wanted a new track to come in, you'd have to type it in manually. It was just painful. It took so long. And there was so much trial and error . . . there was no visual interface to show you what was going on. That was the main difficulty we faced."

The Dust Brothers' secret weapon—"without it, we would not have been able to make records"—was a device called the J. L. Cooper PPS-1. It converted the two forms of time code commonly used by musicians, MIDI and SMPTE, back and forth; this electronic dialogue allowed loops to be synchronized to tape. Although crucial to their work, the Dust Brothers grew to hate the gadget. "It was a little piece of shit box that looked like it was made as a high school metal shop project," Simpson says with some asperity. "And it wasn't a thing that worked every time, either. It was a finicky little machine."

While those struggles were taking place in the seedier part of Hollywood, there was also unrest not far away within the Capitol Tower. In a harbinger of the music business's turbulent, merger-happy nineties, the EMI Music Group—Capitol's parent—had reached outside the industry in May 1988 and hired former General Mills executive Jim Fifield to head the company. The move would begin a new era of corporate accountability, in which "the suits" would assume greater control of decisions, and the bottom line would trump artistic considerations.

It was ominous news for Capitol executives David Berman and Joe Smith, then into the second, "prove-it" year of a three-year deal, and badly needing to justify their risky expenditure on the Beasties. Smith would set the label's new agenda soon afterward: "Our careers, our salaries, our future, is ours to win or lose in this next year," he told employees at Capitol's 1988 annual convention. "I want you to leave here with a sense of urgency, a sense of intensity, a sense of determination, and even a little desperation."

The A&R man who represented the only real link between Capitol and the Beastie Boys was feeling the desperation. At times, Carr simply adopted an if-you-can't-beat-'em approach. Knowing the band's fondness for egg-related jokes, he once bought dozens of the plastic egg-shaped containers that held L'Eggs pantyhose and filled them with Velveeta cheese, then booby-trapped the Beasties' hotel rooms. But soon afterward, Carr received a forceful reminder that he was certainly not in his charges' league as a prankster.

"They went to the afterparty of the MTV Music Awards, and they had Mario dressed as a security guard," Carr remembers. "Then they found a stairwell with a balcony, and they went upstairs, and Mario wouldn't let anybody in. So then it became this private party, inside the party, and people like Cyndi Lauper would come by and go, 'What's up there?' And Mario would say, 'The Beastie Boys are having a private party up there.' And they'd say, 'Can I go up there?' And he'd say, 'I don't know. Are you on their list?'

"So then Arsenio Hall wants to come up, and Mike says, 'See if you can borrow $100 from Arsenio, Mario.' So Mario says, 'I know this is weird, but Mike D wants to borrow $100. Would that be OK?' And Arsenio looks around and goes, 'Yo, man, you gotta be shittin' me.' And Mario goes, 'I wish I was, but he's pretty serious.' So Arsenio gives $100 to Mario. Then afterwards, Mike comes down and talks to Arsenio, and Arsenio says, 'What about that hundred?' And Mike goes, 'What hundred?'"[5]

Carr boarded a plane for New York the next day, still amazed at how the Beastie Boys had made fools of so many of their music industry peers. Whether he and Capitol were next on the list was something he tried to put out of his mind.

* * *

The G-Spot has entered Beastie Boys lore as the house that allowed them to indulge their deepest, darkest blaxploitation fantasies. It is imagined as a mansion-slash-museum of perfectly preserved seventies chic, which the band and its associates would thoughtlessly trash in orgy after *Licensed to Ill*–inspired orgy.

In fact, an argument can be made that the one-bedroom house on Torreyson Drive, owned by Alex and Marilyn Grasshoff, actually provided the Beastie Boys some much-needed stability at a time when *Paul's Boutique* was threatening to get lost in a morass of recreational drug use and hotel bills. If nothing else, the $11,000 rent the band paid each month still beat the cost of three $200-a-night hotel rooms. "It never had occurred to us that you don't have to live in a hotel," admits Diamond with a laugh. "But I think we had all become more serious about thinking, 'OK, we've gotta finish this record.'"

The property offered a view of all the major movie studios and the Griffith Observatory, while the band's neighbors would have included actress Sharon Stone; the old Errol Flynn estate (later owned by singer Justin Timberlake), was close by on Mullholland Drive. A less glitzy, but still important, benefit was the large gold "G" on the front of the house, making the location's new nickname both perfect and inevitable.

When they attempted to rent from the Grasshoffs, the Beasties' reputation—for once—did not fully precede them. As Marilyn Grasshoff remembers it, "The agent didn't tell us anything about the Beastie Boys. He said they were three young men who were writers."

The Grasshoffs would soon learn the rest of the story. "When I said, 'The Beastie Boys are living in my home,' people said, 'Oh my gosh, you let them in your home?!' Because they had made this movie where they trashed this house," says Mrs. Grasshoff. Once again, "Fight for Your Right (To Party)"—via its video—had come back to haunt the band. "And of course, I don't watch those kinds of movies, so it made me a little nervous. Maybe we made a mistake."

It was not as if the Grasshoffs were unworldly rubes. Alex Grasshoff was a producer and director who had helmed episodes of "The Rockford Files," and "ChiPs," as well as several films, including the Emmy-winning 1973 documentary *Journey to the Outer Limits*. His wife, better known under her stage name Madelyn Clark, owned a Los Angeles studio, which A-list musicians would often rent for tour rehearsals.

The couple, who traveled frequently, also had experience turning their home over to showbiz personalities. Actor Bill Murray had lived at the Grasshoffs' in 1980 while playing gonzo writer Hunter S. Thompson in the film *Where the Buffalo Roam*. (Thompson himself stayed in the guesthouse.) And even rocker Jon Bon Jovi had once been a tenant, pleasantly surprising Mrs. Grasshoff with his tidiness and good manners. "He was very good to the house," she recalls.

Speculation to the contrary, she would say the same of the Beasties. "What happened was, they were absolutely clean and neat," she says, "and took care of the place very, very well."[6]

Of course, the Grasshoffs were also not aware of the activities taking place in their absence. The foremost attraction happened to be Mrs. Grasshoff's closet, which yielded, as Ricky Powell remembers, "Crazy, crazy seventies shit. Fur coats. Crazy pimp hats. Platforms. Lots and lots of velvet." Mike Simpson, who also got a good look at the collection, observes, "I don't think she ever threw anything away." It was this gold mine of a wardrobe that would give the Beasties—in particular, Mike D—much of their retro look for the *Paul's Boutique* era.

The trio managed to get a Ping-Pong table into the house—chipping Mr. Grasshoff's Emmy Award in the process. They also made frequent use of the home theater system, rare for its time, and what Mike Simpson remembers as Mr. Grasshoff's "huge collection of prison movies." Simpson and John King, who had access to the house even when the Beasties were away, spent as much time there as possible.

"Despite the fact that John and I had success from the Tone-Loc and Young MC records, we still hadn't seen a dime. We were sharing a $600-a-month apartment, and we had to step over bums to get into our building, and we were digging in our couches for loose change to buy a burrito at 7-Eleven," Simpson recalls, laughing. "So the G-Spot offered a lot of luxuries that we weren't accustomed to." Yet the only truly crazy thing King noticed there "was a bunch of late teen/early twenties kids hanging out in such a mackadocious—yet dated—pad, partying."

"They didn't trash the place the way they trashed a lot of other places," admits regular guest Sean Carasov, who had seen more than a few accommodations wrecked by the Beasties. "But they *worked* it."[7]

Although Diamond commandeered the home's master suite, while Yauch set up shop in the video room, it would be Horovitz's underground bedroom in the guesthouse, with its window into the swimming pool, that became the G-Spot's best-known feature. Ricky Powell would shoot the inner sleeve photo of *Paul's Boutique* through this porthole, capturing the Beasties clowning underwater. Back on land, however, they were about to get serious.

* * *

After months of incubation in their thousand petri dishes, the songs that would comprise *Paul's Boutique* reached maturity in surprisingly short order. All during the late fall of 1988, the album's creators buckled down; by Christmas, when Tim Carr returned to California for a progress report, the record was almost completely written and recorded.

The track that had turned things around, Carr thought, was "High Plains Drifter." Based on a large, ominous chunk of The Eagles' "These Shoes," it was less complex than many of the creations that surrounded it, and its true-crime verses were written "from beginning to end, based around a really interesting set of samples. And all of sudden they had this complete song." It was a psychological boost—for the beleaguered Carr, at least.

One factor that helped the project overcome its rough patches, Matt Dike thought, was the Beasties' unusual closeness. "I don't think I've ever seen 'em fight," he muses. "They could fuck with anybody else, but they knew just when to give each other space." It was a friendship that even survived what could have been a traumatic romantic dispute, when Yauch began dating Lisa Ann Cabasa, who had gone out a few times with Horovitz. "Yauch had asked him if it was OK to call me, and he said, 'No, it's not OK,'" recalls Cabasa with a laugh. "I didn't wanna be a Yoko Ono, so we kept it hidden for a while."[8]

The work done in Matt Dike's apartment during this period is now "all kind of a blur," confesses Mike Simpson, who still has to hum several songs to remember their titles. No other collaborator offers a clearer recollection. "After we did the first two songs," says Mario Caldato, "there was a break, then it went full-on till we finished."

Most likely, the ingredients Simpson once listed as essential to the making of *Paul's Boutique*—"a blue bong, high quality indica buds, hash, hash oil, freebase, red wine, cigarettes, LSD, coffee and whippets"—have a lot to do with everyone's hazy memories. What is certain is that Capitol's executives, who had the album on the label's spring 1989 release schedule, were finally demanding to hear the music. Carr was dispatched to get it, but instead received proof of that age-old saw about payback being a mother.

"I go there and I say, 'I gotta hear it.' And they say, 'We can't give it to you, but you can hear it,'" Carr recalls. "And Yauch says to me, 'Yo Tim, can I have your key? I need to stuff this joint.' So I give him the hotel key, he stuffs the joint and slaps it back in my hand. And someone says, 'Hey Mike, why don't you drive Tim around?'"

The ride that followed, around the holiday-lit streets of Los Angeles, gave Carr the Christmas present he'd wanted most. "I listen to what they have, which is basically all of the basic tracks for *Paul's Boutique*. I feel this sigh of relief—it's so great," he remembers. "All of the samples are underneath the perfect rhymes, and it's this perfect mixture of New York memorabilia and hip-hop knowledge."

The warm and fuzzy feelings ended the moment he returned to the Mondrian. "I realize I don't have my room key. And I go, Oh, *shit*.'" Carr's L'Eggs prank of months before now seemed like foolishly stirring up a hornet's nest.

After getting another key, Carr would find his room completely destroyed, the handiwork of Horovitz and Yauch. "They had even taken the phone cord from the receiver, so I couldn't call out. I was like, 'These thorough fuckers! I have learned my lesson. I will never, ever, play you boys again!'"

* * *

With the album nearing completion, the Dust Brothers had been instructed to submit to Mike D a list of all the samples used. What happened afterward depends on who you ask.

Sample clearance is the greyest of the many grey areas surrounding *Paul's Boutique*. Finding someone involved with the album willing to fully discuss the dozens, if not hundreds, of samples used to create it,[9] is impossible. It is easy to understand why.

At the time, the Beasties had already been targeted in one sampling-related lawsuit; in 1987, they settled out of court with musician Jimmy Castor, who sued the band for a sample used in "Hold It Now, Hit It." A pair of further, high-profile lawsuits against hip-hop acts De La Soul and Biz Markie would not stop sampling, but they helped set guidelines for sample usage, and insured sample clearance would no longer be optional.

In addition, the Beasties would later endure a long legal battle with jazz musician James Newton, over a sample used on the 1994 song "Flute Loop." (The sample had been cleared, but Newton wanted publishing rights as well.) The band would win the suit, but at the cost of a half-million dollars in legal fees.

It may well be understood that the samples on *Paul's Boutique* are now exempt from litigation, as Adam Yauch explained to *Wired* in 2004: "If ten years have gone by or whatever it is, and there hasn't been a problem, then it's not an issue." But Adam Horovitz's response—"At least that's what we're hoping"—reflects the uncertainty of that claim.

Thus, Caldato begs off discussing samples—"It might not be cool"—while Mike Simpson offers, "I know lots and lots of samples cleared, and I know some samples didn't clear." Tim Carr, on the other hand, counters that "none of the samples were cleared, as far as I know. But in that day, drums weren't part of sample clearance, and now they are." Later, Carr amends his statement: "They cleared what they had to clear."

In a 2002 interview with *Tape Op* magazine, Caldato recalled the band paying a quarter-million dollars in sample clearances for *Paul's Boutique*. Mike Simpson also remembers that when he and John King received their first royalty statement for the record, "there was a huge deduction for sample clearances." And Diamond contends it was the first hip-hop album where an attempt was made to clear every sample.

What all parties involved agree upon is that an album like *Paul's Boutique* would be all but impossible to make today. "You could do it as an art project, if somebody gave you a couple million dollars to make a record like this," muses Mike Simpson. "But commercially, I don't think you could ever do it again."

Yet that, says Matt Dike, was part of the plan from the beginning. "I remember having this discussion with Yauch, and him saying, 'Let's just go completely over the top and sample everything. Let's make this the nail in the coffin for sampling,'" Dike remembers. "And that's kind of what happened. Some of those tracks are total plagiarism of the worst kind, but that's what's funny about that record. It's like 'Hey, we're ripping you off!'"

"Sometimes," he adds with a laugh, "those guys could be pretty profound."

Notes

1. American Expressionist painter Paul Henry Brach.
2. Diamond professes not to remember what made the group sign with Capitol. "I have to think, the paper was better," he says. "John, Paul, George and Ringo gave them more bank than New Edition gave MCA, I guess."
3. That same night, Carr would run into Simmons again at Frankie Jackson's Soul Kitchen. Simmons ignored Carr, but Carr would rationalize this to a friend: "He just doesn't recognize me with my clothes on."
4. "The record was started when we did it," Diamond counters, groaning at the memory, "but that doesn't make it any less dubious, or wrong."
5. For the record, Diamond and Caldato remember this story differently. "I gave Arsenio $100 from the Beasties," Caldato says, "and told his bodyguard they wanted to talk to him." File Carr's anecdote under "If it isn't true, it oughtta be."
6. However, the Beasties would be the last tenants to rent the Grasshoffs' home. The band had wanted to extend the lease, Marilyn Grasshoff recalls, "but my husband said, 'No, I want to come back home.'" The trio would still recall the Grasshoffs fondly in the 1998 song "The Grasshopper Unit (Keep Movin')," comparing the couple to Thurston and "Lovey" Howell from "Gilligan's Island."
7. Perhaps the worst bit of damage the band inflicted on the G-Spot, however, wound up having a unexpectedly beneficial effect. A wooden gate, smashed into by Mike D's car, would be repaired by Caldato's friend Mark Ramos-Nishita—later a valuable musical collaborator as the keyboardist Money Mark.
8. However, soon afterward, Horovitz began dating Ione Skye, with whom he'd been infatuated for months. Skye, who was still living with Anthony Kiedis, had tried to avoid Horovitz, "but it was clear we were gonna end up together." The pair was married for most of the nineties; despite a very public split, Skye still calls Horovitz "the love of my life."
9. Over the years, the Dust Brothers have hazarded several different guesses as to the correct number of samples used; Mike Simpson now says he simply has no idea. His best estimate is "between 100 and 300."

Doolittle

by Ben Sisario

Ben Sisario writes about music and culture for *The New York Times*, teaches at the Tisch School of the Arts at New York University, and is a commentator on the New York public radio station WFUV. He lives in New York City.

1

April 2005. On a brisk spring morning in downtown Eugene, Oregon, the canary-yellow steel hulk of a 1986 Cadillac glides up to the entrance of my hotel like some combination of gondola and cargo ship. The motor purrs unhurriedly as I approach the window and see the driver sitting stiffly upright, his right arm extended over the passenger seat and a look of blank pride on his moon-shaped face. He does not gesture or speak, but the message is clear. The big man is here in the big car. Get in and come along on a journey.

Charles Thompson, aka Black Francis, aka Frank Black, pulls onto the road as we begin a three-day weekend of interviews that take place mostly in his car, cruising aimlessly through the pristine open landscape of western Oregon, where he has lived, in various spots, for the last couple of years. The man who made his reputation with a blood-freezing scream, singing about slicing up eyeballs, about grunting whores and waves of mutilation, is genial and chatty but remote, particularly about his old band, the Pixies. Where was *Doolittle*, the monument of alternative rock that is the band's crowning achievement and biggest seller, recorded? Don't remember. What was going on in his life at the time? Band, girlfriend. Whatever. All that is archaeology. Thompson has just turned forty and is in his first few months of fatherhood, a happy and doting dad. His girlfriend, Violet, threw him a surprise birthday party down in LA the week before, with old friends and stars—cool stars, not plastic-surgery stars: we're talking Jack Black, Polly Harvey, They Might Be Giants—and Thompson is still in the glow of it. He lives in Eugene for family considerations, but being in a quiet, suburban corner of the earth far away from the rock biz or anything having to do with the Pixies seems to suit him in his new life. He is like a great actor adapting to life offstage.

The Pixies' music is distant indeed; the best and most enduring of it was recorded in the waning years of the Reagan administration, a time when "alternative music" barely existed as a market classification. But Thompson is not really so far removed from the band, or the stage. A few months ago, just before the birth of his first son, Jack Errol, he returned home from the Pixies' reunion tour, one of the most significant comebacks in rock'n'roll history. Selling out halls and sheds and festivals from Indio, California, to New York City, from Saskatoon to Paris, it was highly profitable. When I first sat down with Thompson, in New York at the end of the 2004 tour, he mentioned, with no excessive enthusiasm, that it was fun to be back playing Pixies songs with his old bandmates. But he was unequivocal about one thing: "It's very nice to finally be making good money."

Thompson, Kim Deal, Joey Santiago, and David Lovering well deserved their payday. But they were also returning to claim a big slice of the rock-history pie, one that had long been out of reach. As the Pixies, they have had a most unusual career. The archetypal college band, they were a not-quite-next-big-thing who played sold-out gigs everywhere they went and were festooned with critical praise, but were aborted while still young and still far from the top of the charts. Then a weird thing happened. Throughout the 1990s their posthumous legend grew and grew, and they emerged as one of the most admired and namechecked bands of the decade of alternative rock. They became gods in absentia.

With modest but steady record sales and a never-ending stream of tributes from other musicians, but a murky legacy that left no clear school of descendants, the Pixies represented a peculiar pinnacle of the art of rock'n'roll. They played bitingly melodic miniatures, little spasms barbed with noise and Surrealistic lyrics. There was scant precedent for the prickly kind of pop the Pixies played, and their sound is recognizable on the slightest whiff. It's a series of opposing forces that fit together incongruously but exquisitely: a bouncy yet firm bassline (Deal called it "boingy-boingy-sproingy") joined to a demented choir of punky guitars; Thompson's harsh primal scream beside Deal's coy and smoky harmonies; explosive, grating riffs in songs crafted from prime bubblegum. Behind it all is Thompson's songwriting, playful but also insular, inscrutable.

Thompson is a master puzzlemaker, and he has made no puzzle greater than *Doolittle*. Released in April 1989, it marked the midpoint of the Pixies' career and was their first to be released on a major label, Elektra. Their exhilarating previous album, *Surfer Rosa*, had established the band as one of the brightest lights in underground rock, but *Doolittle* improved on it, showing the intricacy, depth, and breadth of vision they were capable of. It is deliberately both attractive and repellent, a pleasure that makes you squirm—a trick Thompson picked up from two of his heroes, Luis Buñuel and David Lynch, the masters, decades apart, of Surrealist film.

Doolittle is, on one hand, among the most violent pop albums ever recorded, if not in body count then in the starkness of its calamities. It features rape, mutilation of the eyes, vampirism, suffocation, smothering by tons of garbage, and the chaos of blind gunfire; for the punch line, everybody gets crushed to death. When not killing or maiming, the album turns to depraved sexual loathing and visions of apocalypse. And yet, even with its shrieks and its squalls, it is one of the most tuneful and lovable albums in the canon of alternative rock, and Thompson has spent the better part of two decades insisting to journalists that there is no real meaning to all the horror and dread, that the lyrics are just words that fit together nicely. "There is no point," he says. "The point is to experience it, to enjoy it, to be entertained by it."

History will eventually sort out how important or unimportant the reunion was to the meaning of the Pixies. Nineteen eighty-nine, besides giving us *Doolittle*, was also a landmark year for rock bands returning from the grave—the Rolling Stones, the Who, the Allman Brothers, the Doobie Brothers, and members of Yes were all reassembled—and a smart person then might have predicted that the naked greed revealed in such a masquerade would forever tarnish a band's memory. That person would have been half-wrong, because *Who's Next* still kicks my ass every time I hear it, no matter how much of a pathetic whore Roger Daltrey becomes with age. (Before you complain, did you see him as Ebenezer Scrooge in Madison Square Garden's musical version of *A Christmas Carol* in 1998, as I did?) But he would have been half-right, too, because every time "Bargain" is used in a car commercial I die a little.

Back in the *Steel Wheels/Join Together* era, the reunion tour seemed a cynical effort at brand preservation, a way for dinosaurs from the 60s and 70s (and whatever corporate entities stood behind them) to retain a moneymaking hold on popular culture. But by the time the Pixies got back together, the idea of the reunion itself was being transformed. A number of important revivals were taking place on a smaller scale, as Mission of Burma, Gang of Four, Wire, the Buzzcocks, and Dinosaur Jr. all had exciting and surprisingly fruitful second (or third) runs; many, in fact, wound up releasing records, and not-half-bad ones at that. Their success served as an oblique rewriting of rock history, a delayed canonization: once marginal, these groups had accrued a significance that was now unquestionable.

The Pixies' reunion topped them all. In their time they barely cracked the top 100 of the Billboard album chart and got only minimal attention from the mainstream press in the United States (though in Britain and Europe they had a much easier time), but now, years later, were being received as major rock heroes. It was a heartwarming change. Throughout the 80s and 90s, it had been an unspoken rite of faith in underground music to believe that there was a meritocratic alternate universe in which groups like the Pixies were the superstars, the ones who made triumphant comeback tours before crowds of thousands, and that albums like *Doolittle* should be celebrated as masterpieces. It's thrilling and just that this long-held belief has been confirmed.

Some of us knew it all along.

* * *

Thompson lives with Violet and their growing family in a large but unpretentious house in the hills around Eugene, with a wide view over the city and the fresh, green Oregon horizon. It looks like a fertile spot, a good place to begin again, and he shows the place off like the proud new father and homeowner he is. His half brother, just out of college, is painting the kitchen a funky earth tone, and Thompson talks with excitement about the remodeling work he's going to have done. "Gonna tear all this out, have a great unobstructed view. What do we need this balcony for? Not really practical for little kids anyway." He speaks with a mixture of ordinary American domesticity and rock-star elitism. "Honey, do you know where that David Cross birthday DVD greeting is? Dammit, maybe we were watching it upstairs." There is a huge framed poster of Jacques Tati's 1958 film *Mon Oncle* in striking crimson and a stylish collection of midcentury modern furniture. But besides the scratched, punctured acoustic guitar propped up in the middle of the living room, there are few visible reminders of the Pixies.

Though the house was surely paid for with Pixies tour receipts, the biggest reminder of the band might be Thompson's car. He bought it in 1989, the year of *Doolittle*, with his first royalty check. He got $16,000, he says, and paid $13,000 cash for the thing. The band, founded in Boston a few months after he and Santiago dropped out of college, had existed for only about three years at that point, but was already beginning to fall apart. On January 1, 1990, Thompson packed up the Cadillac and left Boston with his then-girlfriend (and now ex-wife), Jean, heading to Los Angeles at a leisurely pace. He had a CB radio installed in Memphis (he chose a handle, Big Daddy Caddy, but never used it), and stopped here and there to play some gas-money solo gigs. With the others scattered around the country and a growing case of "tension"—that catchall band disease—the Pixies recorded two more albums, *Bossanova* in 1990 and *Trompe le Monde* in 1991, before Thompson buried the band by fax on January 1, 1993. He had other things on his mind, including a solo career as Frank Black that, at least through 2005, encompasses ten albums.

He had his own music on his mind right up until the Pixies reunion in April 2004. In the days before the tour began, Thompson recorded a set of gentle, confessional songs in Nashville with star R&B players including Steve Cropper and Spooner Oldham. The material from those sessions, released in July 2005 as *Honeycomb*, is about 10,000 light-years from his old band. But it didn't take him long to turn around. When he finished those recordings, Thompson headed up to Minneapolis for the first Pixies gig in twelve years, driving all the way in his yellow Cadillac.

2

The Pixies had existed for barely two years when they began to work on *Doolittle*, and things had moved fast. They had come together in the most prosaic way a band can—through a classified ad in the local weekly. In early 1986, Charles Thompson and Joey Santiago, recent dropouts from the University of Massachusetts at Amherst, were newly installed in Boston and looking to form a band, but lacked a bassist and a drummer. Their listing in the Boston *Phoenix* was jokey though not so aesthetically inaccurate: seeking female bassist into Hüsker Dü and Peter, Paul & Mary. "Charles put that ad out," Santiago says now, "and when he showed it to me, I go, that's perfect, that'll weed out the, um. . . . Whoever calls is gonna have good taste. They're gonna get it. You know. Turns out we only had one call."

The respondent was Kim Deal, a toothy former cheerleader from Dayton, Ohio, who had just moved to Boston with her new husband, John Murphy. She came over to Charles's apartment and they played through some nascent Pixies songs over hummus. And though she was four years older than Joey and Charles, and played guitar instead of bass, she got the job. ("I'd played guitar before," she said, "so I figured, 'Four strings—no problem.'") But they still needed that drummer. They tried and failed to recruit Kim's twin sister, Kelley. She flew out from Dayton "to have a talk and a listen to the songs in consideration of her playing (and learning) the drums," Thompson remembers.

After at least one more false start, Kim remembered another drummer: David Lovering, a square-jawed former Radio Shack co-worker of her hubby's, whom she had met at their wedding reception. Lovering, the only Bostonian among them, was a gearhead and a Rush fan, but he was a monster behind the kit, and that's all that mattered. The lineup was complete by July 1986, and they headed to Lovering's parents' garage in the suburbs for rehearsals. Within fifteen months their first record was out and journalists were flying over from England.

* * *

Thompson and Santiago had been assigned to the same dorm suite their freshman year at UMass. Thompson was there to study anthropology; Santiago remained without a major as long as the university would let him, whereupon he settled on a tough one, economics. Both arrived at school eager to start a band, but not just any band—had to be Original. "I didn't want to do any covers whatsoever," Santiago says. "I always wanted to make something different."

As decisive as he may have been about his rock ambitions, Santiago did not bring his guitar to school that first semester. He had been too studious, he says, or maybe just too shy. Born in the Philippines, the third of six sons of an anesthesiologist, he came to the United States when he was seven. After two years in Yonkers, New York, the Santiagos settled in Longmeadow, Massachusetts, a leafy and affluent suburb of rust-belt Springfield. Joe grew up as the deepest kind of teenage rock nerd, naming his first computer program Iggy and his second computer program Pop. He seems to have never lost the caught-in-the-headlights eyes and nervous half-smile that peers out from so many Pixies photographs. Even today, rounding forty and establishing himself in Los Angeles as a composer of commercial music—he landed a gig doing the music for the cable TV series *Weeds* during the reunion tour, and recorded the music in the breaks between concerts—he has a silent, boyish anxiety, hovering around me with shoulders drawn inward as we wait for coffee at a Starbucks near his studio.

Charles Michael Kittredge Thompson IV had none of his suitemate's timidness. He was born in Boston and his parents separated twice by the time he was in the first grade. His family moved back and forth between Massachusetts and Southern California repeatedly throughout his childhood, first with his natural father, a no-nonsense publican who tried business out West for a while before settling down in Cape Cod, and later with his mother and stepfather, a religious man who "pursued real estate on both coasts." In California, when Charles was about twelve, his mother and stepfather joined a church with ties to the evangelical Assemblies of God, and "also attended other services here and there, including of the Pentecostal variety," he says. Young Charles drank up the fire-and-brimstone oratory, and by his early teens had absorbed a concordanceful of Old Testament drama. The Sunday school indoctrinations would fade from his conscience, but the lessons of charismatic storytelling would not. "Bible stories are great!" he told the *NME* in 1988. "Everything you want: sex, violence, it's all there. Brutal, too. The hardcore stuff, whoooo, that stuff'd make *spicy* movies." At a religious summer camp around age thirteen he saw a performance by Larry Norman, the Gregg Allman of Christian rock, whose catchphrase was "come on, pilgrim!"

Other scenes from youth have passed into the Charles Thompson apocrypha: how his family encountered a UFO while driving through Nebraska when he was an infant, how as a teenager he received vocal instruction from a Thai former rock star—his neighbor or his employer, the stories vary—who encouraged him to "scream it like you hate that bitch!" Perhaps they're true, perhaps not, although Thompson has told the stories himself. What matters more is that they helped establish his persona as an Everydude, a pudgy blank slate who lacked the looks or poise or stage presence of any rock god yet matched them by force of screamy will.

* * *

One day first semester, Santiago happened to hear Thompson and his roommate screwing around on guitars. Charlie was strumming chords and the other guy was noodling in a blues scale, the traditional paint-by-numbers jam technique of the small-minded. Santiago was both excited and appalled. Anything but plain old blues scales! "That's exactly what I wanted to get away from," he says now. But it was enough to get him to retrieve his guitar from Mom's house forty minutes away, and soon he and Thompson were playing all kinds of non-blues-scale, non-cover-song rock.

As a guitarist Santiago was a self-conscious amateur—he still speaks of his "insecurity" on the instrument—but he had a few moves to bring to a dorm-room jam session. He had learned about rock'n'roll from checking out records at the local library—"the Springfield library, not the town library," he states, pausing with the surely-you-know-the-difference look of a true mole. He found Les Paul and Jimi Hendrix, who then led to Wes Montgomery, a pillar of jazz guitar. "And that's when I said, 'Ah, that's a hook,'" he says. "'That's some hooky stuff in this jazz world.' And that's how you do it, you just simplify it. Simplify the hell out of it." Among the tricks he picked up from Montgomery and Hendrix were "those octave thingies." (Santiago is a man of few words, and many of them are "thingy.") Via Hendrix, Santiago also culled a bluesy, dissonant chord, the dominant-7 sharp-9. Groin-thrustingly erotic in Hendrix's hands ("Purple Haze"), when it was played by Santiago, the shyest boy in the dorm, it tapped a hidden rage that matched the horror of Thompson's scream ("Tame").

Thompson had two off-campus experiences during his time at U-Mass that would provide ample inspiration for his songs. One was a summer archaeological dig in Arizona, where he found the bones of infants with jewels stuck in their ribs and teeth. The other was the six months he spent on an exchange program in Puerto Rico. There, while avoiding a "weird psycho gay roommate" who babbled frighteningly about receiving transmissions from Fred Flintstone, Thompson boned up on his Spanish, ate mucho rice 'n' beans, hung at the beach, and inhaled all the passions of a pungent Caribbean metropolis. He was there sans guitar, but the place—and the local Spanish dialect—long haunted his music. "Isla de Encanta" and "Vamos" from *Come On Pilgrim*, "Oh My Golly!" and "Where Is My Mind?" from *Surfer Rosa*, "Crackity Jones" from *Doolittle*, and the B-side "Bailey's Walk" all came directly from his time in Puerto Rico. "You're digging up the bones of Indians in Arizona," he says now, "it's romantic already. Just the whole setup, as opposed to writing about—what, how high school sucked? No, I'm gonna go for the archaeological dig and the streets of San Juan, Puerto Rico. These are independent-young-man experiences."

While on the *isla del encanto* (his *español* was a tad *imperfecto*), Thompson wrote Santiago a letter. Thompson's dad had offered to fuel his son's wanderlust by paying for a trip to New Zealand to see Halley's Comet on its passage in February 1986, but Thompson was itching for something else. "He wrote me saying he's coming back, but not to go to school," Santiago remembers. "This time, we should drop out and start the band." Santiago did not need a great deal of convincing. "I was like, sure. I've had it with this schedule."

In Boston, where both young men promptly got jobs in warehouses, Thompson lived alone in a studio apartment for a time, subsisting, he says, on a tape collection of Hüsker Dü, Iggy Pop, Captain Beefheart, and nothing else. (The Iggy component: *New Values* and the *I'm Sick of You* boot. "That thing's awesome," he says of the latter, still wide-eyed nineteen years later.) He began to amass a small heap of songs and was cranking out new ones all the time, writing in the bathroom, on the T, anywhere. But as working musicians, he and Santiago were impossibly green. When the Pixies lineup was completed and a gig finally booked, Thompson and Santiago realized they had no idea how long a set was supposed to last. Solution: they went out to some clubs and timed the bands. Turned out most of them played for about half an hour.

"I didn't have it all slicked out," Thompson says now. "I wasn't this super-confident guy with a zillion songs sitting down at open mic night every night. It wasn't like I was really established in a way that some people can be. The problem is that people think they're fully formed, but that form is lame. The form is mediocre. That form represents mediocrity, it represents cliché—it represents all the things that you don't want to be when you want to be an original. So I think that Joey being an unformed guitar player and me being an unformed songwriter, kinda lost but at the same time really driven, was a good thing."

* * *

Kim Deal and David Lovering were as unlikely a rhythm section as Charles and Joey were a Mick 'n' Keef. She was older, married, and had never played bass before. Lovering was her age, and though he was the only one with any kind of technical command of his instrument, his experience came from playing in jerkoff bands with names like Iz Wizard and Riff Raff. The upside to this, however, was that he was a drummer with Neil Peart chops who was willing to play in a band called the Pixies, which even the girl bassist admitted was kind of a sissy name.

Deal and Lovering brought something unusual for a college-rock band in the age of Sonic Youth and R.E.M.: a solid rhythm section. Lovering was a powerhouse, and his taste for flashy prog-metal gave him a precision and versatility essential to following Thompson's songwriting quirks. Deal's bass playing was steady if unremarkable at first, but she came to develop a buoyant style that matched her ever-present ear-to-ear. She played with a pick and kept budda-budda eighth notes like a rhythm guitarist—just like Dee Dee Ramone did, in fact. Deal's bass remained the most accessible aspect of the Pixies, and the lady herself, surrounded by young men who barely moved a muscle onstage, became the band's welcoming persona, its source of humor and bonhomie. She seemed tickled by the very idea of playing with these goofballs. In the early days Deal worked at a doctor's office—you had to call her there to book the band—and showed up to gigs in a long skirt and pumps while the menfolk dressed for a morning paper route.

Deal wound up with a variety of roles in the band, ranging from frat-house sister and journalist's loudmouth favorite ("First

I'm gonna piss like a racehorse," she told one charmed *NME* reporter during a night on the town in 1988, "then I'm gonna dance like a black woman") to underappreciated resource and designated antagonist. In time she and Thompson would openly clash; he resented the attention she got, and she griped that he wouldn't let her sing lead. Eventually, in 1990, the band had a big meeting with lawyers and such, in which Thompson had to be talked out of firing her. (Deal's side of the story is unknown to this reporter. She declined numerous requests to be interviewed for this book.)

Those clashes were still far off on Saturday, December 13, 1986, when the Pixies had one of their biggest early shows, opening a Throwing Muses homecoming gig at the Rathskeller, aka the Rat, the beloved Kenmore Square dive that had long been a dank hub of the Boston scene. ("Boston's CBGB," it was called more than once, and remained so until it closed in 1997.) The Muses, from Newport, Rhode Island, had just released their first album on the British boutique label 4AD and played in Europe—pretty major shit for a mid-80s indie girl band. During soundcheck the Pixies were seen by Gary Smith, the Muses' friend and sometime producer. The man was gobsmacked. "It was an otherworldly experience," he later wrote. "They had no parallel. They had no peer. They had no idea what the hell they were doing or that it could change everything." He told the band he wanted to record them at Fort Apache, a newish studio in the Roxbury section of Boston, and eventually booked a freezing three-day weekend there in March. (Smith was then the studio manager and eventually became a co-owner.) Thompson paid for the sessions with a $1,000 grant from his father—not the churchgoing stepfather but the Cape Cod barkeep, whose religious affiliation his son describes as "pagan, totally." (Dad's generosity was a form of recompense. "He wasn't around for a lot of my younger years," Thompson says, "so I think he was doing his best to make up for lost time.")

Smith recorded eighteen songs, put seventeen of them on a cassette with a purple cover and a post office box number on the back, and sent it all over the place. (The eighteenth cut, "Watch What You're Doing," was a cover of a song by Larry "come on, pilgrim" Norman, and has never been released. "I have the only copy of the recording," Smith says, "and, perhaps, by now, it's unplayable.") One copy of this Purple Tape landed with Ivo Watts-Russell of 4AD in London. Known for its slick, gauzy package design and quasi-gothic bands invariably described as "ethereal" (q.v. Cocteau Twins), the label did have an unpredictable streak. It had some success early on with the Birthday Party, who were anything but gauzy, and in 1987 the label scored a fluke hit with M/A/R/R/S's spacejam instrumental mix "Pump Up the Volume." The Pixies had an in. They were now being managed by Ken Goes, who also represented Throwing Muses, 4AD's first American signing and a new critical favorite on both sides of the Atlantic. But the boss did not capitulate immediately. "I was hesitant," Watts-Russell says now. At first blush the Pixies had seemed a tad too straight, too normal, "too rock'n'roll." He might have passed on them if not for the efforts of Deborah Edgeley, the label's publicist and his then girlfriend, whose subtle arguments persuaded him. "Don't be so fucking stupid," he says she told him. "We have to do it."

* * *

Watts-Russell picked eight songs from the Purple Tape for a mini-LP, called it *Come On Pilgrim* after a beguiling line in "Levitate Me" (no Christian-rock Bible camp for the young Ivo, apparently), and released it in October 1987. The week it came out Charles Thompson scoured Boston's record stores in vain—4AD had no American distribution, and it could be bought only as an import.

In honor of Iggy Pop, Thompson had chosen a vaudevillian stage name, Black Francis; his father had once made a gag, understood by nobody outside the bloodline, that he had been saving that name in case he had another son. Deal picked her own, calling herself Mrs. John Murphy as an ironic feminist joke. She stuck with it, on album jackets at least, until her divorce from Mr. Murphy a year or two later.

Smith and Watts-Russell began to hype the band with British journalists, and by the time *Come On Pilgrim* was released, with a cover photograph of a nauseatingly hirsute brute engulfed in Joel-Peter Witkin-esque sepia and blackness—if a free copy of that didn't catch the eye of a rock critic, nothing would—there was significant press interest. Reporters from the British weeklies began to trek their way to the Rat, where they were all charmed by twenty-two-year-old "chubby salt-of-the-earth avuncular poet" Charles Thompson. He was then first asked a question that would forever annoy him: What's with all the freaky lyrics about incest and stuff? "It's all those characters in the Old Testament. I'm obsessed with them. Why it comes out so much I don't know," he told the *Melody Maker*, already a little impatient. "I use the word 'motherfucker' in the way it was used 200 years ago; it's been devalued since." Anyway, he told them, the lyrics don't really mean anything. They're just words that sound good together. Like T. Rex.

To record the Pixies' first full LP, 4AD hired Steve Albini, the butcher of Big Black. He did it in Boston over a couple of weeks in December 1987, placing amps in the bathroom of the studio, Q Division, for that extra-harsh tile resonance. *Surfer Rosa*, released in March 1988, is the Pixies' version of a hardcore album, whose thirteen tracks seem not so much songs as quick and violent crimes. Thompson is a demon with a destroyed body, his voice a frantic whine punctuated by dick-in-a-bear-trap screams. Around him the guitars simply burn. The head rush of Side 1—"Bone Machine" to "River Euphrates"—is broken only by "Gigantic," Kim Deal's greatest moment with the Pixies, and perhaps ever. On its most obvious and enticing level, it is an unabashed praisesong to a well-endowed black man ("Gigantic! Gigantic! Gigantic! / A big, big love!"). But a commonly overlooked theme is its eroticized maternalism: Deal has said that an inspiration for the lyrics was the 1986 film *Crimes of the Heart*, in which Sissy Spacek plays a married woman who has an affair with a teenager. Deal's earthiness, her "sweet humanizing gravity," as Robert Christgau once put it, is the ideal counterbalance to Thompson's abstract ravings, and their interaction—not flirtatious per se, but not exactly brother and sister, either—is an emotional touchstone. Even Thompson's "you fuckin' die!" is directed, with dorky affection, at her.

The band did a short blitz through Europe—eighteen shows in twenty-four days beginning April 8—and got a madly, wonderfully, ego-strokingly rapturous response. "Pixies were welcomed like gods, which I felt was underestimating them somewhat," wrote the *Melody Maker*'s reviewer of their appearance at the Town and Country Club in London. Fans were reportedly pissing off the balconies in sheer *Caligula*like abandon. The weeklies went nuts, competing with each other to put the young band on the cover again and again. *Surfer Rosa* topped the indie charts there—on the NME's chart for the week of April 16, it was No. 1, while Throwing Muses, the Pixies' benefactor and the headliner of their joint tour, was at No. 2 with *House Tornado*—and was named album of the year by the *Melody Maker* and *Sounds*.

In America, Surfer Rosa was greeted with far fewer golden

showers. It was licensed for distribution to Rough Trade, whose retail penetration was minimal. The press response was positive but muted, a tone that would persist for much of the band's career. *Spin* gave it a nothin'-special 120-word review ("beautifully brutal"), though the magazine later chose the Pixies as musicians of the year. The *Village Voice* ran a nice spread on the album ("kicks like no pop record ever kicked"). But there was a sense that the Pixies were being greeted with a thud in their home country. In England they got long, thoughtful stories by leading writers. In America, *Musician* magazine called the album *Suffer Rosa*, *Rolling Stone* didn't review it, nor did it make it onto the annual Pazz & Jop critics' poll in the *Voice*, a survey of, that year, 212 of the country's most prominent music writers.

Still, not bad for four kids who had never set foot in a professional recording studio until a year before. After its victorious run in Europe, the band returned home and rounded out the middle of 1988 with gigs, gigs, gigs—Maxwell's, the 9:30 Club, and such in the U.S.; big halls with names like the Paradiso and the Town and Country Club on a return engagement across the pond—and began to work on what could possibly top *Surfer Rosa*.

* * *

During the summer the group began demo sessions while on breaks from touring. They returned to a studio they had used early on, Eden Sound in the Boston suburb of Newtonville. A small room located in the basement of a hair salon, it was a part-time 8-track facility that recorded to half-inch tape for $15 an hour. They were in there for a week, and the circumstances were similar to those of the Purple Tape sessions the year before, but having released two records and charmed the London critics by the pubful, the band was remarkably more confident this time. Jonathan Claude Fixler, the owner of the studio and the engineer of the sessions, remembers that Charles screamed so loudly on "Tame" that Fixler kept backing him away from the mic until he reached the far wall.

Thompson gave the tapes a working title: *Whore*. It touched on a recurring theme in his new songs, contrasting eros with fear and disgust. "Whore" is still a brutal word. A signifier of an intense and forbidden desire, it is also a moral accusation that has few equals. Thompson says it was suggested by his pagan dad, and was meant to have a broad and provocative resonance. "There are male and female prostitutes, and they're both whores," he said when the album was released. "I only meant it to be in the more traditional sense of the word, the operatic, biblical sense, you know, *whore!*, as in the great whore of Babylon. 'Whore' is a great word with a lot of connotations—mercantile connotations and politics, everything."

The term would also surely have had a snide and ironic meaning for any so-called alternative rock band that found itself signing papers with a major corporation, as the Pixies soon would. *Surfer Rosa* had made enough of a splash that some of the big labels started checking them out, and by the fall the band had interest from Elektra, the coolest major there was. Founded as a folk label in 1950, Elektra got into rock via Love, the Doors, the MC5, and the Stooges, and in the late 80s had a roster that included the Cure, the Sugarcubes, Metallica, and Mötley freakin' Crüe (plus, well, Howard Jones and Simply Red). Peter Lubin, then an A&R man for Elektra, says that there was little serious competition from other labels, and that the band was easily signed. (The Pixies' management, however, says they were fielding calls from a variety of labels in the post–*Surfer Rosa* months.) Lubin first saw them on October 14, 1988, at the World club in New York, opening up for the Jesus and Mary Chain. He was there with other scouts, who convened on the sidewalk after the show. "In typical A&R fashion," he says, "I turned to my comrades and said, 'I don't know what to think.' The others all said, 'Pass.' I remember telling them that any group that can get up there and play for eighty minutes and I don't understand the first note, that's something I've got to be interested in."

Lubin contacted the band's management and began the A&R mating dance, eventually signing the Pixies to a licensing deal. 4AD had worldwide rights to the band, but no distribution in the United States (or, for that matter, anywhere outside Great Britain). The negotiations began in the fall, and after months of lawyering, the deal was finally signed on April 2, 1989—just two weeks before the album was released. Elektra took the American distribution rights; PolyGram had already licensed the band in Canada.

In a sense, the Pixies had hit the indie jackpot. In just a couple of years of existence, they had gotten a taste of stardom, been praised by the press as geniuses, and secured a sizable deal that would get their records into the stores, their music onto the radio, and their mugs into yet more magazines and newspapers. They were about to spend tens of thousands of dollars recording an album with a guy who had a British accent. They had become "whores."

Or not. Selling out was the great cardinal sin of alternative rock in its golden age, but prior to Nirvana's success in 1991, signing to a major had rarely amounted to much for anybody. The Replacements, Hüsker Dü, Soul Asylum, and Throwing Muses, among many others, had all done the Faustian deed, and none had found riches; ready-for-the-mainstream R.E.M. was one of the few that had. Alt-rock in 1988 was, as a music-business proposition, strictly small-time. Without bankable hits that resembled those of the big rock sellers—U2, INXS, Van Halen, Guns N' Roses, John Mellencamp—a band was not likely to go far, and the modest recording contracts of the era reflected this. The Pixies were one of the last bands of the 80s college-rock era to sign to a label that did not expect megahits out of them.

And yet Charles and company had a high-fiving cockiness as they worked on *Whore*. "I remember the first thing we did was, after we made the demo, I went over to Joey Santiago's apartment," Thompson says now. "We just sat around playing the demo tape over and over again. We were just like, fuck. This is good. If they don't get this, fuck 'em."

There's a Riot Goin' On

by Miles Marshall Lewis

Miles Marshall Lewis is founder and editor of *Bronx Biannual*, the journal of hip-hop literature. He has contributed to the *Believer*, *Dazed & Confused*, the *Village Voice,* and many other publications. Lewis is author of *Scars of the Soul Are Why Kids Wear Bandages When They Don't Have Bruises*, a memoir. He currently lives in Paris, at work on *The Noir Album: On Life in Multicultural Paris*, due next year.

Sly Talk

He is at that age where one expects to grow up to become rich and famous, and as this age may differ for everyone, let's clarify: Ploot Parsley is fifteen. Said riches and fame may stem, one day, from rock stardom or Hollywood, so Ploot imagines, and so he's lately become a more avid listener to the idiot-savant ramblings of his enormously informed father. The two speed down I-95 en route to Virginia for a family homecoming, CBS-FM's Mr. Music aka DJ Norm N. Nite spins "Dance to the Music" and recognizes the sixteenth anniversary of Woodstock this August 15, 1985—all Ploot's father needs to launch into his own personal history with Sly Stone and the upstate New York music festival.

"I didn't buy *Dance to the Music*. *Stand!* is the first album that I bought new. And that could've been sixty-nine."

"Why didn't you buy the first two? You told me before you didn't like the covers."

"Nobody was really playing Sly's very first one, *A Whole New Thing*. Probably the first Sly record that broke, I mean really broke, was *Dance to the Music*. Which means that when *Dance to the Music* broke, people went back to the earlier albums. Even then there were DJs, they just couldn't mix. It was almost like, if you went to a club and they played 'Dance to the Music,' people were dancing to it and they'd say, 'Well, if you liked that, you should've liked *this* last year.' And then they would play something from *A Whole New Thing*, and people all of a sudden started realizing, 'There's something happening here, there's something different here.'

"There's a guy, the guy that sings, Ben E. King—"

"'Stand by Me.'"

"The guy that sings 'Stand by Me' and your grandmother's favorite song about . . . 'Save the Last Dance for Me.' He was with the Drifters and he went solo and his career was going pretty well in the early-to-mid sixties. And he made the point, the first time he saw the Beatles and they said 'Wooo!' and shook their hair, he knew that his career days were limited. Because no matter how much he shook his head, his hair wasn't gonna do that. And in those days, if you were—these are stereotypes—but if you were a musician, you played jazz or you backed a singer. If you were black and you sang, you sang R&B. When the whole British Invasion thing happened, all of a sudden there were self-contained bands. And self-contained bands didn't exist in the black community for the most part in sixty-five, sixty-six. Except for maybe Dyke and the Blazers or a group called Charles Wright and the Watts 103rd Street Rhythm Band.

"So when Sly starts breaking in sixty-seven, sixty-eight, he's got one of the first black self-contained bands. The Family Stone don't particularly look like the Beatles. They're trying to look like what they are. And all of a sudden, it's like, wait a minute, we can do this too. I always mention the Chambers Brothers to you. We weren't particularly dancing to the Chambers Brothers, but the Chambers Brothers existed, another all black group that was singing in the British style. And Sly and the Family Stone: they're setting up in the British style, but they sure ain't sounding like the Beatles. They were sounding like us.

"And, uh, what year would it have been? It would probably have been the Christmas show at the Apollo, 1970. One of the big acts in those days was the Five Stairsteps, 'O-o-h Child.' And the Stairsteps were known to be Smokey Robinson and the Miracles clones. So me and your mother go to the Christmas show at the Apollo. The Stairsteps were onstage, and they opened up with 'Purple Haze,' playing instruments. And all of a sudden, it's like, even the Stairsteps are doin' it! And then you knew. Now the handwriting is on the wall that black music's never going to be the same again.

"Even the Ohio Players. Then the next time, next thing you know, every time you look, you don't know what to expect. It's almost the rarity to see four or five guys dressed in the same suit doing moves and singing harmony the way we were used to it. All of a sudden you had to play instruments, you dressed the way you felt, the song didn't have to be two minutes and forty-five seconds. And it opened up everything.

"And so many things were happening that, on occasion, you didn't know what to call Sly. Is this R&B? It's definitely not the Motown style, it's definitely not the Stax style, it's definitely not the British Invasion. What the heck is this? You know, so, he did that. If he had only shown up on time a little bit more it would've never ended. You know, it felt that way: this will never end."

"The first time I played *Purple Rain* in the house, you pulled out *Stand!* and *Electric Ladyland* and lent me your headphones. Interracial bands like the Revolution, Sly and Hendrix did that first, you were sayin'?"

"Yes. Well, that whole sixty-seven Summer of Love and the whole 'hippie love power' is supposed to come so much from San Francisco. Sly is from San Fran, Oakland. So he's the other side of the Grateful Dead, the other side of the Jefferson Airplane, except. . . . Well, not except.

"Like Hendrix in interviews, Sly would never get deeply into the race thing, as I recall. One of the things that threw people was, for example, the Chambers Brothers were brothers, except the drummer was a white guy. But he was still one of the Chambers Brothers. With Sly, the name of the band is the Family Stone. Magazines always asked, 'There's family in the band?' But when they would try to pin him down and say, 'Who's family?' he would say, 'We all are.'

"Hendrix went through that whole learning curve for black folks of, 'What is Hendrix playing? This does not sound like black music to me.' Which is interesting, 'cause he was playing the straight blues, so he was playing blacker music than a lot of black music that Motown was doing. But we had that thing with him: 'This ain't quite black, I'm not gonna throw Hendrix on if I have people over to dance.'"

"It probably didn't help that he didn't seem to take pride in his blackness, either."

"Well, people were thrown by the two white guys in the band,

Mitch Mitchell and Noel Redding. It didn't matter how much the Isley Brothers or Little Richard said, 'Hendrix used to play guitar for us.' It was like, he went to England to come back. So it was almost like, he went to be white to be black. And certain people had a problem with that. People never had a problem with Sly because it was too evident you could dance to it. Couldn't dance to Hendrix. As long as you could dance to it, Sly could do any weird thing he wanted to do, it was okay."

"What about James Brown? Did people see them like Prince and Michael Jackson, like two sides of the same coin or funk competitors?"

"James Brown had been around since . . . I'll say fifty-eight, but he's probably around even before that, right? 'Papa's Got a Brand New Bag' came out around sixty-five, 'Cold Sweat' is around sixty-seven. James Brown had fast stuff. He had 'Out of Sight' and 'Night Train,' he had those things that he was known to dance to. But all of a sudden...What I was saying about, there'd be the group and backing musicians? James Brown kinda did something else, and a couple of years before Sly. It was obvious that James Brown was the main man, but the musicians started coming to the forefront. Also, when the James Brown Revue would come to the Apollo, he'd stay on stage the entire time. When one of the acts would play, he'd play drums. When the other opening act would play, he'd play organ. So it was like, he's the star but he's one of the musicians too. And it was clear that the music would just kind of change rhythm, change everything because he lifted a finger. It was like, he's part of this band and this band is *tight*.

"Usually in black music, when you hit a rhythm, that rhythm stays consistent throughout the song, even if it seems like it changes. Not always with some James Brown stuff. All of a sudden, he'll just leave that initial rhythm altogether. He'll be back later, but he would take detours no one else was taking. And all of a sudden, when you listened to the Ohio Players—like *Pain* and *Ecstasy*—there's some things happening. Even though they were set up like a Sly band, they were doing things lifted straight from JB. So JB gets an edge because he's doing it first, to me. And then other groups a year or two later said, 'You think that's something? Watch *this!*' No doubt Sly has that same counterpoint and stuff happening."

"So in the sixties, y'all didn't see Sly Stone and James Brown as competing at all?"

"No, probably because of the generational thing. Sly is

almost my age. James Brown is your grandma's age. James Brown had been around twelve years before anybody ever heard of Sly. James Brown kind of already had his hardcore audience. This is funny because, well, James Brown is from the deep south, right? He's from Georgia. But he also had urban appeal. So if you went south and you wanted to get the party going, you played JB. If you were in a big city and you wanted to get the party going, you played JB. Nowadays, if you want to get the party going you play JB."

Father and son laugh.

"Or a sample, like with Rakim."

"Who?"

"The rapper, Rakim. Like 'Eric B. Is President'?"

"Right, I don't know about him. Oh, the guy on 'Soul Train' who wouldn't smile?

"Well, I wouldn't say people felt like they were competing. I'll say this: talking about an influence that Sly might've had on JB, he was starting to see he wasn't in the funk by himself. Because he wasn't the only one doing it anymore."

"What about Sly and the Family Stone concerts?"

"Always tight, always late. My first time, I saw him at the Apollo. What would frequently happen, the Apollo would have at least four to six shows in a day, right? Saturday and Sunday, there'd be a one o'clock, a three-thirty, a six o'clock, a nine o'clock, an eleven o'clock, a midnight. Like that. The midnight might not run off till twelve-thirty, one o'clock. And what you'd have is groups of entertainers, maybe six or seven acts that didn't always tour together but would come there because they had a hit record to push, that kind of thing. And the entire thing would be built around a star. When James Brown came he would rent the Apollo and the entire show would be his Revue. There wouldn't be any outside act, okay? So James Brown was kind of an exception, but generally it was, if you were gonna see the Motown Revue you'd see six, seven acts.

"So me and your mother went. When Sly came, instead of them doing seven shows a day, at the max they probably did three. They did a one o'clock, a five o'clock, an eight o'clock. 'Cause Sly wasn't gonna work that hard. And it was a new situation for the Apollo but because he had the drawing power that he had, they went for it. If they said there was a five o'clock show you'd be lucky if it started at six. Sly's audience kind of knew that time was very . . . flexible for him, so you were just glad he was gonna show up at all, right?

"Usually at the Apollo, the curtain would be down and you'd hear the backing musicians getting in tune, warming up. When they would introduce Sly the curtain would come up and there'd be nobody on stage. They'd walk out one at a time. He'd start playing some runs on the organ. And from those runs, the brass instruments would tune, right? So as soon as they hit the stage, even though it felt like there was no rhyme or reason to what they were doing, they were tight. And the next thing you knew, they were in it. So soon as Sly sat down at the organ, the rhythm started, the beat was on, and things were happening. And the show might be a half-hour, the show might be two hours. It was gonna be built around certain songs and you knew that, you just didn't know quite how long the song was gonna go, right?

"So figure, as much as your mother and I went to shows, we were used to seeing a group a couple of times. If we saw a group twice, the third time we saw them we didn't need the group! We knew every grunt, every groan, every little joke, everything. When you saw Sly, you didn't know *what* was gonna happen."

"How many times did you see him?"

"A lot. Well, it feels like so many. But let's say I probably saw the Temptations like a hundred times? I might not have seen Sly more than maybe ten times. Now one of the reasons is, he didn't show up as often, right? He came to the Apollo twice that I remember. I saw him there on June 29 in sixty-nine, the night Armstrong walked on the moon. When he would come, because he'd be there for a week, I might go two or three times during the course of the week. He played where they have the US Open out in Forest Hills? Louis Armstrong Stadium? They used to have concerts, I saw him out there. He got married at Madison Square Garden in seventy-four. We went to that. I saw him at the Fillmore East. He played there with Hendrix in May of sixty-eight, but I missed it."

"What! Why?"

"It could've been that by the time we heard about it, it was too hard to get a ticket. I can't remember. Have you heard David Crosby from Crosby, Stills, and Nash say, 'Anybody who says they remember the sixties wasn't there'? I can't remember many times going to Fillmore. Sometimes I would hear about a concert late and when I would get there it'd be sold out already. So I'd be in the lobby kinda trying to scout for tickets, trying to figure out a way to sneak in and I could never work the thing out. In those days I was working in the post office and I got off work between ten and midnight. So a lot of times I would just run down from the PO and hope that I'd figure out a way to making my way in."

"What about Woodstock? Sly and Hendrix were there too, right?"

"Yeah, but that reminds me of a funny story. In the summer of sixty-nine I was a teenager in college, and every summer I would work for the phone company. In those days there was really only one, it was all AT&T. So it was a cool summer job and the whole company was known for being conservative. You had to be something of a nerd to work there. You know, you had to understand technical stuff. There was a guy who worked with me from Seattle named Brewer, and he was a bona fide, one hundred percent hippie, which used to drive them crazy. He was smart, blond-haired, blue-eyed. I'm pretty sure he evolved into something else after he interviewed for the job so they didn't know what he was when they hired him."

"He was there longer than you?"

"I was just there for the summer. He really worked there."

"He was older than you?"

"Maybe . . . I would've been nineteen, he would've been twenty-two, twenty-three. There was another guy named Roy Vocina, another kind of hidden hippie. He had done Vietnam service so he could've been twenty-five. I was getting into certain music, like Sly, and he was heavy into Al Kooper. You know Al Kooper?"

"No."

"Al Kooper had played on Dylan records, 'Like a Rollin' Stone.'"

"What did he play?"

"He played piano but he wasn't really a good piano player if I'm getting this story right. But because he played on 'Like a Rollin' Stone,' people tried to pick up his style. And he's said since, 'My style was, I didn't really know what I was doing. But everybody copied me.' Anyway, we would constantly bring records back and forth to work; like, 'If you think this is great, listen to *this*.' So we were kind of hipping each other to music that we wouldn't have necessarily gone to on our own. My summer job always ran until the end of August and Woodstock was in August. Brewer talked about going but just sorta kind of."

"Y'all were the only two talking about going?"

"Us and Vocina. So we started hearing Friday afternoon on

the radio how so many people were showing up they were turning the highway into a parking lot and they weren't letting any more people drive and people were just getting out of their cars. That seemed to me to be madness, a good reason not to go. To Brewer it was an excellent reason *to* go. So he was working me, working me. Y'know, 'We gotta go, we gotta go.' I said, 'I'm not going up there, it sounds too strange.' And we separated, it's four-thirty, time to go home.

"Monday comes. All weekend, you hear about Woodstock and what's happening. Every time there's a news story, they're showing these kids in the mud and in the rain on the news and the locals touting them. 'Cause the locals, for the most part they were sorry the kids were there but they were pretty nice to them. So that was how the stories were going. Monday morning comes and Brewer doesn't come to work. Vocina didn't go, Brewer's the only one. He doesn't come to work and everybody's fearing the worst. Tuesday morning comes and Brewer comes to work in the same clothes that he wore at Woodstock."

"And three kids died and two babies were born?"

"Yeah. They always made such a point that it was actually a city population there. People were living and dying, so much was happening. So Brewer had two inches of mud on his shoes and he smelled . . . interesting. I said, 'You were supposed to be at work yesterday,' and he said, 'Yeah, but Hendrix hadn't played yet.' Hendrix didn't play till Monday morning, so he couldn't leave."

"Why did he come straight to work without washing up?"

"'Cause he was, y'know, he's a hippie! They thought nothing of that kind of stuff."

"So he didn't get fired."

"He didn't get fired. His days were numbered but he didn't get fired."

"When was the last time you saw him?"

"That was my last summer but I would always come back to say hi every summer. The next summer he was gone. But they tell me his family was doctors, that he pretty much—"

"He shaved and got a real job."

"Yeah. He went back to Seattle, went back to college like they wanted him to do. Right now he's probably a brain surgeon or something and this is just one of his interesting stories from his early days."

"So did you regret not going?"

"Yeah, because—"

"How soon did you regret not going?"

"Almost immediately. It would've been interesting, because in no way could I have told my family, 'I'm not going to work Monday 'cause I'm gonna go to Woodstock.' Your mother and I weren't married yet. I'm still a college kid, up at CCNY. I'm staying with them at home. I would have had to explain. And for me to just go out of town, especially, you know, I was nineteen. I didn't do that yet. So it would've been too much for them to handle, and it would've been too much of me not doing what they wanted, so I just didn't even bother. As soon as the Woodstock movie came out the next year, I went to see the movie. And when I saw Sly's performance—they did 'I Want to Take You Higher,' 'Dance to the Music,' 'Music Lover' —I said, 'I should've been there.'"

"Was it obvious that Woodstock was one of the sixties' defining moments?"

"Yeah. I mean, as soon as *Rolling Stone* came out. The next issue of *Rolling Stone* was nothing but Woodstock. They did a special book, it's out of print. But what the book amounted to, most of the book was those next two issues after the festival, because there was nothing else to talk about. Everybody was there, if you're talking straight rock'n'roll, everybody was there. And let's say that the true rhythm and blues, the true soul acts weren't there, but what I'll call the crossover soul acts were. Like Sly was there, Richie Havens was there, which was a big deal. Santana."

"And the Doors weren't there?"

"No. Frequently with things that Morrison was doing, it would be such a hassle for them to play. You might have heard, like, he exposed himself at a concert and all of that. So it may have been one of those periods where it was just easier not to play."

"And didn't Janis Joplin have sex with Sly?"

"No, no. Hahaha. . . . That was a guy named Country Joe. Joplin and Country Joe had sex in the hotel with everybody watching, like, 'What are they doing?'"

Sex entering the conversation makes things silent. Wilson Pickett's "In the Midnight Hour" plays on the radio. Then, commercials.

"Did I ever tell you about the time Wilson Pickett tried to shoot the Isley Brothers?"

The Believer Whose Faith Was Shattered

1

Picture thirty years after the Woodstock Festival's three days of peace and music, into the premillennial days of 1999. Visualize through the eyes of a contemporary counterpart of someone like Meredith Hunter, the black teen murdered by Hells Angels at the Rolling Stones' Altamont concert, who'd certainly have thought Sly and the Family Stone at Yasgur's farm in '69 was totally far out. For the sake of argument let's say this modern-day Meredith wears dreadlocks in place of his antecedent's Afro, smokes as much weed as Meredith might've, and rents a brownstone apartment in the heart of bohemian Fort Greene, Brooklyn.

Such a location means he has a neighbor in Erykah Badu, who represents something of particular significance to the young brother. (We'll call him Butch.) Erykah Badu arrived from Dallas, Texas, three years ago, like a hiphop Joan Baez for the incense-and-oils set, to this section of Brooklyn where most of the women already look like her: African headwraps, ankh jewelry pieces, thrift store fashion. For Butch the runaway success of her 1997 debut *Baduizm* and its *Live* album follow-up means something. In specific he thinks the singer's tendency toward preaching her earth mama philosophy to sold-out audiences implies that spiritual knowledge is being spread, that consciousness is being raised to a tipping point, that Erykah Badu fans will spill out of nationwide venues discovering holistic healing and transcendental meditation and Kemetic philosophy and vegan diets for themselves. What would this mean, for the millions who follow Erykah Badu's music to embrace the singer's lifestyle on a mass level at this specific period in time, the cusp of the Aquarian age? Butch wonders.

But that's not all. In April Butch saw *The Matrix* in a crowded Flatbush Pavilion theater and all spring everyone's been talking about how we're "living in the Matrix, man," puffing on blunts of marijuana-filled cigars at house parties and discussing the subversive information laced throughout the film. People really *get* it: the society that we've been led to believe matters only serves the agenda of those who prop it up as the standard. Butch feels that everyone is on the verge of pulling the rubber pipe out the back of his head and redefining the social order. Society is in for an interesting turn; there's no way *The Matrix* can be this popular and millions of moviegoers not understand what it's really saying, he feels.

On top of this, every single day Butch sees someone on the A train to Manhattan with some sort of spiritual personal improvement book. If not Kahlil Gibran's *The Prophet* then Julia Cameron's *The Artist's Way*. If not James Redfield's *The Celestine Prophecy* then Dennis Kimbro's *Think and Grow Rich*. He reads a few of them himself: *Conversations with God, The Alchemist, The Four Agreements, The Seven Spiritual Laws of Success, Heal Thyself, Tapping the Power Within.* Deepak Chopra becomes more of an omnipresent talking head on Butch's TV set. Oprah redefines the mission of her talk show and urges her viewers to "be your best self," *The Oprah Winfrey Show* exposing even exurban housewives to spiritualists like Yoruba minister Iyanla Vanzant on a regular basis. Things are coming together, Butch thinks. The sixties flirted with revolution; the nineties threaten the even greater prospect of evolution.

And as certain things come together, others fall apart—like the recording industry. Butch hasn't bought a CD in quite a while. All the music he wants is available on Napster and he's already laid down a few hundred dollars for a portable MP3 player. After decades of nefarious activities—contractually cheating musicians out of profits; overcharging the public for compact discs; paying artists less than fifteen percent of their music's earnings and owning their master recordings forever and ever—record companies are feeling the big payback, revenge. To Butch, record companies seem like the first crumbling institution in a wave of falling multinational corporate entities to follow.

In the Brooklyn arts community surrounding him, unsigned independent bands all take encouragement from the digital revolution, burning their own CDs, setting up their own websites, selling their own music. Screw the industry. In the new age everyone can have his own record label, be her own CEO. One's artistic worth won't be measured or rejected by a corporation. On the verge of the twenty-first century Butch saw people self-actualizing, believing in themselves without looking for outside approval. How liberating.

To top things off the death of immediate hiphop icons Tupac Shakur and the Notorious BIG has made the power of intention common knowledge to the pop community. At first only a few made the crass observation that Biggie Smalls named his albums *Ready to Die* and *Life After Death* and was then killed;

that Tupac rhymed incessantly about death and dying young and was murdered at twenty-five. The moral slowly spilling over into the mass consciousness? We get what we ask for, all of us. This was the beginning, Butch thought, of folks being more careful of what they put out into the universe, consciously exercising universal laws of cause and effect more carefully. It's the biggest legacy the senseless deaths of the young and talented MCs could have left their generation.

Butch was all ready for the 2000s, bring 'em on. The Y2K computer scare came and went, tail between its legs. The election of George W. Bush didn't bode well. But at the time it seemed at least to bring into question the notion of the Electoral College system, another antiquated structure ripe for rehauling and replacement for the new age.

And then September 11 came.

In 2001 the first foreign attack on US soil ushered in a period of disillusionment as considerable as that of the early seventies, at least for Butch and his peers. The idealism that typified his Brooklyn boho scene gradually dissolved. People moved. They had babies, took nine-to-fives to support families. Beset by the borough's backbiting, Erykah Badu re-relocated back to Dallas with her and André 3000's baby boy, Seven. Radio and listeners alike fell in love with Jill Scott's debut; less preachy, less pretentious. Folks got lax with their meditation, started backsliding on their vegetarian diets, dismantling their altars. Cut their dreadlocks, some of them. *The Matrix* sequels came out. They sucked. The government shut down Napster and the record industry appropriated the whole digital download movement: the iPod came out, and it *didn't* suck. By and large the new age that Butch highly anticipated was a letdown, a non-event. Looking back, his lofty expectations started to appear softheaded as the years passed.

When someone eventually crafts a soundtrack for the disillusionment Butch's generation feels for the thwarted promises of the Aquarian age—any day now, by my watch—it'll without a doubt share a kindred spirit with *There's a Riot Goin' On*.

2

Postmillennial agita is a yet-undiagnosed social affliction. More documented by far is the sense of disappointment faced by the baby boomers at the end of the sixties. My childhood coincided with the birth of hiphop (in the Bronx, no less) and so all my knowledge concerning the spirit of those times is secondhand, but like even the most casual student of American history I still know it like the back of my (second) hand.

On my first birthday, December 18, 1971, *There's a Riot Goin' On* reached the top of the *Billboard* pop chart and its first single "Family Affair" had already been the number one pop single in the country for two weeks. In between the release of Sly and the Family Stone's 1967 debut album *A Whole New Thing* and my turning a year old, both Martin Luther King, Jr. and Bobby Kennedy were assassinated; Meredith Hunter was murdered at the Rolling Stones' Altamont show; Vietnam War casualties were steadily escalating by the thousands; the US National Guard killed four students during a war demonstration at Kent State University; Charles Manson was sentenced to life imprisonment for the death of actress Sharon Tate and seven others; and seventeen-year-old Black Panther Bobby Hutton was killed by Oakland police in a shootout with the Panthers. Somewhere in there, spring 1969, the 5th Dimension's "Aquarius/Let the Sunshine In (The Flesh Failures)" ruled the *Billboard* number one spot for six weeks—how discouraged the hippies must've been by the time I turned one.

This is a story often told: "the death of the sixties." It usually begins by talking about how the decade didn't precisely extend between 1960 and 1970 per se, but instead, for instance, between the Beatles on *The Ed Sullivan Show* and the Rolling Stones' free concert at Altamont Raceway, or the mainstreaming of the Pill and the government corruption of Watergate. I hate to add to the heap of cultural mythology surrounding this done-to-death decade from said angle but there's almost no other "in" to begin explaining the downward spiral of Sly Stone, which is essential to understanding the genesis of *There's a Riot Goin' On*.

In Greil Marcus's excellent essay on *Riot*, "The Myth of Staggerlee," he characterizes Sly Stone as a believer whose faith was shattered. This tells the tale in a nutshell. "Don't hate the black, don't hate the white. If you get bitten just hate the bite," he advised America (reciting lyrics from *Dance to the Music*'s "Are You Ready") onstage at the *Sullivan Show* in December '68. *You can make it if you try, different strokes for different folks*, and *you don't have to die before you live* are just a few of the optimist messages spread in songs by Sly and the Family Stone during the heady days of the Summer of Love and Woodstock, where the septet performed before a countercultural audience 500,000 strong. But by the release of the stylishly mournful *Riot*, the man who once sang of hot fun in the summertime warned, "Watch out 'cause the summer gets cold when today gets too old." Immensely bleak, moody, seductively despairing, and funky, *Riot* laid a sonic backdrop for the nationwide cultural and political disintegration of sixties fallout, as well as the personal dissolution of disillusioned idealist Sly Stone.

3

Critics always say Sly Stone was ahead of his time. I'll go one better and prove it to you. Back in October 1969, Ben Fong-Torres interviewed him backstage at ABC's short-lived "Music Scene." (Sly and the Family Stone were awarded the cover of the three-year-old Rolling Stone in March 1970.[1]) The group's maestro had this to say:

> The record company wants another LP by February. Well, we could do some good songs, but that would be just another LP. Now you expect a group to come out with another LP and another. There's got to be more to it. But what else can you do? The only thing that sounds interesting is something that ties in with a play that finishes what an LP starts to say, and the LP will be important on account of the play.

That's a pretty spot-on synopsis of the concept behind Prince's *Purple Rain* phenomenon fifteen years before the fact, wouldn't you say? Or, you know, Mariah Carey's *Glitter* . . . take your pick.

Notes

1. In this interview Sly Stone also tells Fong-Torres the group will never do a Greatest Hits album or sing for Coca-Cola; no sell-out. Sly and the Family Stone's Greatest Hits was released on November 11, 1970, selling nearly four million copies. Toyota featured "Everyday People" in a 1998 television ad campaign; both AT&T and the National Basketball Association have used "I Want to Take You Higher" in commercials.

The Stone Roses

by Alex Green

Alex Green's interviews and reviews have appeared in *Magnet, Trouser Press, CMJ New Music Monthly, Amplifier, Hits!* and *SOMA*. In addition, he teaches English composition and Greek and Roman literature at St. Mary's College of California. He is currently the editor of the online music magazine www.caughtinthecarousel.com.

Prologue
"Sometimes I fantasize . . ."

When I was in seventh grade, my favorite conversations came at the bus stop. While my friends and I waited for the bus, which was driven by a drowsy-looking guy named Lenny who would only play Styx's *Paradise Theatre*, we would energetically cover a range of topics: which girls were hot, what the best song was on Def Leppard's *Pyromania*, or how Han Solo could still be alive after being submerged in such a deep and heartbreaking freeze for all that time.

But what we were best at were pop culture hypotheticals, wildly imagined scenarios whose possibilities were so intriguing that the next day we'd continue the conversation right where we'd left off without missing a beat, without even first saying hello. We'd wonder who would win if Bruce Lee fought Heavyweight champ Larry Holmes; what would happen if the shark from *Jaws* somehow got in the community swimming pool through the metal drain at the bottom of the deep end; how awesome it would be if Christie Brinkley was our babysitter; or if the rumor was true that Bon Scott was not dead at all, but bearded and sad and rotting away in a Mexican prison, and if it was, maybe we should head down there and do something about it.

The bus stop was like a bar but without any of the drinks, though the conversations we had did prefigure the kind of drunken musings we would have years later as college students. Of course we knew our endless combinations of preposterous pop culture pairings and bizarre, almost supernatural wishes ("And then Jim Morrison would jump down from the sky right on the stage with wings made of snakes and be like, 'I was never dead'") were never going to come true, but they were so inspired, so sublimely hallucinogenic, they made us glow with excitement because they felt like the newest and best ideas on the planet. And as outrageous and illogical as they were, they felt real enough to happen and that was what made them so seductive.

But the fact was, Bruce Lee was dead, and even if he wasn't, it was doubtful he'd come out of retirement and jump both sports and weight classes to fight Larry Holmes; the metal drain at the bottom of the pool was too small for even a baby barracuda to get in; my babysitter was Lisa Gates, a girl who didn't look to be even in the same species as Christie Brinkley; and if Bon Scott really was in a Mexican Prison, and five seventh graders from California somehow slipped under the parental radar and made their way down to Tijuana on a school day, what could they really do once they got there?

Reality, however, has not dampened my desire, even into my thirties, to think of the world in the same terms I did when I was a kid at the bus stop. But instead of dreaming up things that fancifully mutate reality, I have now become obsessed with reality itself, and what might have happened if it hadn't gotten in the way. For example, if River Phoenix hadn't died of a drug overdose; if the Smiths hadn't broken up; or if Björn Borg hadn't retired from tennis at twenty-six. Of course these are all great artists and athletes who left their marks with deep indentations on popular culture, but the mind just takes off when it thinks about what more they could have done: Phoenix was deepening as an actor and his body of work seemed to only scratch the surface of what he was really capable of; the Smiths' last studio album *Strangeways Here We Come* was their most accessible yet; and Borg had eleven Grand Slam titles when he walked away from the sport, which at the time was only two shy of Roy Emerson's record.

As for me, an ardent music addict with far too many arcane facts easily accessed by the right question and with a music collection so absurdly sizable I can listen to a different album every day for the next fifty-five years, for me what hurts the most is the story of the Stone Roses.[1] On the strength of their self-titled debut album, the Stone Roses should not only have ruled the world, they should still be ruling it. Shrugging off time and history and the constantly evolving musical curves of the pop universe, the Stone Roses' harmonious blend of melodic six-string pop and psychedelic rock and roll still remains, after all these years, both fresh and vital. Whether it's the slithering, narcissistic arrogance of "I Wanna Be Adored," the soaring chorus of "She Bangs the Drums," or the funky workout of "Elephant Stone," *The Stone Roses* has more highlights than a David Beckham career retrospective. But more than that, it's a cohesive album, an album not Frankensteined together with one hit single and an array of scraps disguised as songs, but an album whose seamlessly sequenced song cycle begins by devilishly taunting, "I don't have to sell my soul / He's already in me," and then nervily ends with the self-obsessed and deliciously arrogant declaration "I am the Resurrection and I am the Light." True to the words of its bookends, the entire album is pompous and defiant, each song crackling with ambition and hunger.

The Stone Roses' debut finds that lone, peerless groove occupied in temporary installments by precious few superstars, that groove where everything clicks and hums and snaps into place, and even the mistakes look good. In other words, when you've got it, you've got it big and it was here that the Stone Roses had it. Even experimental dalliances with backward recording, or a minute-long number set to an old English folk song about assassinating the Queen somehow work. The mastery of this period for the band is evinced on the songs that didn't even make it on to the record. In fact, not only are the b-sides as good, if not in some cases better than the singles they backed, I'm convinced that the Stone Roses were so untouchable at this point in their career that a recording of the band eating lunch would have been a hit single.

Not that they needed it. After *The Stone Roses* was released in May of 1989, it climbed as high as #19 on the UK charts, and peaked in the US on *Billboard*'s top 200 at #86.[2] Although it wasn't an instant seller on either shore, it did demonstrate a great deal of staying power, lodging itself on the UK charts for forty-eight weeks and the US charts for twenty-six. To date its sales are estimated to be over four million and in British magazines it consistently ranks in reader's polls as one of the best albums of all time.[3]

There are always varying reasons why some albums just stick around, and in the case of *The Stone Roses*, its endless stream of singles certainly didn't hurt. In the UK from July of 1989 to March of 1992, six songs from the album, including "She Bangs the Drums" (#34), "I Am the Resurrection" (#33), "Waterfall" (#27), "Made of Stone" (#20), "I Wanna Be Adored" (#20) and "Elephant Stone" (#8), not only made big impressions on the singles chart, but indicated the enduring power of the album.[4]

The band's apotheosis, however, had as much to do with singular events as chart successes. Over the course of their career they provided celebrated live results, with sold-out shows everywhere from the Hacienda in Manchester to Blackpool's Empress Ballroom to Spike Island in Cheshire, where they played for over 30,000 fans. They burned their bridges in public, splashing paint all over the offices of one former record label, while engaging in a protracted legal battle with another.[5] They signed a multimillion dollar deal with Geffen then vanished for several years before even putting out a record.[6] They appeared on "Top of the Pops" in a performance punctuated by singer Ian Brown's conspicuously mocking refusal to lip synch. They thumbed their noses at history, making claims they were going to be bigger than the Beatles, and that living legends Mick Jagger and David Bowie were insincere. They turned Jackson Pollock's name into a verb by *Pollocking* their instruments in blasts of colorful paint. And like Robin Hood, Brown allegedly strolled the streets of Manchester with £100,000 in a carrier bag, giving money to the homeless. Whether you witnessed it firsthand or read about it in the *NME*, these events forever secured the place of the Stone Roses right next to all the other immortals in pop music lore.

But before we get to the Stone Roses, it's worth spending a minute or two on the rich musical lineage of their Manchester hometown. Located in northwest England, Manchester is considered the world's first major industrial city and after London is judged by many to be England's unofficial second city. Some of its early inhabitants were Flemish weavers specializing in linen and wool, while later, during the Industrial Revolution, the advent of steam powered engines were crucial in making the city known for being the foremost manufacturers of cotton.

However, in spite of its roots in industry, Mancunians have a long tradition of a fierce commitment to the arts. Boasting notable art galleries, museums, theaters and reputed music institutions, Manchester's rich cultural heritage has not only been a continuous source of pride for its citizens, its long list of talented artists, writers and musicians have proven it is more than fertile ground for creativity and expression.

When it comes to pop, many believe that Manchester's music infrastructure was properly established in 1978 when television personality Tony Wilson founded the now legendary Factory Records. Branding every Factory product with fac and a corresponding number denoting its place in the Factory sequence, the label cultivated its own visual mythology, which helped create a mystique for its acts. As the label grew so did its roster, which in addition to its flagship acts like the Durutti Column and Joy Division, also eventually included A Certain Ratio, Cabaret Voltaire, the Railway Children, the Happy Mondays, New Order and for a spell, James, whose brief tenure with Factory was confined to a handful of singles early in their career.

Before Factory, Manchester had the usual pop music outlets of nightclubs and magazines and record stores, but by the end of the seventies, musically, the city found itself to be in a bit of a rut. But when Factory set down its anchor, it ended up performing a kind of musical quadruple bypass and got the blood flowing through the artistic veins of the city in ways that it never had before.

Capitalizing on his success, Tony Wilson (along with Joy Division manager Rob Gretton) opened the Hacienda in 1982, a nightclub that on paper seemed like the perfect base for the bands that were sprouting up all over Manchester. Built in an abandoned yacht showroom, the Hacienda's spartan inner environs and admittedly woeful acoustics at first prevented the club from catching on and instead catered to a small crowd of indie guitar rock devotees. But by the second half of the eighties as dance culture took off and the designer club drug Ecstasy made its way into British youth culture, the Hacienda began to move away from just booking live bands and began hiring DJs who commandeered their own theme nights, spinning acid house, hip-hop, electro funk and techno. With three levels, enough space to hold almost two thousand people, and the quavering beats of a new kind of dance music reverberating throughout, the Hacienda became the hottest nightclub in Manchester.

"The Hacienda was rubbish," says former Creation boss

and current Poptones head Alan McGee.[7] "Then they imported loads of Ecstasy and it became good. Suddenly everyone was dancing to balletic house music and it was insane, but it was fantastic fun. The Hacienda was probably the most rock and roll fun you could have outside of Mexico City."

With a schedule that now included live bands and adventurous DJs playing various species of dance music, the Hacienda made it clear that guitar rock and dance music, two previously warring factions, could not only coexist, they could even merge together without anyone noticing. The result of this experimental sonic coupling created a new pop offspring and bands like the Happy Mondays, Inspiral Carpets and the Stone Roses found themselves emerging as the new sound of Britain. But I'm getting ahead of myself. No one emerges as the new sound of *anything* without a little history of their own.

Formed in 1983 by childhood friends Ian Brown and John Squire, the Stone Roses rose from the quietly smoldering ashes of the two's first band, a Clash-inspired outfit called the Patrol. Although the Stone Roses recorded an album that was never released in 1985, in the nearly five years it took to finally put out their debut, they did manage to amass some pretty impressive highlights.[8] They opened for Pete Townshend, toured Sweden, played late-night warehouse gigs all over Manchester, had two managers (Howard Jones and Gareth Evans), recorded a single with producer Martin Hannett (who had produced both the Buzzcocks and Joy Division), were the first band in almost a decade to play a live radio gig for Manchester's Piccadilly Radio, got banned from the London Marquee nightclub for allegedly spray painting their name in a bold trail across Manchester and they secured the services of well-known producer John Leckie to take the helm for the recording of their belated debut album.[9]

Not a bad way for a young band to cram a resumé.

But keep in mind that when the Stone Roses went into the studio with Leckie in 1988, musically speaking, they were no longer a young band anymore. People around Manchester had been aware of them for years and had perhaps even grown tired of the band that had been hailed as the next big thing talking so much and producing so little. The lack of an album technically made the Stone Roses rookies, but on the strength of their years together, they were rookies who were deeply seasoned.

Initially the rhythm section of the Stone Roses went through several permutations and at various points included former Patrol singer Andy Couzens, future Colourfield and Fall drummer Simon Wolstencroft, and bassist Pete Garner. But for *The Stone Roses* album, the band was a solid quartet that consisted of drummer Alan "Reni" Wren, bassist Gary "Mani" Mounfield, John Squire on guitar and Ian Brown on vocals.

Mani hailed from blue-collar north Manchester, and had cut his musical teeth playing in the Mill with future Inspiral Carpets keyboardist Clint Boon. Wide-eyed and handsome, Mani possessed, according to Jon Stewart, former guitarist of the Britpop band Sleeper, "The kind of straightforward soulful rootsy ballsy bass playing that drives a band—they wouldn't have been the same without him.[10] "He's got everything a band needs in those fingers," seconds former Woodentops singer Rolo McGinty.

With a kind of casual toughness, and a traceable smirk, Reni would lounge behind his drum kit sending out muscular backbeats and improvised jazz fills, the sticks in his hands flashing like chopper blades. Continually compared to Keith Moon, Reni is still considered by many to have been the Stone Roses' secret weapon due to his musical versatility. Wearing his trademark beanie, he was a dangerously good drummer, but he was also an excellent singer. In his biography of the band *The Stone Roses and the Resurrection of British Pop*, John Robb writes of him, "Not only being content with being a great young drummer on the up, he also possessed an outstanding voice, a voice that would play a key role on the first album, underpinning Brown's husky fallen-angel mooch." As for his importance to the band, Brown even went so far as tell *Uncut*: "We had a drummer with soul, so we always had a beat. That's what made the Roses."

As much a visual artist as a guitarist, John Squire's love of painting seemed to inform his musical sensibility. With a dark fringe falling halfway over his eyes, Squire, an unabashed fan of Jackson Pollock, followed the artist's lead and fearlessly let his inventive riffs whirl and sinuate from his instrument in long, helical sparks. With the tendency in interviews to say very little, Squire often described himself as a loner and seemed to prefer to let the music speak for itself. The temptation for many journalists was to compare Squire to Johnny Marr, because not only were both from Manchester, but onstage Squire seemed to hold the same silences as Marr, peering up every now and then as his guitar veered and chimed.

But Love guitarist Mike Randle is quick to point out the differences between the two: "Johnny Marr is organic and sweet and borderless," he says. "Squire's style was brittle, brilliant and melodic. Squire is a very innovative guitarist in that he seems to marry melody and chords quite well together, which was refreshing for that time. If you listen to that first record, even when he's not playing notes you still have previous notes in your head."[11]

Although his lean build suggested a kind of pop pugilist, Ian Brown's face hinted at the brains of an intellectual and the brawn of a bully. He had not quite a villainous sneer, but not exactly one wracked with morality either. With his narrow, well defined cheekbones, and his thin, gunfighter eyes, Brown could be mistaken for either a cocky graduate student or a member of a feral gang who held their meetings under a bridge down by the river. Brown could look sometimes as if he wasn't there at all, but his deep stare also suggested a man capable of a probing focus and a potentially splenetic temperament.

"I still believe," says singer Martin Phillips of New Zealand's beloved indie rock heroes the Chills, "that the Stone Roses would not have done anywhere near as well without the powerful charisma and looks of Ian Brown. He looked good from every angle. Though largely expressionless, he looked as if there was a lot more going on inside his mind than there appeared to be once he opened his mouth. His lyrics show him to be no fool but he did seem determined to come across as a bit of a lad."

Although *The Stone Roses* was only their first album, in interviews the band were as self-possessed and confident as a band with a handful of albums under their belts who had been through it all before. Perhaps their confidence stemmed from the fact that they knew they had just let loose a soon-to-be classic album on the general public, or maybe they were just brash by nature and didn't know any better. Whatever it was, by 1988 some kind of magic had happened that transformed a band with only a few half-decent singles to their name into a cocksure foursome who were absolutely convinced they had recorded one of the best albums ever. And they weren't shy about saying as much.

John Robb tells me the band's shameless belief in themselves and their music wasn't something that happened overnight, as it appeared, but that it had developed over the years they had already spent together. Robb also thinks waiting so long to put out their debut actually worked in their favor. "Luckily for them," he says, "the planned debut album was scuppered; they managed to avoid the first album fumblings and move straight into top gear. They had time to listen to more music, rehearse even harder and assimilate more influences. By the time they came to record the lemon album they were brilliant musicians with a very wide musical vocabulary on the cusp of a scene that they helped instigate."

And like Muhammad Ali who said, "It's hard to be humble, when you're as great as I am" (it's no wonder that Brown once declared "boxers are my heroes"), or John McEnroe who, mid-match, told his opponents they had no business being on the same court with him, the Stone Roses by the end of the eighties knew they were better than great and the evidence of this knowledge came in interviews and hustings where, in bursts of hubris and swagger, they were quick-witted, subversively monosyllabic, confrontational and utterly charming. Always a fanfaron, Brown told Roy Wilkinson of *Sounds* in 1989 that the Stone Roses' debut was better than the Rolling Stones' first offering; he told *NME* the same year that, "None of our obvious contemporaries do anything for me," and he boasted the next month to *NME* again that, "We're the most important group in the world because we've got the best songs and we haven't even begun to show our potential yet."

History shows us that Brown may have been right on the first two of his points but as for the last one, he was dead wrong. *The Stone Roses* shows more than a band with potential—it shows a band sizzling with skill, consumed with drive and aspiration and possessing an almost preternatural mastery of the pop paradigm. On their debut album, they were, for all practical purposes, a band at the height of their powers.

The trouble is, they were not only at the height of their powers, they were using them all up. Evidence of this comes five years later on the soggy follow-up *Second Coming*, which, the band's legal and personal troubles aside, wasn't worthy of their name and didn't live up to its title—instead bringing the band back to earth with the weight of bad reviews, disappointing sales and the command over their audience clearly dimming. So in spite of the fearlessness and brilliance of *The Stone Roses*, it may be that the band, together nearly four years at the time of the recording of their seminal debut, by 1994 had already peaked and simply had little left.

Before we get things started, I should tell you I'm from a small San Francisco suburb called Concord, which is roughly five thousand miles from Manchester. When *The Stone Roses* came out in the US in 1989, I was a sophomore in college and working as the Music Director of my campus radio station. When I put on the album for the first time and read the accompanying press kit RCA had sent me, which was loaded with tasty interviews from *Melody Maker* and *NME*, I was immediately hooked. The music was catchy and infectious, but the things the band said in those interviews blew my mind as much as the songs. Cavalier, blunt and mouthy, the Stone Roses were the cockiest musicians I had ever encountered, sure of themselves down to the last word. As for me, I had never been sure of anything in my life and the sheer fearless braggadocio of the band and their songs was addictive.[12] I had always wanted to live the self-assured life and this was the soundtrack I needed.

As much as I loved the album, I'm not ashamed to admit all these years later that at the time, there was a lot about it I didn't understand. I didn't know "Bye Bye Badman" was referencing the 1968 Paris student riots; I couldn't make out any of the lyrics to "Waterfall"; and on "(Song for My) Sugar Spun Sister" when Brown sang "Every member of Parliament trips on glue," I thought he was talking about George Clinton and Bootsy Collins. So at the time, I didn't get exactly what each song was about, but I was in love with the Stone Roses' confidence and certainty of their place in the world. I had loved a lot of bands up to that point, like the Police, R.E.M. and the Replacements, but the Stone Roses were the first band that I studied and mimicked. I wore the baggiest clothes I could find, started speaking in an English accent and tried to grow a fringe like John Squire—but unfortunately being a scrappy Jewish kid with curly hair, all it would do was rise in a frontal puff above my forehead. It was only a fringe (albeit somewhat of a kinky one) for four minutes after a shower, and then it became the floating curly brownie that was fast becoming my trademark around campus.

I even wrote a glowing review of *The Stone Roses* for the campus newspaper, and at 2,537 words not only did it challenge the normally enforced 200-word length of the paper's record review guidelines, it was also a complete mess. The only bit worth saving was, "Bookended by 'I Wanna Be Adored' and 'I Am the Resurrection,' *The Stone Roses* begins with a plea and ends with a promise."[13]

Although when it comes to describing my favorite albums, I've been known to lapse into a kind of room-clearing adorational hyperbole, enough time has passed since I first heard *The Stone Roses* for my bias to give way to the kind of reason and critical perspective which the passing of years generously affords. But those years have changed nothing, and time has proven rather impotent at chipping away my love for this album.

I'll be honest, I don't know what Ian Brown's favorite movie is and I have no idea where John Squire likes to buy his clothes, but you have to understand this: I love *The Stone Roses* and play it more than any other album I own. Not only that, but I can still do a dead-on impersonation of Ian Brown; at the university where I teach I have the same Stone Roses poster hanging in my office that I had in my dorm eighteen years ago; and I have lost girlfriends on long drives who have begged me after the eighth listen in a row, to put on something else.

No way. Never. *The Stone Roses* is my favorite album of all time. And we are gathered here today to talk about it.

Notes

1. I'm still waiting for a party where a beautiful girl asks me the name of the drummer on the Jazz Butcher Conspiracy's *Distressed Gentlefolk*. I've rehearsed this so much that I'm sure if it ever happens I'll blow it and instead of saying, "Kevin Haskins," I'll say the name of the guy who played keyboards in Curiosity Killed the Cat.
2. A two-disc ten-year anniversary edition of *The Stone Roses*, released in 1999, charted at #9 in the UK.
3. In 2003 the writers of *NME* declared *The Stone Roses* to be the best album of all time, while in 2004 the British newspaper *The Observer* revealed a poll of 100 musicians and critics had voted *The Stone Roses* as the best British album of all time.
4. Although "Fools Gold" (#8) matched "Elephant Stone" in terms of chart position, the Roses' highest charting singles were "One Love" (#4) and "Love Spreads" (#2).
5. The paint throwing, by the way, did get the entire band arrested.
6. It's been said that had the Stone Roses fulfilled this contract it would have been worth an estimated $20 million.
7. McGee got his start as the manager of the Jesus and Mary Chain and is also credited for being the guy who signed Oasis.
8. You can pick through its bones on the bootleg compilation *Garage Flower*. But if you're an intrepid collector you could try to get your hands on *...And on the Sixth Day Whilst God Created Manchester, the Lord Created the Stone Roses*, a highly sought after bootleg album, similar to *Garage Flower*, which is

comprised of early work from 1985–87, and the Martin Hannet–produced sessions they later shelved.

9. Leckie at that point was best known for his tape-op work on solo albums by John Lennon, George Harrison and Paul McCartney, engineering Pink Floyd's *Dark Side of the Moon* and his production on XTC's *White Music* and the Fall's *This Nation's Saving Grace*.
10. "I have rehearsed in a room next to him," Stewart recalls, "and he was unbelievably loud."
11. Although from a historical perspective Squire's chiming swoon might be as memorable as Marr's moody jangle, Randle points out that a major difference between the two guitarists is, "Johnny Marr's canvas has way more colors."
12. Earlier that year a girl I had a crush on came to my dorm room late one night, took off her shirt and crawled into my bed. I remember thinking, *I wonder if she likes me*.
13. Conversely, the low point of the article was, "Seriously, gang, this is the raddest album of the year!"

In Utero

by Gillian G. Gaar

Gillian G. Gaar is the author of *She's a Rebel: The History of Women in Rock'n'Roll*. She served as project consultant on the Nirvana box set *With the Lights Out*. She lives in Seattle.

Chapter 6
The *In Utero* Sessions

Even before Nirvana had signed to DGC, Cobain had been toying with the idea of working with Steve Albini. "We were driving to Madison [Wisconsin] back in '90," Krist Novoselic recalls (where the group would first work with Butch Vig). "And we were listening to something produced by Steve Albini, I think *Surfer Rosa* by the Pixies. By that time we were pulling all our gear in a trailer, so the van was nice and open, and there was this little couch against the back door. And Kurt lifted up his finger and he goes, 'And our snare sound will sound like this!' It was like he proclaimed it, 'cause he was sitting on that couch like he was a ruler on a throne. And then the tire blew out!"

Albini was himself a musician, having been a member of the abrasive Big Black and the provocatively named Rapeman. He was also a producer, though, like Jack Endino, he preferred to use the credit "Recorded By." Along with *Surfer Rosa*, the Breeders' *Pod* was another Albini-produced album that was a favorite of Kurt Cobain's; he had also produced Jesus Lizard, Naked

Raygun, and Jon Spencer Blues Explosion, among many others. In addition, he had a reputation as someone who did not suffer fools gladly, and was blunt about his dislike of the machinations of the mainstream music industry. "I'm not interested in being a part of the music business," he says. "I don't want to develop any relationships with any of these players, these administrative types, record label people. By and large those people are scum; I don't want to have anything to do with them."

Cobain had first seen Albini at Big Black's last show, which was held August 9, 1987 at the Georgetown Steamplant in Seattle. Though he would later tell a journalist he was not really "much of a Big Black fan," he had liked Albini's other work, and after the success of *Nevermind*, the band was interested in achieving a harsher sound in their recordings that better reflected their musical roots. "It was our sophomore [major label] record," says Novoselic. "And everybody was watching. So we thought, let's make a real indie record." The April '92 sessions at the Laundry Room and the January '93 sessions in Brazil had shown that they could still get back to cranking out songs quickly, as in their days at Sub Pop. The release of *Incesticide*, a collection of material from the band's early years, at the end of '92, served as a reminder to their new fans that Nirvana's music had not always had the slickness of the songs on *Nevermind*. The appeal of working with someone like the no-nonsense Albini, who had plenty of indie credibility, was obvious.

The band had spoken publicly about wanting to use Albini so frequently throughout '92 that rumors were circulating that he was officially signed on to produce the album. The problem was that Albini himself had not been contacted about the matter. "The press reported that repeatedly," he says. "I was having to contend with it on a daily basis. People were asking me about it, not just passers-by, but prospective clients, other bands, and it was genuinely affecting my business. So I sent the paper a letter saying, 'I have not been contacted by Nirvana, you didn't contact me before you printed this.'" Albini's denial was published—after which he finally was contacted by the band's management.

Albini had never seen the group live, though he was friends with Sub Pop's co-founder, Bruce Pavitt. "I remember him being all excited about Nirvana," he says. "I was aware of a lot of the things that had happened around that band, and I had heard their record and stuff, but I didn't count myself as a fan. The thing that changed my mind about their validity was seeing them work in the studio."

Albini had preliminary talks with both Cobain and Dave Grohl, "just discussing the approach to making the record and talking to them about records they liked and stuff that I should listen to to acquaint myself with what they wanted to try to do," he says. "It seemed like they wanted to make precisely the sort of record that I'm comfortable doing, and it seemed like they genuinely liked the records that I did make, so the whole thing seemed legitimate to me. The reason I decided to do it was I not only got the impression they were genuine about wanting me to work on it, they were also genuine about wanting to make a record for themselves. That's really all I cared about. I didn't want to be in a position where we were trying to satisfy some outside agency. And I didn't know if they would be allowed to make a record that way. I just figured, if they make a record and give it to their record label, then they will be in a much better situation on an emotional level, and the record will go faster and be better than if they try to make a record where they're trying to clear obstacles with the record label the entire way and trying to get people to rubber stamp it. So I asked the band if I could deal with them directly, and not have to contend with the record label at all, and they said, 'Yes, that's fine.' So all of my dealings were with the band. To this day, I don't honestly know if anyone from Geffen has ever spoken to me."

But he admits that agreeing to work on the album after denying he was doing so, "sort of created the first of many little micro-controversies. Once it was apparent that I was working on the record, it seemed like I had tried to create some sort of Nixonian denial of it, so that if everything went shitty, I could get out of it without ever having been publicly associated with it. That was the beginning of a pretty bizarre period, where my parents, among other people, who had been mercifully insulated from most of everything to do with the music scene, started reading things in the daily newspaper in Montana [where Albini was raised] about me working on this record or some other overboiled micro-controversy. That was the beginning of the 'weird' period."

And Albini's suspicions about the "outside agencies" Nirvana worked with were not inaccurate; those close to the band were none too pleased with their choice of producer. "I don't think they were too happy about it, because Albini's such an iconoclast," Novoselic confirms. "He's an outspoken critic of the major labels, and excess, of musical pomp and excess." Nor were the band's artistic desires taken very seriously by those around them. In trying to reassure Gary Gersh, the band's A&R rep, about Albini, Grohl recalled to writer Phil Sutcliffe, "I said, 'Gary, man, don't be so afraid, the record will turn out great!' He said, 'Oh, I'm not afraid, go ahead, bring me back the best you can do.' It was like, 'Go and have your fun, then we'll get another producer and make the *real* album'" (emphasis Grohl's).

But if the label felt the band was wasting their time, they had to concede they weren't wasting money; Albini's fee was a modest $100,000, and he refused to take any royalties ("Anyone who takes a royalty off a band's record—other than someone who actually writes music or plays on the record—is a thief," he told Azerrad). They would also be recording at the same place Albini had recently finished working with PJ Harvey on *Rid of Me*, Pachyderm Studios, located just outside the small town of Cannon Falls, 40 miles southeast of Minneapolis, Minnesota. It was felt that the remote location would cut down on outside distractions, and it was also inexpensive—recording costs were said to be a mere $24,000. Albini sent Cobain a copy of *Rid of Me* to give him an idea of what the studio sounded like.

Albini had also been sent a cassette by the group, of the songs they had worked on in Brazil. "I preferred them immediately to the stuff that I had heard of *Nevermind*," he says. "The *Nevermind* album seemed very confined in its parameters. Each song had a beginning, middle, and an end, and it was all presented in a way that allowed you to hear each chunk. This new material, some of it was kind of sprawling and aimless, and I liked that, but there were still moments that were really powerful and dynamic. It just seemed like they had made a conceptual break in how they wanted to be and how they wanted to behave as a band, and what they wanted their music to sound like."

Just before leaving, there was a last minute equipment crisis. "The night before they flew out I got this panicked phone call," says Earnie Bailey. "They were practicing the night before and Kurt said that his Echo Flanger was broken. When those things break, they're really complex under the hood, and I don't want to say poorly made, but they weren't built to the highest standards. Kurt said, 'It's the entire album—it's *got* to work!' He had been using his Echo Flanger to do all of this material, and I think he was worried that it wouldn't sound the same. So I said that I would take a look it. We met over at Krist's house, and it was really funny, because they popped the pedal open, and all he'd really done was he'd bumped the AC switch that turns the power on with his foot! It was hilarious, because it was such a simple fix. I was able to fix it with a Phillips screwdriver and a pair of pliers, and the level of gratitude was ridiculous. 'Man, you saved the album!' I had to laugh because I was like, 'Man, this is the easiest thing I've ever done.'"

The band, booked into Pachyderm as "The Simon Ritchie Bluegrass Ensemble," arrived in Minnesota the second week in February. The studio grounds also had a large house where clients could stay, another factor that helped the group focus on their work. "We were isolated," says Novoselic. "I don't know how we survived through that. It was pretty mellow. For two weeks, we were in this house, cooped up in the middle of nowhere, like a gulag. There was snow outside, we couldn't go anywhere. We just worked."

Recording began on February 13, and most days the group adhered to a regular schedule, beginning work around midday, taking a dinner break, then continuing to work until around midnight. "It was pretty simple, straight ahead," says Novoselic. "It was pretty live. Some of those songs were first takes." Their work ethic impressed Albini. "We earned his respect," says Novoselic. "'Cause he would stand there by the tape machine with his arms folded. And we'd play most of the songs in the first, second take, and he'd nod his head, like all right, these guys are the real thing."

There was a moment when Bailey's services were thought to be required. "I got a call the day or two after they arrived and they were having some kind of trouble getting going," he says. "I wasn't really sure what it was about, if it was problems tuning—I don't know if they didn't want to be bothered tuning their own stuff and didn't really feel like it would be a big deal having me along. So they arranged for me to fly out and I was waiting for the call, and then I spoke with Krist on the phone and he said that most of the instrument tracking was finished! They pounded out most of the album very quickly; I wasn't expecting Fleetwood Mac's *Rumours*, but I wasn't expecting it to happen that fast either. I remember being really excited by that, just thinking that they were doing something that raw and spontaneous and not being so critical that they were going to go over everything and kill it, you know?"

As usual, most of the album's lyrics were worked on up to the point of recording; Albini remembers Cobain carrying around a notebook of potential lyrics. "Many people would be expecting me to be writing about the last two years and my past experiences—drugs, having a child, the press coming down on us and stuff like that," he told a journalist a month before the album's release. "There's a little bit of my life on [the album], but for the most part it's very impersonal." It was a remarkably disingenuous claim, for Cobain's recent experiences permeated virtually every track on the record. The key events in his life the previous year had been the success of his band and the resultant media frenzy that had caused, his struggles with drugs, and the birth of his daughter. Accordingly, the record was replete with references to babies, childbirth, and reproduction (the album's very title means "in the womb"), witch hunts, the loss of privacy, illness and disease, and ambivalence about fame. The songs expressed a heartfelt anguish that would later cause some to interpret the entire album as a cry for help, but even at the time of its release *In Utero* could easily be read as an album focused on physical and spiritual sickness. But *In Utero*'s saving grace is that it doesn't fully give in to despair; the bursts of anger and sarcasm throughout the album keep the songs from sinking into abject despondency. Rather than being overwhelmed by circumstances, Cobain's songs on *In Utero* show him—for the most part—still able and willing to fight back. As such, among Nirvana's recorded efforts, it stands as Cobain's most personal work.

The first song on the first tape box from the sessions, dated February 13, is "Chuck Chuck Fo Fuck," an obvious reference to the rhythm of the song's main riff, and only meant as a temporary title; by the end of the sessions it was retitled "Scentless Apprentice." The song was inspired by Patrick Süskind's best-selling novel *Perfume: The Story of a Murderer*. Set in eighteenth-century France, the novel is the story of a man whose own body has no scent, but who has a highly developed sense of smell; apprenticed to a perfumer, his quest to capture the "ultimate perfume" of virgin women leads him to commit murder.

Appropriately, the song is one of *In Utero*'s most aggressive, alternating between the "chuck chuck" riff Grohl had come up with and Cobain's ascending answer call, underpinned by Novoselic's steady bass line and Grohl's powerful drumming. "It's a good example of the Nirvana dynamic at work," says Novoselic. "There's three players but there's a lot of stuff going on." The verses have allusions to the book's storyline, but it's the chorus that captures the attention here. Cobain seems to sum up not only the misanthropy of the book's lead character, but also his own, in his tortured shrieks of "Go away!" ("I just wanted to be as far away from people as I could—their smells disgust me," he told Azerrad in discussing the song.) As he reaches the end of each scream, his anger boils over into pure rage and his voice virtually gives out, in one of Cobain's most tortured and anguished performances. The song is one of the few in Nirvana's catalogue where the music is credited to all three members.

Bodily excretions and illness are the focus of "Milk It," initially entitled "PiL" (presumably after John Lydon's first post-Sex Pistols band), and then "Milk Made." It's a stark portrait of dependency with near-mumbled verses, dotted with words like "parasite," "endorphins," and "virus," none of which were in the version recorded in Brazil; at other points the lyrics are seemingly nothing more than random wordplay. The verses explode into maelstroms of noise and screams as they surge into the choruses, though the fury is somewhat tempered by Cobain's brief chuckle before the final chorus. But the overall bleakness of the scenario is confirmed by the observation that the only "bright side" in the future is suicide, the song screeching to a halt after Cobain's final screams.

"That's a gnarly song," says Novoselic. "The lyrics are pretty heavy. I got the bass nailed and real steady in a way that kind of harks back to 'Teen Spirit.' It's the same formula, but it's way twisted, kind of grotesque—it's a grotesque song."

Yet the twisted elements in both this song and "Scentless Apprentice" are what most impressed their producer. "There's always one or two songs on any given session that strike you as being the money shot, like, 'Wow, this is an amazing song, this is where everything came together, and this is really great,'" says Albini. "For me, that was the 'Milk Made' song or whatever it ended up being called, and 'Scentless Apprentice.' Those are the two that struck me as being the biggest step for the band. They seemed like the biggest break with their aggressive pop style that they were developing for themselves. They seemed the most adventurous sonically, and the most up my alley anyway." Being newer songs, both were also perhaps more indicative of the future direction Nirvana would have pursued. In 2005, Grohl cited both "Milk It" and "Heart-Shaped Box" as his favorite Nirvana songs.

In recording the songs, Albini also recalls, "On both of those, there were two vocal takes. There was one take that was singing the whole of the song, and one take where Kurt was just singing parts of the song to emphasize them or parts of the song with a different sound quality. There's a really dry, really loud voice that comes zooming up at the end of 'Milk It,' a vocal that's really dry and uncomfortably loud. That was something that was also done at the end of 'Rape Me,' where he wanted the sound of him screaming to just overtake the whole of the band." Though Cobain's screams were long noted for being key to Nirvana's sound, nothing the band previously recorded matched the sheer intensity of the vocal performances on *In Utero*.

There was then another go at "Sappy." It was a very unusual choice for the sessions, as the group hadn't played the song live since November 1990 (and after these sessions they would only play it a further three times). This version was the most fully produced band version of the song, slightly shorter than previous band versions, with a faster tempo and a noticeably stronger drum part. This version also begins without the instrumental intro on some of the earlier versions.

As for why the song was again revisited, Novoselic says simply, "We liked to play that song. I put that bass line together four years before that, and I thought it was really great, so I never changed it. It seems like nobody ever changed anything else on it either. You can hear older versions of, like, 'Lithium' or whatever, the bass lines are different, or the guitars, something's different. But why is it that this song, every time we recorded it, everybody did everything exactly the same? Well, I was totally happy with it, so why change it?"

Actually, the song was not "exactly the same" each time the group recorded it. There were always some variations—the Albini version featured a different guitar solo in the instrumental break, and was in a different key—though they were admittedly minor ones. And there still remained some dissatisfaction with it, as "Sappy" didn't appear on any of the proposed track listings for the album. "I actually think it's a pretty good song," is Albini's summation. "I don't remember it being bad. But I think it wore out its welcome on the band, apparently."

Next was "Very Ape," then still titled "Perky New Wave," which would be one of the shortest on *In Utero*. It's essentially the same length as the acoustic home demo of the song featured on *With the Lights Out*, said to have been recorded in 1993, with lyrics that appear to be similar to the version recorded in Brazil. But while the musical structure on the home demo, Brazil version, and the Albini version is basically the same (though the Albini version has a tighter performance), the lyric on the Albini version is vastly different. In the end, "Very

Ape" is a send-up of stereotypical macho behavior, *à la* "Mr. Moustache" on *Bleach*; it's the singer himself who's regressively "very ape," primitive, hiding his naivety behind a wall of braggadocio. Musically, the song's most interesting aspect is the persistent new wave-flavored riff that wails through the song like a siren, not dissimilar from the main riff in "Lounge Act" from *Nevermind*. The jerky rhythms also bring new wave act Devo to mind, one of the few groups whose songs Nirvana covered.

February 14 saw the first run-through of "Pennyroyal Tea," the first take an instrumental. The song had been written during the winter of 1990–91, when Cobain was then sharing an apartment with Grohl in Olympia, Washington. But though it was first performed on April 17, 1991 at the same show where "Smells Like Teen Spirit" had its public debut, and the group subsequently performed it on their fall '91 tour, the song was apparently not considered for *Nevermind*. Cobain later told Azerrad the song was written "in about thirty seconds," the lyrics taking somewhat longer—half an hour. "I remember hearing it and thinking, 'God, this guy has such a beautiful sense of melody, I can't believe he's screaming all the time,'" Grohl later told Harp magazine.

As there was little lyrical variation in the song from '91 to '93 (the lyrics on the home demo on *With the Lights Out*, said to be from 1993, are identical to the released version), the instrumental version recorded with Endino was presumably just intended to nail down the musical arrangement. The verses convey a profound sense of anomie, with each one mentioning some ailment or at the very least disaffectedness (as in the second verse's wonderful longing for a "Leonard Cohen afterworld"). The final verse, with its references to warm milk, laxatives, and antacids, touches on Cobain's well-documented stomach problems, which caused him pain throughout much of his life, but were never properly diagnosed. ("I'm always in pain, and that adds to the anger in our music," he told writer Jon Savage. "I'm grateful to it, in a way.")

The song's title refers to a home abortion method, though the lyric extended what Cobain called its "cleansing theme" to a hope it would wash away one's inner demons, in addition to being a means of eliminating something that was "in utero." And while the song has the Nirvana formula of quiet verses/loud choruses, Cobain's vocal during the chorus still has a lugubrious feel (with the harmonizing vocals adding a degree of tension), as if the singer is suspended in some stage between sleep and wakefulness (also tying in with the song's references to insomnia). This element was something that would be even more apparent in the *Unplugged* performance of the song. His summation of being "anemic royalty" was an image that was indicative of his own contradictory nature; being powerful, yet feeling powerless.

"Radio Friendly Unit Shifter" was titled both "You Said a Mouthful" and "Nine Month Media Blackout" on the tape box, and elsewhere was also referred to as "Four Month Media Blackout" (though while interviews with the band were limited from 1992 on, there was never any official media blackout). A "Radio Friendly Unit Shifter" refers to songs that are both accessible and strong sellers—a hit single, in other words. In any case, the lyrics don't really reflect any of the titles, and are more reflective of what Cobain insisted was his usual songwriting method—stringing together lines he found in his journals. But there are a few lines that hint at a more personal meaning. There's a pointed reference to privacy, as well as the childbirth imagery ("my water broke"). And the desperation of the chorus, which repeatedly begs to know what's wrong, is matched by a bridge that expresses a measure of hopefulness—find where you belong, and the truth shall set you free.

The song begins with a wailing guitar note, then, as Novoselic admits, "There's just one riff through the whole song! I pretty much just play the same riff through the whole song." Nonetheless, the song's propulsive energy is undeniable, and though Novoselic calls the title "cynical, sarcastic," there's also some truth in it—the song has a catchiness that is accessible (something the group recognized by opening virtually every subsequent show with the song). Tellingly, the song didn't get its final title until after the band's label had told the group that the album wasn't "radio friendly" enough.

"Frances Farmer Will Have Her Revenge on Seattle" was a song that "came to the band pretty intact," says Novoselic. "Kurt brought it in pretty finished. Lyrics were left to last. That's why in practice tapes you hear Kurt singing phonetically, just doing the melody." Like "Scentless Apprentice," "Frances Farmer" was inspired by a book, *Shadowland*, William Arnold's biography of the actress, published in 1978. Farmer was born in Seattle in 1914. In the 1930s she found fame in such films as *Come and Get It*, but following an arrest for drunken driving in 1942, her life was set on a downward spiral that resulted in her being committed to a mental institution and lobotomized. She died of cancer of the esophagus in 1970.

Cobain had been fascinated by Farmer's story since reading Arnold's book in high school. And after he himself became a star, he identified even more with her story, especially with Farmer's unconventional nature, her outspoken dislike of commercialism, her hounding by the media, and her sad, unjust fate. Arnold worked as a film critic at the *Seattle Post-Intelligencer*, a daily newspaper, and Cobain made several attempts to contact him in 1993. When he didn't respond, Cobain contacted the Arts and Entertainment editor at the paper, who passed the message on to Arnold. "I said, 'Who is Kurt Cobain?'" he recalls. "She was shocked that I didn't know who he was."

Arnold had not responded as he'd been pestered by "hundreds" of obsessed people about Farmer since the book's publication, and he figured that Cobain was just another of them. But Cobain was persistent. "He called and left this rambling message," Arnold says. "I have this vague memory of him saying he had read this book when he was in high school and he got it from the Aberdeen library. It had a big impact on him. And there was something about him thinking he was related to Judge Frater [who signed the first court order to commit Farmer], and just rambling. I thought to myself, 'I've really got to talk to this guy,' but I was going through other stuff then and I just didn't. Then he killed himself and I felt really bad."

Arnold didn't hear the song until after Cobain's death, and he also wrote a short piece about his missed communications with Cobain. "The weird thing to me is the lesson that when you write stuff, you do influence people in ways that you don't even know," he says. "And that gives you a certain moral responsibility. I don't know what that responsibility is, and I don't know how far you can carry it, but you have that responsibility, whether you like it or not. You can't just say, 'Well, I don't care,' because people can take it any way they want to." It was an observation Cobain might well have benefited from, given his frequent comments he wished there was a "Rock Star 101" course he could've taken to adjust to his unexpected fame.

Instead, "Frances Farmer" seethes with controlled anger, as Cobain drew parallels between the unfair treatment he felt he and his wife had experienced under the scrutiny of "false witnesses" and what Farmer had endured (unsurprisingly, he also draws on witch hunt imagery). But it's also a song of vengeance, with Farmer returning to scorch her enemies into oblivion, a rare case of someone emerging triumphant in a Nirvana song. But such solace eludes the singer himself, who prefers to sink into oblivion, longing for the "comfort in being sad."

The version of "Moist Vagina" recorded at the Albini sessions was not markedly different from the one recorded in Brazil, though the Albini version has a final minute of noise concluding with what sounds like a dry gargle from Cobain. In essence, it's a slightly more melodic version of the improv material Nirvana recorded in Brazil, and though the title and its harsh music wouldn't have made it out of place on *In Utero*, it was apparently never considered for the album's final lineup. Nor was it ever known to have been played live. Perhaps, as in the jams played during the last session with Endino, it was only meant as a means of taking a break.

"Punk Rock," later called "tourette's," is a song that Novoselic says dates back to the Go Team era, the Go Team being an ad hoc collection of Olympia musicians that Cobain recorded a single with. It has the distinction of being *In Utero*'s shortest track, one minute and thirty-three seconds of pure sonic assault, after the jokey spoken intro, "Moderate rock!" The final name, "tourette's," refers to Gilles de la Tourette syndrome, more commonly called Tourette's syndrome, a condition that compels the sufferer to involuntarily blurt out obscenities. Cobain may well be screaming obscenities during the song, but it's hard to tell—the most distinguishable word is "Hey!" The music itself consists of a four note riff pounded out repetitively; this version is a good 40 seconds shorter than the instrumental take recorded with Endino, simply cutting back on some of the repetitions. Cobain himself admitted to writer Dave Thompson the number "isn't that good a song" but it nonetheless made the final cut because "it fit the mood."

The band then made a first attempt at what was arguably the defining track of the album, "Heart-Shaped Box." Cobain wrote the song in early '92, but then had trouble developing it with the band. Before putting it aside for good, he decided to have the band jam on it once again and this time it came together, "instantly," Cobain said. This clearly occurred before the Brazil session, by which time the bulk of the song had been worked out.

"Heart-Shaped Box" was the Nirvana formula personified, with a restrained, descending riff played through the verse, building in intensity to the cascading passion of the chorus. Cobain told Azerrad the song's "basic idea" was about children with cancer, a topic which made him unbearably sad. But while the song does reference the illness, the lyrics appear more to address the physical and emotional dependencies inherent in relationships. The imagery is particularly striking, with phrases like "tar pit trap," "meat-eating orchids," and "umbilical noose." That these female symbols each hold a potential danger means they all convey a fear that ultimately equates intimacy with a suffocating claustrophobia. Yet the singer is unable, or unwilling, to tear himself away, snarling at his own submissiveness in the sarcastic chorus. Cobain's vocal on the song is one of his most evocative. The fact that so many of Nirvana's songs end in strenuous screaming means that his emotive delivery in quieter moments is sometimes overlooked, as in the haunting way his voice slightly catches while singing the words "baby's breath" or "highness," contrasting with the manic glee with which he sings of his newest complaints in the chorus. Another of the song's inspirations was the heart-shaped box filled with seashells, teacups, pinecones, and a doll that had been Love's first gift to her future husband.

Though pleased with the performance on the whole, Novoselic strenuously objected to a shimmering effect used on the guitar solo that he found "really grating. These were the words I said: 'Why do you want to take such a beautiful song and throw this hideous abortion in the middle of it?' And they're like, 'Well, I don't know, it sounds good.' They didn't have any good arguments, because they were sabotaging it is what they were doing. Kurt was being self-conscious. 'Why can't you just make it beautiful?' 'I don't know.' I argued and argued and argued and argued about it, and they just wouldn't listen." Novoselic's assessment was right; the discordant sound of the effect broke the haunting mood of the song.

Also recorded on the 14th was another song destined to be as anthemic as "Heart-Shaped Box"—a song then called "La La La," but ultimately titled "All Apologies." This version was more stripped down than the version recorded in 1991 with Craig Montgomery, without extra touches like the tambourine. Like "Radio Friendly Unit Shifter," the number is deceptively simple, with a single insinuating melodic line played throughout most of it. But again, the strength of the performance keeps the song from sounding repetitive, due in part to the addition of a bittersweet cello line (played by Kera Schaley, the only other musician to appear on the record).

Cobain's lyric and resigned delivery also invest the song

with an elegiac quality. In the verses, the singer effectively takes all the problems of the world on his shoulders, assuming all the blame, even turning his back on his work, in a song that's wracked with guilt (though Cobain insisted it was "a very, very sarcastic song"). As in "Dumb," the narrator is caught looking in from the outside, torn between the desire to be included and the urge to maintain the independence of standing alone. It was a conflict Cobain never worked out, and after his death, more than one observer described this song as being akin to a suicide note. Again, there's a glimmer of hope in the chorus, with the singer finding some sense of unity with the sun, though singing of being married as being "buried" was a comparison that would inevitably result in media speculation about the state of Cobain's own marriage—exactly the kind of attention he disparaged on the rest of the album (in interviews, he said he wrote the lines before meeting Love).

"I remember really liking the sound of that song as a contrast to the more aggressive ones," says Albini. "I remember thinking it sounded really good in that it sounded lighter, but it didn't sound conventional. It was sort of a crude light sound that suited the band."

On the 15th, the group recorded the song that would eventually be titled "I Hate Myself and I Want to Die" but on the tape box was represented by a drawing of a fish. "That was just one of those dirty little songs that we'd do," says Novoselic. "They're just really fucked up, demented. They're trashy, but they're tight; they have a lot of good energy. They're catchy." The song is largely the same as the version recorded in Brazil, minus the lengthy intro, and with a different guitar solo. Musically, it occupies a middle ground between *In Utero*'s more aggressive material and songs like "Heart-Shaped Box" and "Pennyroyal Tea"; the underlying pop sensibility makes it not unpleasant to listen to, though lyrically it remains unmemorable. Nor was it apparently of much interest to the band; Cobain dismissed it as "a typical, boring song," and they never performed it live. The group also put together a version with a jokey spoken-word vocal overdubbed on the main track.

Then came "Rape Me," which was written around the time of the *Nevermind* sessions and was performed during the fall 1991 tour. By the time the song was released, it was easy to read it as a condemnation of the media harassment Cobain felt he had suffered, especially as the song's intro reworks the opening chords of the group's biggest hit, "Smells Like Teen

Spirit." But in fact most of the lyric was complete before *Nevermind* was even released, though Cobain conceded the "favorite inside source" line, added to the bridge later, was intended as a direct jab at the media (among the album's thank-yous was a listing for "Our favorite inside sources across the globe").

Interestingly, the acoustic demo of the song on *With the Lights Out*, said to have been recorded in 1992, has different lyrics; curious, as the song had already been performed in concert with the same lyrics that would be used in the *In Utero* version. The verses seemingly welcome abuse, though there is an implied threat of comeuppance in Cobain's grim delivery. This was something that was particularly true of the song's ending; as in "Milk It," Cobain's vocal was recorded so that it "just overwhelms the band and becomes this really uncomfortable presence," says Albini, though "frightening" would be a more appropriate description than "uncomfortable."

The end result was a song that was part submissive invitation, part defiant taunt, a mix that confused and disturbed many listeners. Cobain found himself having to explain repeatedly that the song was not meant to advocate assault of any kind; "It's an anti-, let me repeat that, anti-rape song," he patiently explained to MTV. That there were still those who missed the point was evidenced by the fact that *In Utero* was initially banned in Singapore and South Korea because of the track and other profanities on the album. In a letter to the South Korean authorities, the band's manager, John Silva, stressed the song's relation to media harassment, writing, "[Cobain] used the analogy of a 'rape' to highlight the degree to which he felt violated as a result of his newfound celebrity." His justification for the use of the word "shit" in "Milk It" was more convoluted, stating the song addressed the exploitation of Cobain's talent by a greedy music industry; "When taken on face value with a predisposition towards subjective language requirements, I think you'll agree that the effectiveness of this song is due largely to the graphic nature of this [obscene] refrain," Silva wrote.

"Serve the Servants" is a song that Novoselic remembers Cobain bringing in "pretty much done" (it's the only song on *In Utero* that wasn't previously demoed by the band). It was also a song that was his most openly autobiographical, as even Cobain had to admit—the first two verses dealing with the aftermath of fame, the second two with family. Musically, the track was a straight-ahead rock song, arguably the most straightforward on *In Utero*, with the tempo steady throughout, as is the volume, in a departure from the soft/loud Nirvana formula.

Cobain's sense of persecution is made clear when he again likens his targeting by the "self-appointed judges" of the media to a witch hunt in the first verse. His portrayal of his troubled relationship with his father in the second verse revisits a familiar theme in his work, unhappiness with one's family, as in "Paper Cuts" from *Bleach* and "Even in His Youth," a 1991 B-side (in comparison, the home demo on *With the Lights Out* has completely different lyrics). Yet in the chorus, he sardonically dismisses the impact his parents' "legendary divorce" had on him, in the same way he claimed in interviews his own songs "don't have much personal meaning at all." But in this instance, Cobain's meaning was clear; "This is the way Nirvana's Kurt Cobain spells success: s-u-c-k-s-e-g-g-s," David Fricke wrote in his review of the album for *Rolling Stone*. But the question of why a young man who'd enjoyed such unexpected acclaim and monetary rewards now found himself left "bored and old" remained unanswered.

Two and a half years after it was written, "Dumb" was finally recorded. "That's a beautiful song," says Novoselic. "That's a really good one. I like the BBC version of that song [recorded in 1991, which features identical lyrics to the *In Utero* version]. It's real raw, but still the beauty is strong. A sweet pop song."

"Sweet" in sound perhaps, but dark in sentiment; "Dumb" has a lyric thoroughly steeped in melancholy. This time, the outsider is also a recluse, fully immersed—drowning?—in the "comfort in being sad," the same state that the narrator of "Frances Farmer" yearned to attain. Yet, as is true of many of the album's quieter songs, the sadness is laced with resignation, not despondency. The narrator is again on the outside looking in, and this time seems to be too filled with apathy to have much desire to change the situation. Cobain's world-weary vocal conveys the exhaustion of a man who hasn't slept for days, but is past caring—even when he sings of being happy (a highly unusual sentiment to be expressed in a Nirvana song), he qualifies that with a "maybe." The song is shorter than the instrumental recorded at Word of Mouth, eliminating one of the verse repetitions. A cello line adds a mellow undercurrent to the song's chorus and bridge.

Albini remembers Pachyderm's studio tech, Bob Weston, primarily working with Grohl on his material, which was recorded next. "Dave Solo" was a quick minute and a half of heavy metal-style riffing, along the same lines as "Dave's Meat Song," perhaps intended as a warm-up. It couldn't have made more of a contrast with what was called "Dave's Mellow Song," a song Grohl had already released as "Color Pictures of a Marigold."

Grohl had previously released the song in 1992 on his solo cassette *Pocketwatch*, recorded under the name Late!, on which he plays all instruments himself. This version of the song is shorter, and features better production, which heightens its delicate, brooding quality. Two instrumental versions were recorded before Grohl recorded one with vocals; when the song was released, it would surprise many who hadn't realized Grohl had been recording his own songs for years.

Following "Marigold" is another improv number, the instrumental "Lullaby." Organ, bass, and drums swirl around each other for three minutes in an aimless jam that ends with a spate of wild drumming.

On the 16th, more takes of "Pennyroyal Tea" and "Heart-Shaped Box" were recorded, and then the basic tracks for the album were completed. "Recording was very straightforward," says Albini. "They recorded the basic take as a band, all recorded live. And on almost every song, Kurt would add one, sometimes two additional little guitar parts. I would say that was basically it."

Cobain then recorded the vocals with dispatch (one account claims all vocals were laid down in six hours). By this time, he had become a far more expressive singer than he had been on *Bleach*, and without the double-tracking and other effects used on *Nevermind* one gets a far greater sense of what he was capable of as a vocalist. Especially notable is the immensity of his emotional range, from frenzied shrieks to a gentle, even soothing, delivery. Similarly, the album also highlights all three member's skill as musicians. Nirvana wasn't a one-note band that was only capable of rocking out; they were also a group that could actually play. The melodic strengths of Nirvana's songs were later clearly revealed in their *Unplugged* performance.

Mixing was done over the course of five days. "That was also very straightforward," Albini recalls. "We basically just pushed the faders up and take it at a decent balance, and then put it down. So we didn't really screw around a lot on any of it. I think we got two or three songs mixed every day."

The group took time to relax as well, going into Minneapolis to see the Cows one evening. They also made various prank phone calls. At one point Grohl called Silva, claiming that after three days he was still doing a soundcheck on the snare drum—then having to rush to assure Silva he was only joking. Bailey was also kept up-to-date about the sessions. "Dave described to me at one point an idea that Albini had about hanging suspending microphones overhead and having them swing back and forth over his cymbals," he says. "I don't think that they ever utilized that, but it was an idea I was excited about because I liked the idea of something kind of chaotic in the recording like that." Courtney Love turned up during the second week of the sessions with Frances and there was some resulting friction. But overall, the working atmosphere was positive, with a camaraderie that was evident to Albini. "Kurt was the principle songwriter and he was the lead vocalist, but the other two guys in that band had far more to do with the ultimate sound and direction of the band than anyone has given them credit for," he says.

Albini also had a favorable impression of the members as people. "Dave and Kurt and Krist had a very overtly goofy take on things," he says. "I really liked and enjoyed their company. Kurt was more withdrawn initially, but I think that's only to be expected because he didn't know me; he didn't have any reason to trust me or whatever. I didn't try to get on any sort of intimate level with him, out of respect for the pressure he must feel under every day—having people try to get close to him all the time. I figured I'd allow him as much distance as he wanted. It was obvious that what was going on in his head was as important to him as what was going on between him and other people."

Novoselic suggested opening the album with one of the harsher tracks. "I wanted to start the record off with 'Scentless Apprentice,'" he recalls. "I remember saying, 'Let's get some mall rat girls that'll buy this record and just freak them out! And freak their moms out!' We were laughing." "Rape Me" was also considered as the opening track, but it was felt it would draw too much of a parallel to *Nevermind*, as that album's first track was the song the opening of "Rape Me" plays off of, "Teen Spirit." "I Hate Myself" was originally considered for the final lineup, but was dropped to keep the album from sounding too noisy; it later appeared on the compilation *The Beavis and Butthead Experience*. The remaining songs were apparently not considered for the album, but were released elsewhere: "Sappy," renamed "Verse Chorus Verse" appeared on the compilation *No Alternative*, and "Moist Vagina" and "Marigold" were used as B-sides.

Novoselic later told a journalist it took two weeks to decide the running order for the album. Ultimately, *In Utero*'s final running order would be: "Serve the Servants," "Scentless Apprentice," "Heart-Shaped Box," "Rape Me," "Frances Farmer Will Have Her Revenge on Seattle," "Dumb," "Very Ape," "Milk It," "Pennyroyal Tea," "Radio Friendly Unit Shifter," "tourette's," and "All Apologies."

The sessions were wrapped up by February 26, and everyone smoked cigars to celebrate. "It worked in precisely the same way as any session that I do," Albini says. "The band shows up, they know their material, they have their equipment together, they set up, they play, we add a few things, and we mix it. It was very, very straightforward." But the road to *In Utero*'s release would not be.

Highway 61 Revisited

by Mark Polizzotti

Mark Polizzotti's previous books include the collaborative novel *S.* (1991), *Lautréamont Nomad* (1994), *Revolution of the Mind: The Life of André Breton* (1995), *The New Life: Poems* (1998), and a study of Luis Buñuel's *Los Olvidados* for the British Film Institute (2006). His articles, reviews, and poetry have appeared in the *New Republic, ARTnews, Parnassus, Partisan Review,* and elsewhere. He is also the translator of over thirty books, including works by Gustave Flaubert, Marguerite Duras, André Breton, and Jean Echenoz. He lives in Boston.

3. You Got a Lotta Nerve

Just as "Like a Rolling Stone" was entering the charts, Bob Dylan made his annual appearance at the 1965 Newport Folk Festival. Even accounting for the difference between historical time and real time—the recognition that not everyone would have caught up with the new hit record mere days after its release—we might still have anticipated that the wide airplay Dylan's latest single was receiving would help ready the audience for his new musical direction. But of course, it didn't.

Dylan's involvement with the Newport festival has become yet one more legend attached to his name, dissected, reported, and misreported in countless histories. It was at Newport '63 that he first cemented his stardom, following a guest set on Joan Baez's stage. At Newport '64 he elicited the first stirrings of discomfort among folk purists by replacing the "finger-pointing" songs they expected with the more personal ballads of *Another Side*. His appearance at the 1965 festival, in a mod black leather jacket and Carnaby Street peg legs instead of faded blue denim, Stratocaster in hand (like his teen idol Buddy Holly) and band in tow, constituted a slap in the face whose violence is barely comprehensible today. After that, Dylan would not play Newport for another thirty-seven years.[1]

When Dylan stepped onstage on the evening of July 25, 1965, he was the undisputed star of the Newport event. He had already performed the acoustic “All I Really Want to Do” the previous afternoon at a songwriters’ workshop, his fame draining so much of the crowd away from the other workshops that he had to cut short his appearance. Soon afterward, he met up with members of the Butterfield Blues Band, who were also performing at Newport (earning them a snide introduction by Alan Lomax about white boys playing the blues—which earned Lomax a fistfight with Dylan’s and Butterfield’s manager Albert Grossman). It is unclear whether this inspired Dylan to prepare an electric set or whether he already had one in mind—chances are, the latter—but that night he, Bloomfield, Butterfield bassist and drummer Jerome Arnold and Sam Lay, pianist Barry Goldberg, and Al Kooper (who had come as a regular concert-goer, only to find himself drafted ad hoc) quickly rehearsed three numbers in a borrowed mansion. The following afternoon they did a cursory sound check (which quashes theories that Dylan’s electric music was a complete surprise even to the festival organizers), and at a little after nine o’clock Peter Yarrow of Peter, Paul and Mary came out to introduce the man of the hour:

> The person that’s coming up now is a person who in a sense has changed the face of folk music to the large American public, because he has brought to it a point of view of a poet. Ladies and gentlemen, the person that’s gonna come up now has a limited amount of time [protests from the audience]. His name is Bob Dylan.

You can hear the crowd’s cheering fade as the band starts to plug in behind Dylan. A few test notes on the keyboard, some rapid strumming on an electric guitar, and Dylan shouts, “Let’s roll!” The band launches into an especially raucous version of “Maggie’s Farm,” its already grating cadences made sandpaper rough by Bloomfield’s deafening, insistent, attention-hogging guitar licks, constantly pushing themselves forward, screaming to be heard. This wasn’t the first electric music ever played at Newport, but it was surely the loudest. At the end the audience is still cheering, though some dissent is audible. Then a slow, almost lilting build-up to "Like a Rolling Stone," which must have placated at least some of the fans. Then one more song, a rapid-fire version of "Phantom Engineer," and it's over, almost as soon as it has begun.

Though circulating tapes of the concert suggest that the audience's response was more positive than legend would have it, by now the fury is unmistakable. After some coaxing by an audibly shaken Peter Yarrow, Dylan returns to the stage holding a borrowed Martin ("he's coming: he's gotta get an *acoustic* guitar," Yarrow reassures) and sings "It's All Over Now, Baby Blue," according to some reports with tears in his eyes. (Footage of the concert does in fact show water running down his face, but it might have been sweat: Dylan, too, sounds a bit shaken at this point.) Mollified, the audience now cheers without reservation, believing they've won their champion back from the Dark Side. No one seems to have recognized this as another restless farewell.

Some have claimed that it was the brevity of Dylan's performance that caused the protests: most acts played for a good forty-five minutes as opposed to Dylan's fifteen, and he was the headliner to boot (there are clear chants of "We want Dylan" from the crowd as Yarrow tries to pacify them). Others have blamed the painful volume, or the poor sound system that made his singing inaudible. Listening carefully, one can hear booing mixed in with applause from the moment Dylan appeared in what the purists branded his "sellout jacket"—and even then, it was the attitude that rankled more than the clothes: Dylan had performed in the same leather jacket throughout his ecstatically received tour of England that April. (When the British booed the following April, he was wearing a houndstooth suit.)

The broad, but I think accurate, generalization is that Dylan's performance drew a sharp dividing line between the Old Left, the children of Woody Guthrie for whom folk music was intimately connected with advancing the people's cause, and the younger generation who felt the emergent new music articulated their concerns in ways that neither "Be-Bop-A-Lula" nor "Kumbaya" had been able to.* As Dylan's contempo-

---

* Primary among the old guard was Pete Seeger, who has gone down in Dylan lore as the man who threatened to cut the power cables with his woodsman's axe (the one he had been using shortly before to conduct a labor songs workshop). Seeger had been one of the earliest and most fervent supporters of Dylan the

rary Richard Fariña put it, "Only when popular music was in its very worst period, when nothing was happening there, did we turn to folk music. . . . Folk music, through no fault of its own, fooled us into certain sympathies and nostalgic alliances with the so-called traditional past . . . almost as if Chuck Berry and Batman had really nothing to do with who we were, and Uncle Dave Macon or Horton Barker could do a better job of telling us."[2]

Whether or not Dylan meant to provoke a scandal is, like much surrounding the event, open to speculation. What does seem certain is that, fresh from the thrill of making "Rolling Stone," he had little interest in endlessly dusting off his old material. "I get very bored," he told Robert Shelton the following month. "I can't sing 'With God on Our Side' for fifteen years." But more than this, there was an exhilaration that I believe Dylan genuinely wanted to communicate. Years later, he looked back on the period surrounding *Highway 61* as "exciting times. We were doing it before anybody knew we would—or could. We didn't know what it was going to turn out to be. Nobody thought of it as folk-rock at the time. . . . It was the sound of the streets. . . . That ethereal twilight light, you know. It's the sound of the street with the sunrays, the sun shining down at a particular time, on a particular type of building. A particular type of people walking on a particular type of street. It's an outdoor sound that drifts even into open windows that you can hear."[3]

In going onstage that evening, Dylan was both sharing the headiness of his new music and thumbing his nose at those who wouldn't keep up. What he was either ignoring or intentionally flouting was the "strict and rigid establishment" (as he later said) of the folk community, which didn't cotton to his new flamboyance; the degree of self-righteous protectionism, at a

---

protest singer, and he took his putative protégé's "going electric" as a personal affront. He has also put a variety of spins on his reaction to Newport, ranging from "I was ready to chop the microphone cord" to "I did say, If I had an axe I'd cut the cable! But they didn't understand me. I wanted to hear the words. I didn't mind him going electric." None of this prevented the Byrds from scoring a hit with an electrified version of Seeger's "Turn, Turn, Turn," nor Seeger from recording his own electric album (if you can't axe 'em, join 'em) with the Blues Project the following year.

time when "commitment" was already on the verge of turning into commodity. "It was the antithesis of what the festival was supposed to be doing," commented folksinger Oscar Brand. "The electric guitar represented capitalism . . . the people who were selling out."[4] As with his acceptance speech in December 1963 for the Emergency Civil Liberties Committee's Tom Paine award—at which he compared himself to Lee Harvey Oswald and denigrated the "old people" in attendance—Dylan's performance mainly ended up confounding those who would try to pin him down, and ultimately expressed his own refusal to be defined. If Woody's machine killed fascists, Bobby's was set to steamroll anyone who got in his way.

Still, other folk musicians were experimenting with electric backing without provoking anywhere near the furor, and ultimately the intensity of the reaction had less to do with the gesture than with Dylan himself. From the moment of his arrival in Greenwich Village, Dylan had managed to project an aura of little-boy-lost helplessness that drew both women and men toward him. As Joan Baez put it, "He'd bring out the mother instinct in a woman who thought her mother instinct was *dead*." Like Robert Johnson before him, Dylan had an extraordinary talent for being taken care of. He had perfected the myth of the itinerant musician reliant on the kindness of strangers, whether fellow entertainers and their wives eager to feed the waif, journalists eager to further his career, or *eminences grises* such as Izzy Young and Howard Leventhal eager to show him off—so many "Jewish mothers," as Dave Van Ronk said.[5] The Dylan these people saw, aided by his undeniable charisma and adaptive instinct, was a projection made of every frustrated desire by every folksinger scrambling to make a living, every well-meaning pamphleteer striving to make a difference in an indifferent world. When he became a star on the folk circuit, many saw it as a vindication of the Cause. Now, for the "Jewish mothers," it was as if their honor-roll son had suddenly turned delinquent.

Dylan's own public reaction to the Newport events was typically noncommittal. "I'm not really bothered by Newport, because I know in my own mind what I'm doing. If anyone has imagination, he'll know what I'm doing. If they can't understand my songs, they're missing something," he told Shelton. But to the Beatles, in an odd moment of embarrassment, he vehemently denied having been booed at all. And some months later, he allowed that he did "resent somewhat . . . that everybody that booed said they did it because they were old fans."[6] For Dylan, too, this was personal.*

Dylan had vented spite in song before: the apocalyptic "When the Ship Comes In," to take just one example, originated with a hotel clerk who'd refused him a room. Four days after Newport, he returned to the studio with a new musical put-down. Originally named "Black Dalli Rue," it was retitled—removing all ambiguity—"Positively 4th Street," after his former Greenwich Village address:

> You got a lotta nerve to say you are my friend
> When I was down you just stood there grinning
> You got a lotta nerve to say you got a helping hand to lend
> You just want to be on the side that's winning

It was as if all the slights Dylan had endured since his arrival in New York, all the resentments that had built up, all the attempts to pigeonhole him—whether by Suze, Baez, Wilson, or his fans—were now condensed in this one blast of vitriol.

Addressed to a nameless, universal "you," more an embodiment of the static folk ethos than an actual individual, "Positively 4th Street" is an unremitting piece of character bashing, as if Dylan had taken the motor of "Rolling Stone" and cranked it up to full capacity. In the course of it, the singer lashes back at the subject's insincerity ("you know as well as me you'd rather see me paralyzed"), dissatisfaction with life ("it's not my problem"), and, as a finale, utter lack of redeeming virtues:

> I wish that for just one time you could stand inside my shoes
> And just for that one moment I could be you
> Yes, I wish that for just one time you could stand inside my shoes
> You'd know what a drag it is to see you

---

* Though maybe not so much as all that: Bloomfield recalled Dylan at a party the evening after the concert, "sitting next to this girl and her husband and he's got his hand right up her pussy and she's letting him do this and her husband's going crazy. So Dylan seemed quite untouched by it the next day" (Nigel Williamson, *The Rough Guide to Bob Dylan* [London: Rough Guides, 2004], 54).

With its unvarying a-b-a-b rhyme scheme and lack of chorus (Dylan called the song "extremely one-dimensional, which I like"[7]), "Positively 4th Street" is unrelenting, unmerciful, and unforgiving. It is this quasi-monotony that drives some listeners to distraction, and it is also what makes the diatribe so effective. It is a nice irony that Dylan, in striking back at the folk purists, is in fact challenging the rigid verse-chorus-middle eight conventions of pop music much more than the structures of traditional folk, which can easily accommodate such unvarying patterns. In fact, "Positively 4th Street" is practically Dylan's only song from the *Highway 61* sessions that could be considered amplified folk, that would work equally well with just an acoustic guitar. The electric backing seems, more than anything, just one more jab at those who wasted their time heatedly debating the relative demerits of so-called "folk-rock" (a term Dylan despised).

If the theme relays this song back to "Rolling Stone," the music does even more so. The chord progression and Kooper's organ strokes unmistakably echo their predecessor, while Dylan's vocals build with the same triumphant glee. "Positively 4th Street" became his next single, released on September 7 (backed with "From a Buick 6") and reaching no. 7 on the *Billboard* chart.

"I don't write songs to critics," Dylan later commented on the song. The hostility at Newport proved to be only a prelude, mirrored in the reactions of many of his Greenwich Village cronies (who felt personally targeted by "Positively 4th Street," and with good reason), continuing in his concert at Forest Hills on August 28 and in appearances throughout the fall, and exploding in his next British tour. But by combining what began as an angry response to audience incomprehension with a deeper, more personal fury at people's presumptions of ownership, he showed that hostility was one of the most effective spurs to his performance. As he told Anthony Scaduto, in a different context but one that seems to carry a similar emotional charge, "I'm known to retaliate, you know. You should know I'm known to *retaliate*."[8]

4. Gypsy Davy with a Blowtorch

"Mama was in the kitchen, preparing to eat / Sis was in the pantry looking for some yeast / Pa was in the cellar mixing up the hops / And Brother's at the window, he's watching for the cops."[9] The song is "Taking It Easy" by Woody Guthrie, Dylan's first great model and his "last idol." Often cited as a basis for "Subterranean Homesick Blues" ("Johnny's in the basement mixing up the medicine," etc.), "Taking It Easy" more loudly echoes through "Tombstone Blues's" famous refrain and in the distorted Depression-era dreamscape that springs up around it:

> Mama's in the factory, she ain't got not shoes
> Daddy's in the alley, he's lookin' for food
> I'm in the kitchen with the tombstone blues*

Many of the song's references, from the title nod at the Arizona badlands to its name-checking of the nineteenth-century Oklahoma bandit Belle Starr, carry the unmistakable scent of America's hardscrabble past. "Tombstone Blues" is not about the Depression of the 1930s, the Wild West, or any specific historical period. But in its mood, tempo, and much of its imagery, it conjures up an atmosphere of American hardship, and of Guthrie the Dust Bowl troubadour.

"Woody turned me on romantically," Dylan told Robert Shelton in 1966. "Woody used his own time, in a way nobody else did. . . . What drew me to him was that hearing his voice I could tell he was very lonesome, very alone, and very lost out in his time." Nearly four decades later, he added: "He was so poetic and tough and rhythmic. There was so much intensity, and his voice was like a stiletto. He was like none of the other singers I ever heard. . . . Woody made each word count. He painted with words. That along with his stylized type singing, the way he phrased, the dusty cowpoke deadpan but amazingly serious and melodic sense of delivery, was like a buzzsaw in my brain and I tried to emulate it any way I could."[10]

This was hardly news to anyone who encountered Dylan in his first years as a performer: the "Woody Guthrie jukebox" adopted not only his hero's set list but his sound, dress, and manner as well. According to Bonnie Beecher, he even insisted for a time on being called "Woody." "In Guthrie," writes music historian David Hajdu, "Bob found more than a genre of music, a body of work, or a performance style: he found *an image*—the

---

* Lyrics consistently has Daddy "lookin' for a fuse" (which Dylan later used in live performances) and places the narrator "in the streets." But what's there to hear is what's there to hear: on *Highway 61*, Dylan sings "food" and "kitchen," as any listener for the past forty years can attest.

hard-travelin' loner with a guitar and a way with words, the outsider the insiders envied, easy with women, and surely doomed. An amalgam of Bob's previous heroes, the Guthrie he found in [Guthrie's autobiography] *Bound for Glory* was Hank Williams, James Dean, and Buddy Holly—a literate folksinger with a rock and roll attitude."[11]

Guthrie provided the ideal vessel into which young Dylan poured his self-mythologizing, from his supposed orphanhood to his stint as a circus performer to his travels with various legendary bluesmen. So devoutly did he emulate folk's elder statesman, both onstage and off, that he was floored to discover another performer, Ramblin' Jack Elliott, had beaten him to it by several years: it was "like being a doctor who has spent all these years discovering penicillin and suddenly [finding out] someone else had already done it," he said.[12] And so we can easily imagine his relief and hilarity at discovering that Ramblin' Jack was actually Elliott Adnopoz, a Brooklyn doctor's son, as much a product of the Jewish middle-class as Dylan himself. "As far as Bobby knew, Jack Elliott was absolutely gold coin *goyisha* cowboy," recalled Dave Van Ronk. "In the course of the conversation it came out somehow that he was Elliott Adnopoz, a Jewish cat from Ocean Parkway, and Bobby fell off his chair. He rolled under the table, laughing like a madman. . . . He'd be laying under the table and just recovering from his fit and every once in a while somebody would stick his head under the table and yell 'Adnopoz!' and that would start him off roaring again."[13]

By 1965, Dylan had to a large extent left Guthrie behind, the "last idol" having "taught me / face t' face / that men are men / shatterin' even himself / as an idol." But "Tombstone Blues," more than practically any other song on *Highway 61*, revisits the spirit and myth that informed Guthrie's persona and Dylan's early fascination with it. Dipping deeper into the wellspring that had earlier produced "Hard Rain" and "It's Alright, Ma," Dylan brushes a panorama of distinctly American violence and the venality of its institutions—"the gulf," as one commentator put it, that "Guthrie saw between America's ideals and its practices."[14]

From the start, the topography is established as native. In contrast to the underside of urban sophistication that "Rolling Stone" evokes, this is grassroots America, small-town, Main Street America, the America of Dylan's youth, which he once described as "still very 'straight,' 'post-war' and sort of into a gray-flannel suit thing, McCarthy, commies, puritanical, very claustrophobic."[15] From the "city fathers" voting "the reincarnation of Paul Revere's horse" (clinging to long-dead national myths) to the Chamber of Commerce, from shoeless Mama in her non-union factory to the swaggering medicine man, from the National Bank selling road maps for the soul to "Gypsy Davy with a blowtorch" (a nod to a Guthrie standard), the reality sketched here comes straight out of American folklore, the flora and fauna of a thousand time-tested verses underlying thousands of attitudes Americans hold about themselves. (The song also makes reference to the English Jack the Ripper, the Italian Galileo, and the German Beethoven, but even these are absorbed into Dylan's melting pot.)

One other specifically American reality that hovers behind the song, out of time with the imagery but synchronous with its composition, is the Vietnam War, visible in the verses about the "king of the Philistines" who sends his slaves "out into the jungle" (often read as a swipe at then-president Lyndon Johnson) and about the Commander-in-Chief condemning "all those who would whimper and cry" (a line I can never hear without flashing on Robert Duvall in *Apocalypse Now* rhapsodizing about the "victory" smell of napalm).

But to call it a song about Vietnam would be too limiting, as "Tombstone's" mini-episodes limn a broad canvas of violence, of innocent flesh ripped from the bone, of jingoism for all seasons, of privilege abused—whether Jack the Ripper masking his atrocities behind his position on the Chamber of Commerce, the doctor who detours the hysterical bride away from her natural desires (unless, like his colleague in "Leopard-Skin Pill-Box Hat," he is arrogating them for himself), or the National Bank defrauding both old folks and college kids with their bogus guidance. Dylan famously described writing the song in "this one bar I used to play where cops would always come and hang out, mostly off duty, they'd always be talking stuff, saying things like 'I don't know who killed him or why, but I'm sure glad he's gone,' that kind of stuff."[16] However fanciful the testimony, Dylan's recollection captures the sense of corrupt and dangerous power that infuses "Tombstone Blues" (a theme brought into sharper focus in "Tom Thumb's Blues" and "Desolation Row"). The topology might look different, but the territory hasn't changed since the early protest songs: a distrust of authority, of the arbitrary exercise of power that invades people's lives.

A mix of historical, fictional, mythical, and musical figures, the protagonists of "Tombstone Blues" intermingle to form a world at once recognizable and wholly alien, an outsized American landscape made up not only of our daily reality, but also of our myths, dreams, cultural archetypes, and barely formed nightmares—"history recast as phantasmagoria."[17] The landscape traversed is an unholy alliance of the scientific and the spiritual (Galileo throwing his math book at Delilah), the familiar and the uncanny (the city fathers and the ghost of Revere's horse), the sacred and the abject (John the Baptist torturing a thief), the modern and the classical (Ma Rainey and Beethoven in their bedroll: the same marriage that Dylan was attempting in his music)—a veritable "cast of thousands," directed by Cecil B. DeMille himself.

Whether traditional ballads or his own tales, the songs Dylan sings are often grounded in specific character and place names, real or imagined; names drawn from song and story, tabloid and history book. In *Tarantula*, their number is legion, a seemingly endless panorama that ranges from J. Edgar Hoover, James Cagney, Crow Jane, Mae West in a closet, Bat Masterson, and Edgar Allan Poe to Galileo "the regular guy," Mickey Mantle, Cole Younger, Little Red Riding Hood, John Lee Hooker, Jackie Gleason, Yogi Bear, Elvis, Baby Huey, Lord Buckley, John Wayne, Cardinal Spellman, and the Black Ace. On *Highway 61*, their fellow denizens jostle in as best they can—names famous and obscure, insistent or overheard, filling out a landscape as vast as the disparities of all America.

This was among a spate of new works Dylan composed in the wake of "Rolling Stone," between mid-June and late July, when he went back into the studio to record the rest of the album. The songs were written in a newly acquired home in Byrdcliffe, New York, a stone's roll from Woodstock and from the Grossman home in Bearsville. "Do you know what I did when I got back from England, man?" he asked Shelton. "I bought me a thirty-one room house . . . can you imagine that?" The Arts and Crafts-style mansion, named Hi Lo Ha and purchased shortly after Dylan's visit to John Lennon's English manor, was the site of his new burst of rock 'n' roll creativity. Dylan later commented that he felt he'd "broken through with ['Tombstone Blues'], that nothing like it had been done before. Just a flash, really." Because of this, however, his dream house soon turned into a "nightmare." "I wrote *Highway 61 Revisited* there and I don't believe in writing some total other thing in the same place twice," he explained. "I just can't stand the smell of birth. It just lingers, so I just lived there and tried to go on, but couldn't."[18] By the following spring, Hi Lo Ha was back on the market.

"Tombstone Blues" was recorded on July 29, at the same lengthy session that produced "Positively 4th Street" and the remake of "It Takes a Lot to Laugh," as well as an early version of "Desolation Row." As the second cut on the album, following the majestic, swelling roll-out of "Rolling Stone," it comes on like an out-of-control freight train, the fast, bass-heavy strum of Dylan's acoustic guitar setting the pace like a bandleader's baton before drums, piano, a fuzzed-up bass, Bloomfield's electric, and Kooper's organ come crashing in.

Unlike "Rolling Stone," "Tombstone" seems to have undergone little revision. The known outtakes sound more or less like the official take (the last completed), and everything—false starts to final cut—was done in one day.* The incomplete Take 9 (the one on the *No Direction Home* soundtrack) is notable for the slightly countrified tone of the chorus, in which Dylan harmonizes with members of the band. Another circulated version features the gospel/soul group the Chambers Brothers—whom Dylan had probably heard at Newport, and whose hit "Time Has Come Today" was still three years off—overdubbed on the chorus. "I thought [the Chambers Brothers version] was great," Kooper later said. "But I think the deciding criterion was that Mike Bloomfield was great on the take they used."[19]

As Kooper recognized, the star of this show is Bloomfield, whose between-verse solos build from heated to blistering, jackrabbiting helter-skelter over the fret board, anticipating and pointing the way to Alvin Lee, Johnny Winter, and any other late-sixties guitarist who took blues riffs and fed them uppers. It is practically the only time on the album that he'll get to shine like this. A photo of Bloomfield and Dylan at Newport catches them grinning at each other in amazed delight at the sounds they're producing: two Jewish cats making the music come to life, reviving the blues, a faith more real to them than the religion of their fathers.

---

* The partial vignette "Jet Pilot" (a.k.a. "Jet Pilot Eyes") is described on *Biograph* as "the original version of 'Tombstone Blues,'" but this seems unlikely—not only because "Jet Pilot's" stated recording date of October 1965 would have made it the only "original version" to postdate its final draft by three months but also because the two songs have almost nothing in common lyrically or musically. If anything, "Jet Pilot" sounds like a reprise of "From a Buick 6," with a little of the upcoming "Obviously 5 Believers" thrown in for good measure.

In "Tombstone," Bloomfield uses his axe like a flamethrower, spewing liquid fire over the space between the vocals, he and Dylan marauding the tune like twin Gypsy Davies burning out the camps, leaving only scorched earth. Take him away and the song remains lyrically strong but musically weakened, its engine a few cylinders short. You can hear it in the version Dylan attempted on his *MTV Unplugged* concert. You can hear it in the one he and the Band played at Berkeley in December 1965, in which Robbie Robertson wisely avoids competing with his predecessor. Energetic as these versions are, they lack the heat of Bloomfield's performance.

Although this first return to the studio came a full six weeks after the "Rolling Stone" sessions, the personnel remained essentially the same, with Bloomfield and Kooper continuing to develop their distinctive duo, and Gregg and Griffin ably filling in the rhythm. One change involved session bassist Russ Savakus. Bloomfield noted that Savakus, a stand-up player, was intimidated about recording with an electric bass, which he was touching for practically the first time. According to one witness, Savakus "freaked out a bit during the ending"[20] of "Tombstone"—you can hear his bass sliding frantically up the neck several times in the fade-out—and had to be replaced shortly afterward by a friend of Kooper's, Harvey Goldstein (later known as Harvey Brooks).

But the most significant personnel change happened in the control booth, when Bob Johnston took over for Tom Wilson as Dylan's producer. Dylan later affected ignorance of the reasons behind the switch: "All I know is that I was out recording one day," he told Jann Wenner in 1969, "and Tom had always been there—I had no reason to think he wasn't going to be there—and I looked up one day and Bob was there." Wilson, for his part, made reference to a huge disagreement with Dylan at around the time of the "Rolling Stone" sessions, prompting Dylan to suggest sarcastically that they bring in "wall of sound" maestro Phil Spector. One hint of such a disagreement revolved around Al Kooper: during playback, Wilson tried to hold Kooper's part to a minimum, arguing that "that cat's not an organ player." But Dylan snapped back at him to turn up the organ track: "Don't tell me who's an organ player and who's not."[21] History has come down on Dylan's side: the guitar-organ-piano blend forged here became one of the most potent elements of his (and, in his wake, others') sound at the time. As for Wilson, his gentlemanly gesture at letting Kooper sit in might have proved his undoing.

Dylan would always have complicated relationships with his producers: any authority, even one on his side, was suspect. Bob Johnston, who holds the record for the number of Dylan albums produced, claims that he and the singer never had a cross word; but even he would find himself replaced after 1970. Somewhere along the line, there always had to be a restless farewell. Still, while it lasted, there seemed to be a vast difference in tone between Dylan's relations with the two men—between his and Wilson's manic laughter at the beginning of "Bob Dylan's 115th Dream" and the more settled, collegial question he puts to his producer on *Nashville Skyline*: "Is it rolling, Bob?"

A contemporary of Tom Wilson's, and like him a native Texan, Donald "Bob" Johnston had a family musical pedigree and a brief career as a pop singer under his belt. "I grew up in a musical element and I was very sure of myself when it came to music," he told an interviewer.[22] After producing for small labels in Nashville, he was hired by Columbia in 1965 and assigned to waning country singer Patti Page. His success with her established the new kid as someone to watch.

Johnston's chance to work with Dylan came soon after his arrival at Columbia. Hearing that Wilson was on his way out, and hankering to produce an artist he considered a prophet of the age, Johnston went to see company president Bill Gallagher. "Gallagher said, 'We don't know who we're going to pick, but don't say anything to Tom Wilson.' And I said, 'Great, I promise.' Then I left his office and went over and told Tom [that he was about to be fired]. He said, 'I know, man, I know all of that.' He said, 'I'll help you, don't worry about a thing.'" Johnston lobbied strenuously, ultimately overcoming a rival bid from Terry Melcher, who had produced the Byrds' covers of Dylan's songs. "One morning I walked in the back of the studio on West 52nd Street and Dylan was sitting there on his haunches. And I went up to him and said, 'Hi, I'm Bob Johnston.' And he said, 'Hi, I'm Bob, too.' And he gave me the sweetest smile." Beginning with *Highway 61*, the two men's association would stretch over five years and six albums, including the revered *Blonde on Blonde*, the reviled *Self Portrait*, *John Wesley Harding*, and *Nashville Skyline*.

Apart from Dylan, Johnston went on to produce a number of landmark albums, both for Columbia and on his own, including Simon & Garfunkel's *Sounds of Silence* and *Parsley, Sage, Rosemary and Thyme*, Leonard Cohen's *Songs from a Room* and *Songs of Love and Hate*, Johnny Cash's renowned concerts at Folsom and San Quentin prisons (against Columbia's strict orders), and albums by the Byrds, Marty Robbins, and Willie Nelson, among many others. Now in his seventies, he has retained the engaging manner and mellifluent drawl that must have helped him negotiate some of the craggier corridors of "Black Rock," CBS's corporate headquarters on Sixth Avenue. There is a certain modesty in his presentation: to hear Johnston tell it, his main contribution was to provide a support for his artists' self-explorations and to stay out of the way. "My gig was not to lose anything he came up with," he says of Dylan, "and I didn't." But it's the modesty of someone who wants you to understand there's more to the story. "Staying out of the way" doesn't preclude having set Dylan on his country road in the late sixties, or allowing for experiments such as "Sad-Eyed Lady" and "Rainy Day Women #12 & 35" that are now considered high-water marks. (Al Kooper, no fan of Johnston's, nonetheless credits him with suggesting the signature Salvation Army band arrangement for "Rainy Day Women.") In a moment of candor, Johnston was willing to admit, "I just told everybody, all I do is let the tapes roll. But that isn't true."

Unlike auteur-style producers like Phil Spector or Don Was, Johnston has always maintained that the artist is the sole valid judge of the work. "Dylan's king, and I'll not tell Dylan what I think of his material unless he asks me," he once remarked, later adding: "If Dylan wanted to record under a palm tree in Hawaii with a ukulele, I'd be there with a tape machine"[23]—a claim fairly borne out by such Johnston-produced oddities as "All the Tired Horses" and "If Dogs Run Free." This deferent style has won him his share of admirers and detractors: Johnny Cash called Johnston "an artist's dream," while Kooper said his "only quality as a producer" was knowing "how to pat the artist on the back."[24] Dylan, typically, remained ambivalent. "Bob was an interesting cat . . . short but with a personality that makes him seem bigger than he really is. . . . He had that thing that some people call 'momentum.' You could see it in his face and he shared that fire, that spirit," he later wrote. But his recollections of the 1970 *New Morning* sessions, their last album together, suggest a dissatisfaction similar to what he was feeling toward Wilson in 1965: "He's thinking that everything I'm recording is fantastic. He always does. He's thinking that something is gonna strike pay dirt, that everything is totally together. On the contrary. Nothing was ever together."[25]

One of Johnston's first actions with Dylan was to put his own stamp on "Like a Rolling Stone" before its final release. As he told Greil Marcus:

> "The thing that I tried to do—the first time I walked in with Dylan . . . I said, 'Your voice has got to come up.' He said, 'I don't like my voice, my voice is too goddamn loud.' And I'd say ok, and I'd turn it up a little bit, and he'd say"—and Johnston affects a clipped, effete voice—"'My voice is too *loud*.' Finally he quit saying that. My guess is he didn't want to fuck with me anymore, *but that's what I wanted*."[26]

Credit where credit is due, however: when first copies of the record sleeve came in, with Wilson's name absent, Johnston insisted it be reprinted and his predecessor restored next to his one contribution.

The curious thing about "Tombstone Blues," for all intents and purposes the first song Dylan recorded with Johnston, is that it sounds more like a Wilson production than "Like a Rolling Stone." While the latter boasts an integrated sound in which musicians, vocals, and overall atmosphere blend into a seamless whole, "Tombstone" seems more in the harsh, clattering vein of "Subterranean Homesick Blues" and "Maggie's Farm." In this one regard, it would be the last of its kind: by the end of the June 29 session, a sound unlike any of Dylan's previous records was being captured on Columbia's tape decks, and there was no turning back.

Notes

1. Many sources claim that he also sported Ray-Bans and a polka dot shirt, but this was at the afternoon sound check, not the evening performance.
2. David Hajdu, *Positively 4th Street: The Lives and Times of Joan Baez, Bob Dylan, Mimi Baez Fariña, and Richard Fariña* (New York: Farrar, Straus & Giroux, 2001), 227.
3. "For 15 years": Robert Shelton, *No Direction Home: The Life and Music of Bob Dylan* (Cambridge: Da Capo Press, 2003), 306; "you can hear": Ron Rosenbaum, "The *Playboy* Interview" (March 1978), in *Younger Than That Now: The Collected Interviews with Bob Dylan* (New York: Thunder's Mouth Press, 2004), 122–23.
4. "Rigid establishment": *Biograph* booklet, 8; "selling out": Howard

Sounes, *Down the Highway: The Life of Bob Dylan* (New York: Grove Press, 2001),182. For an insightful analysis of Newport, see Mike Marqusee, *Wicked Messenger: Bob Dylan and the 1960s* (New York: Seven Stories Press, 2005), 149ff.

5. "Instinct was dead": Scorsese, *No Direction Home*; "Jewish mothers": Shelton, 99.
6. "Missing something": Shelton, 306; "were old fans": Clinton Heylin, *Bob Dylan: Behind the Shades* (New York: Summit Books, 1991), 145.
7. Patrick Humphries and John Bauldie, *Absolutely Dylan: An Illustrated Biography* (New York: Viking Studio Books, 1991), 183.
8. "Songs to critics": *Biograph*, liner notes to Side 7; "known to retaliate": Anthony Scaduto, *Bob Dylan: An Intimate Biography* (New York: New American Library, 1973), 334.
9. "Taking It Easy" by Woody Guthrie and Pete Seeger (alias "Paul Campbell"), as quoted in Shelton, 271. The verse largely echoes an anonymous Prohibition-era poem. The first line might also have been inspired by Kerouac: "sitting in my mother's house all day while she worked in the shoe factory" (*Desolation Angels*).
10. "Out in his time": Shelton, 356; "any way I could": Bob Dylan, *Chronicles, Volume One* (New York: Simon & Schuster, 2004), 244–47.
11. Hajdu, *Positively 4th Street*, 70.
12. Robert Hilburn, "How to Write Songs and Influence People" (interview from 2004), *Guitar World Acoustic* (Feb. 2006), 30.
13. Scaduto, 81.
14. "As an idol": Bob Dylan, "11 Outlined Epitaphs" (late 1963), quoted in Shelton, 74; "and its practices": Hilburn, "How to Write Songs," 30.
15. *Biograph* booklet, 5.
16. *Biograph*, liner notes to Side 3.
17. Marqusee, *Wicked Messenger*, 141.
18. "Imagine that" and "go on, but couldn't": Shelton, 357–58; "just a flash": *Biograph*, liner notes to Side 3. Daniel Kramer, who often saw Dylan at the time, told me that some of these songs had already been written by April, the month when the *Highway 61* cover photo was taken and when Dylan left for his UK tour.
19. Andy Gill, *Don't Think Twice, It's All Right: Bob Dylan, The Early Years* (New York: Thunder's Mouth Press, 1998), 85.
20. Clinton Heylin, *Bob Dylan: The Recording Sessions, 1960–1994* (New York: St. Martin's, 1995), 42.
21. "Bob was there": Jann Wenner, "The *Rolling Stone* Interview: Dylan" (Nov. 1969), in Craig McGregor, ed., Bob Dylan, *The Early*

Years: A Retrospective (New York: Da Capo, 1990), 324; Phil Spector: Heylin, *Behind the Shades*, 136; "who's not": Al Kooper, *Backstage Passes & Backstabbing Bastards: Memoirs of a Rock 'n' Roll Survivor* (New York: Billboard Books, 1998), 36.

22. Quotes and information about Johnston: Dan Daley, "Bob Johnston," *Mix* (1 Jan. 2003), mixonline.com/recording/interviews/audio_bob_Johnston, 10/22/2004; Richard Younger, "An Exclusive Interview with Bob Johnston," www.b-dylan.com/pages/samples/bobjohnston.html, 7/20/2005; MP, interviews with Bob Johnston, 2 Aug. 2005 and 9 Dec. 2005.
23. "He asks me": Shelton, 278; "with a tape machine": Heylin, *Behind the Shades*, 136.
24. "Artist's dream": Younger, interview with Johnston; "on the back": Gill, *Don't Think Twice*, 84.
25. Dylan, *Chronicles*, 134, 137.
26. Greil Marcus, *Like a Rolling Stone: Bob Dylan at the Crossroads* (New York: PublicAffairs, 2005), 144.

Loveless

by Mike McGonigal

Mike McGonigal has written about music and art since 1984, when he started the fanzine *Chemical Imbalance*. An occasional curator, sculptor and DJ, Mike edits the arts journal *YETI* and resides in Portland, Oregon. He really needs to get out more.

Chapter Ten
Forever and Again

Drummer Colm O'Ciosoig is the phantom of *Loveless*. Most of the percussion tracks on the album were painstakingly programmed from samples. It's like he's there, but he's not really there. Sure, he contributed the awesome, minute-long, ambient "mating whales" track, "Touched." But mostly, he's there as an electronic ghost; like a Xerox stuck into a painting, the way Basquiat used to throw color Xeroxes of his own drawings made at Ed's Copy Shop onto his canvases, and then paint on top of them.

Colm's absence is really weird, as live, and on their previous recordings, Colm is MBV's secret weapon. He had to be one of the only drummers in the world loud enough to compete with the rest of the band's wall of squall. Check his drumming on *Isn't Anything*. He's really *on* like a metronome, but he throws these little, melodic, jazzy accents all over the place. "Emptiness Inside": it's Steve Shelley on steroids! Those fills on "You Never Should" are almost off, but they're perfect. "Feed Me With Your Kiss" is Keith Moon after taking lessons from Milford Graves; it's sick.

Speaking of sick, that's what Colm was for much of the recording of *Loveless*, which was a long-ass time obviously, and that's why so much of the recording happened without him. "He had a really hard time when we were doing the record," Bilinda Butcher relates. "It's such a shame, 'cause he's such a brilliant drummer. He just wasn't at his best at all. I think it all just really took its toll on him, having trouble with just about everything in his personal life: nowhere to live, and his girlfriend had to go back to America—she was going through some hard times herself and stuff—and he just couldn't function the way he normally would. He just couldn't drum the way he normally would. The drums ended up being compromised because of that; Kevin's not a drummer. He's got a good sense of rhythm, but he couldn't just take over for him and do his job, so a lot of that [translated to] more programming than was anticipated, which caused a lot of stress." Later, when the band toured the songs, "He actually learned all the stuff after not having done it; it was a sort of different process, you know."

"With the arrangements—it's exactly what Colm would have done, it just took much longer to do." Kevin Shields stresses that the drums sound exactly the way they would have if Colm had played them all live. "Colm only played proper drums on two tracks," Shields says. "The song 'Only Shallow' has Colm playing live drums, 'cause he'd gotten better then." Shields brings at least part of O'Ciosoig's predicament to bear on the record label. "We were in the studio and didn't have any equipment. We were promised two grand by Creation and we never got it. It was a cold autumn; we were both homeless and had been squatting, which gave us a better lifestyle than being in some crummy flat. So we did a deal with Creation. We were on the dole for 50 pounds a week and once we were paid 70 pounds by Creation, which doesn't pay for rent and living, we lost the dole money and had to apply for income-based assistance. It's all complicated and harder to get a place to live than even if you're on the dole, because you're on a ridiculously low income. Colm and his girlfriend got thrown out of the place they were living in and Creation were completely broke at the time. They'd just left Rough Trade distribution and were penniless and literally couldn't afford like 100 pounds."

"So they stuck us in the studio and hoped for the best, which wasn't really working out because Colm needed somewhere to live and he needed 300 pounds for a deposit," Kevin says. "Creation just wouldn't give it to him; they just told him to fuck off and not to even ask for money. It all became too much for him. He hadn't anywhere to live and couldn't find another squat. They were telling him to look for a squat after recording, which would be like one in the morning. Then he got really bad flu mixed with all that stress. His girlfriend was being deported. She was from America and caught working in an after hours bar. It all got too much and he just lost it. He couldn't even use his legs! That's why he ended up not being involved in the normal way."

"We would be trying to do these tracks and Colm wouldn't be able to; we tried to program the bass pedal because he couldn't use his legs any more and he wanted to play live over the top," Shields says. A slew of drum tracks were recorded this way, but when time came to play guitar over the top, "it was like playing along to a human and a machine with no groove to it, and we realized it was a waste of time. So we had to program all the stuff he was playing. We sampled his sounds, not trying to have them sound like a machine, [although] his parts were quite like that anyway. It wasn't a terrible tragedy; it was more like, 'This is a fuck up but we're gonna get there any way.' We didn't know how to work the machines and didn't have anyone there to do it for us—we were totally out there in the wilderness. But we managed to do it with people who had little roles, like Harold Burgon helped with the operating of the computer."

Oh, wait. Maybe I should have called Debbie Googe "the phantom of *Loveless*"? After all, she doesn't play a note on the record, even though she's listed as "bass" in the credits. When asked if she felt left out, Deb replies "Yes, definitely. On the one hand I completely understood Kevin's motives. I mean you wouldn't expect a painter to feel happy about other people coming in and putting their little marks all over their painting. *Loveless* was very much Kevin's thing; it was impossible to know what was going on his head. Even if I had played the bass lines he'd made up, I wouldn't have had the same feel or touch as Kevin and that would have bothered him, which I completely appreciate. But it's not nice to feel totally superfluous. And I think the knock-on effect of that was that I didn't go in as much as the others and that resulted in me feeling like a bit of an outsider at times, plus of course Kevin and Colm had known each other forever and Kevin and Bilinda were living together. That added to that feeling of alienation at times."

Bilinda confirms that Debbie isn't on the record, and adds that "the guitar parts that I would play live, Kevin basically did all of it on the record," too. I wondered if that was ever tough on her ego or anything. Bilinda answers that she "was never a great guitarist, and for Debbie—for Kevin to actually translate to Debbie what he had in his head and play it right would have been an agonizing process. I think Debbie, because she later went off and did her own music, would have liked to do that. And the whole thing with the band deteriorating when we had the studio later, maybe there were issues with people wanting to do more, but it's not like there wasn't room for someone to make up a song. I think Kevin would have welcomed that, and I know he was really pleased to have Colm's piece included."

"The really important thing about Colm's drumming on the record is that the drums sound exactly how they were supposed to sound," Kevin stresses. "Of course there's the exception of songs where we wanted it to sound sampled, like on 'Soon,' the parts were supposed to sound like that. Otherwise, people can't tell the difference between Colm's playing and his not playing, when it had been sampled and sequenced. We worked very hard to make it relatively seamless. I've had people in the studio, playing them the master tapes, and asked them if they could tell which tracks had live drums and which didn't, and they couldn't tell the difference. We had lost the Who-type influence and were going for something more simplistic, more pure. And with Bilinda and Debbie—you have to remember that they really just weren't there for so much of the recording, especially Debbie. She was never there."

Chapter Eleven
I Only Said

> Sometimes when I want to write lyrics, I'll listen to *Loveless*. Because of the way the vocals are buried, you can almost listen to the songs as if they're instrumental pieces.
>
> —Bob Pollard of Guided by Voices,
> interviewed by the author in 2001

Part an abstraction of 60s backing vocals and partly a wholesale improvement on the Cocteau Twins' moaning croons, MBV's breathy vocal style is unique and lovely. It's also impossible to describe without using the word "ethereal." That's partly due to the low volume they're usually at in the overall mix, but also the lovely high pitch that Kevin and Bilinda often sang in. Bilinda disallows that there's much special about her vocal style, arguing that she was just copying the way that Kevin used to sing back up for Dave.

"Because it took so long to do the vocals, and because the melodies were in my head since '89 and we didn't do them until '91, I couldn't tolerate really clear vocals, where you just hear one voice," Kevin explains. "I'd heard it indistinctly in the studio for so many years (with scratch vocals on the tracks) that it had to be more like a *sound*. So that's why, when we'd had all the vocals, what was slightly eccentric about it, slightly only, was that we had so many vocals on one reel. We had a separate twenty-four track reel with between ten and seventeen vocal tracks on there. And because they couldn't really face analyzing them, I realized just by a wonderful coincidence that Bilinda and I have a tendency to sing things really similarly each time. So it was easy just to bring all the vocals up, eliminating the ones that weren't good all the way through. And what you hear there is all the ones that are left. And then we'd just take one, one that I particularly like, and ever so slightly edge it forward, so that the articulation's coming more from that. But then the sound and the whole thickness of it's coming from ten or fifteen vocals on each track." If you'll allow me to be a master of the obvious, the way the vocals are recorded, with shit-loads of layers, is not how the guitars were done, even though it's how most folks assume the guitars were done! Meanwhile, the Internet legend about the vocals has them being recorded in one take while half-asleep.

The indecipherability of MBV's lyrics is deliberate, and is a key element of their sound. Lyrics aren't printed anywhere on the band's albums, except in Japan where lyrics have to be printed out, and those are hilariously inaccurate. The only way I know any MBV lyrics at all is by rewinding tracks obsessively, or trolling obsessive fan sites to see whose take on the tunes seems most likely. Kevin laughs when I ask him if any of these are correct. "They're all wrong," he says gleefully. "It bothers me only in the sense that all of the lyrics are much more stupid and pretentious and flowery than what we wrote. On our website for a laugh I was thinking we would rate these sites on a percentage of rightness. Instead of saying which lyrics are right or wrong we'll say, 'This site is 90 percent wrong,' or, 'This site is 75 percent wrong.'"

"How all the lyrics come about is that when I make up a tune I just sing whatever and I realize that there's actually most of the song there when you listen to it," Kevin says. "I'm singing stuff unconsciously, and then if it does make sense but it's not proper grammar, and I like the way it sounds, I'll just leave it. People will be going, 'I can't work the lyrics out,' but if I were actually to tell you word for word what they are, you would say, 'Of course I can hear that, it's totally clear.' The sentences are broken so a line will finish like halfway through and then the next bit will come afterwards. If you were to see it on a piece of paper it does actually make sense."

When I was eight or nine and first started to become a music freak, I was really drawn to pop and rock songs that were scary and indecipherable. Glossalalic, obscure lyrics shouted, chanted and sung atop music that implies volume—I dug that shit a lot. There are songs that scar you for life because they just sounded so big and heavy and impenetrable (that's the kind of babble Patti Smith was going on about in *Babel*, no?) at one point. Later, they usually sound ridiculous. There was a hit song in 1977 called "Black Betty" by Ram Jam, basically a cocaine unicorn proto-rap delivered by sleazy Southern rockers. To my young ears, though, the speed of the lyrical delivery sounded alien and really cool. It took me many listens to decipher the words. I think I liked the song best before I understood it. It was a puzzle; don't all kids love puzzles?

Lyrics are one area where Shields was more open to input from others. Bilinda wrote about a third of the lyrics on *Isn't Anything* and *Loveless*. Most rock lyrics are ridiculous, even before you cut and paste them out of one of those websites that shoots twenty-two pop-ups at your face to try and see what the words to "Popozao" are. Not enough rock music has words that you simply cannot understand. "Wolves, Lower" by R.E.M., "Pay to Cum" by the Bad Brains, "Madame George" by Van Morrison—part of what makes these songs such total classics is that no matter how many times you listen, you never really know the words.

"Words are extremely important in the sense that we've spent way more time on the lyrics than ever on the music," Shields says. "Music is spontaneous and it's either good or bad so you just take it or leave it. Where lyrics, all the stuff comes out and then we usually just finish them right before we have to sing so it's usually these nights of eight or ten hours just trying to desperately make sure it's going to be as good as possible, even though most of it's there anyway and it's always been there. There's nothing worse than bad lyrics. For me a bad lyric is a lyric that jumps out at you, and that's offensive, it takes you completely away from enjoying the music." Amen to that.

Chapter Twelve
When You Wake You're Still in a Dream

ME: You spoke with Kevin about the sleep deprivation thing going on?

GUY FIXSEN: I'm not sure what this is about; I know he often had problems sleeping though.

I've always been attracted to songs about being dizzy, confused and/or lost in dreams—"Circles (Instant Party)" by the Who, "Dizzy" by Tommy Roe, "Mixed-Up Confusion" by Jimi Hendrix, "The Sound of Confusion" by Spacemen Three, "I Dreamed I Dream" by Sonic Youth, "Dream Baby Dream" by Suicide—absolute favorites, all of them. I especially dig the way these tunes use certain structural elements to reinforce the lyrical content, generally employing exaggeratedly woozy and/or nursery rhyme-ishly swoopy sounds to mimic a loss of control.

MBV's sound is so clearly bent and disorientating, as are what lyrics one may easily discern, and several of the band's tunes deal with dreams: "(You're) Safe in Your Sleep (From This Girl)," "(When You Wake) You're Still in a Dream" and "When You Sleep." It's no surprise that *Loveless* is often associated with altered states of consciousness, whether through dreams, sex, the state of being in love or drugs. It's often assumed that MBV were total drug fiends but not so, according to Bilinda. "Kevin and Colm took ecstasy but not a lot," she says. "I tried it and didn't like it, you know, palpitations and stuff. Kevin, the whole time he was with Alan McGee, and Colm, they were pretty into it, you know. And later hanging around with Primal Scream there was a bit of coke going around, and parties. We never got into it really, but Colm did a bit. But doing *Loveless*, the only bit of relaxation afterwards was before we went to bed, you know. Later, [the pot use] really accelerated when we moved to the house in Streatham."

But Shields' favorite method of achieving altered states was not such a rock star cliché as drugs. Especially while recording an album, he would not sleep much at all during the process, and would record late at night as well, at times achieving what's called a hypnagogic state. Andreas Mavromatis' *Hypnagogia: The Unique State of Consciousness Between Wakefulness and Sleep* roughly defines hypnagogic experiences as "hallucinatory and quasi-hallucinatory events taking place in the intermediate state between wakefulness and sleep."

"The *Isn't Anything* phase was big time about sleep deprivation," Kevin says. "I was young enough and strong enough and not into drugs enough. I wasn't smoking lots of dope or anything, because if you smoke enough pot you can't stay awake. I would get off on just having two or three hours of sleep a night and work constantly and it was very enjoyable. For *Loveless*, I had become more immersed in a general state of slight dislocatedness. You see, there's a subconscious kind of way of using language that's more impressionistic than the normal way. The way that people speak in their sleep—people are slightly incoherent but it's not less real. The structure isn't as formed and as focused. It was just a case of having all of our unconscious stuff and just honing it into something that was acceptable. That was a big part of my life for a long time."

While recording *Isn't Anything*, Shields was "in an extreme lack of sleep state" at the studio in Wales. "And it was out there, that's the only way I can describe it. I was having experiences like real classic stuff from cheap UFO movies. I'd be by myself in the studio, which was a barn away from where everyone else was staying, and there in the middle of nowhere in this barn trying to write lyrics, and one night I couldn't stay awake but I had to finish the lyrics, and then, while falling asleep, I heard this huge roaring noise. And the room was all bright and I was crawling across the floor, desperately crawling under the desk trying to stay awake long enough to finish these lyrics, while feeling completely surrounded by the presence of things."

"We found out later that the whole place is supposed to be haunted, and all sorts of weird things had happened" Kevin says. "The engineer wasn't telling us that it was haunted. That's part of the policy of the studio, that you don't tell the clients it's haunted because they start getting freaked out, because weird things happen and because it's in the middle of nowhere and all that shit. And, also it's near the military base, so there were weird planes flying above all the time and pulling sonic booms. My whole memory of making that record was just this constant sense of presence, like it was a mixture of angels and, funnily enough, cow ghosts, ghosts of cows. I don't know why, but I kept having this impression of bloody animals and cows all the time—really big, weird faces with big brown eyes. But not like aliens."

"By and large most of the lyrics come from, not so much the hypnagogic half-awake half-asleep state, but more the slightly trancey state that you're in when you're writing songs," he (sort of) explains. "And that does involve being quite tired. Most tunes I write it's really late at night, or if it's in the studio it's after a few weeks of being in the studio not really getting good sleep. And being in a room full of electronic equipment I find quite mind altering as well, somehow. I don't know why, but I feel very affected by a lot of electricity. And that's why for me the record making process involves a lot of getting away from the studio. Being in there for a long time it's kind of like, I'm going off; I'm losing reality, day by day, slightly. Do you know what I mean?"

Of course, similar experiments were conducted by such spiritual-minded aesthetes as the Surrealist-associated *Grand Jeu* group headed by Rene Daumal in the 30s. Kevin isn't familiar with them in particular, and claims to only have glanced through one book on Surrealism, but he obviously took away a lot from it. "Surrealism wasn't coming from a social perspective, by taking social things and making juxtapositions of them," he says. "It was coming from inner information, it was coming from in the inner worlds, those combinations of imagery and situations are natural. They weren't superficial; it was deep, and that's why it has a deep resonance."

I ask Kevin if he's aware of the Dream Machine experiments that Brion Gysin and William S. Burroughs got into in the 60s. "Actually, that's funny," he says. "I was thinking about that the other day, because we played this gig with Primal Scream in France, at a festival in Rennes. The guy who does our lights has the tendency to make the strobes really extreme sometimes. I closed my eyes, and whatever frequency it was, I suddenly was totally tripping, and I was going into inner space, right there on stage, and it was really cool, and then he stopped the light and it was just that particular frequency. Usually it's just, you know, the strobe effect where you see stuff in front of your eyes when you close them and it's really interesting. But this time it immediately kicked in to encourage the theta brainwaves. It's probably about time that I found out what those frequencies are and do something with that, just for the hell of it."

There are kits on the Internet where you can assemble your own Dream Machine, though if you want to really trip out from simply watching the alternation of bright light, take any chance you ever get to see Tony Conrad's *The Flicker* projected in a theatre (assuming you do not have a heart condition or suffer from seizures). For the post-*Loveless* tour, the band wanted some sort of visual element that matched the music, but they'd stopped receiving any funding from Creation and were broke. Thankfully, Angus Cameron, the guy who shot the cover and videos for the album, had a series of short abstract loops that the group were able to pick up on the cheap. "It was quite haphazard in a way," says Shields, "the way it came together, but [it worked]. The statement for the tour was primarily the energy, using the force of volume to make audiences pay attention whether they wanted to or not. And it was the same with the visuals, which force people to be pay attention, but not really. You know [with the abstract looping] it was a constant sameness in a way, like a modern version of the psychedelic thing in a way. But rather than trying to imitate the effects of acid, we were more trying to induce it, you know what I mean?"

Chapter Thirteen
Honey Power

Taking a break from work, I drop by to visit Kami and April, two thirty-something music fiends who dance at Magic Gardens, a small strip club located in a section of downtown Portland that used to be a funky, excellent Chinatown and is now getting a "facelift" to make it more tourist-friendly. And despite its low-key, neighborhood bar type vibe, Magic Gardens is generally considered to be the best club in a town with more strip clubs per capita than any other in the US. The place is frequented by rock stars, who drop by late at night while road crews pack up their gear. The song "Sometimes" comes on and, ever the egoist, I ask Kami if the tune is being played for me, since I've told her a dozen times I'm writing a book about this record. "It's a mistake," she replies, laughing at me a little bit. "But I can't dance to this shit!," she adds. This surprises me; women at this place dance to stuff you'd never expect anyone to: Iron and Wine, Patsy Cline, Can, Ween, Dungen, Soft Cell, Suicide, even the Sun City Girls. But never "Girls, Girls, Girls."

"It's just too . . . emotional," she explains, about the song. Then Kami rolls her eyes, shrugs and moves very slowly and gracefully across the small, low stage as the song plays. Swathed in red light, she watches with seeming disinterest as bills make their way to the edge of the "rack." This is not the kind of place where people stuff bills into g-strings; people keep their distance. Kami's little dance to "Sometimes" is lovely, despite her reservations about it. I wish I could show it to you, but we're not in that part of the future where books have Quicktime videos imbedded in them, so you'll just have to use your imagination.

What Kami said really got me thinking, though. Just a record or so earlier, MBV had songs with titles such as "Soft as Snow (But Warm Inside)" and lyrics that went, for instance, "Get in your car and drive it all over me" or, "Kiss kiss kiss uh suck suck suck." Bilinda had written a third of the songs on *Isn't Anything*, including the crowd pleasing "Several Girls Galore." "Cupid Come" has the lines "Swallow me into your bed / With glimpses of your thighs / Forget your vanity / Come cupid come," or I think that's what they are. But they're more abstract on *Loveless*, the song titles less sexualized. It's still a very sexy record, it's just more complicated. On the first song, "Only Shallow," Bilinda sings, "Soft as a pillow touch her there / Where she won't dare, somewhere" in her most ultimately sexy voice. The backing guitar line sounds like a mechanical beast gone crazy. As Heather Phares puts it in All Music Guide: "*Loveless* intimates sensuality and sexuality instead of stating them explicitly; Kevin Shields and Bilinda Butcher's vocals meld perfectly with the trippy sonics around them, suggesting druggy sex or sexy drugs."

The sexuality may be charged, but it's ambiguous. James Hunter, writing in the *SPIN Alternative Record Guide*, assumes that the two high-pitched vocalists on *Loveless* are Debbie and Bilinda, when in fact of course it's Kevin and Bilinda: "The women manage great feats because, even when their singing lies several layers beneath the foregrounded accompaniments, the sweet timbres of their voices alternately sting, caress or upbraid." In his Amazon.com review of the album, Douglas Wolk plays up the record's sexual angle, calling it a "pure, warm, androgynous but deeply sexual rush of sound" that is "furiously loud but seductive rather than aggressive . . . pulsing like a lover's body." Bilinda occasionally sang the lower register and Kevin the higher one. I love that, and ask Kevin about it. "Yeah that's the thing; Bilinda always had a very girly voice, but also a bit low," he says. "I had a slight androgynous edge to myself I suppose," Shields continues. "When I was younger, I was half-influenced by female singers as I was by male singers. Sometimes when I'd be having trouble singing a song, I'd just have to think of Dusty Springfield or something. And that sounds mad, but that would really help. And Björk; she would be a bit of an influence just because of her fearlessness."

MBV's very composition appeals in its sexual symmetry: straight dude, gay woman, discreet couple. Sounds like the start of a "casual encounters" post on Craigslist. Speaking of ads, they were no Benetton commercial, but there was a diversity to their sizes: Colm all small and wiry like a soccer forward; Kevin big and strong, a bit of extra weight on his frame but cute with his long hair; Deb all curvy and slightly butch in her shortish hair and penchant for trousers; and then Bilinda with her slight, model-type looks and huge eyes that look straight out of a Margaret Keane painting. The boy-girl-boy-girl make up of the group was really important to Shields. "Yes—it was a balance of energy! Even on tour, we tried to balance the crew. We desperately didn't want a bunch of rock and roll crew people." Along with Kevin's sister Ann-Marie, "We'd have various other girls on tour, like, selling t-shirts, and it kept it good. The female energy is so powerful, and I need that around me, to this day. Even when I'm thinking about doing my own solo stuff, although the first thing I do will be my own thing, I know it will morph into a band with girls in it. I know it will."

Chapter Fourteen
No More Sorry

Everything about this album feels so oblique, so gauzy and hazy and inscrutable, that I never realized the album's title was actually straightforward, almost literal. Then I spoke with Kevin and Bilinda for this book, and it seemed apparent that the title referred directly to the disintegration of their relationship, which was happening right then and there, in the studio. It was happening even more slowly than the recording process itself, but it was happening. (I know I keep inserting myself into the narrative here, but I hope I'm not painting myself as some great close friend with insider knowledge. Yeah, they almost gave me a song for free once, and we had a few pals in common, whoop dee doo. Besides, the few times I was backstage, I was so awestruck by Bilinda and Debbie that I never spoke with them. They were both so rad and beautiful, and at the time, I barely knew how to talk to women at all let alone cool-ass rock star women.)

Asking Kevin about the title, he sighs and pauses for a while before getting more oblique than usual. "The word 'love' is very powerful even when you put anything after it. It's difficult to explain, but it's to do with effect and feel and to have some tangible meaning, with the meaning being less important than the overall effect." It's clear that it still is hard to talk about, and I don't blame him. Kevin does allow that "it would be basically true to say that the lyrics were as much about us as anything, but they weren't completely 'cause as I said there were these other issues that were influencing us. So, her lyrics and my lyrics would be that kind of thing as well."

Asked whether the album's title referred to their relationship, Bilinda replies, "I think it did, in a way, but it was not just us. You know, I think he found the whole process of making *Loveless*, in the end, just such a slog. The songs were so brilliant, and I think the state Kevin had to get into to create those was compromised by just a lot of misery going on around us, nothing particularly terrible happening to anybody, but it was kind of a depressing time. I was not the most bubbling, happy person, you know."

At the time, the two never spoke about their relationship status to the press. "The media here in England are extremely tabloidish—the *NME*, you know what I mean?," Kevin says. "You just don't want to give them anything 'cause everything's an *issue*, so you just say as little as possible really and you get away with it then. What I learned is that you can be as private as you want really, unless you're really famous. But if you're in a position like me, you can have your privacy; you have to just make it happen."

Bilinda's voice brightens considerably as she describes first crushing out on her band mate. "He just seemed really gentle, a really soft-spoken, gentle guy, a bit geeky," she says. "He had these glasses that were always done up with cellotape [*laughs*] and always seemed to wear the same clothes all the time, which I used to do too then, so it really wasn't so unusual. He always had his stripey shirts and a leather jacket, sort of a bomber jacket, and this black jumper that became legendary. It had what started as a tiny hole that probably came from dropping a bit of burning cigarette or something, and then it just ended up in this massive big hole but he still used to wear it, you know. So, he was scruffy, but adorable." "I never wore a bomber jacket in my life; it's amazing that's what she remembers!" Kevin interjects.

When Bilinda joined the band she was having "a bit of a hard time" with the father of her son Toby. "We were sort of together but he was being quite violent and things were going really wrong. He was becoming quite suicidal, and telling Toby that he was gonna kill himself and all this. So there was this whole scenario going on when I first joined the band. And Toby's dad wasn't too happy that I got the audition, even though he latched me up with going to it. He wasn't jealous at first, 'cause he knew that doing backing vocals wasn't really what he wanted to do. But I started playing guitar—and he was a guitarist, and I had never picked up his guitar at home or anything—and now I was suddenly playing guitar. There was a bit of, you know, animosity." Kevin and Bilinda didn't really start going out until six months or a year after she joined.

"We were together properly from '88 till '92," Kevin says. "I mean, it's complicated you know. She was living in the house until '97; we were together on and off for more than ten years. Those two records are a real document of that, in a way—our coming together made that [music] happen, even though I would be 'in charge' of everything musically. I was the leader of the band and everything. But Bilinda, when she joined the band, she brought very good taste in music, and this sort of energy, for want of a better word, and atmosphere."

Bilinda says her relationship with Kevin "was brilliant in the beginning—best thing in the world—but when we did *Loveless*, things were falling apart. But he was always off, and during *Loveless*, the hours were so upside-down. He'd be in the studio all day. And sometimes I would be there too, but I had to be there for Toby [in the day]. There was a yearning feeling, you know. We were living together but not really being together. And, um, a lot of times we weren't really like a proper couple anymore, and we weren't sure if we were going to split up or get back together, you know? We did split up when we went on the tour after *Loveless*; we sort of split up on the week of our first gig. We went to Australia first, and we decided that would be it."

"It was just quicker and easier to live together, and we always thought we would get back together, maybe," Bilinda says. "I was going through my own personal nightmares and I think we were also smoking too much dope. I still really cared about Kevin, even though I knew we couldn't be together, and I think we'll never really stop caring about each other in that way. We really loved each other, but we tend to just push each other's buttons, and being trapped together for the longest time on tour [is not easy]. It was a weird thing, because although we'd have all these big fights, we still always got on together. The only time we really fell out for a time was when I moved out of the house, you know. I think Kevin felt a bit abandoned by everybody then; he was just left having to keep it still going. And I didn't leave because I wanted to leave the band, I just felt like I was the one who needed to sort myself out. It was hard 'cause I felt like there wasn't any connection at all, you know, and I felt really sad. Really, really sad."

The Who Sell Out

by John Dougan

John Dougan received a PhD in American Studies from the College of William & Mary and is an associate professor in the Department of Recording Industry at Middle Tennessee State University.

Jaguar and Coca-Cola

> We've got some ideas to try and get the English pop scene back on its feet again. The drag is that kids over here have seen so much . . . in a few months we'll be ready with something a bit different—something that's going to give them their money's worth and make them appreciate what we're doing.
>
> —Pete Townshend, *Melody Maker*, October 14, 1967

Leisure, argues Simon Frith, is an implicit critique of work and the symbol of leisure is youth. Leisure represents fun, freedom, and pleasure, impulses that contrast sharply with the drudgery, oppression, and alienation of work. It is therefore the charge of employers to trivialize leisure, denaturalizing its potential to liberate, preventing it from interfering with the objectives of labor, namely production and consumption.[1] In this environment rock music is a "leisure commodity," wherein the "consciousness of class became the myth of 'rock brotherhood'; the rock and roll experience became something that would be consumed by middle-class youth, by students; culture became commodity."[2] Frith's use of "commodity" is not strictly pejorative but rather refers to the music industry's creation of "repertoires of goods" designed to attract and incorporate audiences as commodity consumers who, according to John Fiske, excorporate these texts for their own purposes. Though Frith and Fiske would not articulate these points until the 1980s, Pete Townshend and Kit Lambert seemed to implicitly understand how such elements contributed to the complex cultural matrix that was London in 1967. A city on the brink of a three-year period of mediation-revolution[3], London was youth-obsessed and brilliantly day-glo, advertising and pop art were synonymous, skilled pop bands morphed into rock bands, mods grew out their hair and traded in their Fred Perry shirts for kaftans and mandarin jackets, the club scene was still happening, but there were also full-blown, acid-drenched "happenings" like the two-day "Psychedelica-mania" and the "14-Hour Technicolor Dream," pirate radio may have been silenced but not after changing the broadcast landscape, "The Underground was no longer the property of a tiny minority," wrote George Melly in his seminal 1970 work *Revolt Into Style*. "It had thousands of adherents and sympathizers, its own slang, its own meeting places, its own heroes and, more relevant here, its own groups." To hardliners who'd waved their freak flag high, and done so before anyone else, for the Underground to become co-opted by the mainstream meant it was politically and culturally spent. The counterculture newspaper of record, *International Times* (which had debuted less than a year earlier), "officially" pronounced the movement dead in March 1967. A mock funeral for the dearly departed was held in central London.

Had Townshend been equally dour, dogmatic, and proprietary about the cultural import of the underground, it's likely that *Sell Out* might have been an unbearably tedious satire of consumerism. From the beginning, he had (with Lambert's unequivocal support) envisioned the album as a celebration of the zeitgeist, a joyous reaffirmation of the discrete cultural elements that had defined British postwar popular culture and the Who as a pop art musical experience. For one so culturally astute, who thoroughly understood the imbricated nature of pop art (and music), mass media, and youth culture, for *Sell Out* to not embrace and reflect such cultural dynamism would have been inconceivable. Moreover, *Sell Out* distinguishes popular culture as essentially optimistic, potentially progressive, and fueled by the desire for social change, and the impetus to make it happen. More than anything the band recorded over the next decade *Sell Out* represents the full flowering of leisure and its powerfully liberating promise of fun, freedom, and pleasure.[4]

The original idea was to sell ad space between each track. The thankless task of approaching potential advertisers fell to Chris Stamp, who found corporations unenthusiastic about product placement on a rock record with an initial pressing of 50,000 copies. Only Coca-Cola expressed interest having, briefly, employed the Who as pitchmen. On April 24, 1967 during a week of recording at De Lane Lea, a "tough, dirty, rock and roll studio"[5] situated in the basement of a Midland Bank, the band cut two jingles for the soft drink. The first was a variation on the company's ubiquitous catch phrase "Things Go Better with Coke," a line that would take on an entirely different meaning among rock fans in the 1970s. The second attempt proved even less viable. Built upon a driving, distorted guitar riff, the band chants the mantra "Coke after Coke after Coke after Coca-Cola." Undeniably forceful, the company regarded it as too aggressive and only briefly used the spots in the UK. (Both tracks were eventually released on the 1995 CD reissue of *Sell Out.*) Townshend had also written a sports car tribute called "Jaguar" that, along with rejected Coke adverts, started him thinking about a unique concept for the next Who record. "As it stood I could see that we just had an album of fairly good songs but there was really nothing to differentiate it from our last LP [*A Quick One*]," Townshend told *Melody Maker*. "It needed something to make it stand out.. . . . We thought of using the powerful instrumental number that we made for Coca-Cola and then I linked it up with the number 'Jaguar' and then, of course, we thought 'Why not do a whole side of adverts?'"[6] As important, according to Richard Barnes, was that the album pay tribute to the recently silenced pirates, a censorious act that Townshend regarded as an assault on British youth and rock and roll:

> [The Who] wanted to give the album the feel of a British pirate commercial radio station. The Government had recently passed [The Marine Broadcasting Offences Act] banning the pirates and enforcing the BBC on the nation. The Who, Pete in particular, resented the forced closure of the pirate stations and the BBC's pop straightjacket.

> Although the pirates were really rather shoddy, and many of the actual ads amateurish and crude, their news bulletins blatantly right wing, and many of their records simply paid to be played by the big record companies, they were, compared to the BBC Light Programme, bright, full of fun . . . and gave airtime to a lot of new sounds. The Who owed pirate radio a lot. It was Radios Caroline and London that were instrumental in breaking their first four singles. Kit Lambert and Chris Stamp also moved offices from those they shared with [Robert] Stigwood to set up in Caroline House, the headquarters of Radio Caroline in Mayfair. Also, Ronan O'Rahilly . . . used to be part owner of the Scene Club and became friendly with the Who.[7]

Recorded primarily on eight-track equipment and frequently between gigs, *Sell Out*'s basic tracks were cut with remarkable speed and efficiency. While the band crisscrossed the Atlantic, Lambert lugged the tapes with him to a number of American studios (eg, Talentmasters in New York, Gold Star in Los Angeles, even Bradley's Barn near Nashville) to facilitate mixing, overdubbing and, as was commonly done at the time, mono transfers. "I Can See for Miles" was mixed at Gold Star—famously known as the studio wherein Phil Spector perfected his trademark "wall of sound" production technique—because Townshend felt it had the "deepest, clearest sounding [echo chamber] in the world."[8] Just prior to the Herman's Hermits tour, Lambert booked three days at Talentmasters with engineer Chris Huston, a native Liverpudlian and former member of the Undertakers who'd opened for the Who in 1964. The sessions consisted of recording new backing tracks and vocal overdubs to "Rael," *Sell Out*'s longest, most elaborate, and perplexing song, a politicized slice of sci-fi futurism in which the Red Chins (who Richard Barnes affirms are the communist Chinese), threaten to conquer the world, eliminating all established religions. (Townshend's interest in spiritual matters during this time was affected by his recent introduction to the teachings of Merwan S. Irani, or Meher Baba, the messianic figure who would become his avatar.) According to Al Kooper, who'd been brought in to add organ to the track, the tape accidentally ended up in the trash, ruining the song's opening fifteen seconds. Once informed of this error, an infuriated Townshend heaved a chair through the glass partition in the control room. While this sounds behaviorally consistent, Huston has since amended Kooper's claims noting that, while the tape did end up in the trash (Huston fished it out of a dumpster in back of the studio), he was able to rescue the track by copying parts of the mono mix onto the stereo master. Townshend was extremely annoyed but exhibited considerable restraint; no chairs or glass partitions were harmed during the making of *Sell Out*.[9]

Though the sessions began in July, the majority of *Sell Out* was recorded during a frenzied October in three London studios: De Lane Lea, Kingsway, and IBC. The pub round the corner from Kingsway provided John Entwistle and Keith Moon with pint glasses of inspiration that led to their creating short ad parodies plugging products they already used, in the hopes of getting more free goods. But what had worked for Rotosound strings ("Hold your group together with Rotosound strings") and Premier drums (Moon pounds his kit furiously as the group chants "Premier drums," though for the longest time I thought they were yelling "Let it Rock!") did not work for John Mason, a luxury car dealer in Ealing, whom Entwistle and Moon thought might come across with a couple of Bentleys for their inebriated efforts. He didn't and the track was left off the album. Entwistle's other spoofs, "Heinz Baked Beans" (which is simply "Cobwebs and Strange" from *A Quick One* with different lyrics), "Medac," and the "Charles Atlas" spot, were slightly less spontaneous, learned by the rest of the band from his demos.[10] Townshend's lone parody to make the LP was "Odorono," a "tragic" tale of a young woman's budding singing career undone by underarm odor and perspiration. An insightful critique of the entertainment industry's elevation of style and appearance over talent, as well as a satire of products as salvation, the song is unexpectedly heartfelt, partly the result of the anguish expressed in Townshend's voice and the story's cinematic quality. By this I'm not suggesting anything grand or expansive, on the contrary, the song's brilliance is due to its being a succinct 2:16. "Odorono" (the title coming from an actual product Odo-Ro-No a deodorant for women) is cinematic in the way it conjures up the image of the plucky but unknown chorus girl who, finally, gets her chance at stardom (sort of like Ruby Keeler in *42nd Street*). The "triumphant" heroine (the adjective given added import in the song courtesy of a booming tympani) is distraught when her dreams of stardom and the attentions of one Mr. Davidson (a reference to famed London booking agent Harold Davidson) are ruined by her poor choice of deodorant. "She should have used Odorono," the song's final line (and only product mention), is delivered as more of a weary shrug than snappish I-told-you-so. "Odorono" is by far the album's most complex fake ad because Townshend didn't approach it as a smug joke; there is a narrative arc and character development that leaves you feeling bad for the singer, and slightly peeved at Mr. Davidson's insensitivity and superficiality. But before any of this can register, the song's fading final chord flows seamlessly into another PAMS jingle sung by an unreasonably cheerful woman who tell us, "It's smoooooth sailing with the highly successful sounds of wonderful Radio London."

These deftly inserted, delectably crass jingles, along with emphasizing *Sell Out*'s playfulness (my favorite is a stentorian-voiced choir intoning, "Radio London reminds you / Go to the church of your choice"), perform a secondary function as powerful cultural signifiers. Embedded in every jingle is the history of pirate radio, not as nostalgia, but a rebuke of the BBC's (Labour party–sanctioned) paternalism. The Who were reminding listeners of the end of a vigorous era of cultural independence brought about by a bunch of renegade, money-fixated entrepreneurs undone by a government and radio corporation that were quite comfortable defining the moral parameters of youth culture. It is, therefore, thematically consistent, unsurprising, and a tad perverse that *Sell Out* opens with a PAMS bumper: a synthesized voice (sounding similar to the cadence of Steven Hawking's computerized speech) announcing the days of the week, each day punctuated by a fusillade of blatting horns. Lasting a mere twenty-seven seconds, it begins to fade around mid-week, and by the time the weekend arrives it's almost inaudible. It's a haunting farewell, a ghostly reminder that in the ecology of culture extinguished species are rare; it is a voice that, despite having been officially silenced, survived. Used at the album's beginning it reaffirms the cultural shift brought about by the pirates, acknowledging that vernacular culture adapts rather than disappears.[11]

As if opening the record with a jingle wasn't perverse enough, *Sell Out*'s first track, "Armenia [pronounced 'arm and ear'] City in the Sky," was an equally confounding bit of mindfuckery. Loaded with backward guitars, sculpted feedback, soaring blasts of fuzztone, John Entwistle's legato French horn, and suitably trippy lyrics ("The sky is glass / the sea is brown / and everyone / is upside down") it is, arguably, the most overtly psychedelic track, not just on *Sell Out*, but in the entire Who catalog. It is a pure studio creation, a dense sonic mélange impossible (hell, unthinkable) to recreate onstage. Its appearance, however, begged some salient questions: Who exactly was singing? The song was credited to someone named Speedy Keen. Was Townshend composing under a pseudonym? For years it was assumed the vocalist was Keith Moon, the dubious logic being that the song's key was too high for Roger Daltrey but somehow adequate for the barely tuneful Moon. It is, in fact, Daltrey singing with help on the chorus from Speedy Keen.[12] John Keen (the nickname "Speedy" indicating a fondness for motorcycles rather than amphetamine sulfate) was a Who fan who'd bonded with Townshend (eventually working for a time as his driver) over big cars and big sound systems, "[Pete and I] had a lot of things in common, we liked really good cars with big engines. We liked high energy music, and just the whole thing of how he set up his life was just phenomenal to me at that point because of [his] sound system. . . . At that time you couldn't get a long paper between us. We were close."[13] Though he occasionally treated Keen abominably, Townshend encouraged him to write songs and put a band together. As rendered by Keen, "Armenia City in the Sky" sounds like a Townshend song, which may explain why it made the album in the first place. Keen's efforts were later rewarded when his new band, the idiosyncratic Thunderclap Newman, had a mega-hit with the Townshend-produced track "Something in the Air" in 1969. Keen, who later produced records by the Heartbreakers (featuring Johnny Thunders) and Motörhead, died in 2002.

"Armenia" employs some of the sonic appurtenances common in psychedelic rock, what Jim DeRogatis describes as "circular mandala-like song structures; sustained or droning melodies; altered and effected instrumental sounds; reverb, echoes, and tape delays that created a sense of space, and layered mixes that rewarded repeated listening by revealing new and mysterious elements."[14] Compared to "Armenia," however, the rest of *Sell Out* is judiciously psychedelic. Lambert is creative but restrained in the use of "far out" studio trickery, there is no meandering westernized raga rock, or ponderously over-elaborate art rock, but rather complex, inscrutable, metatextual songs like "Rael"—"No one will ever know what ['Rael'] means," Townshend admitted, "it has been squeezed up too tightly to make any sense"[15]—and in the compressed, ecstatic intensity of "I Can See for Miles." Dabbling with acid doubtlessly impacted Townshend creatively, but *Sell Out*'s lysergic tinge is as much a reflection of an exuberant zeitgeist as it is the product of chemically induced mind expansion. By being relatively circumspect when it came to psychedelia's sonic trappings, *Sell Out* retains its enduring vitality because the conceptual apparatus never overwhelms the songs.

Following "Armenia," "Mary Anne with the Shaky Hand" comes as a bit of a shock. Propelled by luxuriously thick acoustic guitars (two earlier less successful attempts featured an electric guitar) and Latin percussion (it's the only Who song I'm aware of with castanets) it's an unabashed, decidedly unpsychedelic pop song about, ostensibly, masturbation; the shaky handed Mary Anne being an expert in administering hand jobs. Daltrey and Townshend's unison vocals, given a choir effect by Kit Lambert, tell how Linda, Jean, and Cindy, all good dancers, don't seem to measure up to the sexually accommodating Mary Anne. In such an appealing melodic context even the song's glib chauvinism ("Linda can cook / She reads books / Cindy can sew"), sounds like a parody of anti-feminist rhetoric. Had it been released as an A-side and been successfully promoted by Decca there's no reason why such a cheeky male fantasy couldn't have been a huge hit. After all, it's not as if rock and roll suffers from a dearth of horny, frustrated teenage boys.

The same is true of Townshend's coming of age miniature "Tattoo." The only song from *Sell Out* regularly featured in the band's live set (there's an excellent version on *Live at Leeds*), and a nice bookend to "Mary Anne" and "Odorono," it's quintessential Townshend (pre)adolescent angst—a young boy and his brother searching for an answer to the question what makes a man a man ("Is it brains or brawn / Or the month you were born?"), decide to get tattoos, an idea that greatly displeases their parents. It's an astonishingly compact song, one that establishes conflict almost immediately ("Our old man didn't like our appearance / He said that only women wear long hair") and reifies postwar generational divisiveness. Once inked, the brothers face the wrath of their parents, and the song's undercurrent of domestic violence is casually, almost comically referenced ("My dad beat me cause mine said 'Mother' / But my mother naturally liked it and beat my brother"). The story ends with one brother getting "tattooed all over" and marrying a wife who's "tattooed too." Originally Townshend thought only he could articulate the song's longing, confusion, and uncertainty. "'Tattoo' is me examining that divide between me and Roger and his idea of what made a man a man and my idea," he recalled. "I thought it was going to be one of those songs where Roger would turn around and say to me, 'No, you sing this, I don't need to question whether I'm a man or not.' But he did sing it, and he sang it really well. And I realized then, 'Hey, he doesn't know. He doesn't know if he's a man or not. He's got the same insecurities I do.'"[16] One listen proves Townshend correct; there is a vulnerability and plaintiveness to Daltrey's singing that gives "Tattoo" its emotional weight, a performance that, even now, remains one of his finest on record.

Before side one explodes into tiny fragments at the conclusion of "I Can See for Miles," there is "Our Love Was," a stunning, almost completely forgotten love song. Though initially likening love to "famine" and "frustration," the sudden, dramatic emotional shift in the chorus ("Our love was flying / Our love was soaring / Our love was shining / Like a summer morning") while lyrically precious, is exhilarating, bolstered by a magnificent, kinetic instrumental performance, heightened by Kit Lambert's emphasis on volume and mass. As songs go it's more poignant than sophisticated but, more importantly, it's impossible not be caught up in its passionate undertow, a feeling evinced by the band's determined playing and the ardor of Townshend's vocal (he's singing at the top of his range). In much clumsier hands this would be filler, a track worthy of only a passing mention. Here it strains against such limitations executing a rarely successful act of musical legerdemain by turning cliché into insight.[17]

This breakneck pace and constant barrage of music and noise—a remarkable display of pop art music—is more restrained on side two. Principally, it's due to the absence of the PAMS inserts, a decision influenced by practical considerations that effectively ditched the pirate radio theme. While the majority of basic tracking was done quickly there were regular interruptions for tour breaks, as well as sessions recorded for John Peel's Radio 1 show "Top Gear" and the odd appearance on "Top of the Pops." Exacerbating this was the laborious, time-consuming tape assembling process wherein the balance of the PAMS inserts, fake ads, and real songs had to sound seamless.[18] The album's release had already been delayed once and there were concerns that it might not be out in time for the lucrative Christmas sales season. Despite the loss of the Radio London jingles the ad parodies remain intact—side two opens with Entwistle's short, humorous "Charles Atlas" spoof promising that any 90-pound weakling can be remade into (cue the bassist's extremely low, heavily reverbed voice) "a beast of a man." Equally funny and surprisingly touching (considering it was written by Entwistle) is "Medac," a 57-second advert for pimple cream with (another surprise) a happy ending. The only non-spoof Entwistle track to make the album is "Silas Stingy," a song that, quite honestly, took me a long time to warm up to. While I consider Entwistle one of the greatest rock bassists to have walked the face of the earth, I've never much cared for his songwriting or solo work; the notable exceptions being *Who's Next*'s powerful, funny, unrepentantly sexist "My Wife," and the autobiographical satire of rock star excess, "Success Story" from 1975's *The Who by Numbers*. His violence and horror vibe always sounded rote and one-dimensional (though he could be profoundly unsettling and disturbing as in "Cousin Kevin" from *Tommy*) and, loathe though I am to spout heresy and disparage the memory of such a great musician, "Boris the Spider" is a lousy song.

"Silas Stingy" is not about a specific, Scrooge-like character (though the name Silas was nicked from George Eliot's novel *Silas Marner*), but rather Entwistle himself. The first one in the band to purchase a house, he "found it very hard going because our expenses were so ridiculous and our [earnings weren't] that big, so I saved every penny to put a deposit on the house and [bought] furniture. . . . So Silas Stingy buying a house and a watchdog and a safe is exactly what happened to me."[19] There is a childlike, singsong quality to the verses ("Once upon a time there lived an old miser man / By the name of Silas Stingy") accentuated in the chorus's bratty chant, "Money, money, money bags / Money, money, money bags / There goes mingy Stingy / There goes mingy Stingy," and propelled by Entwistle's aggressive bass. Disliking the song for its nyah-nyah cadence is understandable; over the years friends and acquaintances have singled it out as the album's weakest track, arguing that it was too jokey and lacked substance. Though I was once in such company, I now hear it as one of Entwistle's cleverest efforts, a song that suffers only when compared to Townshend's contributions to side two: "Relax," "Sunrise," "I Can't Reach You," and "Rael."

"Relax," accurately described by Chris Charlesworth as "acid rock à la early Pink Floyd [and] not the Who's natural territory,"[20] articulates trippiness through its vibey, turn-on and tune-in lyrics ("Relax and settle down / Let your mind go round / Lay down on the ground / Listen to the sound / Of the band / Hold my hand") and Townshend's swooping, billowing organ. Still, it's a Who song and therefore has considerably more guitar muscle than Syd-era pop naiveté like "Bike" or "Arnold Layne." *Sell Out* doesn't lack pop naiveté, it's simply and more directly expressed on the album's penultimate track "Sunrise." On the surface it's decidedly unWho-like (Townshend is alone and unplugged) not to mention sounding jazzish, the influence of Mickey Baker's *Jazz Guitar* instruction books. "At the time I was studying [Baker's books]," Townshend recalled, "and I had two of [them], both of which were magnificent. It's all that I've ever needed to get into slightly more complex chord work. I played that song on a Harmony 12-string. It was written for my mother to show her I could write real music."[21] Recorded on November 2, 1967, the same day the band appeared on "Top of the Pops" as leather-clad biker types with Townshend sporting blacked out front teeth promoting "I Can See for Miles," "Sunrise" was an eleventh hour replacement for the more raucous "Jaguar," a decision made despite Moon's strenuous objections. It's a gorgeous song, featuring rich, intricate (at times too intricate) guitar playing, and is sung by Townshend (purposely?) in such a high register as if to preclude Daltrey from even attempting it. Lyrically it appropriates the strong emotionalism of "Our Love Was" to the point of being unabashedly sentimental ("You take away the breath I was keeping for sunrise"), but given Townshend's recent enthusiastic embrace of Meher Baba's philosophy ("Baba is the avatar of the age—the Messiah," he rapturously declared in late 1967. "He can't do anything but good. He has utterly changed my whole life . . . "[22]), it's not unreasonable to think that the romanticism of lyrics such as "My everyday is spent / Thinking of you all the while" or "Each day I spend in an echoed vision of you," express both the trepidation and exhilaration of a spiritual crisis and awakening. None of which is surprising considering Townshend's penchant for passion, intensity, and openness when it came to personal expression. The operative word being *personal*; Daltrey, Entwistle, and Moon, for the most part, didn't give two fucks about Meher Baba and were more inclined to prick Townshend's spiritual pretensions by referring to his Messiah as "Ali" Baba. Even if the spiritual yearning of "Sunrise" was more implicit and accidental than explicit and premeditated, the same quest theme animates Townshend's strongest contributions to *Sell Out*, "I Can't Reach You," and "Rael."

Originally titled "See, Feel, Hear You" (add "touch" and "heal" and you have the mantra that forms the thematic nucleus of *Tommy*), "I Can't Reach You" is one of Townshend's earliest attempts at composing on the piano—the song's simplicity, he has often claimed, the result of his mediocre keyboard skills. Although he wrote it before being introduced to Baba's teachings (the interlocutor in this spiritual epiphany was UFO club regular and *International Times* art director Mike McInnerney), Townshend later admitted that, while not aware of it at the time, the song reflects his yearning for spiritual sustenance, something that he frighteningly learned he could not get from hallucinogens. Never an enthusiastic proselytizer of the "acid lifestyle," Townshend was more of a psychedelic dilettante. What changed him was a protracted bad trip on the plane to London after the Monterey Pop gig:

> On the plane, I looked through my pockets, and I found a pill, which had been given to me by Owsley [Augustus Owsley Stanley III, the Grateful Dead's notorious pharmaceutical dispenser] which was called STP, a very powerful hallucinogen supposedly twenty times more powerful than acid. Keith Moon produced a similar one and said "Let's while away the hours with a trip." I thought, "I can't leave him go off on his own," so I swallowed mine. About fifteen minutes later I was having visions of the most unbelievable nature.
>
> Now, I'd had LSD before many times and I'd had bad trips before on LSD many times, but nothing like this. At one point, I was so disgusted with what I was and what I was thinking and my body and the way I felt, that I actually left my body. I was looking down at myself in the seat, and in the end I realized that I must go back otherwise I was gonna die. About three weeks later, I thought about it, and I thought it really did happen, I really did leave my body to avoid these horrible sensations. And I did avoid them, and yet I could still see, and I could still hear, and I still existed and then I went back in again. I would never have touched acid again after that, because the shock of the bad trip was so stunning and so awful. I didn't even smoke a cigarette again for four years.[23]

"I Can't Reach You" was recorded on July 5, 1967, about two weeks after this incident, and contains moments that, while not exactly mirroring the event, reflect its post-traumatic intensity ("My body strains but the nerves are dead," "You're so alive and I'm nearly dead"). The song's references to flying, long thought to be the result of the frightening circumstances (the emergency landing in Nashville being one) faced traveling across the US in a dilapidated charter plane with Herman's Hermits, were more likely due to Townshend being trapped on a plane for twelve hours enduring an extended, unpleasant psychedelic experience. The melancholic frustration of the chorus ("I can't reach you / With arms outstretched / I can't reach you / I crane my neck") indicate vulnerability (a quality intensified by Townshend's singing) and the need to "see, feel, and hear," a sign that spirituality was, for Townshend anyway, the only panacea for acid's false consciousness. He seemed ready for such an epiphany, if only for a lack of alternatives, as he told writer Michael Watts, "Baba's coming was directly coincidental with a lack of available things to turn to."[24] Similarly spiritually inclined "Rael" ("The home of my religion / To me the center of the earth") which concludes *Sell Out* (and at just under six minutes is the album's longest song), suggests that Townshend was preparing for *Tommy* insofar as he and Lambert realized that certain thematic concerns and narratives were best expressed and grasped not in one three-minute rock song, but on a thematically linked LP full of them—a lesson doubtlessly learned while making *Sell Out*. Musically it foreshadows *Tommy* through the use of riffs and chord progressions that would reappear on "Sparks" and "Underture," and while coherence is not among its strengths, its complex structure, lush, multi-tracked harmonies, and inscrutable yet emotionally charged lyrical images, evoking war, paranoia, and nationalism, articulates how far Townshend had come as a writer (in such a short time and at only 22) and the risks, no matter how puzzling or unsettling, he was willing to take. To me it remains *Sell Out*'s most intriguing and frustrating track, not because it resists interpretation, but rather because it's a veritable Pandora's Box of ideas and meanings. "Rael," inchoate though it may be, is more beginning than end, more future than past or present. Not bad considering it nearly ended up in the trash.

On November 2, Kit Lambert continued mixing the record at De Lane Lea and finalized the track sequence. There was plenty of material from which to choose and Lambert, with input from the band, chose wisely. It would have been nice had "Jaguar" been included, but not at the expense of "Sunrise." Two Eddie Cochran songs, "Summertime Blues" (which would become a live staple) and "My Way," were recorded but left off so as to not detract from Townshend's efforts. As for the other selections, those decisions were more clear cut: Entwistle's "Someone's Coming" (sung by Daltrey), the flipside of the UK single "I Can See for Miles," is a fine brass-driven pop song, but isn't as good as "Silas Stingy"; Townshend's tantalizing "Glittering Girl" has potential, but sounds unfinished and too much like a demo; "Early Morning Cold Taxi," written by Daltrey and former Who roadie Dave Langston, is pleasant enough, but only as a B-side; the instrumental version of "Hall of the Mountain King" from *Peer Gynt* is pure pisstake; an electric "Mary Anne with the Shaky Hand," even with Al Kooper on organ, when compared to the luminous acoustic version, is completely unnecessary; and finally, the Keith Moon–penned and sung(!) "Girl's Eyes," needlessly rambles on for nearly four minutes, and is glutted with oh-wow lyrical bons mots such as "Girl's eyes / Butterflies / How she cries / Can't get through to you." (These tracks and more can be found on the 1995 CD reissue, which provides a more complete picture of the album's creation.) Once the running order was set, it took three weeks to prepare the album for pressing and the cover for printing—cover art that proved to be of great significance. For *Sell Out* to maintain its conceptual consistency, the packaging had to articulate the notion, with tongue planted firmly in cheek, that the band was indeed "selling out." It needed to be funny and smart, slightly crass but in a manner that reinforced its pop art intentions and "[embraced the] world [of advertising], in all its mind-wrenching, sometimes stomach-churning contradictions and disarray."[25] All of which it accomplished brilliantly, much to the chagrin of the band's American record label.

Notes

1. Simon Frith, *Sound Effects: Youth, Leisure, and the Politics of Rock'n'Roll* (New York: Pantheon, 1981) 262.
2. Ibid., 263.
3. George Melly coined the expression "mediation-revolution."
4. This approach to popular culture as both empowering and a site of resistance is informed by the work of John Fiske.
5. Producer Mike Thorne (Wire, among many others) described De Lane Lea in such glowing terms.
6. Andy Neill and Matthew Kent, *The Who, Anyway, Anyhow, Anywhere* (New York: Virgin Books, 2005), 101.
7. Richard Barnes and Pete Townshend, *The Who, Maximum R&B* (Medford, NJ: Plexus Publishing, 2004), 48.

8. Dave Marsh, *Before I Get Old: The Story of the Who* (Medford, NJ: Plexus Publishing, 2003), 275.
9. Brian Cady, www.thewho.net/linernotes/WhoSellOut.htm
10. Chris Charlesworth and Ed Hanel, *The Who: The Complete Guide to Their Music* (New York: Omnibus, 2004) 26.
11. The case for vernacular culture's adaptability is persuasively made by W.T. Lhamon, Jr. in *Raising Cain: Blackface Performance From Jim Crow to Hip Hop* (Cambridge, MA: Harvard University Press, 1998).
12. Charlesworth and Hanel, 27.
13. Marsh, 254.
14. Jim DeRogatis, *Kaleidoscope Eyes: Psychedelic Music from the 1960s to the 1990s* (London: Fourth Estate, 1996) 10.
15. Charlesworth and Hanel, 31.
16. Cady, www.thewho.net/linernotes/WhoSellOut.htm
17. Keith Moon, in a letter to his wife Kim, claims that this track was actually recorded at Bradley's Barn in Nashville during a rare day off from touring.
18. Marsh, 279.
19. Cady, www.thewho.net
20. Charlesworth and Hanel, 29.
21. Cady, www.thewho.net
22. Neill and Kent, *Anyway, Anyhow, Anywhere*, 100.
23. Ibid., 116.
24. Ibid., 100.
25. Dave Marsh, liner notes to *The Who Sell Out* CD reissue (MCAD-11268), 1995.

Bee Thousand

by Marc Woodworth

Marc Woodworth is the author of *Solo: Women Singer-Songwriters in Their Own Words* (Dell, 1998) and a volume of poetry, *Arcade* (Grove Press, 2002). He edits the international quarterly *Salmagundi* and teaches at Skidmore College in Saratoga Springs, New York.

A SONNET—MADE FROM *BEE THOUSAND* FRAGMENTS (THEMSELVES OFTEN FRAGMENTS)

With the same old fears and frustrations waiting
for a contact, you chose a giant step
down from broken-down buildings, the cup
of wisdom a little worn and bearing
the sweet milk of the new church to sustain
miraculous recovery. The end
is better than ever. Skin-tight old friends
join him in the red wing, nothing to gain
but the word to signify fertile land.
Now here's the plan: to face their dreams of gold.
Heart, love the most sad, incurable old
fears and all of a sudden understand
nothing else can lift us up to taller windows
like a siren or a simple hello.

Guided by Voices Narrative #4: Robert Griffin

The secret of Bob Pollard's talent is that his process is completely organic. When he was young he immersed himself so deeply in records that the language of the music he liked, after it had filtered through his personality, became his language. There's a whole vocabulary that he particularly likes. He has his words: circuses and pies and queens. And he's incredibly spontaneous—you give him two or three words and he'll just start singing a song. The words he uses have the right number of syllables to work with the music and the melody immediately lodges itself in your brain. There's always something just vague enough that listeners can read themselves into a lyric. What Bob does is so intuitive and natural that if he could have stopped himself from writing songs and playing music as he planned to do after *Propeller* I don't think he or the people around him would have been very happy. He has a restless imagination that he has to use. That restless quality seems integral to what he does. He has the ability to create quickly, not overthink it, and then go on to the next thing before it becomes boring.

Maybe working like that is part of the reason why *Bee Thousand* succeeds as a record. At the time, some critics wrote that there were too many fragments and that the songs were too short. They complained that there weren't enough full songs to make *Bee Thousand* a great record. I have a feeling that the people who bought the album really liked those fragments and short songs and wouldn't have cared about a more conventional record with ten three-minute songs in the same way.

I don't buy the argument that we need to see through what the songs actually are or the production of the record to enjoy it. It's not as if the album is good in spite of those things. At the end of the day the songs have to carry emotion and for that to happen the performances have to feel right. If we'd redone certain things because they had technical problems, the record wouldn't have had the same spirit and the spirit of the songs is the bottom line.

There are sudden shifts on *Bee Thousand*. There's drama in the pacing as it moves from one part to the next. All of a sudden everything will open up. In that way, it's psychedelic. The record has a very late sixties, early seventies feel, part psychedelic, part progressive rock. It's dream-like. A door is opened and when you go through it instead of being in the room you thought you were walking into, you're somewhere you don't expect to be, in a different room altogether or maybe somewhere outside. It not only plays with your sense of where you are but also with your sense of time. What's actually very short can feel long while you're inside of it, but then your sense of time changes. Because things happen suddenly, the record can also feel like it's moving very quickly. Its indulgences are not the sort that test your patience even if you don't always know how you got from point A to point B. It's a record that has a very short attention span and I mean that as a compliment.

When we were mastering the album, Bob and Tobin Sprout were really coming up with ideas on the fly: "let's save this little bit here" or "chop off that part." They were creating a sense of change and compression. The way they worked together seemed pretty open. Toby was quiet, but whenever he had an idea, Bob always listened to it. I think for Toby, who was already an accomplished painter, music was more of a hobby than it was for Bob. Toby was a really great foil for Bob. His songs were good enough to stand alongside Bob's songs and they really broke the album up. He certainly wrote plenty that all fans would put on their lists of best Guided by Voices songs. Bob is more wide-ranging as a writer and his songs sometimes leave the stratosphere, so Toby's songs grounded the record even though in some ways his lyrics are more illogical. Bob's writing can be very bizarre but you can always find some line through it, even if he wouldn't agree with me about that, whereas I don't know what some of Toby's songs are talking about at all—and I don't mean that as a criticism. Toby's role was special, too, because he provided the means for Bob to get more fleshed-out versions of his songs onto tape. Bob had always recorded onto his boombox, just singing with a guitar, but with a four-track and someone who knows how to record with it he had so many more options. So Toby definitely provided the means as well as being the perfect complement as a songwriter to Bob.

When we were mastering *Bee Thousand*, everyone stayed at my girlfriend's place and we'd go out to this little Polish deli over in Tremont. We worked at Landmark Recording, which was a very professional studio for the time. I imagine they did a lot of commercial work. It didn't have much in the way of ambiance. If you haven't been to a lot of recording studios, it's exactly what you imagine they're like. I didn't know the people there, but it was the one place in Cleveland that was set up to do what we needed to do. The engineers we worked with were professionals. They did their job. If they had any disparaging thoughts about the music, they kept them to themselves.

We worked on the sequence of the album there. We'd had a lot of problems editing the record and I knew that it would appeal to Bob to have complete control over its flow. The way it flowed was a big part of what sold him on the sequence I suggested. I was especially interested in making the right changes in tempo from song to song. Side one consisted of more complete songs. Putting them in sequence, I knew, for instance, that if "Buzzards and Dreadful Crows" started exactly on the beat after "Hardcore UFO's," it would move in the right way. It was a bit like making a mix-tape for a friend. There was a lot of trial and error. I messed around with different sequences for a week or so before I came up with the one I thought worked best. There were some changes to that sequence—Bob put "Yours to Keep" between "Smothered in Hugs" and "Echos Myron" on side one and I had "Scissors" instead of "Mincer Ray" on side two. Including "You're Not an Airplane" as the closing song was part of my intended sequence.

Because it's the opener, I wish that "Hardcore UFO's" didn't have the guitars dropping out, but the first time I heard the song I knew it should be at the beginning of an album. It's such a great song. It's about rock. That's one of the things that I love about Guided by Voices and Bob's songs. He's one of the few guys who writes about rock in a way that's authentic. He actually can sing about amps in a song and make it work. People who are enthusiastic about rock music connect with those lyrics. It's another way that *Bee Thousand* works on listeners emotionally. So, we felt that "Hardcore UFO's" would make a great opener despite its technical faults. When we made the master for the record we corrected the problem as best we could by bringing up the volume of the guitars for 4/10 of a second, but you can only bring them up so much.

We were making a lot of changes and edits, but there wasn't any sense of pressure. Bob was already doing a lot of interviews at the time, but the snowball was just gathering speed . . . it was maybe a quarter of the way down the hill. The process at that point was still very pure. Rather than pressure, I think everyone felt excited: "Wow, we can record songs and they will actually come out on someone else's record label . . . let's do this all the time!" And they did. When I first called up Bob about doing a single for Scat he said, "Well, you know, we broke up"—and this is literally how the conversation went: I groaned, "Oh, man," and he said, "Well, we *pretty much* broke up. . . . No, wait! I can get something together. I can put together a single." A week later, I had it. When we put out that first single, there really wasn't a buzz yet. I knew people only had to hear the band and they would like them. After I saw Guided by Voices live there was no question about it at all. After *Bee Thousand* I felt that for once I had busted my ass promoting a band and it actually worked.

One way Guided by Voices' career could have gone was to keep the smaller, devoted following that *Vampire on Titus* won for them by putting out an album every year that roughly the same three or four thousand people would buy. But because *Bee Thousand* was such a great record, their success went much further. It's probably even more apparent now than it was then that in our culture there always has to be a story. The fact that Bob was almost 40 years old and hitting his creative stride after making all of these albums that nobody really paid attention to was a compelling story for the press. Because 1994 was pre-Sound Scan, no one could check the number of copies *Bee Thousand* had sold before deciding to devote four or five pages to this obscure band. Today, an editor would pull up the statistics on a computer before giving a record like that so much attention. People started hearing about Guided by Voices and pretty soon everybody was talking about them. As word got out, there was a lot of genuine enthusiasm.

Maybe I loved it because I listened to the same records that Bob did. That's how I thought about it—"Oh, he's speaking my language." Not everyone agreed. My girlfriend at the time said, "This record's good but why does he sing with that accent? I don't think this band is that great. I don't think you should put them out." And I told her, "No, no, this is it. This is the band. They're going to do it"—and with *Bee Thousand*, they did.

Bee Thousand Word Cluster
STATES (OF BEING)

bliss / cold / love / down / high / nice / right / lost / painful / sad / better / worse / safe / tight / good / sentimental / worry / awful / fine / sweetness / broken / cool / weak / armored / sane / pleased / worse / left out / fears / frustrations / pity / hateful / paranoia / doubt / cynical / shocked / removed / bored / disappointed

Fiction, Man & Hardcore Facts
Part Four

Another well-rehearsed aspect of the *Bee Thousand* story concerns the way it shines as a beacon of DIY brilliance. This is true enough, as far as it goes, but to limit the album to an example of what was becoming in the early and mid-nineties a small movement within the world of independent rock is to see things too narrowly and miss some of the broader, more compelling elements of the record's achievement. If DIY culture opened up around the time of *Bee Thousand* because of specific technological advances in the late eighties and early nineties—notably, the affordability and availability of multi-tracking cassette recorders and consumer-priced quality microphones—it's also the late-season flower on a deep-rooted native perennial as old as the idea of the colonized American soil itself—the same ground over which a writer like Ralph Waldo Emerson looked for stalky specimens in the mid-nineteenth century and then praised them for their ability to thrive in an inhospitable climate. *Bee Thousand* is not only a result of its means of production—though those means determine and inspire to a real and identifiable degree the resulting music—or a recent and self-contained movement—whether DIY or lo-fi—but the result of a much deeper and more comprehensive impulse that Pollard, Sprout, and company embody as they harbor and release a particularly American kind of energy. It's not contemporary politics I think of when I hear Pollard sing about Echos Myron's endurance "like the Liberty Bell," but the way that cracked emblem reminds us that *Bee Thousand* is a kind of declaration of independence, a recent example of a long-standing American tradition of self-reliance and personal freedom.

But before considering in more detail the Emersonian dimension of the project at the heart of *Bee Thousand*, let's take a moment to make an account of the process of self-production that led to the music on the record. There's a dead-wrong sense that the DIY process enables anyone with half a notion and a four-track to make great music. Like the philistine at MoMA who looks at a Jackson Pollack and says "I could do that; a kid could do that," so the casual or foolish listener to a record like *Bee Thousand* might be tempted to think he could do it too. It's much harder to make a messy masterpiece that carries the sense of how hard it is to make anything worth hearing while nevertheless making it worth hearing, than it is to make a competent radio-ready version of the music everyone else it making. Writing and recording a record that has the presence of Bee Thousand is incalculably harder than making a smooth, palatable kind of sound that listeners can simultaneously take in and ignore the first time they hear it. For all its apparent artlessness and unchecked force of being, music like this is the product of artists whose ability to disappear behind the seeming naïveté of their work is a trick no ordinary blokes banging around in the basement could pull off. That's because it's not a trick. It's a rare form of apprehending reality by means of art, an example of true being, even a kind of spiritual accomplishment.

Perhaps the strangest and most winning thing about *Bee Thousand* is that the recording process—or rather the recording *processes* given the range of ways the songs were committed to tape—serves to give life to the music rather than leeching life from it. In part, this success is a response to the newfound self-confidence that the band exhibited during this period. "A noisy, weird record" by Pollard's account, *Vampire on Titus* put Guided by Voices on some map, even if it was a map consulted only by a few people who weren't going to take the main roads anyway. "We made this bizarre record that people loved," Pollard says, speaking of *Vampire on Titus*, "so that opened a door for us to do whatever we wanted to do next. I was fearless after that. It was liberation." And it's that sound of liberation that defines *Bee Thousand*.

One of the distinguishing features of the *Bee Thousand* sessions—if events so informal and impromptu can be called sessions at all—was their inventiveness, even if, as we've seen, some of the songs had a history as they evolved through a long process of artistic maturation. Like Franklins launching kites, the musicians sent up song after song to see if any of them would be struck by lightning. This kind of recording was an experiment and like all experiments began in hope as well as with the real possibility of failure. Think of Franklin the self-taught polymath who pursued every avenue by consulting his own sense of things rather than deferring to established precepts and authority. No one else was standing out in the storm in order to test what seemed to his contemporaries a ridiculous hypothesis. As with Franklin's experiment, the experimentation that led to *Bee Thousand* carries the whiff of something quintessentially American: self-reliant, self-taught know-how and invention compelling maverick souls to do what no one else thought to do. "After an hour or two hours, we'd have six or seven songs taped and ready to go through to see if they were going to be on the album or not," Sprout recalls. "It's the same thing that happens when I paint. You just get into a groove and time just flies by; you don't know where it goes but that's what happened when we worked with the songs for *Bee Thousand*, too." In those lost and found hours, that time spent in a "groove" when the inner life accelerates and, at the same time, slows down enough to render itself real, the results often became conclusive: lightning struck.

And it struck not only at Toby's but also at Kevin's and Bob's. There were tapes taken out of the not-exactly-a-suitcase Pollard used to store cassettes once they were filled with music, tapes which contained instrumental jams or fragments of songs he had recorded years before on his General Electric boombox at home in the middle of the night while everyone slept and the neighborhood with its familiar layout of driveways, basketball hoops, and weedy lawns disappeared. Those initially private recordings which ended up on the first Guided by Voices record that a larger public heard are the purest examples not only of doing it yourself in the limited terms of its nineties alt-rock provenance, but of the more fundamental self-reliance that gives the music its force and authenticity. These tapes found a further kind of life as they were augmented at Toby's, fed into the four-track and furnished with new tracks. "It was a revelation to me," Pollard remembers, "that I could find a tape of a live jam from the basement from ten years before, take it to Toby, put it on the four-track and then add guitar and vocals to create an entirely new song. 'Second Moves to Twin,' which was on an earlier version of *Bee Thousand*, and 'Big Fan of the Pigpen' were done like that." The final versions created a rich, alternate reality that combined the conscious work accomplished in Toby's garage with the spontaneity of the most private consultation with the self, divulged only to the boombox.

In "Self-Reliance," Ralph Waldo Emerson wrote "Let us affront and reprimand the smooth mediocrity and squalid contentment of the times." The use of the word "smooth" here is a testament to the continuity of the understanding, however differently absorbed, that is shared by Pollard and Emerson. In describing authentic achievement, Emerson's "smooth" reminds us of Pollard's "creamy." Both words describe the same quality: what's false and unaffecting because of the way it conforms to and reiterates received ideas. Society, Emerson argues, deriding the powerful and deadening influence of what's smooth, "loves not realities and creators, but names and customs." Emerson, like Pollard, Sprout, and company, loves realities and creations rather than names and customs.

In this spirit, Pollard and Sprout are quick to disavow the labels DIY and lo-fi as merely convenient tags applied later to what they had done. "We were being championed as the pioneers of the lo-fi movement," Pollard says, "[but] all it meant to me was that you didn't have enough money so you had to record songs yourself in your own house." Lo-fi, he remembers, was "a term I was not very familiar with at the time." Sprout agrees: "There was no sense of doing something lo-fi. It was just the way we were recording. We were using one of the first Tascam Portastudio 1 four-tracks that had DBX noise reduction. . . . A lot of people were picking up these machines at the time because they were coming out and there was a market for them. Using a four-track became common enough that they had to find a category for it: DIY, lo-fi, whatever."

The record's distance from the genre to which it's been assigned is almost as great as its distance from the culture into which it emerged. Though it bears no trace of cultural or political motive, *Bee Thousand* is nevertheless a record that sounds like a reaction against the slickness of the mid-nineties, a time when two Elton John numbers from the *Lion King* were on the charts and Bill Clinton's smooth politicking had (thankfully) replaced the deceptively bland faux-populist rhetoric George Bush the Elder used to forward a radical right-wing agenda. If *Bee Thousand* in this context sounds like a kind of revolt, however unconscious, against the reigning climate where kitsch, mock-patriotic bullshit, and market research were kings, it is also an act of conservation, an act that kept alive a kind of music and a kind of art-making that was increasingly absent and entirely antithetical to that which defined the mainstream. Along with DIY and lo-fi of varying qualities, there was a lot of new-school pretty on the ground and in the air in 1994, but there wasn't quite anything as self-made, sublime, strange, full of memory and hard-won authority as *Bee Thousand*.

As our culture (whatever such a proprietary and inclusive category might presuppose), as *all* culture becomes further focused on what can be mass-produced, sent to and consumed efficiently by millions of people separated only by geography, the presence of what's homemade, intimate, rough, human, and resistant to lowest-common-denominator transparency becomes more and more important—an affirmation of what is still possible on a human scale, that what is defined by "neighborhood," or "hometown," or "friendship," still carries the clarifying charge of reality—a kind of presence we forget exists as we slowly or not so slowly give in to the notion that what is mass-made, generic, and universal offers the only kind of reality because it has nearly eclipsed other, fuller forms of the real. Listening to *Bee Thousand* we remember the scale of life implicit in the rasp of breathing left on a recording or the creaking of a door behind the strumming of a guitar because someone—some*body*—is coming in or out of a room (to bring in news from upstairs: a family squabble of who owes whom—or perhaps a visit from a friend who was in the neighborhood: "Hey. Brought some beer").

The person who is recording this moment of making music does not choose to separate art from life so radically that he must keep the incidental sounds apart from the intentional ones. Instead, noises made by people alive in a particular space where they are making music remain audible, are even, in some cases, added to music that did not originally include non-musical sounds. The effect of creating songs this way is not only to make them less "creamy" or "smooth," but also to assert the presence of human beings in the process of making art. When we hear the sound of breathing or the opening of a door, we are listening to the product of the will and desire of a person, alive and making noise, artful or accidental—"Here I am going to add the sound of snoring throughout the song." Sometimes the act is a joke, but even so, as in *Alien Lanes*' "Ex-Supermodel," it is nevertheless essential, a live example of following a spontaneous impulse that always leads toward life and flux and openness: because the rhythm of the snoring fits, somehow, with the rhythm of the song, it is artful and also assertive, even as it remains funny. *Because I am creating music for my own pleasure, in my own basement, to satisfy my own sense of what I am making, I'm adding the snoring here*—a thought never expressed or even formulated as a thought, but instead finding expression as an action. It's surprising, even disruptive, to hear an unexpected noise, but in the surprise or disruption is a resistance to art that is made mostly to court an audience.

Three years after the release of *Bee Thousand*, Guided by Voices included the song "I Am Produced" on their 1997 LP *Mag Earwig!* A plaintive fragment timing out at one minute six seconds, "I Am Produced," cowritten by Robert Pollard and Tobin Sprout, the architects of the band's mid-nineties ascent from utter obscurity to vanguard acclaim, relates in a coldly descriptive first-person voice the process of becoming "product." Although the writers don't abandon the sound-driven impulse that creates their characteristic verbal surrealism for anything like direct polemics, "I Am Produced" expresses the dehumanizing and even violent nature of what it means to make a product and, more to the point, be a product, even as it retains the non-commercial format, relatively speaking, of a fragment aggressively cut short from what might have been a longer, "finished" song:

I am pressed, printed, stomped
And strategically removed
I am everybody
Insane without innocence
I am trapped, tricked, packaged
And shipped out
I am produced
I am produced
Pressed, printed, stomped, tripped
Trapped, tricked, packaged, shipped . . .

Are Sprout and Pollard imagining themselves as a record? Are they recounting the way a "real" studio can "strategically remove" a stray note or an off-key vocal line? The process is violent: the speaker is tripped, tricked, trapped, and stomped. Being produced and being beat up seem identical. The speaker is "everybody." No one escapes a bruising in a climate dominated by product. In the wake of the acclaim for Guided by Voices following *Bee Thousand* and *Alien Lanes*, "I Am Produced" reveals the fear of losing "innocence" as a result of getting caught up in commerce. The process can make you "insane." When *Bee Thousand* is most at risk of seeming crazy—consider its cast of freaks and queens, robots and renegades, it abortive jabs of noise, the sometimes maniacal energy or arresting melancholy—it comes closest to providing a record of an imagination that's robust and healthy. The utter sanity of *Bee Thousand* derives from its independence from being mere product in a culture of mere product.

"Dispense with the popular code," Emerson writes. To refuse to follow the usual rules, he continues,

> demands something godlike in him who has cast off the common motives of humanity, and has ventured to trust himself for a taskmaster. High be his heart, faithful his will, clear his sight, that he may in good earnest be doctrine, society, law, to himself. . . . If any man consider the present aspects of what is called by distinction society, he will see the need of these ethics.

Or, in Pollard's more personal account, "There were people who said I still shouldn't quit teaching, because I'd been doing it for fourteen years and had benefits and a family to think about, but I knew this [devoting himself to music] was something I needed to do. . . . My decision caused difficulties later on—being on the road eventually led to a divorce—but I still can't regret making that decision to take a chance because I got to do what I sometimes feel I was meant to be doing." Here's a real example of pressure to reject what you yourself know to be right in order to follow a socially sanctioned course. It's not that Emerson's advocacy of individuality is without its costs—we see in Pollard's example the cost of losing a marriage—but for all the costs and despite the complexities that attach to this vision of self-reliance, Pollard's story is real and moving, the result of his decision to look inside himself. "For the first time," he says, "I was really happy with one of our records, which is particularly gratifying because it was the first time we did it ourselves."

Pollard is called a "genius" so often that the category ceases to mean anything. Emerson's definition of "genius" helps to show just how appropriate that overused term is: "To believe your own thought, to believe that what is true for you in your private heart is true for all men—that is genius." After a long immersion in his chosen means of expression, Pollard had come to believe in his own thought and the value of what was in his "private heart." The most direct expression of this inward turn, the realization that what's essential comes from the self, appears in "I Am a Scientist" where Pollard writes, "I seek to understand me." It's not surprising that this is one of the two songs on the album that was both written and recorded during the period when *Bee Thousand* was made. If *Bee Thousand* is the result of Pollard's newfound confidence—"this wide avenue had opened up where I could do whatever I wanted"—"I Am a Scientist" is the song that most directly embodies that achievement. Pollard writes that "nothing else behaves" like him. There's a direct line from mid-nineteenth century American Romantic individualism to Pollard's understanding of what it was necessary and possible for him to do as an artist. The attempt to discover the contours of this self might be like digging a hole that is "bottomless," but "nothing else" aside from such a process of self-discovery can "set" Pollard "free."

In making music in the way they did, the musicians who recorded *Bee Thousand* discovered the power that was in them. You can hear this discovery in the delicious friction generated in "Echos Myron" as the ascending chord progression rubs against the lyrics about bringing low what's high. There's joy in the leveling of the "tower to the skies" and the "academy of lies." In the midst of a "mighty blowup" that brings the walls down, the observer says serenely and rather pedantically, a Scouse schoolmaster providing perspective for his young charges with a superfluous "surely": "what goes up surely must come down." The song ends with a communal affirmation that "we're finally here" as the song celebrates its final destination—"shit yeah, it's cool and shouldn't it be." But to what place, exactly, have we come? The vertiginous towers and their institutionalized lies have come down in the mighty blowup. There's no need to consult what the institutions think is right—they're all false and falling down. Emerson writes, "There is a time in every man's education when he arrives at the conviction that envy is ignorance; that imitation is suicide; that he must take himself for better or worse as his portion." Pollard, Sprout, and company find that conviction as they joyfully dance in the rubble of the fallen monuments to received wisdom. In its place is Myron's credo of individual intuition: "when it's right you can tell." It's the new founding truth, the fact that allows you to discover your real identity. You don't need towers to the sky, institutional lies, or men of wisdom to tell you what you feel and know to be right.

It took time to arrive at this discovery—"we're *finally* here . . ."—but by the time of *Bee Thousand* Guided by Voices had learned who they were. They'd learned to "watch that gleam of light which flashes across the mind from within, more than the luster of the firmament of bards and sages." Go dark, Brothers Davies and Pete T.; to the other side of the moon Syd Barrett (you're already there); in eclipse, Davey Jones, you little satellite; keep turning away, slow planet of Genesis. What Guided by Voices saw, shaded from the luster of rock's glowing firmament, what they enacted, was new; however much the music had evolved out of the love they had for the work of the fabled greats of the pop-rock pantheon, the process by 1994 had moved inside. Most of us may be pleased with the same old song, but Pollard and Co. were not among that majority. There's no need to travel to New York or LA to find yourself—or even outside of Dayton. You don't need to leave your basement: *Let us not rove; let us sit at home with the cause.* This has been Pollard's choice for a long time now: to be at home with the cause. Remaining in Dayton, choosing to stay away from it only as long as absolutely necessary, he trusts his instinct to remain where he is most himself, least subject to the authority of the tall towers looming over the capitols of culture. It's an understanding that comes from experience and self-knowledge: *nothing else behaves like me*. You only have to discover your own giant, as Emerson called it, the colossus in the room who's always been there but, for all its size, remains invisible until you find a new perspective, a fresh way of seeing that emerges from self-reliance, "when you have life in yourself."

Guided by Voices Narrative #5: Dan Toohey

When we were recording *Bee Thousand*, Toby would be sitting down at the four-track not more than ten feet in front of the drum set. We were all crammed into Kevin's basement playing together and he would be down there working very hard. I don't remember if he was sitting on a box or something else, but he was a lot lower than he would have been if he'd been sitting in a normal chair. He'd lean down over the four-track, really focusing on getting a good sound.

Toby had the ability to help each musician really see the potential of the music. He was able to make us into more of a group. For *Bee Thousand* there were many people playing in different combinations and at different times, so it was more challenging to bring everyone together. It's in Toby's nature to be able to fit into a lot of different areas and situations. He was a songwriter, so he knew music from that perspective. He was also good at recording with the four-track. He could play guitar, bass, piano, and drums, but he wasn't just a musician in the band because there were so many other ways he contributed.

What was fun about the *Bee Thousand* period was that everybody in the band was pretty much on the same page. I think it might come down to the fact that each of us found a purpose. It was like a team. I really function well in cooperative relationships—I guess we all do—and it was that kind of situation at the time, more so than it was later. For some reason, the mix of personalities just worked. There was that atmosphere where almost anything could happen, especially considering how we typically recorded and how free it was in most ways. We were all excited and that excitement made everyone bring a lot to the table.

Bob would bring in a piece and might say he wanted it to sound a certain way. We would play it a couple times, then, from that initial practice, the reins were off. The process was open and we were all trying to make the song better. It was really fun because you could really create as you were playing. The songs were made to be creative. I can't control the way I play. It just has to come out. All I'm trying to do is make the song better by adding melody and bass at the same time without sacrificing either one. I started playing the trombone in high school and learned not to play the main melody, but a countermelody. Because I did that for so long it influences the way I play the bass. I'm not even conscious of what I'm doing. It's almost like something takes over when I start playing. You're using all of your knowledge—mental, physical, and spiritual—and hopefully you're hitting the right notes.

I always tried to play not just to the structure of the music—the way it was meant to be played—but also with a feel for the guys in the band. I wanted to be sensitive to how they were playing and to be complementary. I didn't want to step on anybody's feet because that's just not my way. So, hopefully, that's not what my playing sounds like. I remember the bass on "Queen of Cans and Jars" as being very melodic. It just felt right. That may have had something to do with playing with Toby on that song because we've always had an unusually strong musical connection. I mostly played higher on the neck without sacrificing the low end too much. I felt that moving from low to high added to the song. I remember thinking "this is going to be fun to play the song so melodically."

There are some songs from those days that may never see the light of day even though they also had a good feeling. The album went through at least four different incarnations. After the second one, I stopped paying attention until it was out. I learned that going through so many changes was somewhat normal for Guided by Voices, but it was unusual for me. I played on *Propeller*, but I was really an outsider then, so I didn't understand that part of the process. I still enjoy the first version of *Bee Thousand* a lot. It seemed more consistent to me. I also liked certain songs that weren't on the final version. I remember one particular song, "The Way to a Man's Heart," that really had a sense of humor to it. I think Jimmy was playing violin. I'm a pretty calm person but I was laughing so hard when I heard it that I fell to my knees. It was just one of the funniest things I'd ever heard in my life.

I never thought about what might happen with the album when we were recording the songs. I couldn't have guessed that the record was going to be thought of as really important. I just knew that at a point in time I enjoyed playing a particular piece. Recording was always a joy. Bob really loved it and we loved it. If you enjoy something and what you're playing seems right, then the song develops a good feel. You didn't have to force anything—it all seemed so natural. I think that's why *Bee Thousand* started attracting people . . . because it was so natural.

Listener Response #12: John Wenzel

Nick Kizirnis, a bespectacled Dayton-area musician and clerk at Gem City Records, had been trying to pimp Guided by Voices on me since 1993's *Vampire on Titus*. I'd walk into the store, he'd point knowingly to the listening station, and I'd don the headphones. No dice. It sounded like dogs being faxed through a cheese grater. But eventually I took the plunge and bought *Bee Thousand* when it came out, partly because I was familiar with the band name ("They're from Dayton! And they're fucking great!!" everyone told me) and partly because I was sick of hearing about it and not being able to form my own opinion.

During that summer before my senior year in high school I was working on my dad's farm near Spring Valley (about twenty minutes south of downtown Dayton). I'd stumble in from the fields, absent-mindedly put on *Bee Thousand*, and down lemonade and ham sandwiches while the sweat cooled. The one song that immediately grabbed me was "Echos Myron," and then only because I thought it sounded like an inspired They Might Be Giants outtake. The recording fidelity made me nauseous. The song titles hurt my brain.

Then, as often happens to budding/helpless GBV fans, the melodies and lyrics started to take hold. Call it lo-fi, indie rock, space-pop, or whatever; the slew of beautiful, hummable melodies stuck to me like hot glue. Each song became associated with a specific scene in my mind, like the pungent odor of blood and dirt that reminds you of the time you broke your elbow on the playground slide.

"Hardcore UFO's" was the way the insects buzzed about my ears while I lounged on the front porch after a taxing day. "Buzzards and Dreadful Crows" was a sweltering August afternoon, the shadows of scavenger birds darkening my field of vision. "Tractor Rape Chain" communicated more about Midwest culture in a single cryptic line than the entire run of "WKRP in Cincinnati." "The Goldheart Mountaintop Queen Directory" was the weirdly quiet ass-end of a drunken night, a Camel Light hanging from my soured lips. And on and on. In fact, album closer "You're Not an Airplane" was so instantly gorgeous to me that anytime I'd hear the sound of crickets (audible in the song's background) it prompted me to start singing the song. And does to this day.

Eventually my curiosity compelled me to seek out Guided by Voices' live set that fall, and the band's plainness and accessibility were intoxicating. That and the *Bee Thousand* songs found a satisfyingly muscular dimension onstage. Mitch Mitchell's windmill chops transformed tinny stompers like "Gold Star for Robot Boy" into headbanging epics. Greg Demos's punchy bass and Kevin Fennell's thunderous drums bolstered the considerable sex-mojo of "Hot Freaks." When Tobin Sprout stepped aside to let Kim Deal sing harmony on "The Goldheart Mountaintop Queen Directory" (during a Dayton show at Special Occasions on 9/30/04) I thought my head might explode with glee.

These swarthy gents seemed to know intimately my wretched life. Every cracked, urine-stained corner of it. How could something so bizarre and visceral come from my hometown? These non-sequitur lyrics that sounded like Richard Brautigan on PCP, the Daltrey-aping stage antics and fake UK accent, the grand allusions to science and aerospace and incestuous royalty. How could this band possibly be from the Birthplace of Flight? I ask you!

Over the last eleven years *Bee Thousand* has effortlessly stood as my favorite all-time album. It is perfect, in that same subjective and tautological way that all great works of art are perfect. Its quality cannot be overstated, but it can certainly be overanalyzed, and that I usually try to avoid. Let its mystery lie, like the alien corpses rumored to exist in Wright-Patterson Air Force Base's Hangar 18. Perhaps that's where the album's magic came from, some toxic alien blood infiltrating the water table of Northridge, somehow birthing a modern classic in the mind of a beer-fueled ex-jock schoolteacher.

MARC WOODWORTH

Dayton Ode

Dayton, underloved Dayton, now our darling of the middle state, our barely discovered beauty.

Holy Dayton with its premise of flight, its understaffed airport, the goings and comings of trippers who stop only for the next plane and render America false by moving on to either coast or even Cleveland.

Dayton, you are now in our dreams, strongbox of memory and hope.

Big Daddy Dayton, we total our purchased and unpurchasable pleasures on your novel cash register which rings with the liberty and clarity of its steel bell every time we bite the dental, two-beat syllables of your name.

Nearby, the ghosts of the Appalachias haunt the haze rising from your sulfur lights, singing in a thin quavering trill the notes of ballads transplanted to hardwood forests by tooth-bare pioneers lost to Englands, old and New.

Dada Dayton, we are singing in your pale streets, driving through your drive-through beer stores, remembering the hard glories of our school days nearly lost to us now through work, and love, and less than love, and age, and our bodies moving up and down through broken down buildings.

In March, that liminal month neither winter nor spring, your wires hung low and wet and cold from their poles, and the pavements were washed with the spare grit from the sandpaper factories, the streets abandoned as if there'd been a plague or a run of vice that left lovers to hide in their brown rooms.

And even the abandonment was beautiful as we inhabited it to fill a tent risen like a cartoon approximation of a tent.

The kegs and taps stood like a pale chorus of girls about to dance a slow, leg-lifting pantomime of desire, mechanical and fluid—and then there were people, fine or damaged, beautiful in their need or full of some strange self-love (it didn't matter which): the white vacuum, omphalos and womb, filled by us instantly, slowly, our appearance a hallucination, and none of us, then, were alone.

In Dayton, the music, Dayton drums and Dayton drunks, lifted us along with the streets, the tent, the taps into a second city that hovered and glowed above the first, the sound a stairway of glass risers and oxygen treads, an ineffable stairway that linked the two cities, the created and the conjoined, a stairway on which we invented the shape of our soul as we walked between these intersecting and distinct planes, both invented, both sublime, each as real and as unreal as the other.

The *Destroyer* Tour in Dayton, the thousand and one dreams of Needmore, Dayton's blue address, reinvented nightly, kiln and emporium, locus of salute, regression, and command.

Damn it Dayton, when will you be worthy of your heroes? When will we be worthy of you?

We are standing in the place where we live, each place, like this place, its own center and fulfillment, undone and remade by each raw second, unnamed, unnamable, replaced, irreplaceable.

Dayton, you are home and we have come home to you, shining from the journey, broken back to bone and whispers, the crying streets and the smile of sweet disinterest.

As we arrive, you disappear into your own live and inaccessible hit, playing it again and again, the needle running out the groove like a mind tracing to its end a spiral nebula in the ground glass of good optics, our subterranean telescope aimed at the hardcore originary event that we all share and recognize, Dayton, in yours and in you.

Listener Response #13: Bela Koe-Krompecher

"Hardcore UFO'S" was going to be the first in a series of singles. Bob came up to Columbus one Saturday and dropped off the song at Used Kids Records. He said, "This is the single," and he left the store. It was on a cassette, of course, so I put it in the cassette player, hit play, and the machine ate the tape. Oh Shit! So I threw the cassette in the box at the back of the store and said to myself, "I'll worry about this later," thinking that I would just call Bob and tell him to send me another copy. Three or four weeks go by before Bob calls and says, “Bela, I need that tape.” I asked him why and he said, “I have another song, a better song that I want to give you for the single. We’re going to put ‘Hardcore UFO’s’ on our new record.” I asked, “Didn’t you make a copy of it?” Bob said, “No, that’s the only copy I have.” I never told him that it was eaten by the tape machine, but if you listen you can hear where it happened. Some people think that sound was intentional, but it was really caused by a cheap tape deck at Used Kids.

Kicks

At the end of a main set, or often as an encore, Guided by Voices, on certain tours, offered a mini-set that included a suite of *Bee Thousand* songs. Robert Pollard has called this the *Bee Thousand* set, as in, “Hey, kids—here’s the *Bee Thousand* set.” Not only is this set comprised of a number of *Bee Thousand* favorites, but, given the excitement of the moment, the nearly universal sing-along aspect of this portion of the show, the band’s increasingly unbuttoned energy, the pushing in gleeful aggression of bodies toward the stage, there are, during this *Bee Thousand* set, the most extravagant displays of Robert Pollard’s accomplished stagecraft—viz, single-leg high kicks, crotch-level microphone clutching, crisp military salutes, deadpan and dead-level gazing over the heads of the audience, Daltrey-esque microphone swinging. But it is the single-leg high kick that I want most to focus on, the one stage move that best exemplifies the ebullient and unironic beauty of *Bee Thousand*.

1. The act itself: There is the planting of the other foot, the non-kicking foot. Video evidence is inconclusive, but the planting foot seems most often to be the right foot, in which case the preferred kicking foot is the left. Mr. Pollard plants the kicking foot by executing a small but powerful hopping motion, not unlike the one a diver executes on a diving board before leaping into the air.

2. Once the planted foot completes its diver-like hop and braces against the floor of the stage, the kicking foot begins to ascend—the kicking foot at the end of a stiff leg that is locked from ankle to hip in a straight line. A bent knee would diminish the effect and has never, to our knowledge, marred even the most challenging effort at the high kick.

3. The shoulders and head move forward as the leg and foot ascend, the motion a punter makes following through after he has kicked the ball. Where are the hands and arms? We hardly see them, but, if we focus on these appendages rather than the leg itself, we note that they are in the air, presumably to balance the body in the act of kicking, of forcing the foot to be at the opposite extreme from where the anatomy of a human body dictates it most usefully should be. The ascending leg and foot and the forward-moving shoulders and head create a bend at the waist, itself not a focus, in the same way the hands and arms are not a focus, for viewers of the event—the leg commands the eyes and the rest of the body becomes invisible as we watch the astonishing height of the kick. But the kick's power comes from another unseen source—the core, as a dancer would say, the viscera, the guts, that generates this bodily movement even as it plays no visible part in the movement as visual spectacle.

4. The return—a form of recoil—is sudden and therefore becomes a blur, though it is no faster than the upward movement and therefore, somatically speaking, no less visible than the ascending kick which we seem to witness with perfect clarity. The downward motion of the leg and foot is the necessary but post-climactic result of the leg having risen so high, so quickly. The kicking foot reaches the ground—the stage—with a matter-of-fact reentry that is—as quick as it is—unspectacular. The one-legged high kick is complete.

As with all movement on a stage, the kick takes place within a cultural context and becomes an allusion—most often cited are the kick's connections to arena rock posturings, its opposition to the stage demeanor of so-called "shoe-gazing" musicians, its freshness when considered in the context of the anti-theatrical rock of the early nineties when Robert Pollard's particularly well-executed kicks debuted in New York in the years just before *Bee Thousand* was released.

But if the kick's meaning as an allusion is derived from its context, what keeps the kick from becoming simply an allusion is also its context. We witness a man (Robert Pollard) and a band (Guided by Voices) who do not dress in the manner of the arena rock showmen who brought such stage moves to the peak of their visibility and popularity in the seventies. The difference between the most famous and mass-audience uses of the kick and the way Mr. Pollard employs it might suggest his use of this move is meant to be ironic. The kick minus the trappings of the arena rock stars of an earlier decade, in this way of thinking, becomes a comment on that excess that points out the distance between the domestic values of homemade do-it-yourself simplicity and the bombastic artifice of another genre of rock music. But this way of thinking of the kick—as irony—is wrong, just as the idea of Guided by Voices music as a comment or implicit criticism of a certain kind of mass-market arena rock is wrong.

The kick in the form that Robert Pollard executes it is not an ironic act, but one of pleasure and, in part, homage—to the musicians that Mr. Pollard grew up listening to, seeing live in venues like Hara Arena in Dayton. For Guided by Voices fans of various ages, the kick is likely to be a very differently charged piece of public performance. Stripped of excess—silk scarves, quasi-medieval tunics, revolving stages, mundane melodies of love or pseudo-philosophical treatises-cum-lyrics, skin-tight pants, etc—that marked the ascent of the arena rock gods who employed such stage business to the delight of their teenage acolytes, the kick becomes for Mr. Pollard's contemporaries—give or take several years on either side—a plausible reiteration of a move that would not be plausible were it accompanied by the paraphernalia of the seventies. Without the accoutrements, the kick is unembarrassing, somehow pure, even "natural." Of course, it is an unnatural movement—hence its power to excite and represent a surge of emotion—but conducted in, say, a pair of neutral colored corduroys and unexceptional athletic shoes, it seems as natural an expression of joy as such a contrived and freighted gesture can be. For a younger viewer, however, the kick may evoke a lost time—a time before the viewer was alive, a time discovered by means of photographs, books, recordings, and hearsay. For such a viewer, the kick is a link to this lost time. Depending upon the viewer's relationship to the music and theatrics of the arena-rock past—guilty pleasure or genuine love or ironic appreciation—he will respond to the kick in different ways. In some younger fans, the kick will trigger what is perhaps the most evocative of nostalgias, the nostalgia for what it was never possible to experience first-hand.

Daydream Nation

by Matthew Stearns

Matthew Stearns is a regular contributor to *Resonance* magazine. A onetime graduate student in comparative literature, he has also held down jobs as a seasonal construction worker in Alaska, black-market babysitter in Paris, bookseller, editorial assistant, and record store clerk.

Intro

Silence gets knocked-up. Ghosts haunt the run-out groove. Desperate whores probe yellowed ankles. Reagan boils. Atrocious crimes loom at the far edge of the vinyl horizon.

The pregnant void waits.

Listen close and you'll hear it in those moments of not-so-silent silence before the music surfaces. It lives in the split seconds of emptiness that teeter on the edge of any album. It happens *juuuuust* after the needle engages the vinyl (or the magnet snuggles up against the tape, or the laser beam hits the CD, choose your media—for me, the needle landing on wax seems the most potent format, the physicality of the procedure the most visceral) and *juuuuust* before the start of recorded sound. It also lives in the space between tracks. And it's there lingering at the end of an album, in that brief pulse of quiet that happens after the last notes have dissolved. Like me, you've probably seen it hush large roomfuls of people—inciting a pin-drop silence similar to that of sacred rituals (group meditation, prayer, public moments of silence), focusing the collective attention and introducing a sense of drama, anticipation, fidgeting. But it can be menacing too. Witness the acute agitation and mass anxiety that sweeps like a virus across dance floors whenever a DJ makes a less than seamless transition between records. Notice, too, the correlative relief (usually marked by a swell of applause) that descends upon the crowd once the awkward, taboo silence has been swallowed up by the next track. This noisy silence exists in a kind of liminal, in-between state: it is audio, but not music. It lacks substance, but in the context of our favorite records, it can evoke whole fields of emotion, memory, and narrative associated with the music it surrounds. It's a riveting, confounding paradox: emptiness with content, pregnancy in a void.

By some small auditory miracle, these *empty-fulls* mnemonically incorporate themselves into the overall listening experience of our most treasured records. Over time, these chasms undergo a kind of consecration. Integrating themselves into the neurological hardwiring, they become as fundamentally important as the music itself. Sequences of sizzles and knocks on vinyl, a slight fluctuation in the hiss of a cassette tape, even the immaculate rhythmic cadence of the digital breaks between tracks on CDs—all get ensconced in our memory as permanently as the songs they bracket. On the albums most familiar and essential to us, during the pauses before, after, and between tracks, you can literally *hear* the upcoming song before it starts. This phenomenon is both confirmed and reinforced when we hear a track from some revered album on a mix, stream, or the radio. Displaced from its proper place amidst the album's sequence, the song sounds like an audio refugee forced into temporary sonic exile. When the track that precedes or follows isn't the one found on the record of origin, a vague disorientation takes hold. An internal alarm sounds. There's a mild but very real sense that something is *off* as the slot in your brain where the record lives goes a little haywire. Sometimes when this happens to me, I need to pull out the album at issue and listen to it all the way through so as to set the various planetary bodies that make up my audio cosmos back into correct alignment.

There are whole lives and entire worlds contained in these vacant spaces of records. Like margins and paragraph indentions on the printed pages of books—particularly in the physical placement of poems on a page—the spatial layout informs the impact of the language. The empty, blocked-out nothingness that hovers around the words helps activate our receptors, framing the material contained within its delineation, clearing the way, focusing down our attention.

On our favorite records, the quiet gaps surrounding the tracks act in much the same way. Their presence is actively involved in the registering of the music. They seem to house semi-mute electromagnetic ghosts hung permanently in suspended orbit, each hushed spectral figure silently telling part of the album's story. And no matter how many times we've heard them, these ghosts' stories resist tediousness and refuse to age.

These spaces matter.

Just before the opening guitar strains emerge on Sonic Youth's *Daydream Nation*, we're given a moment to collect ourselves, take a deep breath, and brace for impact. In the space of those first few seconds, with the right ears, I swear you can hear all of the following:

1. New York City (including but not limited to: rumbling subways, bleating taxis, various municipal operations in disarray, the distribution and receipt of goods and services both legitimate and criminal, the accrual of filth in every conceivable metro-crevice, jabbering hookers with renal failure shooting gack into their jaundiced feet on 10th Avenue).
2. An over-boiling frustration with the sucking oblivion of eighties, Reaganized America and its attendant cultural anesthetization.
3. The necessary culmination and white-heat regeneration of a rock sound that helped change how rock *could* sound.
4. Walls closing in around four people about to throw an extended claustrophobic fit.
5. A brutal, pitiless revision of the role of femininity in rock.
6. The meticulous mapping, careful assembly, and consummate pacing of a uniquely indie double album.
7. An experimental rock band about to do something, ironically, *perfect*.
8. The sound of a drumstick being forced into the body of a guitar.
9. The soothing, electric hum of an H3000-D/SE Ultra-Harmonizor Effects Processor.

10. A record hurtling headlong toward the most gruesome, and, in some ways, the most logical of all possible conclusions: *rape and murder.*

In navigating *Daydream Nation*'s sonic landscape, this book will take certain stylistic and formal leads from the record itself. The central chapters will consist of four parts, each tracing the four-sided layout of the original vinyl release. Sections within these chapters will concentrate, sequentially, on each of the album's fourteen tracks (counting "Trilogy" as three distinct tracks under one rubric). As *Daydream Nation* does, the book will take frequent prefatory and peripheral liberties (hence the preface, intro, outro, and footnotes).

Like the record, there are implied, structurally built-in pauses encompassing the "sides"—these pauses will come in the form of digressive (but, I hope, helpful) explorations of tangential items: the album's artwork and packaging, background and influences, and some perspective from Sonic Youth on the making of *Daydream Nation*. All of this is done in an effort to get at the heart of the record—a heart driven by a pulse that pushes *Daydream Nation* forward in relentless pursuit of its ultimate goal: *total rock catharsis and sonic regeneration*.

This book is meant to function as a close critical listening of *Daydream Nation* as well as a bolstering companion-piece for those inspired (or re-inspired as the case may be) to make the trek across some of the most gripping, adventurous seventy minutes fifty-one seconds in contemporary rock.

I should point out that this book spends zero time discussing chords, notation, or tablature. If you're into that kind of thing, I'm sorry to say that I can be of no service to you. There are many reasons why Sonic Youth's sound is so unique, not the least of which is the fact that they have nine hundred million thousand guitars and each one is tuned according to highly insane plans known only to Lee Ranaldo, Kim Gordon, Steve Shelley, Thurston Moore, a couple guitar techs, and the Godhead Alternate-tuning Superbrain.

Chapter 1.
This Record Eats Ears

Bullet to the face. Sonic Youth meets Calvin Coolidge. Flushes of energy through the lobes and sternum. Some concerns about dangerous records. "Let me out of here! These hornets are slammed on acid!" Blessed be our cousins in juvie. Off with your pants!

> Stop being such a Goddamned sissy! Why can't you stand up before fine strong music like this and use your ears like a man?
> —Charles Ives, 1931

Certain records arrive like howling bullets at crux moments and split the face of music wide open, exposing long-concealed sonic musculature, ripping tonal tissue from previously unexplored sockets, and melding it all back together into a form at once oddly familiar but, at the same time, unrecognizable. These records often have a peculiar relationship to time. On the one hand, they manage to appear as precisely what was needed at their current point of entry, necessary and unique to the environment from which they sprung. On the other hand, these albums can feel slightly removed from limited, local continuums, appearing in the present but with a sense of having brought back news about music from the future. Many of these become the records that constantly appear on all manner of admiring critical lists, get reissued with embarrassing regularity, and retain their place in our collections, from one purge to the next, with steady resilience. Despite the legitimacy of these consequences—and, by all means, please; compile your all-time lists, reissue until your brains squirt out, and cultivate those permanent collections—they have an unfortunate tendency to obfuscate the reality of the initial impact and residual force of some of these albums. Rock historicizing can be a diluting, cheapening business. There are some records in this category, however, that are totally impervious to the dulling-down that results from excessive and protracted critical handling. Put them on the player today and they'll blow holes through the moldy, sagging boundaries of music with as much force and violence as they did the first week they were fired out of the distributor's warehouse. *Daydream Nation* is a dead-to-nuts example of just such a record.

Resoundingly canonized as a breakthrough landmark in the chronicles of avant-rock expression, *Daydream Nation* has garnered copious accolades, critical acclaim, and honors since its relatively modest release back in the early fall of 1988. Recorded for a distinctly affordable thirty-five thousand dollars (give or take), *Daydream Nation*'s release in October of '88 was marked by immediate and universal critical adulation. The record finished a more than respectable second to Public Enemy's *It Takes a Nation of Millions to Hold Us Back* in that year's (always nail-bitingly anticipated) *Village Voice* Pazz & Jop poll. CMJ shot it into the top slot of its year-end chart, while it landed second on that year's *Rolling Stone* critic's poll. In Britain, *NME* and *Melody Maker* both listed *Daydream Nation* as first in its category. And, if you're into this kind of thing, in the Fluffy Cloud Land of All-Time Best Album Lists: *Rolling Stone* places *Daydream Nation* in the number 45 slot, *Spin* says it's 14th, and, more recently, the trusty and considered, if brand-spanking-new in the grand scheme of things, *Pitchfork* gave *Daydream Nation* the number 1 nod on their Best Albums of the Eighties chart. Based on the consensus, and in my experience, I think it's safe now to go ahead and assume that all of this excitement has been entirely, rightly deserved. (Notwithstanding the fact that the type of thinking that results in assigning superlatives to records is, let's be honest, kind of suspect to begin with, like declaring someone King or Queen of the rock prom.)

In its way, admittedly, this book is an extension of the applauding critical discourse that has swirled, and continues to swirl, tornado-like, around *Daydream Nation* since its release nearly twenty years ago at the time of this writing. The record's excellence and vitality are presupposed here, while, at the same time, the book argues implicitly for *Daydream Nation*'s decisive historical relevance. That relevance is instantiated both in terms of Sonic Youth's trajectory as a band and in light of *Daydream Nation*'s permanent impact on the development of contemporary independent, avant-garde, and noise rock. As if more evidence was needed to corroborate the record's epochal significance, in 2006 the US Library of Congress added *Daydream Nation* to the permanent archives of the National Recording Registry—a collection of audio recordings, according to the Library, deemed "culturally, historically or aesthetically important," and which "inform or reflect life in the United States." One can't help but celebrate this as a legitimate accolade for Sonic Youth while at the same time seeing it as a triumphant victory for all things marginal, daring, and edgy. *Daydream Nation* shares this archival honor with such co-inductees as Calvin Coolidge's inaugural address and a recording of the first official transatlantic telephone conversation. From Calvin "Keep Cool With" Coolidge to a cross-oceanic phone call to *Daydream Nation*—a historic arc indeed.

When I first learned about the induction of *Daydream Nation* into the Registry, something struck me that hadn't struck me previously—*Daydream Nation* actually is an American rock record that, in its own singular way, "reflects life in the United States." The discomfiting aspect of this follows from the fact that, while there are many of us out here in the world who have tacitly known full well that *Daydream Nation* "reflects life in the United States," this fact was not something we would have ever expected to be explicitly articulated by a federally sanctioned body of these very United States. It's like being told by your parents that your clothes are cool. "I *know*! You don't have to tell *me*!" The teenage resistance to all manifestations of grown-up authority is slow to dissolve, I suppose. Still, the Library has a point in singling out *Daydream Nation* for its archives: the record does represent a uniquely American aesthetic point of view—a point of view rooted in both the New York noise-rock underground and in the wider emergence of a fertile vanguard of independent American rock music.

All of that business being said, however, this book's primary concern is of a more urgent, pressing nature. The real plan here, apart from pursuing all of that important, perfectly reasonable, historico-administrative stuff laid out above, is to get right down into the burning star-core engine that sends *Daydream Nation* careening down its incandescent, combustible path and figure out what the hell kind of fuel allows it to race at such velocities without spinning out into the ether.

There are moments on *Daydream Nation* when the record's aggregate narratives, boggling sound composites, and distributed energies reach a level of intensity so pitched that the whole thing seems to hover on the brink of self-implosion. These moments, when the record is played at appropriately upsetting volumes, have physical corollaries that often involve shooting waves of alarm up the spine, flushes of energy through the lobes and sternum, lockjaw, palpitations, and visual disorientation. If the act of listening to music requires some degree of participatory commitment from the listener, and if that commitment itself takes place as a kind of merging and identifying with the action and drama of the record, then *Daydream Nation* asks for one hell of a commitment. Based on the sheer scope of its attack, *Daydream Nation* poses a direct, imminent threat to the safety and well being of its listeners. At the very least, it threatens the security and structural viability of its listener's ears. This record eats ears—chews them up with its gnarled sonic teeth (something covered later) and swallows them whole.

In this sense, it's perfectly appropriate, and not shameful at all, to be slightly frightened by *Daydream Nation*. By reputation and in size, it stands as a kind of outsized rock 'n' roll behemoth—an overwhelming monstrosity (in the sense that monsters typically tend to be born of extremes, rife with power, difficult to contain, and mythic in proportion—*Daydream Nation* certainly meets all of these qualifications) capable of crushing the will of the most resilient, well-intentioned listener if the necessary preparations haven't been made.

Yet, for all its intensity, seriousness, and voltage, *Daydream Nation* is not beyond lighthearted, reflexive self-critique. Employing various playful gestures and ironic strokes that verge on self-satirization, Sonic Youth laudably resist the temptation to take themselves, and by extension, *Daydream Nation* (and, I suppose, rock 'n' roll itself) too seriously. Some of those strokes include: Assigning themselves "symbolic rock identities" (♀ , W, ¥,) within the album art à la Led Zeppelin at the height of their grand mytho-mystical rock god ridiculousness, circa 1971; using a Heavy Metal-ish Bavarian/Germanic/Slavic typeface on the track listing and liner notes; and incorporating a prog-style song trilogy. These elements of *Daydream Nation* at once reveal Sonic Youth's genuine, collective affection for the gestures and accoutrements of rock 'n' roll-ism while at the same time evidence a healthy, slightly smirking acknowledgment of the form's more ludicrous tendencies. (I mean, *pictogrammatic identities!?*) This levity bumps up against the potent gravity permeating much of Daydream Nation's musical landscape. A counterbalancing happens in the process, which, in effect, helps allocate different types of energy across the record's canvas. As Steve Shelley corroborates: "You know, Thurston's writing 'Teen Age Riot'—*which is a great song*[1]—[emphasis added, see footnote] and his working title was 'Rock 'n' Roll for President,' and it's sort of about J Mascis. I mean, that's not a very serious subject if you know J. Maybe humor's best in small doses on albums. We had a lot of fun with *Daydream*: there's the Gerhard Richter painting on the cover and then there are the four symbols on the labels—which is us poking fun at ourselves: 'This is a pompous double LP! We're just another rock band with a double LP! And there's even a trilogy!' We were having fun with the typical rock album ingredients, but *knowing* they were typical."

As a double album, *Daydream Nation* keeps company with two other notable indie rock records of the eighties—both tremendous in their own right, and which you'd be well-advised to spend some time with by way of proper contextualization—Hüsker Dü's warped hardcore and psych-carnival *Zen Arcade* and Minutemen's forty-four-track skull-diddler *Double Nickels on the Dime* (both released in 1984 on one of Sonic Youth's former labels—the era-defining, if questionably administered, SST). These three records represent a commanding Holy Trinity of early indie rock doubles and together mark a period of unprecedented creative expansion in terms of the possibilities of underground (or otherwise) American rock music. However, *Daydream Nation* wasn't originally planned as a double. Perhaps this is an indication of the degree to which Sonic Youth's creative energy was expanding in ways that even they weren't quite prepared to handle. When they started pounding out song ideas for *Daydream Nation*, the band quickly discovered that the music, flush and brimming as it was, demanded more breathing room. The standard two-sided long-player format didn't have enough girth to accommodate the unwieldy amount of material they were generating. Thurston remembers: "We decided to let the songs stretch in ways that were prohibitive for a single LP, knowing that a double would take care of biz. We were also inspired by the SST releases of Hüsker Dü and Minutemen to do so. The idea of a double was still somewhat radical in its scope for bands like us—they harkened to a previous era of Yes and Deep Purple."

The rich, fertile groundwork laid by music generated stateside in the eighties from indie, post-punk bands like Dinosaur Jr, Black Flag, Butthole Surfers, Royal Trux, Laughing Hyenas, Green River/Mudhoney, Minor Threat/Fugazi, and on and on has only recently begun to be excavated. Like a Doppler sound warp, the impact of the remarkable, forward-thrusting racket made by outfits like these is just now, and in very limited capacity, starting to register and receive its long-overdue critical assessment.[2]

Sonic Youth was tuned into the transformations that were happening in indie rock in the eighties with a heightened sensitivity. They watched closely as hardcore punk reached maximum energy expenditure earlier in the decade, and saw the reorientation of punk's impulse taken in fresh directions by a new breed of young, loud, smart, eager, and curious bands coming out of suburban garages across America. As Thurston writes: "There was certainly a new aesthetic of youth culture at this time—exemplified by the emergence of J Mascis/Dinosaur

Jr, wherein anger and distaste, attributes associated with punk energy, were coolly replaced by head-in-the-clouds outer limits brilliance (Mascis, Cobain, My Bloody Valentine—MBV as somewhat clones of this sensual/appealing stance)—therefore, a new politic, mistakenly manifest and tagged 'shoegazing' which was really what could only be UK'sters—the teenage riot was a head-case, where the outsider musician came forth from the underpinnings of above ground rock 'n' roll and ripped shit on the poof core of Hollyweird."

Well, yes, exactly . . .

"I think *Daydream Nation* came at a significant yet transitional time in American underground rock mitosis," continues Thurston. "Form and content were aching to break all parameters and run into the new decade. It was a liberation from the heady collectiveness of hardcore-infused scene dynamics and an embracing of what we wanted to do beyond that world, one which we predated artistically and one we knew we had to blast forth from."

* * *

I should say here, early on, that all of these preliminary remarks come by way of a blushing confession. When I first heard *Daydream Nation* it quite frankly scared the living shit out of me. I had little or no idea what the hell I was listening to—all of those de/re-tuned guitars chiming and veering around, heroic banshee drumming, extended stretches of atmospheric discord, three different vocalists (representing two different genders!), thickets of feedback, preludes, intermissions, trilogies, and, *for the love of god*, perhaps the most unnerving, haunting element: that silent candle standing there screaming mercilessly across the cover. But there was something lurking in the shadowy, disorienting unfamiliarity of this music, something that made perfect sense, something that expressed nascent sonic realities desperate for expression. But how could this music, which seemed to have gained access to impossibly original and startlingly beautiful forms of rock 'n' roll, even exist? Who the hell is Sonic Youth? What's going on with this spooky, quiet candle on the cover? How did they get the guitars to yowl like that?

The whole experience was mystifying and overpowering and it absolutely terrified me. But, like any record worth a goddamn, the countless rewards of *Daydream Nation* revealed themselves despite the initial trauma it afforded. While those rewards came at significant hazard to the stability of long-standing equilibriums and listening habits (hence, my strong belief that successfully listening to this record requires courage, stamina, and support!), they turned out to be lasting and immense. Like learning a new language, speeding in a snowstorm, or finally discovering a long dormant perversion, listening to *Daydream Nation* can be nerve-racking, perplexing, and rocket-to-the-stars exhilarating in equal measure.

So, one way of putting it, and it's probably best to establish this at the outset: *Daydream Nation is not to be trifled with*. There is some treacherous, gaga material contained on this record and unless you've got the ears for getting deep into it, you might want to put this book down and find a warm, safe place to hide out and drool over your twee pop records because, friend, we're going inside this astonishing beast, and we're going in *the whole way* . . .

* * *

Here's the standard yarn: Sonic Youth is one of those archetypically "important" outfits, notorious for carrying a name of unquestionable validity and integrity, universally acknowledged as heavyweight champions in the break-new-ground-with-a-jackhammer-an-arc-welder-and-a-guitar tournament, but whose recorded output is often met with resistance by the casual, innocent listener due to certain difficulties posed by the music's occasional lack of aural ease-of-use.

Total bullshit.

Substandard magazine writer music journalist record guide critic's poll–generated caked-on *bullshit*. More accurately, the immediate, electrifying appeal, even to the uninitiated, of Sonic Youth's sound derives from the band's ability to penetrate and mark out typically prohibitive musical territory that, in turn, serves as a direct and vital analogue to complexes of human emotion rarely, if ever, represented within rock's sound palette. In my experience, those "casual, innocent" listeners (like me when I got my first Sonic blasting), who supposedly have a tough time with Sonic Youth's exploratory leanings or their fearlessness in the face of dissonance, have more likely had their faces happily blown clear off of their casual, innocent little heads in a frenzy of near-religious ecstasy when exposed to this music. Sonic Youth records may, in part, articulate certain forms of distress or uneasiness, but those articulations themselves aren't "difficult" so much as they're *imperative*; like fresh, nutrient-rich blood being transported through untapped veins to outlying, poorly supplied aesthetic capillaries.

I mean, what the fuck is rock music for anyway? Why are we drawn to certain bands in the first place? What is it about a particular sound that can sink its teeth into us with such ferocity, yet we never want it to release its hold? Why do we want to *inhabit* certain records? Consider the grip that a band like Sonic Youth can have on its audience. There is a quality that inheres in the prototypical Sonic Youth passage, where the various tonal (or atonal) elements have coalesced into a concentrated, resonant hum, crystalline in its integration of disparate elements—clangor enveloped in a whisper, hammering blasts of noise wrapped in trilling lullabies, sobs contained in a scream. In these moments, we see that music is capable of eliciting undisclosed, perpendicular sensibilities and accessing internal economies that typically operate without regulation, without oversight. These passages are capable of giving shape to formless sorrows, voicing mute joys, exposing hidden emotional architectures. When you hear Sonic Youth coming through your speakers or your headphones or in some concert venue, the beauty of the connection that happens derives from a kind of clear, direct contact that the band manages to establish with the ecstatic, emotional lift of rock 'n' roll itself. While the rush and elevation that occurs in these moments is often celebratory, spastic, or playful, Sonic Youth's wide-open aesthetic availability also ensures the frequent presence of a translucent *ache* within that lift as well.

And come to think of it, hasn't rock 'n' roll always been more than just a little bit about that translucent ache? The ache of the thick, heavy weight of unreported affections, of long-suffered shames that stay lodged in the gut like a stinging cast-iron rake, of encouragements and advices quickly and precariously dismissed, of humid teenage nights gone forever, of unfortunate habits pursued without regard to consequence, of the shitty agony of memories, of the swollen melancholy of rainy Sunday afternoons, and, always, always, always *right there* in the music, the relentless background ache of that frantic, lonesome, inevitable curve toward the absolute end of the line. Sonic Youth captures and articulates these things, sometimes explicitly, sometimes implicitly. Their music comes at you from unanticipated angles, across chasms largely assumed to be unbridgeable, but they get there somehow and invite you over. You meet them there, in that territory that few rock bands inhabit, and you don't ever want to leave.

"We tend to see music as *exultational*, or something like that; as cathartic," Lee explains. "When it's working well, whether it's just the four of us in a room, or it's in a room with a couple thousand people, on the right night when everything's aligned correctly, you're *lifting off*, there's a certain transcendent quality to it that everyone's involved with and there's a symbiotic thing between the audience and the performers. It's not like you're leading them, it's something that you do together in a way. We've always felt it was about extrapolation and openness and inclusion. I think that's a word we've used a lot over the years to talk about our music—we've thought it was very inclusive; it wasn't exclusive or trying to be elitist in any way. Some people felt that about our music just because it was weird and in these strange tunings and it didn't sound normal so they thought we were these elitist punks or something. When really for us it was just the opposite. In terms of the tunings I think we always felt like we were more in touch with the base reality, the kernel nuggets of what rock 'n' roll was about than people who were just following along chord progressions. We couldn't follow along chord progressions because the guitars were all in these weird tunings. So we'd be just literally making it all up by ear. We were removed from the whole, 'Well if you play an E chord and then a B and E you've got the basis of the blues' thing. A lot of that stuff comes out in our music, it just doesn't come out in that sort of rote, pre-scripted mentality. It's all discovered. In a sense that's part of the key to our music—we're discovering it rather than just regurgitating it in a sense. It has never, to me at least, been a nostalgic exercise."

As a result of this resistance to rock's nostalgic instinct, Sonic Youth's sound can have a vertiginous effect on us. Common contextual reference points are often nowhere to be found in their music. Fortunately, there are certain listening tactics we can employ to help maximize our engagement with Sonic Youth records; one such tactic is especially appropriate to *Daydream Nation*.

As with most other organs, if not properly exercised, inertia will take hold and the ears will atrophy. In this sense, the physiological metaphor of the ear as housing a *listening muscle* seems an apt one. I find it rejuvenating and bolstering sometimes to put my ears through an extended, active listening session—devoting an uninterrupted span of attention focusing exclusively on one record, from start to finish. To the sullen and unimaginative, this kind of close listening approach may seem sort of old-fashioned, boredom inducing, or hokey. Be that as it may, I can vouch from years of experience that the process yields pleasures of pornographic magnitude. At the same time, this kind of listening unquestionably helps rejuvenate the auditory ossicles,[3] keeping the ears agile and fresh. There are many records to which this type of attentive listening would be inappropriately applied. Luckily, however, there are some outstanding records that are very effective in helping to achieve this goal. It may go without saying at this point, but let's say it anyway: *Daydream Nation* is an ideal candidate for this type of listening exercise. Like *Daydream Nation*, many of these records have an impact that extends far beyond the proper maintenance of our ears.

Some records take us *all the way out*, freak the bejesus right up out of us. Throughout my listening history, I've personally experienced this freaking all the way out a select few times. Occasionally, and I'm very serious about this, I've stood by and watched as certain albums brought people to fits of panic, speechlessness, or the shakes. In some extraordinary cases I've witnessed a grisly combination of all three! This is a disturbing experience and confirms beyond any doubt the notion that certain records, of a particular quality and under specific conditions, can be *really fucking scary*.[4]

The following anecdote illustrates a case in point: I remember riding in my car once with a square friend from high school. I was blaring a Grateful Dead (no shit) bootleg from the late seventies. I'm sure it was a combination of the tape's unfamiliar sound quality (hissy, muddy, *bootleggy*), my neo-hippy-dippy car-dancing, and the late-psychedelic, intergalactic meanderings of the Dead that caused my tightly wound friend to respond the way she did. At first, she just squirmed nervously around in her seat. Then her confused eyes darted back and forth from the tape deck to me and back to the tape deck. Next came a kind of jabbering as she sputtered haltingly. She grew increasingly more agitated and uncomfortable, until, finally, with her arms flapping around like water-desperate fish, she screamed (and I mean blood-curdling style *screamed*) in a trembling voice (verbatim): "I DON'T UNDERSTAND THIS MUSIC!" I honestly thought, and still maintain, that I saw tears forming in her eyes. Poor thing had reached the breaking point. Her mind? *Blown*.

I distinctly remember, her *entire body* lurched up and back into the passenger seat while she shouted. She was physically trying to escape the music! It was like watching someone being chased by acid-damaged hornets. Imagine her reaction if it had been "Silver Rocket," "Rain King," or—oh my—"Eliminator Jr" stinging away at her raw, pink ears . . .

Typically, scary records blast into our lives just as things are going along without incident musicwise—we know what we like, what we don't like, and we know how to explain the difference. Hunky dory. Suddenly, from the shadows, some monster album springs on our unsuspecting little ears (tender and vulnerable, swaddled in complacency, kootchy kootchy koo) and—BOOM—*all auditory hell breaks loose*. Albums like these often serve as crux demarcation points by which we map the landscape of our music life. ("My brains were scrambled when I heard ______ by ______!") These albums resonate, recur, and haunt. But initial exposure can be unnerving . . .

Following is a not unlikely detailing of the circumstances under which first exposure to Sonic Youth typically happens: You're up late on a summer night with some criminally dangerous older cousin (the cigarettes/weed/booze cousin), all parents, bloated with cocktails, have gone to bed. They've put you up in your cousin's dank bedroom above the garage. Things have been pleasantly squalid so far; your cousin smokes menthols while the two of you listen to album after album in an agreeable series of familiar titles. Then your cousin asks if you've ever heard ______ by ______. You sheepishly admit that you haven't, and your cousin stares at you with sinister, mischievous eyes (they're red and yellow, mustard on fire, the eyes of someone destined to spend time lurking around casinos and rehabs). Your cousin nods silently, reaches deep into the album stacks, pulls out a copy of some suspicious-looking record with a cover that makes you think of all the deflating disappointments, impossible longings, and bittersweet regrets you have yet to suffer in your life, and slides it onto the player. . . . What comes out of the speakers is so foreign to your sensibilities that your mind, out of its depth of comprehension, lurches, jolts, and, finally, seizes. De-realization and vertigo set in as your music vocabulary struggles in vain to accommodate what your helpless ears fail to understand. A frightening havoc is wreaked on all of your presumptions and tastes. Your poor little ears are traumatized. You question who you are and what you know. Your cousin is the devil and his music is devil music.

Whatever record that was; it just *blew your tiny mind*. Things will *never* be the same again . . .

After a period of recovery, adventurous listeners (or those with an attachment to music so imperative and consuming they have little choice in the matter) will come to embrace these disorienting experiences, relishing the riotous upheaval and welcoming the expansion of their sense for what's possible in music. You'll do research on the scary record, assuaging your fear while broadening your interest with background and criticism culled from magazines and books. You'll call your cousin: "Hey, dangerous cousin! What else can you tell me about that scary band? Will you make me a devil mix?" Soon, you'll muster the courage to buy your own copy of the felonious album. Gradually, after repeated listens, it becomes a permanent part of your personal music archives and you'll announce resolutely that you're *into* a new band. Entire sections of your record collection will suddenly sound obsolete as a result of all this. You'll hang new posters and subscribe to new magazines—past editions of which you'll bring to your cousin, with a carton of Newports, at the youth detention center.

Like any aesthetic experience worth pursuing to its conclusion, listening to *Daydream Nation* is a perilous, soul blowout–type affair. For a record with a cover image so stark and serene, *Daydream Nation* features inordinately bracing turbulences, ghastly imagery, and hair-raising momentum. It challenges, overwhelms, and exhausts. Of course, let's not forget (*why, whhhh-fucking-yyyyyyy*, is this point so under-served in discussions of the band's merits and achievements?) Sonic Youth is capable of reaching places of stunning, drop-your-pants beauty and rapturous grace with their music. *Daydream Nation* is rich with first-order examples of this kind of material. Aside from the transcendent aural respite provided during these, what we'll call *the shimmering*, passages, Sonic Youth, in their reliably humane fashion, helps the listener along by taking pains to structure the album as four maneuverable, self-contained (but interrelated) sides. For all of my blustering on about *Daydream Nation*'s daunt, this actually was an aspect of the record not lost on Sonic Youth. At once acknowledging the potential challenges posed by the album's scope and evidencing the band's basic decency, Lee Ranaldo explains that the track layout of *Daydream Nation* was conscientiously designed to afford our ears certain stretching-out periods: "We really shaped those sides very carefully; a single side of a vinyl record is the perfect experience in terms of time—about twenty or twenty-five minutes—the perfect amount of time to sit and listen to something without too much taxation."

If, in your listening, you proceed through the record according to the itinerary Sonic Youth has provided, take breaks when they tell you to, and keep this book close at hand—everything will be fine. I promise.

Notes

1. Standard editorial practice would have me remove Steve's brief, subjective celebration of "Teen Age Riot" from this quote. But I'm going to leave it there because it exemplifies a quality in this band that deserves bearing out. It's difficult to re-create tone of voice in writing, inflection is lost, acknowledgments contained within subtle physical cues are missed—but let me try to explain the tone with which Steve dropped that little comment about "Teen Age Riot" and what it says about the nature of Sonic Youth. "Teen Age Riot" is almost twenty years old at this point: Steve was there bashing away at the drums when it was recorded and he's been playing it with Sonic Youth ever since, but when he paused, mid-sentence, and turned to look me square in the face, his eyes gleaming with his trademark boyish earnestness, to tell me how good he thinks "Teen Age Riot" is, it was like he had just heard it for the first time earlier that afternoon. This refreshing enthusiasm and affirmative sincerity must have something to do with why Sonic Youth is still intact and functioning in vital, creative ways after so many years as a cohesive unit, while so many of their New York no-wave nihilist contemporaries are caput.
2. For example, in preparing to write this book, I relied on Michael Azerrad's *Our Band Could Be Your Life* (Little, Brown and Company, 2001) for its thorough behind-the-scenes accounting of the American indie rock culture of the eighties.
3. Vital middle ear components, the ossicles are comprised of three small bones known as the hammer (malleus), anvil (incus), and stirrup (stapes); collectively, they form what's called the ossicular chain. The function of this chain is to lead sound from the eardrum farther down into the inner ear. I mention this because it's like there's a miniature audio blacksmithing operation going on in there. And what with the hammers, anvils, stirrups, bones, and chains, the whole system strikes me as reminiscent of a Sonic Youth–style guitar abuse index.
4. Oh, sure, an entire field of heavy music overtly preoccupies

itself with "scariness." There are no doubt plenty of legitimately scary recordings of this type. But the narrow, short-lived, obvious kind of "scariness" found on these albums (they all have words like "corpse" or "mausoleum" or "dialysis" in their titles. *Zzzzzzzzzzzzz*!) has little to do with the notion of *deep and confusing scariness* I'm trying to convey here. To help get a sense for that notion, here's an exercise that might be useful: Compare the list of records below, all of which have genuinely, deeply scared or confused me, to a similar list of your own. If your list exceeds five entries, look at it again and ask of each one: "Did this record really take me *all the way out*?" Eliminate those that didn't. In my experience, records legitimately capable of doing this are exceedingly, count-them-on-one-*maybe*-two-hands-type rare. If you're puzzling over what criteria to use in determining whether or not you were genuinely taken *all the way out* by a particular record, skip ahead, finish this chapter, and come back to the exercise. My list:

- Boredoms *Soul Discharge* (Shimmy Disc)
- Butthole Surfers *Rembrandt Pussyhorse* (Latino Bugger Veil)
- John Coltrane *Ascension* (Impulse!)
- Fennesz *Hotel Paral.lel* (Mego)
- Public Enemy *Fear of a Black Planet* (Def Jam)

Court and Spark

by Sean Nelson

Sean Nelson is a writer and musician in Seattle, and is a partner in independent label Barsuk Records.

A Broader Sensibility

> *I suppose people have always been lonely, but this, I think, is an especially lonely time to live in. So many people are valueless or confused. . . . Things change so rapidly. Relationships don't seem to have any longevity. There isn't a lot of commitment to anything; it's a disposable society.*
>
> —JM, 1974

Of course, at this point, it feels as though I'm circling the airport of *Court and Spark*, trying desperately to clear the air of my deep admiration for the albums that preceded it before going in for a landing. Fair enough. Still, a fundamental question persists: How can you pick one album? How can you say, even tacitly, that *Court and Spark* is better than *Blue*, *For the Roses*, or *Hissing of Summer Lawns*? Or even *Don Juan's Reckless Daughter*, *Dog Eat Dog*, or any of the other Mitchell records *C&S* is empirically way better than. What does "better" even mean? And so forth.

But again, the premise isn't that *Court and Spark* is the best Joni Mitchell album. As we all know, the best Joni Mitchell album is the one that's playing right now. You don't hear "All I Want" and long for "Down to You," or vice versa. No, the premise is that if you regard the period between 1971 and 1975, from *Blue* to *Summer Lawns* as a single narrative—a musical Freitag's Triangle of sorts—then *C&S* is the unquestionable climax. It's the point at which Mitchell stepped outside herself just enough to communicate the breadth of the lonely time she felt herself living in, and by doing so, revealed more of herself than she ever had before. *Blue* is sharply first person (and presumably autobiographical) throughout. *For the Roses*, meanwhile, steps back somewhat to engage in overreaching social metaphors ("Banquet," "Barangrill," "Electricity"), but also features a second person voice that often sounds like direct address to specific people ("why do you have to be so jive?"; "you imitate the best and the rest you memorize"; "where are you now? Are you in some hotel room? Does it have a view?" etc) and which therefore functions as first person in drag. *Court and Spark* is energized by a wider, more adventurous perspective than either of its predecessors: third person narratives delivered by first person narrators, which is to say character studies, which is to say songs that manage to be personal—often devastatingly so—without needing to be autobiographical. After inspiring such intense one-to-one identification in her listeners, Mitchell was now taking expeditions outside herself, trying to identify with the people she met there, to better illuminate the dark corners of their inner lives as she had her own. The women of *Court and Spark*—the ones who find themselves at people's parties "fumbling, deaf, dumb, and blind," the ones who stay up for hours waiting for their "sugar to show," the ones who know there's going to be trouble because they're falling in love again—are everywomen, at least in the context of a certain corner of California and a certain corner of the 70s. By those same standards, the men are universal, too. The "Free Man in Paris," though famously modeled on David Geffen, doesn't leap off the grooves because Geffen is such a fascinating person, or because of the lurid secrets he was still keeping when the song was written; the song conveys, with forceful grace, the pathos of a prosperous man feeling trapped inside his own life. The simultaneously poetic and novelistic lyrics to this song come out of nowhere for Mitchell—the Free Man owes as much to Sinclair Lewis as to Dylan or Cohen or any of her other folk-rock contemporaries—and are the best representation of the quantum leap her perspective took on the album. *Blue* is about the self. *For the Roses* is about the self as reflected in others. *C&S* is about the city, and all the selves that collide—and fail to collide—within it.

"Court and Spark"

"Love came to my door," the album opens, "with a sleeping roll and a madman's soul." A few years prior, this kind of hippie calling card would have gained anyone happy entrance to a Joni Mitchell song. Back when she was a lady of the canyon, she might have cooked him a meal and sang him a song, then waxed wistful as he rambled onward. But this "Love" is an altogether more complex beast than the ones who had populated Mitchell's universe in the past. The "madman's soul" factor that had once seemed so compelling and agonizing in the lovers she sang about, now begins to seem burdensome, exhausting, not worth the effort. This would-be lover's rap about guilty people and "clearing" himself and the whole litany of ascetic sacrifices he's made—having "buried the coins he made in People's Park"—and presumably expects her to make, can't beat out the comfort of her own life. Though she may be tempted ("the more he talked to me, you know, the more he reached me"), the narrator of "Court and Spark" can't let go of whatever she'd have to let go of in order to be worthy of this Love. In the song, it's called "LA, city of the fallen angels." And what LA means is the subject of nearly every song on the record. This opening song establishes much of the tone that follows: ambivalent, unconvinced, torn, circumspect, wary of love's price even while in its thrall, "mistrusting and still acting kind." These aren't entirely new ideas, even in Mitchell songs. What's new is the worldliness of the voice that communicates them; there's no prostration or angst in her rejection of this suitor, just a choice. She admits a pang of sadness, perhaps, that she "couldn't let go of LA," but that's more about herself than it is about him. The operative contrast here isn't between two star-crossed lovers, it's between People's Park—the student/hippie enclave in Berkeley that represented the best of the 60s counterculture energy and some of the harshest retribution against it—and the city of fallen angels, the seat of decadent decay. This isn't "My Old Man" (though, notice that he, too, was a singer in the park) or the absentee "nonconformer" of "Little Green." Or if it is, the woman singing about him has really changed her tune. No more wistful sighs about his charming unavailability; this "Love" sounds like some kind of raving zealot: with all his talk about glory trains, clearing one's self, and sacrificing one's blues. And at the risk of over-literalizing the whole scenario, can you blame her for choosing LA? I always picture the song starting at 3a.m.: intense guy carrying a sleeping bag and nothing else pounding on the wooden door of a house in the Hollywood Hills, making loud pronouncements about "all the guilty people" and offering his host the privilege of completing him, while pledging to return the favor. There's something vaguely sinister about the whole scenario (a song about a raving hippie with a madman's soul showing up at your door in LA wasn't exactly a lullaby in the post–Helter Skelter early 70s). The choice she's really making isn't about a guy, however, or even a lifestyle. She's choosing between a life of realism—however painful that reality might be to accept—and a romantic ideal she simply doesn't subscribe to anymore. The angels in question are fallen not from heaven but from the naïve grace of being willing to sacrifice their blues to go "dancing up a river in the dark." The great tragedy in "Court and Spark" lies in having outgrown the romance of youth without having lost the thirst for romance.

And while there's nothing in the song to mark it out as autobiography, the stark tonal contrast of "Court and Spark" with previous Mitchell songs makes it feel like a signifier of a new chapter in the artist's evolution. It's clear enough that the lyric need not be about any specific man, much less a famous one. It might not even be a man at all. "Court and Spark," like *Court and Spark*, is a story about a woman's on-again/off-again relationship with love. The love that came to her door. The love that buried its coins and came looking for her. The love that read her mind. The love that made her worry sometimes (she worries sometimes). Personified by a man, or at least by male characteristics—although, her description of eyes "the color of the sand and the sea" can't help but suggest a more elemental nature—this love is full of insane demands, and packed with fitful abstractions. The woman in this song, whoever she is, sounds like she might have been seduced by Love a number of times in the past; he does, after all, know where she lives. But where her predecessors in Mitchell's oeuvre would likely have made the sacrifices Love demands and lived to rue them or not, "Court and Spark" heralds the end of the author's surrender to love. Not the end of her desire for it, nor even the end her quest for it, but the end of her willingness to subsume herself under it. This particular incarnation of love has a rival for her (self-destructive) impulses: the city. "I couldn't let go of LA" is why she turned love away. But why should love and a city be mutually exclusive? Because love, in this instance, is all strings, all contempt for "all the guilty people," many of whom presumably are among the fallen angels who live there. LA in this song—and as filmmaker Thom Andersen pointed out in his heroically ambitious documentary, *Los Angeles Plays Itself*, it's always significant when the city's name is truncated to just two letters; it always constitutes a spiritual, as well as a syntactical reduction—is the antithesis of the 60s, of hippies, of the free love experiment. This LA knows that love is never free, and its denizens, particularly the woman who stars in this song, are jaded enough to know better than to trust a madman who offers to complete you if you'll complete him first. Whether she's too scared or too smart to take love's hand is an open question (one that'll be addressed in the very next song). What's significant is that she chooses not to, and that choice reflects a larger freedom than most Joni Mitchell women—to say nothing of real life women—claimed for themselves in the years behind. You could call it cynical or cold, but the 70s iteration of freedom—the rebellion after the rebellion—constituted a lot more "no" than its freewheeling predecessor had. That's because the 60s version left a lot of women (Mitchell women, I mean) holding the bag for "nonconformers" who felt free to treat them like property. The new version of freedom, as evinced by *Court and Spark*, involved the principle of self-preservation, not just against the bastards in power, but the bastards in People's Park, as well.

This question of freedom, or rather the questioning of it, of its primacy in the culture (and the freedom-loving counterculture in particular), of its very nature, was always one of Mitchell's ripest subjects. Her early quasi-folk song "Urge for Going" seems like a simple celebration of freedom in among a bunch of florid lines about geese and weather, until the little verbal twists ("I get the urge for going but I never seem to go" and "he got the urge for going and I had to let him go") complicate the pretty picture. These complications are taken far further on "Cactus Tree," the last song from her first LP—a song she later called "a grocery list of men I've liked or loved or left behind." The verses describe elaborate courtship rites (sailing, mountain climbing, letter writing) performed by a string of men to try and woo a woman who, in the last line of each verse is too busy (or "off somewhere") "being free." The surface irony of the refrain lies in the assumed tragedy of the woman's failure to land—or be landed by—any of these avid lovers. But there's a deeper irony that comes from Mitchell's delivery; while the line plainly says "she chooses not to accept their proposals because to do so would mean being possessed," her voice says, "I'm not so sure all this freedom is so much better than the alternative." She's not rejecting the lovers—any of the dozens the song offers up—so much as accepting them on her own terms: "She will love them when she sees them," she explains, then warns that "they will lose her if they follow." And then the killer ending: "And her heart is full and hollow like a cactus tree / While she's so busy being free."

That "hollow" is more than just a handy rhyme. The woman in this song isn't so terribly different from the one in "Court and Spark"—except inasmuch as her language has become less baroque. More notable is that the suitor in "C&S" comes offering even less than his "Cactus Tree" forbears: just intense words and a sleeping roll (and a madman's soul). It's as if, year by year, would-be lovers have decided that courtly love isn't worth all the hassle.

"Help Me"

Freedom is also the crux of "Help Me," one of the most emotionally ambivalent pop songs of all time. After a strummy instrumental preamble, a stack of Jonis sings the title phrase in a dying fall. "Help me," she sings. "I think I'm falling . . . in love again," and then later, "in love too fast," and finally "in love with you." Each repetition raises the stakes of the help she's asking for. The first time is almost like a joke, a casual aside to the gods of romance who give her "that crazy feeling," an admission of helplessness from a woman whose casual confidence can be detected not only in her leaping melody, but in the swinging groove of the band that backs her. The sound of that band, combining the rhythmic sensibility of jazz with the assuredly four-square structure of folk-rock, is the surest sign that *Court and Spark* lives in a whole other time zone from previous Mitchell records. It's also the way that "Help Me" most dramatically steps out from the songs and albums that came before. The full band sound will continue throughout the record, receding on occasion to make way for orchestral embellishment ("Down to You"), stepping up to center stage in rock 'n' roll drag ("Raised on Robbery"), or downshifting to establish an even mellower beach-at-sunset vibe late in the album ("Troubled Child").

These shadings of characterization in the music—sometimes subtle, sometimes blatant—allow the lyrics to lean back into their panoptical perspectives. With the aid of a groovy jazz-rock band taking care of the foundation (under her undoubtedly strict direction), Mitchell is set free to become other people, or at least other versions of herself, when she sings.

The second request for help is directed to herself. Falling in love "too fast" is a very different problem from falling in love "again." It suggests that she can't trust her own responses, or the system of checks and balances she has in place to guard against such occurrences. We already know that the lover who's getting her "in trouble" is "a rambler and a gambler and a sweet talking ladies man." Now we discover that the real issue isn't his nature, but hers. Enthralled by a(nother) roguish fella, she's suddenly "hoping for the future and worrying about the past." She needn't be falling in love, too fast or otherwise, to feel that way. The trouble is that, in the past she's worrying about (she worries sometimes), she has "seen some hot, hot blazes come down to smoke and ash." In other words, as we all know, nothing ever works, at least not when you fall in love too fast. But the real culprit for all the doubt and ambivalence of this seemingly ebullient "love" song is lurking as a secondary refrain at the end of the verses, a bonus hook (you can never have too many), and the line that ties "Help Me" to *Court and Spark* like a sailboat to a dock: "we love our loving, but not like we love our freedom." The electric guitar figure that follows this refrain is a wistful, eloquent evocation of the sentiment expressed in the words, a taste of the freedom that prevents us from allowing ourselves to fall too thoroughly in love with someone else—the freedom that is, at its basest level, selfishness itself. It's catchy as hell, tinted by shades of emotion, and shrewdly brief—this is, after all, a pop song, in which the job of each part is to leave you wanting to hear it again.

Again, freedom turns out not to be a palliative measure, but a preventive one. It's not the salve that allows one to live without constraints, but the quintessence of confinement. A freedom that lets you do anything but give yourself to someone else is a prison. The characters on this album wander around that prison (let's call it "LA") in varying stages of despair and despondency, eventually landing in "the sterilized room where they let you be spacy." In the bridge of "Help Me," the narrator gets nostalgic—maybe pre-nostalgic given the present tense of the verses—and indulges in an evocation of pure, effortless joy.

"Didn't it feel good?" she asks. "We were sitting there talking or lying there not talking. Didn't it feel good?" The bridge ends with the question being asked again and again, her solo voice echoed by a chorus of incantatory selves who answer each repetition with another, until the whole part resolves by shifting into yet another of the song's multiple hooks, the five-hit instrumental riff (with flutes!) that followed verse one.

The final verse is a confrontation of sorts. "Help me, I think I'm falling . . . in love with you," she sings, in a sort of indirect direct address. (I don't believe the words are spoken aloud; I think she's imagining what she might say to the guy if she had the nerve or the chance.) When she asks if he's going to let her "go there" by herself, there being "in love," it becomes clear that the preceding verses, with their worries about falling in love "again" and "too fast," were really just preludes to this more acute concern that the love won't be returned, which is really what every lover worries about, and what most good romantic anxieties ultimately amount to. The freedom we keep hearing about allows the two would-be (or would they?) lovers to spend time "flirting around," but only the one singing this song acknowledges, with a very simple rhyme, that while they're "flirting and flirting," they're "hurting, too." And because this exchange is one-sided (if not, indeed, imaginary), she's left to comfort herself, however coldly, with the reminder that "we love our lovin', but not like we love our freedom." On this final refrain, the "we" seems to make the jump from the personal to the universal, and the lead guitar figure returns to underscore that transformation and ease "us" into the recognition that love and freedom are the twin cornerstones of life's profoundest contradiction.[1]

"Free Man in Paris"

There's no missing the centrality of freedom in the thematic construction of "Free Man in Paris." Most obviously, it's in the title—signals don't come more explicit than that. But the way Mitchell treats freedom in this song—as something remote, savored in memory but impossible in real life, as purest fantasy—is the real signifier. Let's forget (briefly) that the lyric was inspired by David Geffen, and that the freedom ever so coyly alluded to ("that very good friend of mine") was a specifically sexual one. Because whether or not that piece of lore is true (and how could it not be?), the song remains one of those rare perfect constructions, a character study in pop so deftly and concisely rendered that it doesn't even need a bridge. While everything on *Court and Spark* is of interest, and most of the album rides a twin wave of ambition and execution that would humble any recording artist, "Free Man in Paris" has to be the pinnacle of Joni Mitchell's career as a songwriter. It's the ultimate extension of her effort to be personal without being autobiographical. Here is pure biography, if not pure fiction: the imagining of an inner life wholly invented, shared, understood—but not confessed. Because of what we know (or presume to know), one imagines the Free Man as scrawny, sad faced David Geffen, sitting behind a broad brown desk atop shag carpet, a few lines of cocaine scraped out on the latest Jackson Browne acetate, a mountain of hundred dollar bills stacked neatly in the corner, his ear cupped to a retro-modernistic phone while some fanciful artist or irate music lawyer ("dreamers and telephone screamers") blathers on about this or that career in jeopardy or this or that unpaid royalty, his eyes glazing over as he remembers his lusty, misspent youth in the city of lights. Wipe away the rock legend, however (it takes some doing), and the Free Man might look a little more like Sinclair Lewis's Babbitt, or some other nonhero from contemporary literature, an acquaintance of Manheim from *What Makes Sammy Run?*, maybe a more prosperous cousin of Tommy Wilhelm from *Seize the Day*, or a neighbor of one of John Cheever's indistinguishable suburban hell-dwellers. In any case, the powerful longing of the Free Man for his free days distinguishes him from the stock characters of the pop song canon. We expect such complicated desire from a first person narrator in a pop song, someone expressing their own feelings, be they assumed or deeply felt. But even though this song is told by an "I," an interlocutor shows up in the very first line. " 'The way I see it,' he said, 'you just can't win it . . .' " It's likely enough that the "he said" is there because it scans, or because Mitchell wanted to clearly acknowledge the gender divide. The rest of the song maintains the first person voice. But the fact that a third person is telling the tale remains significant; it points out the fact that the story is being written, that the anguished longing, the dreary doldrums, all the subtle colorations of character are the work of a crafty inventor (and a generous, empathetic friend/client) who's capable of recognizing in the world that surrounds her a despair very like the kind she had evoked so eloquently on her previous albums.

The opening lines of this three-minute soliloquy are accurate enough to sound like straight reportage, and yet cunning enough to reveal the narrator's mild unreliability. "Everybody's in it for their own gain" (as if he's any different?), "you can't please them all" (spoken like a man with a messiah complex), "there's always somebody calling you down" (and a persecution freak to boot). "I do my best and I do good business" (if I do say so myself), "there's a lot of people asking for my time / they're trying to get ahead" (note the contradictory tones of self-aggrandizement and self-effacement; he knows he's important, but not for the reasons he might like to be). "They're trying to be a good friend of mine" is the unkindest cut, as we'll learn in the next verse. The contrast between the greedy people pretending to be his "good friend" and the "very good friend" he knows he'll find in Paris is the locus of the Free Man's alienation. After all, it's not like he didn't volunteer to suffer these fools. You have to assume that in addition to being good at what he does ("I do good business . . . ") he's also ambitious, and that at some point he'd had to choose between being a free man in Paris and a rich man in LA (you have to assume he's from LA), stoking the starmaker machinery behind the popular song. Still, in his memory, the very good friend brings a sense of being "unfettered and alive," of not having to be important because of what he can do for his dreamers and screamers, but because, to someone far away, he's beautiful. Despite the heraldic flutes that form the song's central melodic hook, despite the breezy tempo, strummy feel, and defiant major key–ness of the whole song, it's the pathos of the Free Man's fantasia that lingers when the song comes to a close. The nostalgic reverie of a bourgeois climber—and a record company suit at that—isn't the most obvious subject matter for an artist who emerged from the folk underground; it seems more likely that Mitchell would have treated the Free Man more like Dylan treated his Thin Man: with blatant (if obtuse) contempt. "You're a cow," or something along those lines. But that kind of harsh judgment never really rolled off Mitchell's tongue. Her songwriting was always invested with a greater sense of empathy than that. She wasn't a take down artist. Not that she ever shied away from calling out the uncomfortable truth. Consider the protagonist of "The Last Time I Saw Richard" (the final song on *Blue*), whose dismal life of consumer comforts and marital torpor are worse than his own worst fears could have told. Last spotted in Detroit in '68, Richard declared that "all romantics meet the same fate someday: cynical and drunk and boring someone in some dark café." Instead, a few years later, he could be found married to a figure skater (recipient of "a dishwasher and a coffee perculator [*sic*]"), and drinking not in some heroically seedy café, but in the nexus of suburban normalcy: "at home . . . with the TV on and all the house lights left up bright." But despite the death of even Richard's meagerest dream—it's pretty sad when alcoholic dissolution is your Plan A—Mitchell's song aims at his faded humanity, not at his moral lapse. Back in Detroit, when she calls him out on his dark predictions, she does it by pointing out the romance that's intrinsic to his whole demeanor, however cynical and drunk he already is. Everything's romantic in the opening verses of "The Last Time I Saw Richard": the looming despair, the glimmering hope, the barmaid in her fishnets and her bow-tie, even the "Wurlitzer" that plays the songs that sing of "love so sweet." It's important that it's not just any old jukebox. And later, when she starts describing Richard now—highball in one hand, remote control in the other—she's not mad that he let the folks down by selling out and marrying up; she's worried that he gave up on himself. And in the final verse, we realize that she (the narrator) is the one who's really romanticizing things. With the leap from Richard's blaring house lights to a candle that's suddenly too bright to stay lit, Mitchell illustrates that Richard's prophecies actually were prophetic, that his warning to her in Detroit in '68 has come true, and that no matter how much she protests that these days of "hiding behind bottles in dark cafés" are "only a phase," her eyes remain as "full of moon," as ever. What he can't know, of course, is that even years later, he remains the object of *her* romanticism. The key difference between them is that he talks about the romantic's fate with hostility (" 'You laugh,' he said. 'You think you're immune' "), and when she does it, she speaks with patience and understanding ("all good dreamers pass this way someday"), however upset ("I don't want nobody comin' over to my table / I got nothing to talk to anybody about") or self-conscious ("only a dark cocoon before I get my gorgeous wings and fly away") it makes her.

"Richard" is a fine case study in Mitchell's empathetic leanings, but even in a song like "Woman of Heart and Mind" from *For the Roses*, which offers some stinging personal observations about a lover (past or present) amid a larger declaration of authorial integrity, her impulse doesn't seem to arise from a desire to shame her subject (even if, as she explains, "you come to me like a little boy and I give you my scorn and my praise"). Rather, it sounds like she wishes he would live up to the qualities she recognizes in him. There's no missing the harshness of lines like "looking for affection and respect, a little passion / and you want stimulation, nothing more. That's what I think." Nor is it possible to deny the tenderness of the promise that follows: "but you know I'll try to be there for you when your spirits start to sink." The song is full of powerful conflict between the heart and mind, with the latter trying to convince the former that the cad in question ("win your medals / fuck your strangers / don't it leave you on the empty side?") isn't worth the bother, and failing. Even though she's been cast as "your mother or another lover or your sister or the queen of your dreams," this woman of heart and mind understands that her true role is "just another silly girl when love makes a fool of me." Still, the anger and frustration of the analysis is tempered by the will to help. "You criticize and you flatter," she observes. "You imitate the best and the rest you memorize." Harsh words, but the admonition that follows is full of love, however stern: "you know, the times you impress me most are the times when you don't try."

No matter how savage her eye for the cutting detail, Mitchell's character studies never veer toward cruelty (not until later albums, anyway). They criticize and they flatter, but they never try to embarrass. Nor, however, do they lionize. That's why "Free Man in Paris" doesn't have to be about David Geffen to be true. For the sake of this song and this album, "Paris" is as mythical and metaphorical (or as literal) as "LA"—it serves as a photo negative to the city that serves at *Court and Spark*'s anxious backdrop, while its central character steps forward for three perfect minutes of individual identification before slinking back into the chorus of "lost and lonely ones."

It's also why it's okay if it is about David Geffen, because, really, was ever anyone a better embodiment of the luster and the pathos of 1970s LA? It's only fitting that this enigma of the starmaker machinery—equal parts visionary and hustler, the simultaneous symbol of prosperity and self-denial—should be humanized by the woman whose career he helped invent. Joni Mitchell could find the humanity in anyone.

"People's Parties"

After the one-two punch of "Help Me" and "Free Man in Paris," which lands at the tail end of "Court and Spark" without so much as a pause, *Court and Spark* takes a breath. The song that follows then takes a turn away from the voice and approach of the three opening songs, and toward a style that forms a miniature model for the entire album. The narrative style of

"People's Parties" isn't entirely new in the Mitchell songbook. Its clearest predecessor is "Banquet" on *For the Roses*, a song that extrapolates the details of a single event into a free-standing metaphor for something much larger. The results are a mixed bag. "Banquet" is melodically stirring, and full of minor folk-pop delights, but its lyrical ambition seeks to encompass the whole of society. While full of crafty epigrams ("some turn to Jesus / some turn to heroin"), the song suffers from its efforts to summarize too much, from having too general a trajectory. "Some get the gravy / And some get the gristle / Some get the marrow bone / And some get nothing / Though there's plenty to spare." There's nothing untrue or unrighteous about these lines. They're even poetically rendered, with their recurring "gr" sounds, their shrewd incrementum of image, from outer to inner bits of food, and from literal portions to their broader figurative ramifications and so forth. But something about the overtness of the banquet table's symbolism, something about the lengths to which Mitchell extends the metaphor, makes the song feel a little overstretched. Within the brief running time, the table, "laden high" with food and fraught with meaning, manages to stand for the gulf between rich and poor, between environmental purity and pollution, between the freedom of the independent life and the shackles of the conventional family, between political awareness and apathetic decadence, and even between savory and sweet. In short, the banquet is meant to mean every possible thing about every possible thing: the whole wide world wrapped up in a pop song, which is great when it works, but pop is better at accidental profundity than the intentional kind. Mitchell herself seems to acknowledge the futility of her efforts in the very last verse, which repeats the lines about the gravy and the gristle and the nothing and the plenty, this time with the caveat that the lines are aphorisms drawn from a fortune cookie ("in the cookie, I read . . . "). Whether or not they really were is beside the point. at issue is the urge to cram a world of wisdom and observational commentary inside a fortune cookie.[2] It makes for a tall order, and an interesting failure.

At a glance, "People's Parties" attempts a similar feat. The narrow little world of glamour and despair described in the lyric is clearly a microcosm for the wider world of glamour and despair that *Court and Spark* is all about. It even employs similar descriptive strategies and language: "Some are friendly / some are cutting / some are watching it from the wings / some are standing in the center, giving to get something." And some get nothing, though one imagines there's plenty to spare. The most glaring difference between the two songs, however, is that while the microcosmic party does serve as a tidy little metaphor for society (or at least a privileged section of it) its real function is to mirror the inner world of the narrator, which is the real microcosm here.

Throughout the song, Mitchell modulates her perspective with a cinematographer's precision. She begins with a wide shot—"All the people at this party, they've got a lot of style"—then moves into snatches of detail ("stamps of many countries," "passport smiles") and casual assessments of a roomful of characters (and their various characters), all from the outlook of a person entering a room. Next, she zooms in on a specific character, the "photo beauty" who makes a spectacle of herself for the sake of attention ("she's got a rose in her teeth and a lampshade crown"). Within the space of a few lines, the narrator witnesses this woman, her beauty nullified by desperate pathos, devolve into a bipolar mess, veering from joy to tears in a single couplet. An honest observer but never a cruel one, Mitchell allows her photo beauty the best line in the song: "laughing and crying, you know it's the same release." It's precisely the kind of line Robert Altman would cut on (Sally Kellerman, in feathered hair and lipgloss, plays the photo beauty in my imaginary Altman film of this song, and she comes sharply out of hysterical sobbing to deliver the line completely straight, then more tears). It's also the kind of sentiment—simultaneously vacuous and profound, utterly false and weirdly true—that perfectly renders the altogether LA madness of the character who says it, and the party that hosts her.

From there, the camera is turned on the narrator herself, but only for a moment—not quite long enough to make her out. "I told you when I met you I was crazy," she says to an absent companion, then directs her attention back to the a wide shot of the room. She instructs the hysterical beauty to "cry for us all," then takes in a few more of the rogues in the gallery: "Eddie in the corner thinking he's nobody" (Eddie is played by John Schuck or Rene Aberjonois), "Jack behind his joker" (I know it doesn't quite fit, but I can't help seeing Nicholson—the Nicholson of *Five Easy Pieces*, or better yet, *A Safe Place*), "stone cold Grace behind her fan" (has to be Geraldine Chaplin), and, as if to complete a 360-degree pan "me in my frightened silence thinking I don't understand" (could she honestly be played by anyone other than Joni Mitchell, making a rare film appearance? No one says no to Altman, even in my imagination).

Our guest says a lot for someone in frightened silence, and the person she says it to—whoever he is—is charged with a heavy responsibility. “I feel like I'm sleeping,” she explains. “Can you wake me? You seem to have a broader sensibility.” That sensibility could encompass anything, as long as it's broader than sleepwalking through a life of parties with people she doesn't know or like, people she pities and empathizes with, people who wear her down simply by needing to be observed. The contempt she spares all the characters Photo Beauty cries for she reserves for herself, a creature reduced to “living on nerves and feelings, with a weak and a lazy mind.” But it might be the parties themselves, and not merely her narrow sensibility, that reduce her to this state, and to this low self-appraisal. The feeling of “fumbling deaf, dumb, and blind” isn't uncommon at gatherings of strangers, after all, particularly when the guest list is full of famous photo beauties. The narrator of “People's Parties” feels like a cipher among the beautiful people, but not (necessarily) because she isn't beautiful, too. It's because she can detect the unspoken pain lurking in every exchange, in every fellow traveler standing in the corner thinking he's nobody, and it prevents her from being a good party guest. As the song moves toward its close, the party still presumably raging on, she wishes for “more sense of humor / keeping the sadness at bay / throwing the lightness on these things / laughing it all away.” The final line expands into a stack of Mitchells singing in tight harmony, and is soon joined by another Joni chorus offering a shrill, teasing counterpoint (“laughing it all, laughing it all, laughing it all”). And as the final word stretches into a long, multi-syllabic sound—“away-ee-hee-ee-ee-heeeee”—the outro takes on the character of a chant, like her wish for increased levity were being pulled taut to reveal what she really wants: to be away. It's telling that she wishes for more sense of humor rather than, say, the resolve to stay away from the parties in the first place—but she told you when she met you she was crazy. It's not that she wants to belong (the sad fact is that she already does belong); she wants to be able to mask the way she really feels, the better to endure the incredible sadness all around her. The ultimate reveal in this little Altman film—and the real reason why only Altman could direct it[3]—is that while the narrator is spending all her time feeling separate from all the people at this party, she never quite grasps the fact that she is perfectly one of them, and perhaps more poignantly, that the alienation she feels keeping her separate from her counterparts is precisely what unites them all. As the picture fades, to the tune of a dozen Joni Mitchells in an incantatory crisscross, the image of a roomful of prosperous guests, all angels in various stages of falling, all convinced they're alone, no matter how together they are.

Notes

1. A side note: I recently heard "Help Me" performed at a wedding reception as a serenade to the happy couple. Because I had this book on the brain, I started feeling uncomfortable, as though it were being offered as some kind of warning or rejoinder to everyone present, though the singer and the couple were all friends. "Listen to the words," I thought. "This isn't something you sing to people who are consecrating the beginning of a life together! Better you should sing it at a divorce proceeding! What are you thinking?" But then the song ended and everyone clapped and the bride and groom smiled honestly, and the singer stepped down off the stage to embrace them and all was well. Such, I was reminded AGAIN, is the eternal power of a hit song: it can mean what it says, and it can mean the exact opposite of what it says depending on the context in which it's heard. Amazing.
2. Though that would be a pretty cool fortune to get.
3. His protégé, Alan Rudolph, made a very similar movie in 1976, called *Welcome to LA*. The main character is a songwriter. Altman was the producer.